MACHINE LEARNING

IN PURE MATHEMATICS AND THEORETICAL PHYSICS

MACHINE LEARNING
IN PURE MATHEMATICS AND THEORETICAL PHYSICS

Edited by

YANG-HUI HE

London Institute for Mathematical Sciences, UK,
Merton College, University of Oxford, UK,
City, University of London, UK &
Nankai University, China

World Scientific

EW JERSEY · LONDON · SINGAPORE · BEIJING · SHANGHAI · HONG KONG · TAIPEI · CHENNAI · TOKYO

Published by

World Scientific Publishing Europe Ltd.

57 Shelton Street, Covent Garden, London WC2H 9HE

Head office: 5 Toh Tuck Link, Singapore 596224

USA office: 27 Warren Street, Suite 401-402, Hackensack, NJ 07601

Library of Congress Cataloging-in-Publication Data

Names: He, Yang-Hui, 1975– editor.

Title: Machine learning in pure mathematics and theoretical physics / edited by
 Yang-Hui He, London Institute for Mathematical Sciences, UK, Merton College,
 University of Oxford, UK, City, University of London, UK & Nankai University, China.

Description: New Jersey : World Scientific, [2023] | Includes bibliographical references.

Identifiers: LCCN 2022058911 | ISBN 9781800613690 (hardcover) |
 ISBN 9781800613706 (ebook for institutions) | ISBN 9781800613713 (ebook for individuals)

Subjects: LCSH: Machine learning. | Mathematics--Data processing. | Physics--Data processing.

Classification: LCC Q325.5 .M342 2023 | DDC 006.3/1015--dc23/eng20230327

LC record available at https://lccn.loc.gov/2022058911

British Library Cataloguing-in-Publication Data

A catalogue record for this book is available from the British Library.

For any available supplementary material, please visit
https://www.worldscientific.com/worldscibooks/10.1142/Q0404#t=suppl

Desk Editors: Logeshwaran Arumugam/Adam Binnie/Shi Ying Koe

Typeset by Stallion Press
Email: enquiries@stallionpress.com

Preface

We live in the Age of Data. Certainly, one could argue that since the dawn of science, we have always lived in the Age of Data. From the astronomical observations of antiquity to the spectral analyses of atomic emissions, our interactions with, and our attempts to understand, Nature have always been grounded on data. Yet, something fundamentally different should be ascribed to our Civilization in the last few decades, something which justifies the capital letters in the "Age of Data", something which has reshaped, and will continue to propel, humanity. I speak, of course, of the conjunction between the personal computer and the Internet. All of a sudden, at every person's finger-tips, is the instantly available plethora of data, as well as the technology to analyze it. Imagine the time when, in order to quantify the precise motion of the planets, Kepler had to travel hundreds of miles, likely on foot, to Tycho, in order to obtain the most accurate data of his time.

The influx of data should only be accompanied by the ability to digest it. Tycho's telescope would have been meaningless without Kepler's geometry. Over the last decade or so, the processing power of our laptops has entered the realm of machine learning and, with it, our initiation into the possibility of rapidly processing the data. In some sense, neural networks are so successful at describing the world because they are *not analytically* modeling the world. The traditional quantitative understanding of Nature is *reductionist*: a relatively simple set of, typically, partially differential equations is proposed and one checks whether the solutions fit the experimental data. In fundamental physics, this paradigm has worked remarkably well through the ages and constitutes the Positivist and Reductionist search for the Theory of Everything. In emergent sciences such as biology or sociology, where noise is often comparable to the signal, it is not entirely clear that such a paradigm is optimal. Meanwhile, deep learning, which acquires complexity via emergence, quickly fits to the data here: instead of trying to model and solve a single analytic set of PDEs, machine learning algorithms such as deep neural networks are optimizing over an intertwinement of myriads of such systems. Perhaps, this is how the brain and indeed how biological, ecological and sociological systems function. Reductionism is being accompanied by Structuralism as a scientific principle.

But, therein lies the rub. The sacrifice of analyticity renders the juxtaposition of "machine learning" and "pure mathematics and theoretical physics" almost a contradiction. Of course, AI and machine learning techniques have long been an indispensable tool in the experimental sciences; in fundamental physics, for instance, the Higgs particle could not have been found by CERN without deep-learning of the detector data. But, it seems counter-intuitive that a methodology grounded upon the statistical inference of data should be of any utility to the rigorous world of proofs in mathematics and derivations in theoretical physics. Nevertheless, from the introduction in 2017 of machine learning into the mathematics of algebraic geometry and the physics of superstring theory, by a few small groups including myself, to the recent advances of Google's DeepMind collaboration with mathematicians in studying knot invariants in 2022, there has been an explosion of activity over the lustrum.

Not only is machine learning used as a tool for speeding up numerical computations that lie at the core of problems from combinatorics to number theory, from geometry to group theory, etc., more importantly, it is helping with the pattern recognition that forms the heart of conjecture formulation.

With an initial attempt to summarize the progress in, and to advocate the necessity of, machine learning in geometry, especially in the context of string theory (YHH, *The Calabi–Yau Landscape: From Physics, to Geometry, to Machine Learning*, LNM 2293, Springer 2021), I speculated — borrowing terminologies from physics — that mathematics and AI could be in conjunction in two complementary ways (YHH, *Machine Learning Mathematical Structures*, arXiv:2101.06317, to appear in *Int. J. Data Sci.* in the Mathematical

Sciences, WS, 2023). In (1) "Bottom-up Mathematics", one builds theorems and proofs line by line, using type-theoretic computer languages such as Lean. This is the automated theorem proving program, which has had a distinguished history since the 1960s, and with recent proponents such as K. Buzzard, H. Davenport, *et al.* (q. v. ICM 2022 addresses by K. Buzzard and by G. Williamson). In (2) "Top-down Mathematics", one creates pure, noiseless datasets of various mathematical structures, such as representations of finite groups, the arithmetic of algebraic curves and the types of superstring vacuum solutions. Such data are then fed into various machine learning algorithms, supervised and unsupervised, in order to find new patterns, raise new conjectures or find alternative exact formulae.

It is this second direction of "Top-down Mathematics" that has been gaining attention and momentum in the last few years and thereto is this present volume devoted. Organized alphabetically by the contributing author, this unique collection of research and survey article is, I believe, the first of its kind in bringing together experts in pure mathematics and theoretical physics, to present their ideas on how machine learning is used to understand the pertinent data and to speed up computation, to formulate new conjectures and to gain intuition on the underlying structure.

As one could imagine, there is a vast expanse of disciplines which produces the mathematical data, and these will be discussed in detail: explorations in the string landscape, Calabi–Yau manifolds, combinatorics of polytopes, the arithmetic geometry of curves, the number theory of the Birch–Swinnerton-Dyer conjecture, volumes of Einstein manifolds, etc.

Conversely, one might also wonder how ideas from modern mathematics and physics help with understanding machine learning. Indeed, this is also an emerging field which is destined to prove fruitful. In this volume, we have perspectives from theoretical physicists on inferencing as a dynamical system, as well as correlation functions as a handle on symmetries in neural networks. Finally, since machine learning is also taking over natural language processing, it is natural and expedient to perform meta-studies where one analyzes the *language* of theoretical physics and mathematics; this is the subject of one of the chapters.

I sincerely hope that this volume offers the first glimpse onto a fertile land, a cross-disciplinary world of mathematicians, physicists and computer scientists. This nascent collaboration between machine learning and pure mathematics as well as theoretical physics, a taste of the spirit of which we hope to capture here, will undoubtedly continue to flourish.

About the Editor

Yang-Hui He is a mathematical physicist, who is a Fellow at the London Institute, Royal Institution of Great Britain, Professor of mathematics at City, University of London, Chang-Jiang Chair Professor at Nankai University, as well as Lecturer at Merton College, University of Oxford. He obtained his BA in physics with Highest Honours from Princeton University, a Distinction in the Mathematical Tripos from Cambridge University and PhD in mathematical physics from MIT. He works at the interface between quantum field theory, string theory, algebraic geometry, and number theory, as well as studying how AI and machine learning help with these problems.

About the Contributors

Laura Alessandretti is Assistant Professor in modeling of human dynamics at the Technical University of Denmark. She works in the area of computational social science and has researched aspects of human behavior combining the analysis of large-scale passively collected datasets with mathematical and computational models. Her research has largely focused on the understanding of human mobility, smartphone application usage, and online behavior in digital markets. Previously, she was a Postdoctoral Researcher at the Copenhagen Centre for Social Data Science and at DTU Compute. She received her PhD in mathematics at City, University of London, and her Master's in physics of complex systems at École normale supérieure de Lyon.

Andrea Baronchelli is an Associate Professor at the Department of Mathematics of City, University of London, Token Economy theme lead at the Alan Turing Institute, and Research Associate at the UCL Centre for Blockchain Technologies (CBT). His research interests include spreading phenomena on networks, the dynamics of social norms, online (mis)information and polarization, collective behavior change, and cryptocurrency ecosystems. His work has appeared in a wide range of journals including *Science, PNAS*, and *Nature Human Behaviour*, and has been recognized by the 2019 "Young Scientist Award for Socio and Econophysics" of the German Physical Society.

David Berman completed his graduation from the University of Manchester in 1994. He completed a PhD at Durham University with a sojourn at CERN theory division. He then took postdoctoral researcher roles at the universities of Utrecht, Groningen, and Jerusalem. Following this, he became an EPSRC Advanced Research Fellow at the University of Cambridge. In 2004, he accepted a faculty position at Queen Mary University of London and became Professor in 2014. He now also works as a Senior Consultant for Cambridge Consultants in Artificial Intelligence and Machine Learning. His work has been focused around string theory and ideas in fundamental theoretical physics. This has included various geometric aspects like noncommutative geometry and its extensions, black hole physics, and quantum gravity. He is most known for exceptional geometry and its possible role in M-theory. His most recent work has been at the interface between machine learning and physics with a focus on using ideas for machine learning from theoretical physics.

Tom Coates is a Professor of mathematics at Imperial College London, working in algebraic geometry and scientific computation. He co-leads a research group that aims to find and classify Fano varieties, which are "atomic pieces" of mathematical shapes, by combining new methods in geometry with cluster-scale computation, data mining, and machine learning. He has won numerous prizes and awards including the Philip Leverhulme Prize, the Whitehead Prize, and the Adams Prize.

Andrei Constantin is a Stephen Hawking Fellow at the University of Oxford, a Research Fellow at Wolfson College Oxford, and a Tutor in physics and mathematics at Mansfield College Oxford. He studied physics in Bremen and received an MSc in theoretical and mathematical physics from LMU Munich. He did his doctoral studies at the University of Oxford, followed by two postdoctoral positions, one in Oxford and one in Uppsala. His work lies at the interface of string theory, algebraic geometry, and machine learning and focuses on developing mathematical and computational tools to investigate String Theory and its implications for particle physics, cosmology, and quantum gravity.

Harold Erbin obtained his PhD in theoretical physics from Pierre et Marie Curie, Paris 6 University. He is currently a Marie Skłodowska-Curie Fellow at MIT and IAIFI (Boston) and CEA-LIST (Paris). Besides working at the intersection of machine learning, physics, and mathematics, his interests include string field theory, two-dimensional gravity, black holes, supergravity, and tensor models.

Riccardo Finotello is currently a Postdoctoral Researcher at CEA-LIST. His research interests cover physical and computational problems, the common thread being the relation between mathematics and artificial intelligence, from data acquisition to the analysis. At present, he focuses on two principal research areas. The first is the segmentation of hyperspectral images using mathematical and unsupervised methods to extract relevant information from complex and diverse data. The second is the compression of neural networks using tensor methods to isolate and propagate the main information contained in deep learning models. He is also interested in applications of machine and deep learning to the theory of mathematics and physics, such as algebraic geometry and string theory, for their fascinating structures and their ability to provide geometrical insights on the behavior of neural network architectures.

James Halverson is an Associate Professor of physics at Northeastern University in Boston, Massachusetts. His research is at some of the interfaces between string theory, particle physics, cosmology, mathematics, and deep learning. He is particularly interested in the string landscape and its implications for particle physics and cosmology beyond their standard models. These implications often follow from the structure of extra-dimensional geometries, of which there are many possibilities. Halverson's research therefore requires importing techniques from mathematics and computer science. Recently, Halverson's interest in the interface of physics and deep learning has continued to grow. To that end, he is a co-PI and serves on the institute board of the NSF AI Institute for Artificial Intelligence and Fundamental Interactions (IAIFI) and co-organizes Physics ∩ ML.

Jonathan Heckman was born and raised in Chicago, where he attended the University of Chicago Laboratory School for high school. He received his AB in physics at Princeton University with undergraduate research supervised by C.G. Callan Jr. and S.S. Gubser, and his PhD in physics at Harvard University under the supervision of C. Vafa. After a membership at the IAS at Princeton and a postdoc appointment at Harvard, Jonathan took a faculty position at UNC Chapel Hill, and subsequently moved to the University of Pennsylvania where he is currently an Associate Professor in the department of physics and astronomy. Heckman's research interests include string theory and quantum field theory, and the application to a range of questions in particle physics, mathematics, information theory, and machine learning.

Johannes Hofscheier is Assistant Professor in Geometry at the University of Nottingham, UK. He obtained his PhD in mathematics from the Eberhard Karls Universität Tübingen, Germany, in 2015. Dr. Hofscheier was a Postdoctoral Researcher at Otto-von-Guericke-Universität Magdeburg, Germany, from 2015 to 2017 and another two years at McMaster University, Canada, before he was awarded a Nottingham Research Fellowship from the University of Nottingham, UK, in 2019. His research interests include combinatorial algebraic geometry, an area of mathematics that uses combinatorial techniques to solve questions in geometry. In his research, he takes advantage of data science and machine learning to discover unexpected new structure in mathematical data, leading to intriguing new results.

Early in his scientific career, **Vishnu Jejjala** switched from vertebrate paleontology to astronomy. He was 7 years old at the time. His interest in explicating the origin of the universe and playing with cool mathematics led him to string theory. He completed a PhD in physics at the University of Illinois at Urbana-Champaign in 2002 and subsequently held postdoctoral research appointments at Virginia Tech (2002–2004), Durham University (2004–2007), the Institut des Hautes Etudes Scientifiques (2007–2009), and Queen Mary University of London (2009–2011). Since October 2011, Vishnu has been the South African Research Chair in Theoretical Particle Cosmology at the University of the Witwatersrand in Johannesburg. He is also a Professor in the School of Physics. Vishnu's research interests are broad, but focus on exploring quantum gravity and the structure of quantum field theories with the goal of bringing string theory into contact with the real world. Black holes are one theoretical laboratory for investigating these issues. Another is string compactification on Calabi–Yau spaces. Vishnu has recently been applying techniques from machine learning to study large datasets in string theory and mathematics.

Alexander Kasprzyk is Associate Professor in Geometry and Head of Pure Mathematics at the University of Nottingham. His research focuses on the classification of Fano varieties — the "atomic pieces" of geometries — and brings together ideas from algebraic geometry, theoretical physics, combinatorics, and increasingly, data science. As part of this work, he has pioneered the use of massively parallel computational algebra and big data, and is increasingly using machine learning to accelerate the process of human-driven mathematical discovery.

Marc Klinger is a PhD student at the University of Illinois at Urbana-Champaign. He is primarily interested in mathematical physics and the role of theory in bridging the gaps between quantum information, machine learning, and gauge theory. Some of Marc's recent work involves developing information theoretical approaches to the Exact Renormalization Group (ERG) by leveraging its interpretation as a functional convection-diffusion equation. This approach facilitates a tight correspondence between ERG and Dynamic Bayesian Inference, resulting in new outlooks for the use of ERG both as a tool for exploring the space of quantum field theories and as a device for constructing and interpreting machine learning algorithms in data science contexts.

Anindita Maiti is a PhD student at Northeastern University and the NSF AI Institute for Artificial Intelligence and Fundamental Interactions, supervised by Professor James Halverson. She is interested in theoretical particle physics, string theory, and theory of machine learning. In particular, Anindita aims to enhance the science of artificial intelligence through fundamental physics, especially quantum physics and quantum field theory. She has worked on establishing a foundational connection, the first of its kind, between field theories and neural networks, the structural basis of deep learning.

Brent Nelson is a theoretical particle physicist whose work connects string theory to testable observations in high-energy physics and cosmology. His 60+ scholarly publications over the last 20 years include highly cited research into hadron collider phenomenology, supersymmetric model building, dark matter phenomenology, mathematical physics, and computational approaches to string theory. With colleagues at Northeastern University, Professor Nelson helped establish the rapidly growing field of machine learning applications in theoretical particle physics, including the use of network science to study the vacuum selection problem and the use of reinforcement learning as a tool to study the string landscape. Dr. Nelson came to Northeastern in 2006 after having served as a Postdoctoral Fellow at the University of Pennsylvania and at the Michigan Center for Theoretical Physics in Ann Arbor, Michigan. He received his PhD in physics from the University of California, Berkeley under the supervision of National Academy member Mary K. Gaillard.

Thomas Oliver is a Lecturer in Mathematics at Teesside University. He completed his undergraduate degree at Durham University and his PhD at the University of Nottingham. His primary research area is number theory and adjacent areas include algebraic geometry and representation theory. He is increasingly interested in the interface of pure mathematics with data science, and is an organizer of the recent DANGER (data, numbers, and geometry) workshops. He often wears a hat.

Rak-Kyeong Seong obtained his PhD in theoretical physics at Imperial College London in 2013 and stayed as a Postdoctoral Research Fellow at the Korea Institute for Advanced Study and at the Angstrom Laboratory at Uppsala University. In 2017, he became a tenure-track Assistant Professor at the Yau Mathematical Sciences Center at Tsinghua University in Beijing, and stayed 2 years as a Senior Researcher and Project Manager at the AI Advanced Research Lab at Samsung SDS in Seoul. In 2021, he returned to academia and became a tenure-track Assistant Professor at the Department of Mathematical Sciences at the Ulsan National Institute of Science and Technology (UNIST) in South Korea.

Keegan Stoner is a Research Engineer at Systems and Technology Research. He completed his PhD in physics at Northeastern University in 2022 with a focus on the statistics of neural networks. His research interests include developing new ways of understanding machine learning through physics and statistics, and applying novel machine learning models to real-world problems. Recently, he has been exploring language models and the mathematics behind their techniques, focusing especially on transformer architectures.

Acknowledgments

First, I extend heart-felt thanks to all the contributing authors to this volume, for their wonderful chapters. Moreover, I am grateful to the London Institute for Mathematical Sciences and to Merton College, University of Oxford, for providing me with two corners of paradise wherein I could simply dream and contemplate. Above all, I am indebted to my many friends and colleagues, especially my talented and dedicated students Edward Hirst, Jiakang Bao, Elli Heyes, Kieran Bull, Lucille Calmon, Suvajit Majumder, Juan Ipiña, Toby Peterken, Yan Xiao, Tejas Acharya, Daattavya Aggarwal, Maksymiliam Manko, Beichen Zhang, Qinyun Liu, Siqi Chen and Hongrui Zhang, with whom I have had the pleasure of exploring the connections between machine learning and mathematics in the last few years.

Contents

Chapter 1

Machine Learning Meets Number Theory: The Data Science of Birch–Swinnerton-Dyer

Laura Alessandretti[*,†,**]**, Andrea Baronchelli**[†,‡,††]
and Yang-Hui He[†,§,¶,‖,‡‡]

*Copenhagen Center for Social Data Science,
University of Copenhagen, Copenhagen K 1353, Denmark
†Department of Mathematics, City, University of London,
EC1V 0HB, UK
‡The Alan Turing Institute, London NW1 2DB, UK
§Merton College, University of Oxford, OX14JD, UK
¶School of Physics, Nankai University, Tianjin 300071, P.R. China
‖London Institute for Mathematical Sciences, Royal Institution of Great
Britain, London, W1S 4BS, UK

**l.alessandretti@gmail.com
††andrea.baronchelli.1@city.ac.uk
‡‡hey@maths.ox.ac.uk

Abstract

Empirical analysis is often the first step towards the birth of a conjecture. This is the case of the Birch–Swinnerton-Dyer (BSD) Conjecture describing the rational points on an elliptic curve, one of the most celebrated unsolved problems in mathematics. Here, we extend the original empirical approach to the analysis of the Cremona database of quantities relevant to BSD, inspecting more than 2.5 million elliptic curves by means of the latest techniques in data science, machine learning and topological data analysis.

Key quantities such as rank, Weierstraß coefficients, period, conductor, Tamagawa number, regulator and order of the Tate–Shafarevich group give rise to a high-dimensional point cloud whose statistical properties we investigate. We reveal patterns and distributions in the rank versus Weierstraß coefficients, as well as the Beta distribution of the BSD ratio of the quantities. Via gradient-boosted trees, machine learning is applied in finding inter-correlation among the various quantities. We anticipate that our approach will spark further research on the statistical properties of large datasets in Number Theory and more in general in pure Mathematics.

1. Introduction

Elliptic curves $\mathcal{E}$ occupy a central stage in modern mathematics, their geometry and arithmetic providing endless insights into the most profound structures. The celebrated Conjecture of Birch and Swinnerton-Dyer [5] is the key result dictating the behavior of $\mathcal{E}$ over finite number fields and thereby, arithmetic. Despite decades of substantial progress, the proof of the conjecture remains elusive. To gain intuition, a highly explicit and computational program had been pursued by Cremona [11], in cataloging all elliptic curves up to isogeny and expressed in canonical form, to conductors into the hundreds of thousands.

Interestingly, a somewhat similar situation exists for the higher dimensional analog of elliptic curves considered as Ricci-flat Kähler manifolds, viz., Calabi–Yau manifolds. Though Yau [36] settled the Calabi–Yau Conjecture [9], much remains unknown about the landscape of such manifolds, even over the complex numbers. For instance, even seemingly simple questions of whether there is a finite number of topological types of Calabi–Yau n-folds for $n \geq 3$ are not known — even though it is conjectured so. Nevertheless, because of the pivotal importance of Calabi–Yau manifolds to superstring theory, theoretical physicists have been constructing ever-expanding datasets thereof over the last few decades (cf. [18] for a pedagogical introduction).

Given the recent successes in the science of "big data" and machine learning, it is natural to examine the database of Cremona [12] using the latest techniques in Data Science. Indeed, such a perspective has been undertaken for Calabi–Yau manifolds and the landscape of compactifications in superstring theory in high-energy physics, ranging from machine learning [17] to statistics [14,19].

Indeed, [10,17,23,30] brought about a host of new activities in machine learning within string theory; moreover, [17,18] and the subsequent work in [1–3,20–22] introduced the curious possibility that machine learning should be applied to at least stochastically avoid expensive algorithms in geometry and combinatorics and to raise new conjectures.

Can artificial intelligence help with understanding the syntax and semantics of mathematics? While such profound questions are better left to the insights of Turing and Voevodsky, the more humble question of using machine learning to recognizing patterns which might have been missed by standard methods should be addressed more immediately. Preliminary experiments such as being able to "guess" — to over 99% accuracy and confidence — the ranks of cohomology groups without exact-sequence-chasing (having seen tens of thousands of examples of known bundle cohomologies) [18] or whether a finite group is simple without recourse to the theorem of Noether and Sylow (having been trained on thousands of Cayley tables) [20] already point to this potentiality.

In our present case of number theory, extreme care should, of course, be taken. Patterns in the primes can be notoriously deceptive, as exemplified by the likes of Skewes's constant. Indeed, a sanity check to let neural networks predict the next prime number in [17] yielded a reassuring null result. Nevertheless, one should not summarily disregard all experimentation in number theory: after all, the best neural network of the 19th century — the mind of Gauß — was able to pattern-spot $\pi(x)$ to raise the profound Prime Number Theorem years before the discovery of complex analysis to allow its proof.

The purpose of this chapter is to open up dialog between data scientists and number theorists, as the aforementioned works have done for the machine-learning community with geometers and physicists, using Cremona's elliptic curve database as a concrete arena. The organization is as follows. We begin with a rapid introduction in Section 2, bearing in mind the diversity of readership, to elliptic curves in light of BSD. In Section 3, we summarize Cremona's database and perform preliminary statistical analyses beyond simple frequency count. Subsequently, Section 4 is devoted to machine-learning various aspects of the BSD quantities and Section 5 to their topological data analyses and persistent homology. Finally, we conclude in Section 6 with the key results and discuss prospects for the future.

2.   Elliptic Curves and BSD

Our starting point is the Weierstraß model

$$y^2 + a_1 xy + a_3 y = x^3 + a_2 x^2 + a_4 x + a_6 \tag{1}$$

of an elliptic curve $\mathcal{E}$ over $\mathbb{Q}$, where $(x, y) \in \mathbb{Q}$ and the coefficients $a_i \in \mathbb{Z}$. The discriminant Δ and J-invariant of $\mathcal{E}$ are obtained in a standard way as

$$\Delta(\mathcal{E}) = -b_2^2 b_8 - 8b_4^3 - 27 b_6^2 + 9 b_2 b_4 b_6, \qquad j(\mathcal{E}) = \frac{c_4^3}{\Delta}, \tag{2}$$

where $b_2 := a_1^2 + 4a_2$, $b_4 := 2a_4 + a_1 a_3$, $b_6 := a_3^2 + 4a_6$, $b_8 := a_1^2 a_6 + 4a_2 a_6 - a_1 a_3 a_4 + a_2 a_3^2 - a_4^2$ and $c_4 := b_2^2 - 24 b_4$. Smoothness is ensured by the non-vanishing of Δ and isomorphism (isogeny) between two elliptic curves, by the equality of j.

An algorithm of Tate and Laska [24,33][1] can then be used to bring the first 3 coefficients $a_{1,2,3}$ to be $0, \pm 1$, transforming (1) into a *minimal Weierstraß model*. Thus, for our purposes, an elliptic curve $\mathcal{E}$ is specified by the pair of integers (a_4, a_6) together with a triple $(a_1, a_2, a_3) \in \{-1, 0, 1\}$. From the vast subject of elliptic curves, we will need this 5-tuple, together with arithmetic data to be presented in the ensuing.

---

[1]In particular, consider the transformation between the coefficients a_i and a_i' between two elliptic curves $\mathcal{E}$ and $\mathcal{E}'$:

$$ua_1' = a_1 + 2s,$$
$$u^2 a_2' = a_2 - sa_1 + 3r - s^2,$$
$$u^3 a_3' = a_3 + ra_1 + 2t,$$
$$u^4 a_4' = a_4 - sa_3 + 2ra_2 - (t + rs)a_1 + 3r^2 - 2st,$$
$$u^6 a_6' = a_6 + ra_4 + r^2 a_2 + r^3 - ta_3 - t^2 - rta_1,$$

for $u, s, t \in \mathbb{Q}$, then relating the points $(x, y) \in \mathcal{E}$ and $(x', y') \in \mathcal{E}'$ as

$$x = u^2 x' + r, \quad y = u^3 y' + su^2 x' + t$$

yields $u^{12} \Delta' = \Delta$ and hence $j' = j$, and thus the isomorphism.

2.1. Rudiments on the arithmetic of $\mathcal{E}$

This section serves as essentially a lexicon for the quantities which we require, presented in brief, itemized form.

2.1.1. Conductor and good/bad reduction

The conductor is the product over all (finitely many) numbers of primes p — the primes of bad reduction — where $\mathcal{E}$ reduced modulo p becomes singular (where $\Delta = 0$). All other primes are called good reduction.

2.1.2. Rank and torsion

The set of rational points on $\mathcal{E}$ has the structure of an abelian group, $\mathcal{E}(\mathbb{Q}) \simeq \mathbb{Z}^r \times T$. The non-negative integer r is called the rank; its non-vanishing would signify an infinite number of rational points on $\mathcal{E}$. The group T is called the torsion group and can be only one of 15 groups by Mazur's celebrated theorem [25], viz., the cyclic group C_n for $1 \leq n \leq 10$ and $n = 12$, as well as the direct product $C_2 \times C_n$ for $n = 2, 4, 6, 8$.

2.1.3. L-function and conductor

The Hasse–Weil zeta-function of $\mathcal{E}$ can be defined, given a finite field $\mathbb{F}_{q=p^n}$, as the generating functions Z_p (the local) and Z (the global)

$$Z_p(t; \mathcal{E}) := \exp\left(\sum_{n=1}^{\infty} \frac{\mathcal{E}(\mathbb{F}_{p^n})}{n} t^n\right),$$

$$Z(s; \mathcal{E}) := \prod_p Z_p(t := p^{-s}; \mathcal{E}). \tag{3}$$

Here, in the local zeta function $Z_p(t; \mathcal{E})$, $\mathcal{E}(\mathbb{F}_{p^n})$ is the number of points of $\mathcal{E}$ over the finite field and the product is taken over all primes p to give the global zeta function $Z(s)$.

Definition (3) is applicable to general varieties, and for elliptic curves, the global zeta function simplifies (cf. [32]) to a product of the Riemann zeta function ζ and the so-called L-function as

$$Z(s; \mathcal{E}) = \frac{\zeta(s)\zeta(s-1)}{L(s; \mathcal{E})}, \tag{4}$$

where

$$L(s; \mathcal{E}) = \prod_p L_p(s; \mathcal{E})^{-1},$$

$$L_p(s; \mathcal{E}) := \begin{cases} (1 - \alpha_p p^{-s} + p^{1-2s}), & p \nmid N, \\ (1 - \alpha_p p^{-s}), & p \mid N \text{ and } p^2 \nmid N, \\ 1, & p^2 \mid N. \end{cases}$$

In the above, $\alpha_p = p + 1 -$ counts the number of points of $\mathcal{E}$ mod p for primes of good reduction and ± 1 depending on the type of bad reduction. The positive integer N which controls, via its factorization, these primes is the conductor of $\mathcal{E}$.

Importantly, the L-function has analytic continuation [34] to $\mathbb{C}$ so that the variable s is not a merely dummy variable like t in the local generating function but renders $L(s; \mathcal{E})$ a complex analytic function.

2.1.4. Real period

The periods of a complex variety are usually defined to be the integral of some globally defined holomorphic differential over a basis in homology. Here, we are interested in the real period, defined as (using the minimal Weierstraß model)

$$\mathbb{R} \ni \Omega := \int_{\mathcal{E}(\mathbb{R})} |\omega|, \quad \omega = \frac{dx}{2y + a_1 x + a_3} \tag{5}$$

over the set of real points $\mathcal{E}(\mathbb{R})$ of the elliptic curve.

2.1.5. Tamagawa number

Now, $\mathcal{E}$ over any field is a group, thus in particular we can define $\mathcal{E}(\mathbb{Q}_p)$ over the p-adic field $\mathbb{Q}_p$ for a given prime, as well as its subgroup $\mathcal{E}^0(\mathbb{Q}_p)$ of points which have good reduction. We define the index in the sense of groups

$$c_p := \left[\mathcal{E}(\mathbb{Q}_p) : \mathcal{E}(\mathbb{Q}_p) \right], \tag{6}$$

which is clearly equal to 1 for primes of good reduction since then $\mathcal{E}^0(\mathbb{Q}_p) = \mathcal{E}(\mathbb{Q}_p)$. The Tamagawa number is defined to be the product over all primes of bad reduction of c_p, i.e.,

$$\text{Tamagawa Number} = \prod_{p|N} c_p. \tag{7}$$

2.1.6. *Canonical height*

For a rational point $P = \frac{a}{b}$, written in minimal fraction form with $\gcd(a, b) = 1$, $a, b \in \mathbb{Z}$ and $b > 0$, we can define a naive height $h(P) := \log \max(|a|, b)$. Then, a *canonical height* can be defined as

$$\hat{h}(P) = \lim_{n \to \infty} n^{-2} h(nP), \tag{8}$$

where $nP = P + \cdots + P$ (n-times) is the addition of under the group law of $\mathcal{E}$. This limit exists and renders $\hat{h}$ the unique quadratic form on $\mathcal{E}(\mathbb{Q}) \otimes \mathbb{R}$ such that $\hat{h} - h$ is bounded. An explicit expression of $\hat{h}(P)$ in terms of a, b can be found, e.g., in Eqs. (4) and (5) of [8]. The canonical height defines a natural bilinear form

$$2 \langle P, P' \rangle = \hat{h}(P + P') - \hat{h}(P) - \hat{h}(P') \tag{9}$$

for two points $P, P' \in \mathcal{E}(\mathbb{Q})$ and as always, $P + P'$ is done via the group law.

2.1.7. *Regulator*

Given the infinite (free abelian) part of $\mathcal{E}(\mathbb{Q})$, viz., $\mathbb{Z}^r$, let its generators be $P_1, \ldots, P_r$, then we can define the regulator

$$R_{\mathcal{E}} = \det \langle P_i, P_j \rangle, \quad i, j = 1, \ldots, r, \tag{10}$$

where the pairing is with the canonical height and defines an $r \times r$ integer matrix. For $r = 0$, R is taken to be 1 by convention.

2.1.8. *Tate–Shafarevich group*

Finally, one defines group cohomologies $H^1(\mathbb{Q}, \mathcal{E})$ and $H^1(\mathbb{Q}_p, \mathcal{E})$ between which there is a homomorphism (cf., e.g., [26] IV.2 for a detailed description). We can then define the Tate–Shafarevich Group

III of $\mathcal{E}$ as the kernel of the homomorphism

$$\text{III}(\mathcal{E}) := \ker\left(H^1(\mathbb{Q}, \mathcal{E}) \longrightarrow \prod_p H^1(\mathbb{Q}_p, \mathcal{E})\right). \qquad (11)$$

This is the most mysterious part of the arithmetic of elliptic curves; it is conjectured to be a finite abelian group. For ranks $r = 0, 1$, this has been proven (cf. the survey of [31]), but in general, this is not known.

2.2.   *The conjecture*

With the above definitions, we can at least present the celebrated

Conjecture 2.1 (Birch–Swinnerton-Dyer (Weak Version)).
The order of the zero of $L(s; \mathcal{E})$ at $s = 1$ is equal to the rank r,

$$\text{Ord}_{s \to 1} L(s; \mathcal{E}) = r(\mathcal{E}).$$

That is, the Taylor series around 1 is $L(s; \mathcal{E}) \sim c(s-1)^r$ with some complex coefficient c.

In fact, a stronger version of the conjecture predicts precisely what the Taylor coefficient c should be, which is as follows:

Conjecture 2.2 (Birch–Swinnerton-Dyer (Strong Version)).
The Taylor coefficient of $L(s; \mathcal{E})$ at $s = 1$ is given in terms of the regulator R, Tamagawa number $\prod_{p|N} c_p$, (analytic) order of the Tate–Shafarevich group III, and the order of the torsion group T. Specifically, let $L(s; \mathcal{E}) = \sum_r \frac{L^{(r)}(1;\mathcal{E})}{r!}(s-1)^r$, then

$$\frac{L^{(r)}(1; \mathcal{E})}{r!} = \frac{|\text{III}| \cdot \Omega \cdot R \cdot \prod\limits_{p|N} c_p}{|T|^2}.$$

3.   Elliptic Curve Data

BSD arose from extensive computer experimentation, the earliest of its kind, by Birch and Swinnerton-Dyer. Continuing along this vein, Cremona [11] then compiled an impressive of list of 2,483,649 isomorphism classes of elliptic curves over $\mathbb{Q}$ and explicitly computed the relevant quantities introduced above. This is available freely online at [12].

3.1. *Cremona database*

The database of Cremona, on which the rest of the chapter will focus, associates to each minimal Weierstraß model (given by the coefficients $(a_1, a_2, a_3) \in \{-1, 0, 1\}$ and $(a_4, a_6) \in \mathbb{Z}$; generically, these last two coefficients have very large magnitude) the following:

- the conductor N, ranging from 1 to 400,000;
- the rank r, ranging from 0 to 4;
- the torsion group T, whose size ranges from 1 to 16;
- the real period Ω, a real number ranging from approximately $2.5 \cdot 10^{-4}$ to 6.53;
- the Tamagawa number $\prod_{p|N} c_p$, ranging from 1 to 87040;
- the order of the Tate–Shafarevich group (exactly when known, otherwise given numerically), ranging from 1 to 2500;
- the regulator $R \in \mathbb{Z}_{>0}$, ranging from approximately 0.01 to 3905.84.

A typical entry, corresponding to the curve $y^2 + xy = x^3 - x^2 - 453981x + 117847851$ (labeled as "314226b1" and with $\Delta = 2 \cdot 3^3 \cdot 11 \cdot 23^8$ and $j = 2^{-1} \cdot 3^3 \cdot 11^{-1} \cdot 23 \cdot 199^3$ which are readily computed from (2)) would be

$$(a_1, a_2, a_3, a_4, a_6) = (1, -1, 0, -453981, 117847851) \quad \Longrightarrow$$

$$\begin{cases} N = 314226 = 2 \cdot 3^3 \cdot 11 \cdot 23^2, \\ r = 0, \\ R = 1, \\ \Omega \simeq 0.56262, \\ \prod_{p|N} c_p = 3, \\ |T| = 3, \\ |\text{III}| = 1. \end{cases} \quad (12)$$

3.2.   *Weierstraß coefficients*

Let us begin with a statistical analysis of the minimal Weierstraß coefficients themselves. It so happens that in the entire database, there are only 12 different sets of values of (a_1, a_2, a_3); we tally all of the curves in the following histogram, against rank and (a_1, a_2, a_3):

We see that most of the curves are of smaller rank, with only a single instance of $r = 4$. This is in line with the recent result of [4] that most elliptic curves are rank 1; in fact, over $2/3$ of elliptic curves obey the BSD conjecture [7].

To give an idea of the size of the a-coefficients involved, the largest one involved in the database is

$$\vec{a} = \{1, 0, 0, -40101356069987968, -3090912440687373254444800\},$$
$$(13)$$

which is of rank 0.

Even though it is a conjecture that the rank r can be arbitrarily large, the largest confirmed rank [16] so far known in the literature is 19, corresponding (the last term being a 72-digit integer!) to

$$a_1 = 1, \quad a_2 = 1, \quad a_3 = -1,$$

$$a_4 = 31368015812338065133318565292206590792820353345,$$

$$a_6 = 302038802698566087335643188429543498624522041683874493$$

$$555186062568159847. \qquad (14)$$

This extraordinary result is clearly not in the database due to the large rank.

One of the first steps in data visualization is a *principle component analysis* where features of the largest variations are extracted. The minimal Weierstraß model gives a natural way of doing so, since the (a_1, a_2, a_3) coefficients take only 12 values and we can readily see scatter plot of (a_4, a_6). Now, due to the large variation in these coefficients, we define a signed natural logarithm for $x \in \mathbb{R}$ as

$$\mathrm{sLog}(x) = \begin{cases} \mathrm{sgn}(x) \log(x), & x \neq 0, \\ 0, & x = 0. \end{cases} \qquad (15)$$

We present this scatter plot of $(\mathrm{sLog}(a_4), \mathrm{sLog}(a_6))$ in Figure 1. Therein, we plot all the data points (i.e., for all different values of

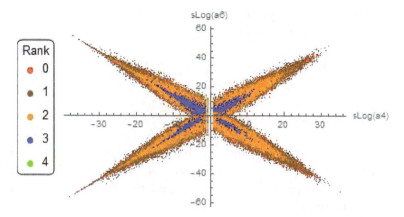

Figure 1.   A scatter plot of (sLog(a_4), sLog(a_6)) for all 2,483,649 elliptic curves in the Cremona database. Different ranks are marked with different colors.

Table 1.   Number of curves per rank (columns) and values of (a_1, a_2, a_3) (rows).

		Rank			
(a_1, a_2, a_3)	0	1	2	3	4
{0, −1, 0}	126135	155604	30236	659	0
{0, −1, 1}	17238	24593	7582	399	0
{0, 0, 0}	172238	213780	40731	698	0
{0, 0, 1}	28440	39235	11187	506	0
{0, 1, 0}	118942	157003	34585	722	0
{0, 1, 1}	18016	27360	9609	426	0
{1, −1, 0}	102769	127198	25793	551	1
{1, −1, 1}	96995	128957	28940	604	0
{1, 0, 0}	66411	98092	25286	612	0
{1, 0, 1}	71309	94595	20907	548	0
{1, 1, 0}	69759	88403	18293	496	0
{1, 1, 1}	67834	91717	21197	458	0

(a_1, a_2, a_3)) together, distinguishing rank by color (rank 4 has only a single point as seen from Table 1).

The first thing one would notice is the approximate cross-like symmetry, even however, this is not trivial because the transformation

$$(a_4, a_6) \longrightarrow (\pm a_4, \pm a_6) \tag{16}$$

is by no means a rank preserving map. For instance, a single change in sign in a_4 could result in rank change from 1 to 3:

$$r(\{0, 1, 1, -10, 20\}) = 3, \quad r(\{0, 1, 1, +10, 20\}) = 1. \qquad (17)$$

Examples of a similar nature abound. The next feature to notice is that the size of the cross shrinks as the rank increases. This is rather curious since the largest rank case of (14) has far *larger* coefficients. This symmetry is somewhat reminiscent of mirror symmetry for Calabi–Yau 3-folds, where every compact smooth such manifold with Hodge numbers $(h^{1,1}, h^{2,1})$ has a mirror manifold with these values exchanged.

3.3.   *Distributions of a_4 and a_6*

Fortified by the above initial observations, let us continue with a more refined study of the distribution of a_4 and a_6. First, let us plot the distribution of each individually, normalized by the total, i.e., as *probability mass functions*. These are shown in part (a) to the left of Figure 2. Note that the horizontal axes (binning) are done logarithmically. We see that the distributions of both a_4 and a_6 are symmetric with respect to 0 (Figure 2(a)), with a_4 spanning ~ 8 orders of magnitude smaller as compared to a_6. This is just to give an idea of the balanced nature of Cremona's data that elliptic curves with $\pm a_4$ and $\pm a_6$ are all constructed.

Next, in part (b) of Figure 2, we plot the joint probability mass function of the pair (a_4, a_6) with color showing the frequency as indicated by the color bar to the right. We see that, as discussed in Figure 1, there is a cross-like symmetry. Here, since we are not separating by rank, the symmetry is merely a reflection of the constructions of the dataset that $\pm a_4$ and $\pm a_6$ are all present. What is less explicable is that it should be a cross shape and what is the meaning of the boundary curve beyond which there does not seem to be any minimal models. For reference, the central rectilinear cross indicates the cases of $a_4 = 0$ and $a_6 = 0$, respectively.

Finally, we compute the Euclidean distance $d := \sqrt{a_4^2 + a_6^2}$ from the origin and study its probability distribution. This is shown in part (c) of Figure 2. We find that half of the data lie within a radius of $\sim 10^6$ from the origin. The logarithm of d can be well fitted with

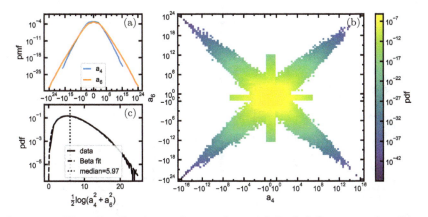

Figure 2. **The distributions of a_4 and a_6.** (a) Probability mass of a_4 (blue line) and a_6 (orange line). (b) Joint probability of a_4 and a_6. The color indicates the density of points within each bin (see color bar). Note that the figure axes are in symlog scale (linear scale between -1 and 1, logarithmic scale for other values in the range). Hence, we can see also the density corresponding to $a_4 = 0$ and $a_6 = 0$ (cross in the middle). (c) Probability density distribution for the logarithm (in base 10) of $\sqrt{a_4^2 + a_6^2}$ (when $a_4 > 0$ and $a_6 > 0$, filled line); the corresponding Beta distribution fits with parameters $\alpha = 4.1$, $\beta = 25.0$ and $s = 44.1$ (dashed line) and the median value (dotted line).

a Beta probability distribution:

$$f(x, \alpha, \beta, s) = K \cdot \frac{x}{s}^{\alpha-1} \left(1 - \frac{x}{s}\right)^{\beta-1}, \tag{18}$$

with parameters $\alpha = 4.1$, $\beta = 25.0$ and $s = 44.1$. Thus, while there are a number of coefficients of enormous magnitude, the majority still have relatively small ones.

3.3.1. *Differences by rank*

As with our initial observations, we now study the variation of (a_4, a_6) with respect to the rank r of the elliptic curves. First, in Figure 3(a)–(d), we plot the joint distributions of a_4 and a_6 for $r = 0, 1, 2, 3$, respectively. We can see that they differ significantly from each other, under permutation test [29] at confidence level $\alpha = 0.01$.

Next, Figure 3(e) shows the probability distribution functions for our Euclidean distance $\sqrt{a_4^2 + a_6^2}$ for the different ranks. We find that the median Euclidean distance from the center decreases for higher

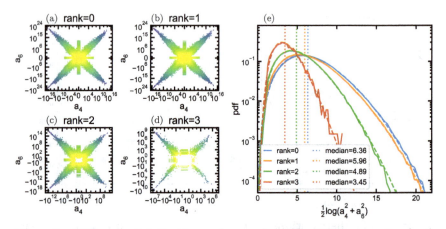

Figure 3. **Different distributions of a_4 and a_6 for different ranks.** (a–d) Joint probability distribution of a_4 and a_6 for values of the rank $r = 0$ (a), $r = 1$ (b), $r = 2$ (c) and $r = 3$ (d). (e) Probability density distribution for the logarithm (in base 10) of $\sqrt{a_4^2 + a_6^2}$ (when $a_4 > 0$ and $a_6 > 0$, filled lines) for various values of the rank r, the corresponding Beta distribution fit (dashed lines) and the corresponding median values (dotted lines).

values of r. In fact, we see that the median values of a_4 and a_6 increase with the rank r (see Figures 4(d)–(e) which we will discuss shortly). Again, each is individually well fitted by the Gamma distribution. In Tables C.1 and C.2 in Appendix, we show some statistics of a_4 and a_6 including their mean, standard deviation, median and the number of zero entries, for given rank r and values of (a_1, a_2, a_3).

3.4.   *Distributions of various BSD quantities*

Now, the coefficients a_i are the inputs of the dataset, each specifying a minimal model of an elliptic curve, and to each should be associated the numerical tuple $(r, N, R, \Omega, \prod_{p|N} c_p, |T|, |\text{Ш}|)$ for the rank, the conductor, the regulator, the real period, the Tamagawa number, the order of the torsion group and the order of the Tate–Shafarevich group, respectively. It is now expedient to examine the distribution of "output" parameters.

As always, we arrange everything by rank $r = 0, 1, 2, 3$ and in Figure 4 show the boxplots of the variation around the median (drawn in red). The boxes enclose 50% of the distribution, and the whiskers, 95% of the distribution. We see that, as detailed above,

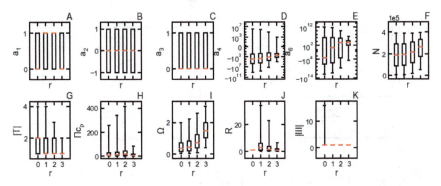

Figure 4. **Characteristics of the elliptic curves based on their rank.**
Boxplots of a_1, a_2, a_3, a_4, a_6 in parts (A)–(E), respectively; boxplots of N, $|T|$,
$\prod_{p|N} c_p$, Ω, R and $|\text{Ш}|$ in parts (F)–(K), respectively, all for different values of
the rank $r = 0, 1, 2, 3$. The red line shows the median value, the boxes enclose
50% of the distribution, and the whiskers, 95% of the distribution.

$a_{1,2,3}$ have only variation $[-1, 1]$ and a_4 has many orders of magnitude more in variation than a_6. The conductor N has a fairly tame
distribution while the other BSD quantities vary rather wildly —
that is part of the difficulty of the conjecture, the relevant quantities
behave quite unpredictably.

3.4.1. *The RHS of Conjecture 2*

We now put all the quantities together according to the RHS of the
Strong BSD Conjecture, which we recall to be $RHS = \dfrac{(\Omega \cdot R \cdot \prod\limits_{p|N} c_p \cdot |\text{Ш}|)}{T^2}$.
We test which statistical distribution best describes these data, by
comparing 85 continuous distributions under the Akaike information
criterion. We find that the distribution best describing the data is
the Beta distribution (see Figure 5(a)):

$$f(x, a, b) = \frac{\Gamma(a + b)x^{a-1}(1 - x)^{b-1}}{\Gamma(a)\Gamma(b)}, \tag{19}$$

where Γ is the standard gamma function, $a = 1.55$, $b = 14.28$, and
the original variable has been re-scaled such that $x = RHS/62.71$.

The selected distribution changes for elliptic with a specific rank r.
For $r = 0$, the selected distribution is the exponentiated Weibull,

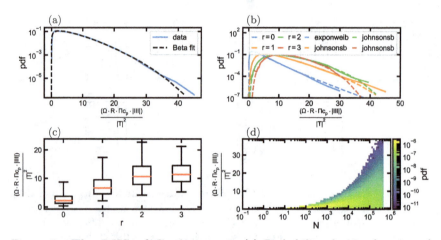

Figure 5. **The RHS of Conjecture 2.** (a) Probability density function of the RHS (filled blue line) and the corresponding Beta distribution fit (dashed black line). Note that, due to the logarithmic y-axis scale, the distance between the curve and the fit appears larger for larger values of the RHS. (b) Probability density function of the RHS for different values of the rank r (filled lines), and the corresponding best fits chosen with Akaike information criterion (dashed lines). (c) Boxplot showing the value of RHS for different values of r. The red line shows the median value, the boxes to the 50% of the distribution and the whiskers to the 95% of the distribution. (d) Joint probability distribution of the RHS and the value of the conductor N.

while for larger values of r, the selected distribution is the Johnson SB (see Figure 5(b)). We find that the median value of the *RHS* increases both as a function of the rank r (see Figure 5(c)) and N (see Figure 5(d)).

4.   Topological Data Analysis

Let us gain some further intuition by visualizing the data. As far as the data are concerned, to each elliptic curve, specified by the Weierstraß coefficients, one associates a list of quantities, the conductor, the rank, the real period, etc. They define a point cloud in Euclidean space of rather high dimension, each point of which is defined by the list of these quantities which enter BSD. In the above, we have extracted the last two coefficients of the Weierstraß form of the elliptic curves and studied them against the variations of the first three which, in normal form, can only be one of the 9 possible 3-tuples of ± 1 and 0. The normal form thus conveniently allows us to at least "see" the Weierstraß coefficients because we have projected to two dimensions. However, the full list of the relevant quantities for the elliptic curve has quite a number of entries and cannot be visualized directly.

Luckily, there is precisely a recently developed method in data science which allows for the visualization of "high dimensionality", viz., persistent homology in topological data analysis [13] (cf. an excellent introductory survey of [27]). In brief, one creates a Vietoris–Rips simplex from the data points in Euclidean space, with a notion of neighborhood ϵ (by Euclidean distance). The Betti numbers b_i of the simplex are then computed as one varies ϵ, whether the values are non-zero for each i gives a notion of whether non-trivial topology (such as holes) persists for different scales ϵ. The result is the so-called **barcode** for the data. In the ensuing, we will use Henselman's nice implementation of the standard methods in topological data analysis, the package Eirene for Julia/Python [15].

4.1. *The Weierstraß coefficients*

We begin by studying the barcodes for the full set of five Weierstraß coefficients a_i (as always, we take sLog for a_4 and a_6 due to their size). Of course, computing the homology of the Vietoris–Rips complex for over 2 million points is computationally impossible. The standard method is to consider random samples. Moreover, the first two Betti numbers b_0 and b_1 are usually sufficiently illustrative. Thus, we will take 1000 random samples (we do not separate the ranks since we find there is no significant difference for the barcodes among different ranks) of the coefficients (with the usual sLog for the last two). The barcodes are shown in part (a) of Figure 6. For reference, we also plot the barcodes for the pair $(\mathrm{sLog}(a_4),\ \mathrm{sLog}(a_6))$ only since $a_{1,2,3}$ do not vary so much.

4.2. *A 6-dimensional point cloud*

Let us now try to visualize the relevant BSD quantities $(N,\ r,\ |T|,\ \prod_{p|N} c_p,\ \Omega,\ R, \text{Ш})$ together. Organized by the ranks

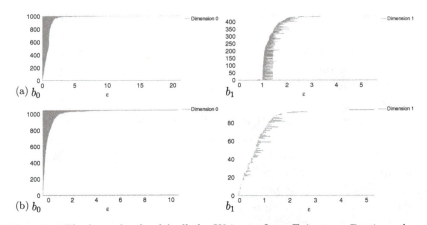

Figure 6.   The barcodes for (a) all the Weierstraß coefficients at Betti numbers 0 and 1 and (b) on the (principle component) coefficients (sLog(a_4), sLog(a_6)).

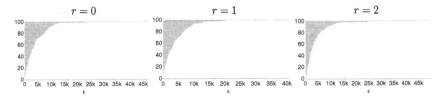

Figure 7.   The barcodes for 6-dimensional point-cloud (N, $|T|$, $\prod_{p|N} c_p$, Ω, R, Ш), with 100 random samples, for $r = 0, 1, 2$.

$r = 0, 1, 2$ which dominate the data by far, the 6-tuple

$$\left(N, \ |T|, \ \prod_{p|N} c_p, \ \Omega, \ R, \text{Ш} \right), \qquad r = 0, 1, 2, \qquad (20)$$

naturally form three point clouds in $\mathbb{R}^6$. Due to the high dimensionality, we sample 100 random points for each of the r values and compute the full barcodes $b_{0,\dots,6}$. It turns out that the main visible features are in dimension 0. We present these in Figure 7 and observe that indeed there is some variation in the barcode among the different ranks.

4.3.   *Conductor divisibility*

The factors of the conductor N are of defining importance in the L-function, which appear to the LHS of BSD, meanwhile, the RHS is

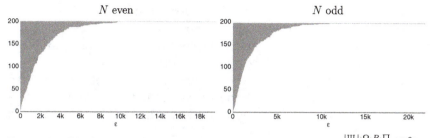

Figure 8.   The barcodes for 3-dimensional point cloud $(N,\ r,\ \frac{|\text{Ш}|\cdot\Omega\cdot R\cdot\prod_{p|N}c_p}{|T|^2})$, with 200 random samples for even/odd N.

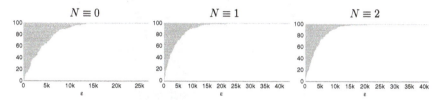

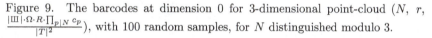

Figure 9.   The barcodes at dimension 0 for 3-dimensional point-cloud $(N,\ r,\ \frac{|\text{Ш}|\cdot\Omega\cdot R\cdot\prod_{p|N}c_p}{|T|^2})$, with 100 random samples, for N distinguished modulo 3.

governed, in the strong case, by the combination $F := \frac{|\text{Ш}|\cdot\Omega\cdot R\cdot\prod_{p|N}c_p}{|T|^2}$. It is therefore expedient to consider the point cloud of the 3-tuple (N, r, F) organized by divisibility properties of N. For instance, one could contrast the barcodes for the triple for N even versus N odd. Again, the features are prominent for dimension 0 and the barcodes are shown in Figure 8.

Similarly, we could group by N modulo 3, as shown in Figure 9.

5.   Machine Learning

In [17,18], a paradigm was proposed to using machine learning and, in particular, deep neural networks to help computations in various problems in algebraic geometry. Exemplified by computing cohomology of vector bundles, it was shown that to very high precision, AI can guess the correct answer without using the standard method of Gröbner basis construction and chasing long exact sequences, both of which are computationally intensive. Likewise, [20] showed that machine learning can identify algebraic structures such as distinguishing simple from non-simple finite groups. At over 99% precision, the requisite answers can be estimated without recourse to standard computations which are many orders of magnitude slower.

It is therefore natural to wonder whether the elliptic curve data can be "machine-learned". Of course, we need to be careful. While computational algebraic geometry over $\mathbb{C}$ hinged on finding kernels and cokernels of integer matrices, a task in which AI excels, problems in number theory are much less controlled. Indeed, trying to predict prime numbers [17] seems like a hopeless task, as mentioned in the introduction. Nevertheless, let us see how far we can go with our present dataset for BSD.

5.1.   *Predicting from the Weierstraß coefficients*

We begin with quantifying the performance of machine learning models in predicting, one by one, the quantities N, $\prod_{p|N} c_p$, R, $|\text{Ш}|$, Ω, r, $|T|$, together with the RHS of the Conjecture 2, given the Weierstraß coefficients a_1, a_2, a_3, a_4, a_6 alone. Straightaway, this is expected to be a difficult, if not impossible task (as impossible as, perhaps, the prediction of prime numbers). This is confirmed by the correlation between the Weierstraß coefficients and the BSD quantities: from the correlation matrix, we see that the relationship is indeed weak (cf. Figure 10), implying this is not a straightforward prediction task. Here, the correlation matrix contains the values of the Spearman correlation [28], that is the Pearson correlation [28] between the rank variables associated with each pair of the original variables.

Our analysis relies on gradient-boosted trees [6], using the implementation of XGBoost [35], an open-source scalable machine learning system for tree boosting used in a number of winning Kaggle solutions (17/29 in 2015). In Appendix B, we present similar results using a support vector machine, another highly popular machine learning model, and see that the XGBoost indeed performs better. Furthermore, based on the learning curves of the XGBoost models (discussed in Appendix A), we have chosen a **5-fold cross-validation**, such that the training set includes 80% of the values, and the validation set the remaining 20%.

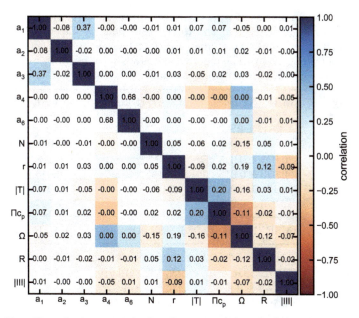

Figure 10. **Correlation matrix for the quantities characterizing ellipses.** Colors are assigned based on the value of the Pearson correlation coefficient between all pairs of quantities. The strength of the correlation is also reported for each pair. Values between –0.01 and 0.01 are reported as 0 in the cell due to space limitations.

5.1.1. *Numerical quantities*

First, we train regression models to predict the values of N, $\prod_{p|N} c_p$, R, $|\text{Ш}|$ and Ω. We evaluate the performance of the regression, by computing the normalized median absolute error:

$$\text{NMAE} = \frac{\text{median}(|Y_i - \hat{Y}_i|)}{\max(Y_i) - \min(Y_i)}, \tag{21}$$

where Y_i are the observed values and $\hat{Y}_i$ are the predicted values, and the rooted mean squared error:

$$\text{RMSE} = \sqrt{\frac{\sum(Y_i - \hat{Y}_i)^2}{n}}, \tag{22}$$

where n is the size of the test set. We desire that both NMAE and RMSE to be close to 0 for a good prediction.

Table 2.   **Performance of the regression models.** The Normalized Median Absolute Error (NMAE) and the Root Mean Squared Error (RMSE), for XGBoost (left column), the dummy regressor (central column) and a linear regression (right column). The reported values are averages across 5-fold cross–validations, with the corresponding standard deviations.

Quantity	NMAE (XGBoost)	NMAE (Dummy)	NMAE (Linear)
N	24.842 ± 0.032	25.175 ± 0.026	25.158 ± 0.027
$\prod_{p\mid N} c_p$	0.028 ± 0.006	0.077 ± 0.016	0.058 ± 0.012
R	0.075 ± 0.015	0.112 ± 0.023	0.108 ± 0.022
$\lvert \text{Ш} \rvert$	0.023 ± 0.015	0.044 ± 0.028	0.043 ± 0.027
Ω	3.120 ± 0.099	6.057 ± 0.189	6.016 ± 0.189
RHS Conj. 2	7.070 ± 0.238	7.548 ± 0.255	7.533 ± 0.250

	RMSE (XGBoost)	RMSE (Dummy)	RMSE (Linear)
N	114687.179 ± 63.171	115784.768 ± 78.329	115774.283 ± 78.302
$\prod_{p\mid N} c_p$	273.912 ± 18.665	286.522 ± 19.679	285.731 ± 19.711
R	13.579 ± 0.886	14.201 ± 0.552	14.197 ± 0.555
$\lvert \text{Ш} \rvert$	6.797 ± 1.550	6.369 ± 1.794	6.524 ± 1.688
Ω	0.449 ± 0.001	0.584 ± 0.001	0.583 ± 0.001
RHS Conj. 2	4.300 ± 0.002	4.554 ± 0.004	4.526 ± 0.003

We compare the result of the XGBoost regression with two baselines: (1) a linear regression model and (2) a dummy regressor that always predicts the mean of the training set. We find that, in all cases, the machine learning algorithms perform significantly better than the baseline models (see Table 2) with respect to the NMAE and RMSE. However, XGBoost performs only marginally better than the baselines in predicting the value of N. We report also the so-called importance of the features for the XGBoost regressor in Figure 11. Here, importance indicates how useful each feature is in the construction of the boosted decision trees and is calculated as the average importance across trees. For a single tree, the importance of a feature is computed as the relative increase in performance resulting from the tree splits based on that given feature [35].

We see that overall our measures, NMAE and RMSE, are not too close to 0, except perhaps $\lvert \text{Ш} \rvert$, for which even a simple linear regression does fairly well. In Table 3, we report the values of the coefficients of the linear regression fit for $\lvert \text{Ш} \rvert$. What Table 3 means

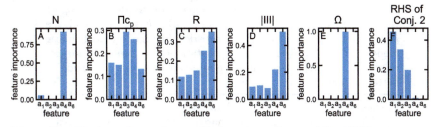

Figure 11. **Feature importance.** Feature importance of the XGBoost regression models for predicting N (A), Q p|N cp (B), R (C), |X| (D), Ω (E) and the RHS (F).

Table 3. **Prediction of $|\text{Ш}|$.** Coefficients of the linear regression for each of the features (inputs), with the associated standard deviation, the value of the t statistics and corresponding p-value. Here, we can reject the null hypothesis that the coefficients are equal to 0 at significance level $\alpha = 0.01$, for all coefficients, except the one associated with a_2 ($p > 0.01$).

	coef	std err	t	$P > |t|$	[0.025	0.975]
const	1.5946	0.004	380.761	0.000	1.586	1.603
a_1	0.0658	0.005	14.524	0.000	0.057	0.075
a_2	−0.0065	0.004	−1.543	0.123	−0.015	0.002
a_3	−0.0518	0.005	−11.473	0.000	−0.061	−0.043
a_4	−0.6320	0.006	−110.282	0.000	−0.643	−0.621
a_6	0.4877	0.006	85.112	0.000	0.477	0.499

is that $|\text{Ш}| \simeq 1.5946 + 0.0658a_1 - 0.0065a_2 - 0.0518a_3 - 0.6320a_4 + 0.4877a_6$.

Likewise, in Table 4, we report the statistics associated with the linear regression models for the prediction of the various quantities, where only the Weierstraß coefficients are used as features (inputs). The low R-squared values indicated that the regression is not so good in terms of the a_i coefficients alone.

5.1.2. *Categorical quantities*

Next, we train classifiers to predict the values of r and $|T|$ because these easily fall into discrete categories: the rank $r = 0, 1, 2, 3$ and the torsion group size $|T|$ can only be one of 16 integer values due to

Table 4.   **Statistics of the linear regression models.** We report the R-squared, the adjusted R-squared, the F-statistics and the p-value associated with the F-statistics for the different linear models. When the p-value of the F-statistics is close to 0, we can reject the null hypothesis that the intercept-only model provides a better fit than the linear model.

Predicted variable	R-squared	Adj. R-squared	F-statistic	Prob (F-statistic)
N	0	0	95.67	3.86e-101
$\prod_{p\|N} c_p$	0.006	0.006	2777	0
R	0.001	0.001	387.2	0
$\|\text{Ш}\|$	0.005	0.005	2522	0
Ω	0.005	0.005	2377	0
RHS Conj. 2	0.012	0.012	6143	0

Mazur's theorem. Again, we use a 5-*fold* cross-validation, and we evaluate the performance of the classifier, by computing the $F1$ score:

$$F1 = 2 \cdot \frac{\text{precision} \cdot \text{recall}}{\text{precision} + \text{recall}} \; ; \quad \text{precision} := \frac{TP}{TP + FP},$$

$$\text{recall} := \frac{TP}{TP + FN}, \tag{23}$$

where we have, in the predicted versus actual, the true positives (TP), false positives (FP) and false negatives (FN). Since we have several possible values for the rank r, we compute both $F1_{\text{micro}}$, by counting the total TP, FN and FP, as well as $F1_{\text{macro}}$, the average value of $F1$ computed across ranks.

In addition, we also compute the Matthew correlation coefficient MCC [37] to describe the confusion matrix:

$$\text{MCC} := \frac{\text{TP} \times \text{TN} - \text{FP} \times \text{FN}}{\sqrt{(\text{TP} + \text{FP})(\text{TP} + \text{FN})(\text{TN} + \text{FP})(\text{TN} + \text{FN})}}. \tag{24}$$

Both $F1$ score and MCC are desired to be close to 1 for a good prediction.

For checks, we compare the XGBoost classifier with (1) a baseline classifier that always predicts the predominant class in the training set, as well as with (2) a logistic regression. We find that XGBoost performs better than the baseline models for predicting $|T|$, but the

Table 5. **Performance of the classification models.** The scores $F1_{\text{micro}}$, $F1_{\text{macro}}$, and the Matthew correlation coefficient MCC, for XGBoost (left column), the dummy regressor (central column) and a logistic regression (right column). The reported values are averages across 5-fold cross-validations, with the corresponding standard deviations.

Quantity	$F1_{\text{micro}}$ (XGBoost)	$F1_{\text{micro}}$ (Dummy)	$F1_{\text{micro}}$ (Logistic)
r	0.502 ± 0.001	0.502 ± 0.001	0.502 ± 0.001
$|T|$	0.582 ± 0.001	0.543 ± 0.001	0.518 ± 0.001
	$F1_{\text{macro}}$ (XGBoost)	$F1_{\text{macro}}$ (Dummy)	$F1_{\text{macro}}$ (Logistic)
r	0.179 ± 0.001	0.167 ± 0.001	0.167 ± 0.001
$|T|$	0.097 ± 0.001	0.059 ± 0.001	0.080 ± 0.001
	MCC (XGBoost)	MCC (Dummy)	MCC (Logistic)
r	0.0172 ± 0.0006	0.0000 ± 0.0000	-0.0002 ± 0.0010
$|T|$	0.1871 ± 0.0010	0.0000 ± 0.0000	0.0299 ± 0.0012

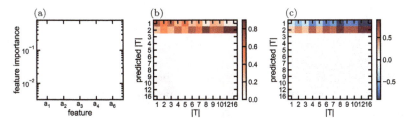

Figure 12. **Prediction of $|T|$.** (a) Importance of the different features (inputs) to predict $|T|$. (b) Confusion matrix (normalized by column) showing the fraction of entries $|T|$ with given *predicted* $|T|$. (c) Difference between the confusion matrix obtained for the XGBoost and the dummy classifier. Results are averaged over a 5-fold cross-validation.

performance of the prediction of r is comparable to the baselines (see Table 5).

Analyzing the confusion matrices (see Figures 12 and 13), it appears clear that it is very hard to predict $|T|$ and r from the Weierstraß coefficients alone. For both the prediction of r and $|T|$, the most important predictor is a_4 (Figures 12 and 13). This is the feature that contributed the most to increase the performance of the boosted tree [35].

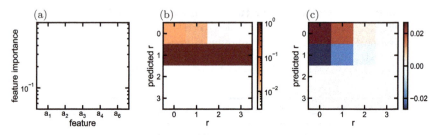

Figure 13. **Prediction of r.** (a) Importance of the different features to predict r. (b) Confusion matrix (normalized by column) showing the fraction of entries with rank r with given *predicted r*. (c) Difference between the confusion matrix obtained for the XGBoost and the dummy classifier. Results are averaged over a 5-fold cross-validation.

5.2.   *Mixed predictions*

While the results in the previous section may seem disappointing in general, they do present a good sanity check: to obtain all the BSD quantities from the elliptic curve data in some straight-forward way would be an almost unimaginable feat in number theory. Nevertheless, in this section, let us build machine learning models to predict the values of N, $\prod_{p|N} c_p$, R, $|\text{Ш}|$, Ω, r and $|T|$ among themselves, i.e., we consider as features (inputs) all the quantities characterizing the elliptic curves (except the predicted quantity) rather than the Weierstraß coefficients alone.

We present the results in Table 6 of the accuracy measure NMAE by the three methods as in Section 5.1: machine learning by XGBoost, dummy regression and linear regression. To read the table, of each of the five quantities given in a row, we use the other four to train the ML in order to predict this row. We see that this is a significant improvement over the previous section and shows that, especially the XGBoost, the machine learning can very confidently predict the Tamagawa number, the regulator and $|\text{Ш}|$. The feature importance is shown in Figure 15, and in Table 7, we report the statistics associated with the mixed predictions' linear regression models. A comparison between the predictions of the linear models compared to XGBoost is presented in Figure 14.

Table 6. **Performance of the regression models considering as features all the quantities characterizing an ellipses.** The normalized median absolute error NMAE, for XGBoost (left column), the dummy regressor (central column) and a linear regression (right column). The reported values are averages across 5-fold cross-validations, with the corresponding standard deviations. Results are considerably improved compared to Table 2.

Quantity	NMAE (XGBoost)	NMAE (Dummy)	NMAE (Linear)
N	23.426 ± 0.031	25.175 ± 0.026	24.408 ± 0.039
$\prod_{p\mid N} c_p$	0.012 ± 0.003	0.077 ± 0.016	0.065 ± 0.014
R	0.014 ± 0.003	0.112 ± 0.023	0.089 ± 0.018
$\lvert\text{Ш}\rvert$	0.006 ± 0.004	0.044 ± 0.028	0.048 ± 0.031
Ω	2.343 ± 0.103	6.057 ± 0.189	5.324 ± 0.174

Table 7. **Statistics of the linear regression models (mixed predictions).** We report the R-squared, the adjusted R squared, the F-statistics, and the p-value associated with the F-statistics for the mixed predictions linear models.

Predicted variable	R-squared	Adj. R-squared	F-statistic	Prob (F-statistic)
N	0.038	0.038	8999	0
$\prod_{p\mid N} c_p$	0.054	0.054	12960	0
R	0.042	0.042	9889	0
$\lvert\text{Ш}\rvert$	0.017	0.017	3891	0
Ω	0.114	0.114	29110	0

Finally, let us use all quantities: the coefficients a_i as well as N, $\prod_{p\mid N} c_p$, R, $\lvert\text{Ш}\rvert$, Ω to predict r and $\lvert T \rvert$. The accuracy measure $F1$ and MCC (which should be close to 1 ideally) are presented in Table 8 and the feature importance is in Figures 16 and 17. We see that these are considerably improved compared to those obtained in Section 5.1 (cf. Tables 2 and 5). This is somehow to be expected in light of the correlations observed in Figure 10. In fact, even logistic

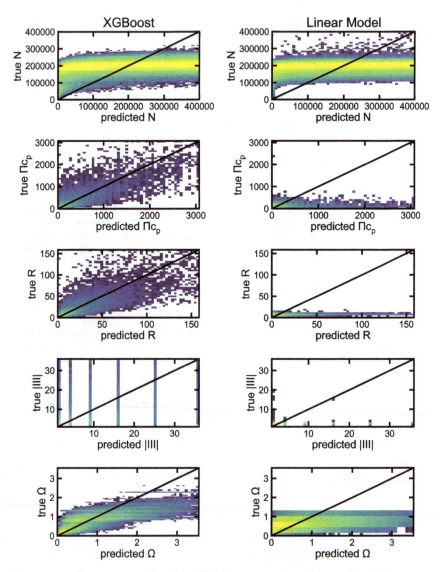

Figure 14.   **True versus Predicted values.** Results are shown for all the quantities, using XGBoost (left column) and the linear model (right column).

regressions behave fairly well, with the $F1_{\text{micro}}$, $F1_{\text{macro}}$ and the MCC scores substantially larger than those obtained by the dummy classifiers (see Table 8). For reference, we include a report of the hyperplane equations of the linear regression models to see how each of the

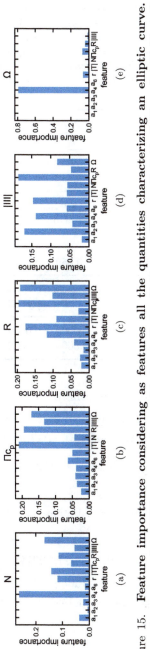

Figure 15. **Feature importance considering as features all the quantities characterizing an elliptic curve.** Feature importance of the XGBoost regression models for predicting N (Part a), $\prod_{p|N} c_p$ (Part b), R (Part c), $|\text{III}|$ (Part d) and Ω (Part e).

Table 8. **Performance of the classification models considering as features all the quantities characterizing an elliptic curve.** The scores $F1_{\text{macro}}$, $F1_{\text{micro}}$ and the Matthew correlation coefficient MCC, for XGBoost (left column), the dummy regressor (central column) and a logistic regression (right column). The reported values are averages across 5-fold cross-validations, with the corresponding standard deviations. Results are considerably improved compared to Table 5.

Quantity	$F1_{\text{micro}}$ (XGBoost)	$F1_{\text{micro}}$ (Dummy)	$F1_{\text{micro}}$ (Logistic)
r	0.900 ± 0.001	0.502 ± 0.001	0.730 ± 0.001
$|T|$	0.908 ± 0.001	0.543 ± 0.001	0.567 ± 0.001
	$F1_{\text{macro}}$ (XGBoost)	$F1_{\text{macro}}$ (Dummy)	$F1_{\text{macro}}$ (Logistic)
r	0.554 ± 0.001	0.167 ± 0.001	0.387 ± 0.001
$|T|$	0.585 ± 0.015	0.059 ± 0.001	0.090 ± 0.001
	MCC (XGBoost)	MCC (Dummy)	MCC (Logistic)
r	0.8311 ± 0.0005	0.0000 ± 0.0000	0.5240 ± 0.0011
$|T|$	0.8302 ± 0.0014	0.0000 ± 0.0000	0.1364 ± 0.0009

quantities can be fitted by all the others:

$$N = 195500.0000 - 1526.8435a_1 + 288.1786a_2 - 806.9174a_3$$
$$- 122.4328a_4 + 16.3690a_6 + 8047.4199r - 10250.0000|T|$$
$$+ 2192.0941 \prod_{p|N} c_p + 3197.1580R + 1293.3455|Ш|$$
$$- 20330.0000\Omega$$

$$\prod_{p|N} c_p = 49.7747 + 14.9069a_1 + 3.6860a_2 + 2.1424a_3$$
$$- 2.4121a_4 + 1.0613a_6 + 17.8877r + 53.2012|T| + 5.3471N$$
$$- 14.5038R - 4.3689|Ш| - 27.7937\Omega$$

$$R = 4.0689 - 0.0028a_1 - 0.1430a_2 - 0.2379a_3 - 0.2995a_4$$
$$+ 0.1230a_6 + 2.1850r + 0.4585|T| + 0.3910N$$
$$- 0.7271 \prod_{p|N} c_p - 0.2167|Ш| - 2.1082\Omega$$

$$|\text{Ш}| = 1.5946 + 0.0517a_1 + 0.0094a_2 - 0.0195a_3 - 0.6322a_4$$
$$+ 0.4875a_6 - 0.5472r + 0.0112|T| + 0.0756N$$
$$- 0.1046 \prod_{p|N} c_p - 0.1035R - 0.3466\Omega$$
$$\Omega = 0.6065 - 0.0252a_1 + 0.0113a_2 + 0.0160a_3 - 0.0030a_4 +$$
$$0.0019a_6 + 0.1147r - 0.0717|T| - 0.0945N$$
$$- 0.0530 \prod_{p|N} c_p - 0.0801R - 0.0276|\text{Ш}|. \tag{25}$$

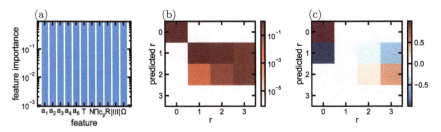

Figure 16. **Prediction of r considering as features all the quantities characterizing an ellipses.** (a) Importance of the different features to predict r. (b) Confusion matrix (normalized by column) showing the fraction of entries with rank r with given *predicted r*. (c) Difference between the confusion matrix obtained for the XGBoost and the dummy classifier. Results are averaged over a 5-fold cross-validation.

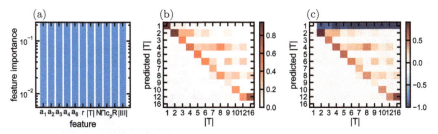

Figure 17. **Prediction of $|T|$ considering as features all the quantities characterizing an elliptic curve.** (a) Importance of the different features to predict $|T|$. (b) Confusion matrix (normalized by column) showing the fraction of entries with value $|T|$ and given *predicted $|T|$*. (c) Difference between the confusion matrix obtained for the XGBoost and the dummy classifier. Results are averaged over a 5-fold cross-validation.

6. Conclusion

In this chapter, we initiated the study of the data science of the arithmetic of elliptic curves in light of the Birch–Swinnerton-Dyer Conjecture. This is inspired by the recent advances in the statistical investigation of Calabi–Yau manifolds, especially in the context of super-string theory [1,19], as well as in the paradigm of machine learning structures in geometry [17,18] and algebra [20]. While we are still within the landscape of "Calabi–Yau-ness", it is expected that patterns in number theory should be much more subtle than those in geometry over $\mathbb{C}$ and in combinatorics. Nevertheless, BSD, residing at the crux between arithmetic and analysis, might be more susceptible to machine learning and to pattern recognition.

From our preliminary examinations on the extensive database of Cremona [11,12], we have already found several interesting features. First, we find that in the minimal Weierstraß representation, where a pair of coefficients (a_4, a_6) clearly constitutes the principle component of the data, the distribution thereof follows a curious cross-like symmetry across rank, as shown in Figures 1 and 2. This is a highly non-trivial symmetry since $a_{4,6} \leftrightarrow \pm a_{4,6}$ does not preserve rank. This symmetry is reminiscent of mirror symmetry for Calabi–Yau three-folds. In addition, the absence of data points beyond the boundaries of the cross is also of note, much like that Hodge plot for the Calabi–Yau threefolds.

Over all, the distribution of the Euclidean distance of (a_4, a_6) to the origin as well as that of the RHS of the Strong BSD, viz., the quantity $\frac{|\text{III}| \cdot \Omega \cdot R \cdot \prod_{p|N} c_p}{|T|^2}$ (cf. conjectures in Section 2.2), are best described by a Beta distribution, which is selected in both cases among 85 continuous distributions using the Akaike information criterion. Organized by rank, these distributions also vary.

One further visualizes the data, the tuples consisting of the coefficients $(a_1, a_2, a_3, a_4, a_6)$ as well as the BSD tuple $(N, |T|, \prod_{p|N} c_p, \Omega, R, \text{III})$ for ranks $r = 0, 1, 2$ using the standard techniques from topological data analysis. The barcodes are shown in Figures 6 and 7. While the Weierstraß coefficients show little variation over rank, the BSD tuple does show differences over r. Moreover, as expected, the divisibility of the conductor N influences the barcodes.

Finally, emboldened by the recent success in using machine learning to computing bundle cohomology on algebraic varieties without recourse to sequence-chasing and Gröbner bases as well as recognizing whether a finite group is simple directly by looking at the Cayley table, we asked the question of whether one can "predict" quantities otherwise difficult to compute directly from "looking" at the shape of the elliptic curve. Ideally, one would have hoped that by training on a_i, one could predict any of the BSD quantities to high precision, as was in the cohomology case. However, due to the very high variation in the size of a_i, one could not find a good machine learning technique, decision trees, support vector machines or neural networks, which seem to achieve this. This is rather analogous to the (expected) failure of predicting prime numbers using AI. Nevertheless, the BSD quantities, when *mixed* with the Weierstraß coefficients, do behave well under machine learning. For instance, the Matthew correlation coefficient between predicted and true values of r and $|T|$ is ∼0.83.

At some level, the experiments here, in conjunction with those in [2,3,10,17,20,22,23,30], tend to show a certain *hierarchy of difficulty* in how machine learning responds to problems in mathematics. Understandably, number theory is the most difficult: as a reprobate, [17] checked that trying to predict the next prime number, for instance, seems unfeasible for simple neural networks. On the other hand, algebraic geometry over the complex numbers seems to present a host of amenable questions, such as bundle cohomology, recognition of elliptic fibrations or calculating Betti numbers. In between lie algebra and combinatorics, such as the structure of finite groups, where precision/confidence of the cross-validation is somewhat intermediate. It is therefore curious that in this chapter one sees that a problem such as BSD, which resides in between arithmetic and geometry, is better behaved under machine learning than a direct attack on patterns in primes.

Acknowledgments

YHH would like to thank the Science and Technology Facilities Council, UK, for grant ST/J00037X/1, Nankai University, China, for a chair professorship and Merton College, Oxford, for enduring support.

Appendix

A.   Learning Curves

To prevent overfitting, we compute the learning curves of the regression (Figure A.1) and classification (Figure A.2) models in Section 5.1. We find that 80% of the data is a good choice for the training set size, suggesting a 5-fold cross-validation.

B.   Comparison with SVM

In this section, we compare the performance of the XGBoost models with Support Vector Machine (SVM) models. SVM models are very long to train, hence we focus, for this task, on a subset of 100,000 examples. In Table B.1, we report the performance of the regression

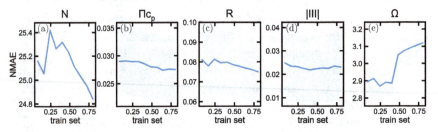

Figure A.1.   **Learning curves for the regression models.** The Normalized Median Absolute Error as a function of the train set size of the XGBoost regression models for predicting N (a), $\prod_{p|N} c_p$ (b), R (c), $|\text{Ш}|$ (d) and Ω (e). The shaded areas correspond to standard deviation across a 5-fold cross-validation.

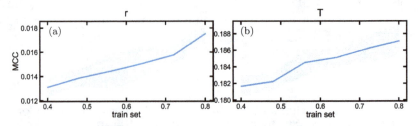

Figure A.2.   **Learning curves for the classification models.** The Matthew coefficient as a function of the train set size of the XGBoost regression models for predicting r (a) and $|T|$ (b). The shaded areas correspond to standard deviation across a 5-fold cross-validation.

Table B.1. **Performance of the regression models.** The normalized median absolute error NMAE, for XGBoost (left column), the dummy regressor (central column) and Support Vector Machine Regression (right column). The reported values are averages across 5-fold cross-validations, with the corresponding standard deviations.

Quantity	NMAE (XGBoost)	NMAE (Dummy)	NMAE (SVM)
N	114881.964 ± 364.409	115664.993 ± 384.936	115690.292 ± 417.181
$\prod_{p\mid N} c_p$	278.372 ± 34.807	273.775 ± 27.528	275.182 ± 27.412
R	17.493 ± 4.178	15.124 ± 4.137	15.417 ± 4.067
$\lvert Ш \rvert$	4.938 ± 1.156	4.868 ± 1.223	4.893 ± 1.218
Ω	0.498 ± 0.004	0.584 ± 0.005	0.607 ± 0.005

models used to predict N, $\prod_{p\mid N} c_p$, R, $\lvert Ш \rvert$ and Ω. Only in the case of Ω, the SVM model performs better than XGBoost.

C. Characteristics of the Weierstraß Coefficients

Table C.1. For given values of a_1, a_2, a_3, and r, the table reports the number of elliptic curves (size) and some statistics of the Weierstraß coefficient a_4 including the mean ($\overline{a_4}$), the standard deviation (s_{a_4}), the median (median) and the number of zero entries (zero entries).

a1	a2	a3	rank	size	$\overline{a_4}$	s_{a_4}	median	zero entries
0	−1	0	0	126135	−5E+09	7E+11	−8E+03	98
1	1	1	0	67834	−8E+10	7E+12	−2E+04	54
1	1	0	0	69759	−2E+11	3E+13	−1E+04	47
1	0	1	0	71309	−9E+10	1E+13	−2E+04	35
1	0	0	0	66411	−1E+12	2E+14	−2E+04	42
1	−1	1	0	96995	−1E+11	2E+13	−2E+04	41
0	1	1	0	18016	−4E+10	3E+12	−2E+03	38
0	1	0	0	118942	−1E+10	1E+12	−9E+03	108
0	0	1	0	28440	−1E+11	2E+13	−3E+03	546
1	−1	0	0	102769	−2E+11	5E+13	−2E+04	97
0	0	0	0	172238	−6E+09	9E+11	−1E+04	832
0	−1	1	0	17238	−1E+10	1E+12	−2E+03	40
0	−1	1	1	24593	−1E+09	1E+11	−1E+03	65
1	−1	0	1	127198	−1E+11	2E+13	−1E+04	150
1	0	0	1	98092	−5E+11	1E+14	−7E+03	77
0	1	1	1	27360	−5E+10	4E+12	−1E+03	54
1	0	1	1	94595	−3E+11	6E+13	−7E+03	62
1	−1	1	1	128957	−2E+10	2E+12	−9E+03	40
0	0	0	1	213780	−5E+10	2E+13	−6E+03	962
0	1	0	1	157003	−8E+09	1E+12	−5E+03	164

(Continued)

Table C.1. (*Continued*)

a1	a2	a3	rank	size	$\overline{a_4}$	s_{a_4}	median	zero entries
1	1	0	1	88403	−5E+10	4E+12	−7E+03	107
0	−1	0	1	155604	−1E+10	2E+12	−5E+03	159
0	0	1	1	39235	−5E+10	7E+12	−2E+03	608
1	1	1	1	91717	−3E+10	4E+12	−7E+03	87
1	1	0	2	18293	−2E+08	2E+10	−1E+03	28
1	0	0	2	25286	−5E+07	2E+09	−2E+03	23
1	−1	1	2	28940	−5E+07	6E+09	−2E+03	17
0	−1	0	2	30236	−3E+07	2E+09	−1E+03	44
1	0	1	2	20907	−2E+08	2E+10	−1E+03	17
0	0	0	2	40731	−6E+07	6E+09	−2E+03	126
1	−1	0	2	25793	−6E+08	8E+10	−2E+03	46
1	1	1	2	21197	−7E+07	5E+09	−1E+03	23
0	0	1	2	11187	−2E+07	9E+08	−5E+02	96
0	1	1	2	9609	−1E+08	1E+10	−5E+02	19
0	−1	1	2	7582	−7E+06	2E+08	−3E+02	22
0	1	0	2	34585	−2E+07	9E+08	−1E+03	36
1	−1	0	3	551	−8E+04	1E+06	−3E+02	1
0	0	0	3	698	−2E+04	2E+05	−3E+02	0
1	1	0	3	496	−2E+04	2E+05	−2E+02	0
0	0	1	3	506	−2E+04	2E+05	−2E+02	2
0	−1	1	3	399	−8E+04	1E+06	−2E+02	1
0	1	0	3	722	−8E+03	4E+04	−4E+02	1
0	−1	0	3	659	−1E+04	6E+04	−3E+02	0
1	0	0	3	612	−6E+03	3E+05	−4E+02	1
0	1	1	3	426	4E+03	9E+05	−3E+02	1
1	−1	1	3	604	−1E+04	7E+04	−4E+02	3
1	0	1	3	548	−1E+04	1E+05	−3E+02	3
1	1	1	3	458	−2E+04	4E+05	−2E+02	0
1	−1	0	4	1	−8E+01	NAN	−8E+01	0

Table C.2. For given values of a_1, a_2, a_3, and r, the table reports the number of curves (size) and some statistics of the Weierstraß coefficient a_6 including the mean ($\overline{a_6}$), the standard deviation (s_{a_6}), the median (median) and the number of zero entries (zero entries).

a1	a2	a3	rank	size	$\overline{a_6}$	s_{a_6}	median	zero entries
0	−1	0	0	126135	−9E+15	4E+18	−5E+02	217
1	1	1	0	67834	−3E+17	9E+19	−1E+03	1
1	1	0	0	69759	−3E+18	6E+20	−7E+02	202
1	0	1	0	71309	2E+17	2E+20	−2E+03	2
1	0	0	0	66411	−4E+19	1E+22	−5E+03	176
1	−1	1	0	96995	−6E+17	3E+20	−3E+03	1
0	1	1	0	18016	−2E+17	3E+19	−4E+02	2
0	1	0	0	118942	−2E+16	6E+18	−1E+03	226
0	0	1	0	28440	−3E+18	5E+20	−6E+02	1
1	−1	0	0	102769	7E+18	2E+21	−8E+02	206
0	0	0	0	172238	1E+16	6E+18	−8E+02	486
0	−1	1	0	17238	−1E+16	4E+18	−2E+02	1
0	−1	1	1	24593	1E+15	2E+17	1E+01	17

Table C.2. (*Continued*)

a1	a2	a3	rank	size	$\overline{a_6}$	s_{a_6}	median	zero entries
1	−1	0	1	127198	−2E+18	6E+20	−4E+00	271
1	0	0	1	98092	−3E+19	9E+21	5E+01	246
0	1	1	1	27360	−1E+17	4E+19	−2E+01	18
1	0	1	1	94595	1E+19	3E+21	2E+01	27
1	−1	1	1	128957	−2E+14	1E+19	4E+01	15
0	0	0	1	213780	−1E+18	6E+20	−5E-01	604
0	1	0	1	157003	−3E+15	5E+18	2E+01	281
1	1	0	1	88403	−1E+17	4E+19	0E+00	271
0	−1	0	1	155604	2E+15	1E+19	0E+00	301
0	0	1	1	39235	6E+17	1E+20	−2E+01	24
1	1	1	1	91717	1E+17	4E+19	7E+00	17
1	1	0	2	18293	8E+13	1E+16	1E+03	42
1	0	0	2	25286	4E+12	4E+14	1E+04	42
1	−1	1	2	28940	−1E+13	3E+15	1E+04	21
0	−1	0	2	30236	7E+11	3E+14	2E+03	58
1	0	1	2	20907	7E+13	9E+15	3E+03	22
0	0	0	2	40731	−2E+13	3E+15	4E+03	82
1	−1	0	2	25793	7E+14	1E+17	2E+03	57
1	1	1	2	21197	−9E+12	1E+15	5E+03	23
0	0	1	2	11187	1E+12	1E+14	1E+03	26
0	1	1	2	9609	−4E+13	4E+15	2E+03	18
0	−1	1	2	7582	4E+10	8E+12	6E+02	24
0	1	0	2	34585	5E+11	9E+13	5E+03	42
1	−1	0	3	551	1E+08	3E+09	2E+03	0
0	0	0	3	698	−2E+06	2E+08	2E+03	0
1	1	0	3	496	3E+06	9E+07	9E+02	1
0	0	1	3	506	−6E+06	2E+08	1E+03	4
0	−1	1	3	399	1E+08	3E+09	6E+02	3
0	1	0	3	722	1E+06	1E+07	3E+03	0
0	−1	0	3	659	3E+06	3E+07	2E+03	0
1	0	0	3	612	−5E+06	2E+08	3E+03	1
0	1	1	3	426	1E+08	2E+09	1E+03	4
1	−1	1	3	604	3E+06	4E+07	3E+03	4
1	0	1	3	548	5E+06	6E+07	2E+03	4
1	1	1	3	458	5E+07	1E+09	1E+03	2
1	−1	0	4	1	3E+02	NAN	3E+02	0

References

[1] R. Altman, J. Carifio, J. Halverson and B. D. Nelson, Estimating Calabi-Yau hypersurface and triangulation counts with equation learners, *JHEP* **1903** (2019), 186. Doi: 10.1007/JHEP03(2019)186 [arXiv:1811.06490 [hep-th]].

[2] C. R. Brodie, A. Constantin, R. Deen and A. Lukas, Machine Learning line bundle cohomology, arXiv:1906.08730 [hep-th].

[3] K. Bull, Y. H. He, V. Jejjala and C. Mishra, Machine Learning CICY threefolds, *Phys. Lett. B* **785** (2018), 65 [arXiv:1806.03121 [hep-th]]; K. Bull, Y. H. He, V. Jejjala and C. Mishra, Getting CICY high, *Phys. Lett. B* **795** (2019), 700 [arXiv:1903.03113 [hep-th]].

[4] M. Bhargava and C. Skinner, A positive proportion of elliptic curves over Q have rank one, arXiv:1401.0233.

[5] B. Birch and P. Swinnerton-Dyer, Notes on elliptic curves (II), *J. Reine Angew. Math.* **165**(218) (1965), 79–108.

[6] J. H. Friedman, Greedy function approximation: A gradient boosting machine, *Ann. Stat.* **25**(5) (2001), 1189–1232.

[7] M. Bhargava, C. Skinner and W. Zhang, A majority of elliptic curves over Q satisfy the Birch and Swinnerton-Dyer conjecture, arXiv:1407.1826.

[8] J. Buhler, B. Gross and D. Zagier, On the Conjecture of Birch and Swinnerton-Dyer for an Elliptic Curve of Rank 3, *Math. Comput.* **44**(170) (1985), 473–481.

[9] E. Calabi, The space of Kähler metrics, *Proc. Internat. Congress Math. Amsterdam* **2** (1954), 206–207; E. Calabi, On Kähler manifolds with vanishing canonical class, in Fox, Spencer, Tucker (eds.), *Algebraic Geometry and Topology. A Symposium in Honor of S. Lefschetz*, Princeton Mathematical Series, 12, PUP, pp. 78–89 (1957).

[10] J. Carifio, J. Halverson, D. Krioukov and B. D. Nelson, Machine Learning in the string landscape, *JHEP* **1709** (2017), 157. Doi: 10.1007/JHEP09(2017)157 [arXiv:1707.00655 [hep-th]].

[11] J. Cremona, The Elliptic curve database for conductors to 130000", in Hess F., Pauli S., Pohst M. (eds.) *Algorithmic Number Theory*. ANTS. Lecture Notes in Computer Science, Vol. 4076, Springer (2006).

[12] J. Cremona, The L-functions and modular forms database project, arXiv:1511.04289, http://www.lmfdb.org/.

[13] G. Carlsson, A. Zomorodian, A. Collins and L. Guibas, Persistence barcodes for shapes, *Int. J. Shape Model.* **11** (2005), 149–187.

[14] M. R. Douglas, The statistics of string/M theory vacua, *JHEP* **0305** (2003), 046 [hep-th/0303194].

[15] G. Helsenman, Eirene, http://gregoryhenselman.org/eirene/.

[16] N. Elkies, Three lectures on elliptic surfaces and curves of high rank, Lecture notes, Oberwolfach (2007), arXiv:0709.2908.

[17] Y. H. He, Deep-Learning the landscape, arXiv:1706.02714 [hep-th]. Y. H. He, Machine-learning the string landscape, *Phys. Lett. B* **774** (2017), 564.

[18] Y. H. He, The Calabi-Yau landscape: From geometry, to physics, to Machine-Learning, arXiv:1812.02893 [hep-th].

[19] Y. H. He, V. Jejjala and L. Pontiggia, Patterns in Calabi–Yau distributions, *Commun. Math. Phys.* **354**(2) (2017), 477 [arXiv:1512.01579 [hep-th]].

[20] Y. H. He and M. Kim, Learning algebraic structures: Preliminary investigations, arXiv:1905.02263 [cs.LG].

[21] Y. H. He and S. J. Lee, Distinguishing elliptic fibrations with AI, arXiv:1904.08530 [hep-th].

[22] V. Jejjala, A. Kar and O. Parrikar, Deep Learning the hyperbolic volume of a knot, arXiv:1902.05547 [hep-th].

[23] D. Krefl and R. K. Seong, Machine Learning of Calabi-Yau volumes, *Phys. Rev. D* **96**(6) (2017), 066014 [arXiv:1706.03346 [hep-th]].

[24] M. Laska, An algorithm for finding a minimal Weierstrass equation for an elliptic curve, *Math. Comput.* **38**(157) (1982), 257–260.

[25] B. Mazur, Modular curves and the Eisenstein ideal, *Publ. Mathématiques de l'IHÉS* **47**(1) (1977), 33–186.

[26] J. Milne, Elliptic curves. http://www.jmilne.org/math/Books/ectext5.pdf.

[27] N. Otter, M. A. Porter, U. Tillmann, P. Grindrod and H. A. Harrington, A roadmap for the computation of persistent homology, *EPJ Data Sci.* **6** (2017), 17. https://arxiv.org/abs/1506.08903.

[28] D. J. Sheskin, *Handbook of Parametric and Nonparametric Statistical Procedures.* Chapman and Hall/CRC (2003).

[29] P. R. Peres-Neto and D. A. Jackson, How well do multivariate data sets match? The advantages of a Procrustean superimposition approach over the Mantel test, *Oecologia* **129**(2) (2001), 169–178.

[30] F. Ruehle, Evolving neural networks with genetic algorithms to study the String Landscape, *JHEP* **1708** (2017), 038 [arXiv:1706.07024 [hep-th]].

[31] K. Rubin and A. Silverberg, Ranks of elliptic curves, *Bull. AMS* **39** (2002), 455–474.

[32] J. Silverman, The arithmetic of elliptic curves, *GTM* Vol. 106, Springer-Verlag (1992).

[33] J. T. Tate, The arithmetic of elliptic curves, *Invent. Math.* **23** (1974), 179–206.

[34] R. Taylor and A. Wiles, Ring-theoretic properties of certain Hecke algebras, *Ann. Math.* (2) **141**(3) (1995), 553–572.

[35] T. Chen and C. Guestrin, Xgboost: A scalable tree boosting system, in *Proceedings of the 22nd ACM Sigkdd International Conference on Knowledge Discovery and Data Mining*, pp. 785–794. ACM (2016).

[36] S.-T. Yau, Calabi's conjecture and some new results in algebraic geometry, *Proc. Nat. Acad. USA*, **74**(5) (1977), 1798–1799.
S.-T. Yau, On the Ricci curvature of a compact Kähler manifold and the complex Monge-Ampère equation I, *Comm. Pure Appl. Math.* **31**(3) (1978), 339–411.

[37] J. Gorodkin, Comparing two K-category assignments by a K-category correlation coefficient, *Comput. Biol. Chem.* **28**(5–6) (2004), 367–374.

Chapter 2

On the Dynamics of Inference and Learning

David S. Berman[*,¶]**, Jonathan J. Heckman**[†,‡,‖] **and
Marc Klinger**[‡,§,**]

*Centre for Theoretical Physics, Queen Mary University of London,
London E1 4NS, UK*
†*Department of Physics and Astronomy, University of Pennsylvania,
Philadelphia, PA 19104, USA*
‡*Department of Mathematics, University of Pennsylvania, Philadelphia,
PA 19104, USA*
§*Department of Physics, University of Illinois, Urbana, IL 61801, USA*

¶*d.s.berman@qmul.ac.uk*
‖*jheckman@sas.upenn.edu*
**marck3@illinois.edu*

Abstract

Statistical inference is the process of determining a probability distribution over the space of parameters of a model given a dataset. As more data become available, this probability distribution becomes updated via the application of Bayes' theorem. We present a treatment of this Bayesian updating process as a continuous dynamical system. Statistical inference is then governed by a first-order differential equation describing a trajectory or flow in the information geometry determined by a parametric family of models. We solve this equation for some simple models and show that when the Cramér–Rao bound is saturated the learning rate is governed by a simple $1/T$ power law, with T a time-like variable denoting the quantity of data. The presence of hidden variables can be incorporated in this setting, leading to an additional driving term in the resulting flow equation. We illustrate this with both analytic and numerical examples based on Gaussians and Gaussian Random Processes and inference of the coupling constant in the 1D Ising model. Finally, we compare the qualitative behavior exhibited by Bayesian flows to the training of various neural networks on benchmarked datasets such as MNIST and CIFAR10 and show how that for networks exhibiting small final losses the simple power law is also satisfied.

1.   Introduction

It is difficult to overstate the importance of statistical inference. It forms the bedrock of how one weighs new scientific evidence and is in some sense the basis for all rational thought. Leaving philosophy aside, one can ask about the mechanics of inference: given new data, how quickly can we expect to adjust our understanding, and in what sense does this converge to the truth?

Bayes' rule [1] provides a concrete way to approach this question. Given events A and B, the conditional probabilities are related as[1]

$$P(A|B) = \frac{P(B|A)P(A)}{P(B)}. \tag{1}$$

As new evidence arrives, the posterior $P(A|B)$ can be treated as a new prior, and Bayes' rule thus provides a concrete way to continue updating (and hopefully improving) one's initial inference scheme.

In physical applications, one typically imposes a great deal of additional structure which allows one to weigh the various merits of new evidence. For example, in the context of quantum field theory, one is often interested in particle excitations where the structure of locality is built into the inference scheme. In this context, "new evidence" amounts to probing shorter distance scales with the help of a higher energy collider experiment or a more precise measurement of a coupling constant. In modern terms, this is organized with the help of the renormalization group [2–6], which provides a general way to organize new data as relevant, marginal or irrelevant (in terms of its impact on long-distance observables).

More broadly, the issue of identifying relevant features as a function of scale is an important issue in a range of inference problems.

---

[1]More symmetrically, one can write $P(A|B)P(B) = P(B|A)P(A)$.

For example, in machine learning applications, one might wish to classify an image according to "dog versus cat" and then proceed to breed and even finer distinguishing features. In this setting, however, the notion of a single quantity such as energy/wavenumber to define "locality" (as used in quantum field theory) is far less clear-cut. This is also an issue in a wide range of systems with multiple scales and chaotic dynamics. In these settings, it would seem important to seek out physically anchored organizational principles.

Our aim in this note will be to show that in many circumstances, there is an emergent notion of scaling which can be traced all the way back to incremental Bayesian updates. The essential idea is that as an inference scheme converges towards a best guess, the Bayesian update equation comes to resemble a diffusion equation. Much as in Ref. [7], the appropriate notion of energy in this context is the Kullback–Leibler divergence [8] between the model distribution $m(x)$ and the true distribution $t(x)$:

$$D_{KL}(t||m) = \int dx\, t(x) \log \frac{t(x)}{m(x)}. \tag{2}$$

In many applications, the model depends on a set of fitting parameters θ^i, and the problem of inference amounts to performing an update $m(x|\theta_{k+1}) \leftarrow m(x|\theta_k)$. Indeed, in the infinitesimal limit where the θ_ks converge to an optimal θ_*^i, we can expand in the vicinity of this point. The second-order expansion in θ^i of the KL divergence then yields the Fisher information metric which forms the basis for information geometry [9,10]. (See Refs. [11–22] for contemporary appearances of the information metric in statistical inference and its relevance to quantum field theory and string theory.)

The processes of inference through Bayes' theorem then amount to specifying the trajectory of a particle in the curved background described by the information geometry. In Bayesian inference, we treat the parameters θ as random variables as well, and these are dictated by a posterior distribution $\pi(\theta, T)$ which updates as a function of data steps T. For any observable $O(\theta)$ which depends on these parameters, its appearance in various averages results in an implicit time dependence and a corresponding flow equation:

$$\frac{\partial}{\partial T} \overline{O}(T) = -\text{Var}(O, D), \tag{3}$$

where the line on top indicates an average with respect to $\pi(\theta, T)$ and Var(O, D) denotes the variance between the observable and D, a KL divergence between the "true" distribution and one which depends on θ at some intermediate stage of the inference scheme. There is a striking formal resemblance between the evolution of the parameters of the model (by taking $O = \theta$) and the evolution of parameters in renormalization group flow. We will explore this analogy further, especially with regard to "perturbations", i.e., new data, which can alter the trajectory of a flow.

In favorable circumstances, we can obtain good approximate solutions to this flow equation for a wide class of observables. In fact, for observables where the Cramér–Rao bound [9] is saturated, we can solve the equation exactly. This then yields a simple $1/T$ power-law scaling. We examine the perturbed flow equation where the Cramér–Rao bound is not saturated and solve the equation numerically to give a power-law scaling with powers greater than -1. Finally, we examine the case where there are "hidden variables". These are non-updated parameters in the model and demonstrate an exponential behavior in this case. The interpolation from this simple $1/T$ to exponential falloff is well approximated by a power-law decay of the form $1/T^{1+\nu}$ with $\nu > 0$.

We illustrate these general considerations with a number of examples. As one of the few cases we can treat analytically, we illustrate how the flow equations work in the case of inference on data drawn from a Gaussian distribution. This also includes the important case of a Gaussian Random Process, which is of relevance in the study of (untrained) neural networks in the infinite width limit [23]. As a physically motivated numerical example, we ask how well an observer can learn the coupling constants of the 1D Ising model. In this setting, "data" amounts to sampling from the Boltzmann distribution of possible spin configurations, and inference corresponds to refining our prior estimates on the value of the nearest neighbor coupling. We indeed find that the trajectory of the coupling obeys the observable flow equation and converges to a high level of accuracy.

It is also natural to ask whether we can apply these considerations even when we do not have a generative model for the probability distribution. A classic example of this sort is the "inference" performed by a neural network as it is learning. From the Bayesian perspective, neural networks are models that contain a large number of parameters given by the weights and biases of the network and training is a flow on those weights and biases induced by the training dataset. See Ref. [24] for an introduction to neural networks aimed at physicists. Due to the large number of parameters, a true quantitative analysis, as we did for the Ising model, is not possible. However, insofar as the neural network is engaging in rational inference, we should expect a flow equation to hold. To test this expectation, we study the phenomenology of training a network as a function of the size of the dataset. We consider simple dense feedforward networks (FF) and convolutional neural networks (CNNs) trained on the, by now classic, datasets of MNIST, Fashion-MNIST and CIFAR10.[2]

Quite remarkably, we find that the qualitative $1/T$ power-law behavior is emulated for the MNIST dataset where the network final loss is very small and other power laws occur for more complex datasets where the final loss is higher. The fact that our simple theoretical expectations match the rather opaque inference procedure of a neural network lends additional support to the formalism.

The rest of this chapter is organized as follows. We begin in Section 2 by reviewing Bayes' rule and then turn to the infinitesimal version defined by incremental updates and the induced flow for observables. After solving the flow equations exactly and in perturbation theory, we then turn to some examples. First, in Section 3, we present an analytic treatment in the context of inference for Gaussian data. In Section 4, we study the inference of coupling constants in the context of the 1D Ising model. In Section 5, we turn to examples of neural network learning various datasets. We present our conclusions and potential avenues for future investigation in Section 6. Appendix A presents a statistical mechanics interpretation of the Bayesian flow equations.

2. Bayes' Rule as a Dynamical System

In this section, we present a physical interpretation of Bayes' rule as a dynamical system. By working in a limit where we have a large number of events $N \gg 1$ partitioned up into smaller number of events

---

[2]These datasets are readily available with supporting notes in https://keras.io/api/datasets/.

$N_k \gg 1$ such that $N_k/N \ll 1$, we show that this can be recast as an integro-differential equation.

To begin, suppose we have observed some events $E = \{e_1, \ldots, e_N\}$, as drawn from some true distribution. In the Bayesian setting, we suppose that we have some model of the world specified by a posterior distribution conditional on observed events $f(\theta|e_1, \ldots, e_N) = \pi_{\text{post}}(\theta)$, which depends on "fitting parameters" $\theta = \{\theta^1, \ldots, \theta^m\}$ and our density for data conditional on θ specified as $f(e_1, \ldots, e_N|\theta)$. In what follows, we assume that there is a specific value $\theta = \alpha_*$ for which we realize the true distribution.[3] A general comment here is that we are framing our inference problem using Bayesian methods, which means that the parameters θ are themselves treated as values drawn from a random distribution. This is to be contrasted with how we would treat the inference problem as frequentists, where we would instead attempt to find a best estimate for these parameters (e.g., the mean and variance of a normal distribution). Rather, the notion of a Bayesian update means that additional "hyperparameters" for $\pi_{\text{post}}(\theta)$ are being updated as a function of increased data. For now, we keep this dependence on the hyperparameters implicit, but we illustrate later on how this works in some examples.

Now, assuming the observed events are conditionally independent of θ, we have

$$\pi_{\text{post}}(\theta) = f(\theta|e_1, \ldots, e_N) \propto f(e_1, \ldots, e_N|\theta) \times \pi_{\text{prior}}(\theta), \qquad (4)$$

where the constant of proportionality is fixed by the condition that $\pi_{\text{post}}(\theta)$ is properly normalized, i.e., we can introduce another distribution:

$$f(e_1, \ldots, e_N) = \int d\theta \, f(e_1, \ldots, e_N|\theta) \pi_{\text{prior}}(\theta), \qquad (5)$$

and write

$$\frac{\pi_{\text{post}}(\theta)}{\pi_{\text{prior}}(\theta)} = \frac{f(e_1, \ldots, e_N|\theta)}{f(e_1, \ldots, e_N)}. \qquad (6)$$

---

[3]A word on notation. We have chosen to write the fixed value of a given parameter as α_* instead of θ_*. We do this to emphasize that the θs are to be treated as the values of a random variable, with α_* indicating what a frequentist might refer to as the estimator of this parameter.

Rather than perform one large update, we could instead consider partitioning up our events into separate sequences of events, which we can label as $E(k) = \{e_1(k), \ldots, e_{N_k}(k)\}$, where now we let $k = 1, \ldots, K$ such that $N_1 + \cdots + N_K = N$. Introducing the cumulative set of events:

$$S_k \equiv E(1) \cup \cdots \cup E(k), \tag{7}$$

we can speak of a sequential update, as obtained from incorporating our new data:

$$\frac{\pi_{k+1}(\theta)}{\pi_k(\theta)} = \frac{f(E(k+1)|S_k, \theta)}{f(E(k+1)|S_k)}. \tag{8}$$

This specifies a recursion relation and thus a discrete dynamical system. Indeed, writing $\pi_k(\theta) = \exp(\ell_k(\theta))$ and taking the logarithm of Equation (8) yield the finite difference equation:

$$\ell_{k+1}(\theta) - \ell_k(\theta) = \log \frac{f(E(k+1)|S_k, \theta)}{f(E(k+1)|S_k)}. \tag{9}$$

To proceed further, we now make a few technical assumptions. First of all, we assume that each draw from the true distribution is independent so that we can write

$$f(e_1, \ldots, e_N|\theta) = f(e_1|\theta) \cdots f(e_N|\theta). \tag{10}$$

Furthermore, we assume that draws from the true distribution can always be viewed as part of the same parametric family as these densities:

$$f(E(k+1)|S_k) = \prod_{e \in E(k+1)} f(e|\alpha_k), \tag{11}$$

where α_k is the most likely estimate of θ given the data $E(k)$. Then, the finite difference equation of line (9) reduces to

$$\ell_{k+1}(\theta) - \ell_k(\theta) = \sum_{e \in E(k+1)} \log \frac{f(e|\theta)}{f(e|\alpha_k)} \equiv N_{k+1} \left\langle \log \frac{f(y|\theta)}{f(y|\alpha_k)} \right\rangle_{E(k+1)}, \tag{12}$$

in the obvious notation.

We now show that in the limit $N \gg N_k \gg 1$, Bayesian updating is well approximated by an integro-differential flow equation. The large N_k limit means that we can approximate the sum on the right-hand side of Equation (12) by an integral:

$$\ell_{k+1}(\theta) - \ell_k(\theta) = N_{k+1} \int dy \; f(y|\alpha_*) \log \frac{f(y|\theta)}{f(y|\alpha_k)} + \cdots, \qquad (13)$$

where the correction terms are subleading in a $1/N_{k+1}$ expansion and we have switched from referring to events e_i by their continuous analogs y. The right-hand side can be expressed in terms of a difference of two KL divergences, so we can write

$$\ell_{k+1}(\theta) - \ell_k(\theta) = N_{k+1} \left(D_{KL}(\alpha_*||\alpha_k) - D_{KL}(\alpha_*||\theta) \right) + \cdots. \quad (14)$$

We now approximate the left-hand side. The small N_k/N limit means we can replace the finite difference on the left-hand side by a derivative. More precisely, introduce a continuous parameter $\tau \in [0, 1]$, which we can partition up into discretized values τ_k with small time step $\delta\tau_k = \tau_{k+1} - \tau_k$ between each step:

$$\tau_k \equiv \frac{1}{N}(N_1 + \cdots + N_k) \quad \text{and} \quad \delta\tau_k \equiv \frac{N_k}{N}. \qquad (15)$$

So, instead of writing $\pi_k(\theta)$, we can instead speak of a continuously evolving family of distributions $\pi(\tau; \theta)$. Similarly, we write $\alpha(\tau)$ to indicate the continuous evolution used in the parameter appearing in $f(e|\alpha_k) = f(e|\alpha(\tau_k))$. The finite difference can therefore be approximated as

$$\ell_{k+1}(\theta) - \ell_k(\theta) = \ell'(\theta; \tau_k)\delta\tau_k + \frac{1}{2}\ell''(\theta; \tau_k)(\delta\tau_k)^2 + \cdots, \qquad (16)$$

where the prime indicates a partial derivative with respect to the time step, e.g., $\ell' = \partial\ell/\partial\tau$. Working in the approximation $N \gg N_k \gg 1$, Equation (14) is then given to leading order by

$$\frac{1}{N}\frac{\partial\ell(\theta; \tau)}{\partial\tau} = D_{KL}(\alpha_*||\alpha(\tau)) - D_{KL}(\alpha_*||\theta) + \cdots. \qquad (17)$$

To avoid overloading the notation, we write this as

$$\frac{1}{N}\frac{\partial\ell(\theta; \tau)}{\partial\tau} = D(\alpha(\tau)) - D(\theta) + \cdots. \qquad (18)$$

Observe that the N_k dependence has actually dropped out from the right-hand side; it only depends on the total number of events N.

In terms of the posterior $\pi(\theta; \tau) = \exp \ell(\theta; \tau)$, we have

$$\frac{\partial \pi(\theta; \tau)}{\partial \tau} = \pi(\theta; \tau) \frac{\partial \ell(\theta; \tau)}{\partial \tau} = N\pi(\theta; \tau) \left(D(\alpha(\tau)) - D(\theta) \right). \quad (19)$$

A formal solution to the posterior is then

$$\pi(\theta; \tau) = \exp N \int^\tau d\tau' \left(D(\alpha(\tau)) - D(\theta) \right). \quad (20)$$

2.1. *Observable flows*

Given an inference scheme over a random variable with parameters θ, we regard an observable as a function of the parameters, i.e., in the classical sense with the parameter space serving as a phase space for the theory. Given such an observable, $O(\theta)$, we now ask about the τ dependence, as obtained by evaluating the expectation value:

$$\overline{O}(\tau) = \int d\theta \, O(\theta)\pi(\theta; \tau). \quad (21)$$

This is subject to a differential equation, as obtained by differentiating both sides with respect to τ

$$\frac{\partial \overline{O}(\tau)}{\partial \tau} = N \int d\theta \, O(\theta)\pi(\theta; \tau) \left(D(\alpha(\tau)) - D(\theta) \right) \quad (22)$$

and using Equation (19). More compactly, we can write this as

$$\left(\frac{\partial}{\partial \tau} - N(D(\alpha(\tau)) - \overline{D}(\tau)) \right) \overline{O}(\tau) = -N\mathrm{Var}(O, D), \quad (23)$$

where $\mathrm{Var}(O, D)$ is just the variance between the operators O and D:

$$\mathrm{Var}(O, D) = \left\langle (O - \overline{O})(D - \overline{D}) \right\rangle_{\pi(\theta; \tau)}. \quad (24)$$

Before proceeding, let us consider the trivial observable $O(\theta) = 1$. This observable determines the normalization condition imposed on

$\pi(\theta; \tau)$ as a formal probability density. Using Equation (22), we find

$$0 = N \int d\theta \, \pi(\theta; \tau)(D(\alpha(\tau)) - D(\theta)) = N(D(\alpha(\tau)) - \bar{D}(\tau)), \quad (25)$$

which implies that

$$D(\alpha(\tau)) = \overline{D}(\tau). \quad (26)$$

Thus, the equation obeyed by arbitrary observables is given by

$$\frac{\partial}{\partial \tau}\overline{O}(\tau) = -N\mathrm{Var}(O, D). \quad (27)$$

To proceed further, it is helpful to work in terms of a rescaled time coordinate $T \equiv \tau N$. In terms of this variable, our equation becomes

$$\frac{\partial}{\partial T}\overline{O}(T) = -\mathrm{Var}(O, D), \quad (28)$$

so that the N dependence has dropped out. By expanding the covariance, we can also write this equation as

$$\frac{\partial \overline{O}}{\partial T} = \overline{O}\,\overline{D} - \int d\theta \pi(\theta; T)O(\theta)D(\theta). \quad (29)$$

We now turn to the interpretation of this equation in various regimes.

2.2.   *Generic observables at late T*

Our approach to analyzing this equation will begin with expanding the observables in a power series to obtain manageable expressions that have interpretations as governing late T behavior. In particular, we will use the expansion of the divergence:

$$D(\theta) \approx \frac{1}{2}\mathcal{I}_{ij}\bigg|_{\alpha_*} (\theta - \alpha_*)^i (\theta - \alpha_*)^j + \mathcal{O}(1/T^3), \quad (30)$$

where $\mathcal{I}|_{\alpha_*} = \mathcal{I}_*$ is the Fisher information metric evaluated at the true underlying mean of the parameter distribution. It is necessary to expand around this parameter value if one wishes to represent the KL divergence as a quadratic form with no constant or linear contribution — that is, we have used the fact that α_* is the minimizing argument of $D(\theta)$ to set the constant and linear order terms in (30) to zero. Then, at late times, any arbitrary observable satisfies the following equation:

$$\frac{\partial \overline{O}}{\partial T} = \frac{1}{2}\mathcal{I}_{kl}^{*}\,\overline{O}\int d\theta \pi(\theta;T)(\theta - \alpha_{*})^{k}(\theta - \alpha_{*})^{l}$$

$$- \frac{1}{2}\mathcal{I}_{kl}^{*}\int d\theta \pi(\theta;T)O(\theta)(\theta - \alpha_{*})^{k}(\theta - \alpha_{*})^{l} + \mathcal{O}(1/T^{3}). \quad (31)$$

2.3. *Centralized moments at late T*

At this juncture, let us turn our attention to a special class of observables. Namely, those of the form

$$C^{i_{1}\ldots i_{2l}}(\theta) = \prod_{j=1}^{2l}(\theta - \alpha_{*})^{i_{j}}. \quad (32)$$

Such observables are precisely the pre-integrated centralized moments of the T-posterior. More precisely, this is true at sufficiently late times in which $\alpha(T) \sim \alpha_{*}$, meaning the parameter distribution has centralized around its true mean. The observable flow equation for these observables therefore governs the T-dependence of the centralized moments:

$$\overline{C}^{i_{1}\ldots i_{2l}}(T) = \int d\theta \pi(\theta;T) \prod_{j=1}^{2l}(\theta - \alpha_{*})^{i_{j}}, \quad (33)$$

which satisfy the differential equation:

$$\frac{\partial \overline{C}^{i_{1}\ldots i_{2l}}}{\partial T} = \frac{1}{2}\mathcal{I}_{kl}^{*}\overline{C}^{i_{1}\ldots i_{2l}}\int d\theta \pi(\theta;T)(\theta - \alpha_{*})^{k}(\theta - \alpha_{*})^{l}$$

$$- \frac{1}{2}\mathcal{I}_{kl}^{*}\int d\theta \pi(\theta;T)C^{i_{1}\ldots i_{2l}}(\theta)(\theta - \alpha_{*})^{k}(\theta - \alpha_{*})^{l}$$

$$+ \mathcal{O}(1/T^{3}). \quad (34)$$

Using our notation, this can be written more briefly as

$$\frac{\partial}{\partial T}\overline{C}^{i_{1}\ldots i_{2l}} = \frac{1}{2}\mathcal{I}_{kl}^{*}\overline{C}^{i_{1}\ldots i_{2l}}\overline{C}^{kl} - \frac{1}{2}\mathcal{I}_{kl}^{*}\overline{C}^{i_{1}\ldots i_{2l}\,kl} + \mathcal{O}(1/T^{3}). \quad (35)$$

2.4.   *Centralized moments for Gaussian distributions*

The analysis we have done up to this point is valid for the centralized moments of any arbitrary posterior distribution. Now, we will specialize to the case that the posterior distribution is Gaussian at late T. This is quite generic and will always be the case when the parameters being inferred over are truly non-stochastic. The aspect of the Gaussian model which is especially useful is that we can implement Isserlis', a.k.a, Wick's theorem, to reduce $2l$-point functions into sums of products of 2-point functions (i.e., the covariance). In particular, we have the formula

$$\overline{C}^{i_1 \ldots i_{2l}} = \sum_{p \in \mathcal{P}_{2l}^2} \prod_{(r,s) \in p} \overline{C}^{i_r i_s}, \tag{36}$$

where $\mathcal{P}_{2l}^2$ is the set of all partitions of $2l$ elements into pairs, and a generic element $p \in \mathcal{P}_{2l}^2$ has the form $p = \{(r_1, s_1), \ldots, (r_l, s_l)\}$, hence the notation in the product. Isserlis'/Wick's theorem implies that for a Gaussian model, it is sufficient to understand the T-dependent behavior of the 2-point function, and the behavior of the other $2l$-point functions immediately follows suit. Therefore, let us consider the equation satisfied by $\overline{C}^{ij}$:

$$\frac{\partial}{\partial T} \overline{C}^{ij} = \frac{1}{2} \mathcal{I}_{kl}^* \overline{C}^{ij} \overline{C}^{kl} - \frac{1}{2} \mathcal{I}_{kl}^* \overline{C}^{ijkl} + \mathcal{O}(1/T^3). \tag{37}$$

Using (36), we can write

$$\overline{C}^{ijkl} = \overline{C}^{ij} \overline{C}^{kl} + \overline{C}^{ik} \overline{C}^{jl} + \overline{C}^{il} \overline{C}^{jk}. \tag{38}$$

Plugging this back into Equation (37), we get

$$\frac{\partial}{\partial T} \overline{C}^{ij} = \frac{1}{2} \mathcal{I}_{kl}^* \overline{C}^{ij} \overline{C}^{kl} - \frac{1}{2} \mathcal{I}_{kl}^* \left(\overline{C}^{ij} \overline{C}^{kl} + \overline{C}^{ik} \overline{C}^{jl} + \overline{C}^{il} \overline{C}^{jk} \right) + \mathcal{O}(1/T^3) \tag{39}$$

$$= -\mathcal{I}_{kl}^* \overline{C}^{ik} \overline{C}^{jl} + \mathcal{O}(1/T^3), \tag{40}$$

where we have used the fact that $\mathcal{I}_{ij}^*$ is symmetric. The equation satisfied by the covariance of a Gaussian distribution at late T is thus

$$\frac{\partial}{\partial T} \overline{C}^{ij} + \mathcal{I}_{kl}^* \overline{C}^{ik} \overline{C}^{jl} = 0 + \mathcal{O}(1/T^3). \tag{41}$$

At this stage, we can recognize our equation as predicting familiar behavior for the $2l$-point functions of a Gaussian posterior.

2.5. *Cramér–Rao solution*

Cramér and Rao [9] demonstrated that there is a lower bound on the variance of any unbased estimator which is given by the inverse of the Fisher information. An estimator that saturates this bound is as efficient as possible and reaches the lowest possible mean squared error.

We now show that the evolution Equation (41) is satisfied when the model saturates the Cramér–Rao bound. That is, at sufficiently late T, we take the bound to be saturated such that

$$\overline{C}_{CR}^{ij} = \frac{\mathcal{I}_*^{ij}}{T} + \mathcal{O}(1/T^2). \tag{42}$$

One can see that (42) is then a solution to (41) by straightforward computation:

$$\frac{\partial}{\partial T} \overline{C}_{CR}^{ij} = \frac{\partial}{\partial T} \left(\frac{\mathcal{I}_*^{ij}}{T} \right) = -\frac{\mathcal{I}_*^{ij}}{T^2} = -\mathcal{I}_{kl}^* \frac{\mathcal{I}_*^{ik}}{T} \frac{\mathcal{I}_*^{jl}}{T} = -\mathcal{I}_{kl}^* \overline{C}_{CR}^{ik} \overline{C}_{CR}^{jl}. \tag{43}$$

We leave it implicit that there could be correction terms of higher order in the expansion $1/T$. The T-dependent behavior of any arbitrary $2l$-point function in the theory is subsequently given by

$$\overline{C}_{CR}^{i_1 \ldots i_{2l}} = \frac{1}{T^l} \sum_{p \in \mathcal{P}_{2l}^2} \prod_{(r,s) \in p} \mathcal{I}_*^{i_r i_s}. \tag{44}$$

2.6. *Higher-order effects*

The assumptions that led to the saturation of the Cramér–Rao bound are based on two leading order approximations: First, that the maximum likelihood parameter is near the "true" value, and second, that the posterior distribution is approximately Gaussian. Both of these assumptions become increasingly valid at late update times, i.e., with more data, hence we have expressed our equations as a power series expansion in the small quantity, $1/T$.

One can look for corrections to these assumptions by systematically reintroducing higher-order effects via a perturbation series. To be precise, as one moves into earlier update times, there will be contributions to the KL divergence which are higher than quadratic order in θ. Similarly, as one moves away from a Gaussian posterior, either by moving back in time or by including some additional implicit randomness to the parameters, one finds new terms in the posterior distribution away from Gaussianity which also lead to new terms in the Observable Flow equations.

We provide an outline of the perturbative analysis including effects both from the additional higher-order expansion of the KL divergence and from the deviation of the Posterior from Gaussianity. To begin, the KL divergence can be Taylor expanded into a power series in the un-integrated n-point functions as follows:

$$D(\theta) = \sum_{n=2}^{\infty} \frac{1}{n!} \mathcal{I}^{(n)}_{i_1 \ldots i_n} C^{i_1 \ldots i_n}(\theta), \tag{45}$$

where

$$\mathcal{I}^{(n)}_{i_1 \ldots i_n} = \prod_{j=1}^{n} \frac{\partial}{\partial \theta^{i_j}} D(\theta) \bigg|_{\theta = \alpha_*}. \tag{46}$$

We will now perturb the posterior distribution away from Gaussianity as follows:

$$\pi(\theta; T) = \text{Gaussian} \cdot e^{-\lambda f(\theta)}, \tag{47}$$

where in the above, $f(\theta)$ is treated as an arbitrary bounded function, and the size of the small parameter λ governing the perturbation is, in general, dependent on the update time T. We take the unperturbed Gaussian distribution to be centered around the maximum likelihood estimate (MLE) with covariance given by the two-point correlator. The expectation value of an observable $O(\theta)$ can therefore be expanded in a series with respect to λ:

$$\langle O \rangle_\pi = \langle e^{-\lambda f(\theta)} O(\theta) \rangle_{\text{Gauss}} = \sum_{n=0}^{\infty} \frac{(-1)^n \lambda^n}{n!} \langle f(\theta)^n O(\theta) \rangle_{\text{Gauss}}. \tag{48}$$

Now, one can input these series expansions back into (29) to obtain higher-order corrections to the scaling behavior of any arbitrary observable expectation value. Doing so explicitly and terminating the perturbation series at order N in powers of λ and order M in powers of $1/T$, we find

$$\sum_{n=0}^{N} \frac{(-1)^n \lambda^n}{n!} \frac{\partial}{\partial T} \langle f(\theta)^n O(\theta) \rangle_{\text{Gauss}}$$

$$= \sum_{n=0}^{N} \frac{(-1)^n \lambda^n}{n!} \langle f(\theta)^n O(\theta) \rangle_{\text{Gauss}} \sum_{n'=0}^{N} \sum_{m=2}^{M} \frac{(-1)^{n'} \lambda^{n'}}{n'!}$$

$$\frac{1}{m!} \mathcal{I}^{(m)}_{i_1 \dots i_m} \langle f(\theta)^{n'} C^{i_1 \dots i_m}(\theta) \rangle_{\text{Gauss}}$$

$$- \sum_{n=0}^{N} \sum_{m=2}^{M} \frac{(-1)^n \lambda^n}{n!} \frac{1}{m!} \mathcal{I}^{(m)}_{i_1 \dots i_m} \langle f(\theta)^n O(\theta) C^{i_1 \dots i_m}(\theta) \rangle_{\text{Gauss}}$$

$$+ \mathcal{O}(T^{-M}, \lambda^N). \tag{49}$$

We will work just to the next to leading order. To see the impact of these higher-order effects, we performed two simple numerical experiments in which the Observable Flow for the two-point function can be solved exactly. In each case, we consider only a single parameter being inferred upon during the Bayesian update.

(1) In the first numerical experiment, we consider a perturbation in which we accept terms in the expansion of the KL divergence up to fourth order, but in which the posterior is assumed to remain approximately Gaussian. In this case, the Observable Flow equation for the second-centralized moment, $\overline{C}^{(2)}$, becomes

$$\frac{\partial \overline{C}^{(2)}}{\partial T} = -\mathcal{I}^{(2)} (\overline{C}^{(2)})^2 - \frac{1}{2} \mathcal{I}^{(4)} (\overline{C}^{(2)})^3. \tag{50}$$

We fix the $\mathcal{I}^{(2)}$ and $\mathcal{I}^{(4)}$ by hand and then use the above equation to solve for the time dependence of $C^{(2)}$. This is done using numerical methods, and subsequently fit to a power law of the form

$$C^{(2)} = \frac{a}{T^b} + c. \tag{51}$$

The resulting curve has a power in which $b < 1$, and typically in the range between 0.65 and 1 depending on the ratio between $\mathcal{I}^{(2)}$ and $\mathcal{I}^{(4)}$ (only the ratio matters). The results of this numerical experiment are given in Table 1.

Table 1.   Result of the first numerical experiment involving perturbations to the KL divergence. This entails numerically solving Equation (50) by fitting to a power law $aT^{-b} + c$, as in Equation (51). In all cases, the R^2 value is $\sim 0.99 + O(10^{-3})$. As the ratio $\mathcal{I}^{(4)}/\mathcal{I}^{(2)}$ increases, we observe that the size of the constant offset increases in magnitude and the exponent b in T^{-b} decreases.

$\mathcal{I}^{(4)}/\mathcal{I}^{(2)}$	a	b	c
0.1	0.96	0.99	-4.7×10^{-6}
0.2	0.92	0.98	-2.5×10^{-4}
0.3	0.88	0.96	-6.9×10^{-4}
0.4	0.83	0.94	-1.3×10^{-3}
0.5	0.78	0.92	-2.1×10^{-3}
0.6	0.74	0.89	-2.9×10^{-3}
0.7	0.70	0.87	-3.9×10^{-3}
0.8	0.66	0.84	-4.9×10^{-3}
0.9	0.62	0.82	-6.0×10^{-3}
1	0.58	0.79	-7.1×10^{-3}
1.1	0.55	0.77	-8.2×10^{-3}
1.2	0.52	0.74	-9.3×10^{-3}
1.3	0.49	0.72	-1.0×10^{-2}
1.4	0.47	0.69	-1.2×10^{-2}
1.5	0.44	0.67	-1.3×10^{-2}

(2) In the second numerical experiment, we consider perturbations away from Gaussianity in which we accept terms of order λ with $f(\theta) = \theta^4$ but regard the KL divergence as sufficiently well approximated at quadratic order. In this case, the two-point function has the form

$$\overline{C}^{(2)} = \overline{C}_G^{(2)} - 15\lambda(\overline{C}_G^{(2)})^3, \tag{52}$$

where $\overline{C}_G^{(2)}$ is the expectation of the second-centralized moment with respect to the Gaussian distribution. The Gaussian two-point function subsequently satisfies the ODE:

$$\frac{\partial}{\partial T}\left(\overline{C}_G^{(2)} - 15\lambda(\overline{C}_G^{(2)})^3\right) = \frac{1}{2}\mathcal{I}^{(2)}(\overline{C}_G^{(2)})^2 - 15\lambda\mathcal{I}^{(2)}(\overline{C}_G^{(2)})^3$$
$$-\frac{1}{2}\mathcal{I}^{(2)}\left(3(\overline{C}_G^{(2)})^2 - 105\lambda(\overline{C}_G^{(2)})^4\right). \tag{53}$$

Table 2. Result of the second numerical experiment involving perturbation away from Gaussianity. This involves numerical solutions to Equation (53) obtained by fitting to a power law $aT^{-b} + c$, as in Equation (51). In all cases, the R^2 value is $\sim 0.99 + O(10^{-3})$. As the ratio $\lambda/\mathcal{I}^{(2)}$ increases, we observe that the size of the constant offset increases in magnitude and the exponent b in T^{-b} decreases.

$\lambda/\mathcal{I}^{(2)}$	a	b	c
0.01	0.78	0.89	-3.9×10^{-3}
0.02	0.63	0.80	-7.7×10^{-3}
0.03	0.51	0.71	-1.1×10^{-2}
0.04	0.42	0.63	-1.7×10^{-2}
0.05	0.36	0.55	-2.1×10^{-2}
0.06	0.31	0.49	-2.6×10^{-2}
0.07	0.28	0.44	-3.0×10^{-2}
0.08	0.25	0.40	-3.5×10^{-2}
0.09	0.23	0.36	-3.9×10^{-2}
0.1	0.22	0.32	-4.3×10^{-2}
0.11	0.21	0.29	-4.8×10^{-2}
0.12	0.20	0.26	-5.3×10^{-2}
0.13	0.19	0.24	-5.9×10^{-2}
0.14	0.19	0.21	-6.5×10^{-2}
0.15	0.19	0.19	-7.2×10^{-2}

Again, this equation can be solved using numerical methods and fit to a power law of the form (51). The resulting curves exhibit scaling in which $b < 1$. The size of b is governed by the ratio of $\mathcal{I}^{(2)}$ and λ. The results of this experiment for various values of this ratio can be found in Table 2.

The upshot of these experiments, and of this section, is that higher-order corrections to the Cramér–Rao solution of the Observable Flow equation can be implemented systematically by considering a bi-perturbation series which takes into account both changes to the KL divergence due to the proximity of the MLE and the data generating parameter, and deviation of the posterior distribution from a Gaussian. The impact of these corrections are to decrease the steepness of the learning curve, in accord with expectations from the Cramér–Rao Bound.

2.7. *Hidden variables and the breaking of the Cramér–Rao Bound*

In the last section, we showed that the Dynamical Bayesian Inference scheme respects the Cramér–Rao Bound as an upper limit on the rate at which the two-point function can scale with respect to the update time. An analogous phenomenon occurs in conformal field theories and is often referred to as the "unitarity bound" (see Ref. [25]), which controls the strength of correlations as a function of distance in the underlying spacetime.[4]

Now, in the physical setting, a simple way to violate constraints from unitarity is to treat the system under consideration as "open", i.e., degrees of freedom can flow in or out. In the context of Bayesian inference, we have a direct analogy in terms of hidden variables h which may also impact the distribution $f(y|\theta, h)$ but which we may not be able to access or even parameterize (see Figure 1). This can lead to dissipative phenomena, as well as driving phenomena.[5]

The basic setup is to consider a data generating distribution which belongs to a parametric family, $p(y \mid \theta, h)$, which depends on two sets of variables: θ (visible) and h (hidden). An experimenter who is observing the data generated by this distribution may, either due to ignorance or by choice,[6] train a model that depends only on the variables, θ, i.e., $f(y \mid \theta)$. Observables involving the hidden variables

---

[4]For example, in a relativistic conformal field theory (CFT) in $D \geq 2$ spacetime dimensions, a scalar primary operator $O(x)$ of scaling dimension Δ will have two-point function: $\langle O^\dagger(x)O(x)\rangle \sim 1/|x|^{2\Delta}$, and $\Delta \geq \Delta_0$ specifies a unitarity bound which is saturated by a free scalar field, i.e., a Gaussian random field. In the context of the Cramér–Rao bound, the limiting situation is again specified by the case of a Gaussian. The analogy is not perfect, however, because we do not have the same notion of spacetime locality in Bayesian inference, and the referencing to the Gaussian case is different ($\Delta > 1$) for a CFT but powers $1 / T^b$ for $b < 1$ in the case of Cramér–Rao. It is, nevertheless, extremely suggestive, and the physical intuition about how to violate various unitarity bounds will indeed have a direct analogy in the statistical inference setting as well.

[5]Returning to the case of a CFT in D dimensions, observe that a 4D free scalar can be modeled in terms of a collection of 3D scalars coupled along a discretized dimension. The unitarity bound for a scalar primary operator in 3D is $\Delta_{3D} \geq 1/2$, while in 4D, it is $\Delta_{4D} \geq 1$.

[6]For example, a model builder may choose to fix the "hidden" variables if they are close to their maximum likelihood values or do not vary greatly across samples.

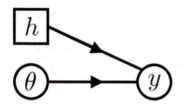

Figure 1. Graphical model depiction of a conditional distribution $p(y|\theta, h)$ we wish to infer, where now we explicitly account for both visible training parameters θ and hidden parameters h. The presence of such hidden variables can impact the inference scheme.

will evolve indirectly over the course of the update due to the changing of the total joint probability density over trained and hidden variables, however this evolution is not necessarily governed by a Bayesian updating scheme. Insofar as we have a reliable inference scheme at all, we can neglect the explicit time variation in the hidden variables, i.e., we can treat them as non-dynamical. Summarizing, only observables in the visible parameters θ will satisfy Observable Flow equations.

Now, although we are treating the hidden parameters as non-dynamical, they still enter in the KL divergence between the likelihood and the data generating model and therefore impact all observable flow equations. To be precise, at leading order,

$$D_{KL}(\Phi_* \parallel \Phi) = \frac{1}{2}\mathcal{I}_{AB}(\Phi - \Phi_*)^A(\phi - \Phi_*)^B. \tag{54}$$

Here, we are using notation in which $\Phi = (\theta, h)$ is the complete set of parameters, and $\Phi_* = (\alpha_*, h_*)$ (by abuse of notation) denotes the actual parameters from which we draw the distribution. The index $A = (i, I)$ spans all parameters, with the index $i = 1, \ldots, n$ corresponding to the trained parameters, and the index $I = 1, \ldots, m$ corresponding to the hidden parameters. In this more explicit notation, the information metric appearing in (54) takes the form

$$\mathcal{I} = \mathcal{I}_{ij}d\theta^i \otimes d\theta^j + \mathcal{I}_{IJ}dh^I \otimes dh^J + \mathcal{I}_{iI}d\theta^i \otimes dh^I + \mathcal{I}_{Ii}dh^I \otimes d\theta^i, \tag{55}$$

where $\mathcal{I}_{iI} = \mathcal{I}_{Ii}$.

In this regard, the hidden variables may more aptly be identified as non-dynamical rather than hidden, but their impact is the same either way.

Consider next the scaling of the two-point function between trained parameters. The scaling of the two-point function over the course of the Dynamical Bayesian Inference scheme is dictated by the differential equation governing $C^{ij}(\theta)$. Using the observable flow equation, and remembering to include the complete KL divergence including contributions from both hidden and trained variables, one finds the following equation[7]:

$$\frac{\partial}{\partial T}\overline{C}^{ij} = -\mathcal{I}_{kl}\overline{C}^{ik}\overline{C}^{jl} - \mathcal{I}_{KL}\overline{C}^{iK}\overline{C}^{jL} - 2\mathcal{I}_{lL}\overline{C}^{il}\overline{C}^{jL}. \qquad (56)$$

The new contributions are the final two terms on the right-hand side which depend on the covariance between trained and hidden variables. As noted above, such observables are to be considered as slowly varying in comparison with observables involving only trained parameters. Hence, for the purposes of this exercise, we can regard these covariances as approximately constant in time.

We now make the well-motivated assumption that the joint probability model between the trained and hidden parameters is such that the covariance among all pairs of trained and hidden parameters satisfies the series of inequalities:

$$\overline{C}^{ij} \gg \overline{C}^{iI} \gg \overline{C}^{IJ} \qquad (57)$$

for all values of i, j, I, J. This assumption (along with the assumption that hidden variable observables are slowly varying) basically serves to justify the distinction between hidden and trained variables. If the hidden variables were rapidly varying and/or highly correlated with observed data, it would not be reasonable to exclude them from the model. Alternatively, we may use these conditions as a criterion for *defining* hidden variables as those variables which vary slowly

---

[7]Here, we have extended the notation $\overline{C}^{A_1...A_n}$ to refer to the expectation value of n-point functions including arbitrary combinations of trained and hidden parameters:

$$\overline{C}^{A_1...A_n} = \int d\theta \, dh \, \rho(h \mid \theta)\pi(\theta;T)\prod_{i=1}^{n}(\Phi - \Phi_*)^{A_i}, \qquad (58)$$

where $\rho(h \mid \theta)$ is a fixed conditional distribution encoding the probability density for hidden parameters given trained parameters.

and have limited covariance with relevant parameters.[8] Under these assumptions, we can then write the ODE governing the scaling of the two-point function as

$$\frac{\partial}{\partial T}\overline{C}^{ij} = -\mathcal{I}_{kl}\overline{C}^{ik}\overline{C}^{jl} - 2\mathcal{I}_{lL}\overline{C}^{il}\overline{C}^{jL}. \tag{59}$$

From Equation (58), we can recognize that the evolution of the two-point function (as well as the n-point functions) depends directly on the covariance between trained and hidden parameters. Note also that coupling to the hidden variables involves the off-diagonal terms of the information metric, $\mathcal{I}_{lL}$, which can in principle be either positive or negative, provided the whole metric is still positive definite. This can lead to a flow of information into the visible system (driving) or leakage out (dissipation).

The presence of this additional coupling to the hidden variables can produce an apparent violation of the Cramér–Rao bound on just the visible sector. To see why, it is already enough to consider the simplest case where we have a single visible parameter θ, with the rest viewed as hidden. In this case, the observable flow equation is

$$\frac{\partial}{\partial T}\overline{C}^{11} = -\mathcal{I}_{11}(\overline{C}^{11})^2 - \beta\overline{C}^{11} + \mathcal{O}(\beta^2), \tag{60}$$

where

$$\beta = 2\mathcal{I}_{1I}\overline{C}^{1I} \tag{61}$$

is twice the sum of the covariances of the trained parameter with the hidden parameters, and we have made it explicit that this is a leading order result in the size of these correlations. Dropping the order β^2 terms, the differential Equation (60) can be solved exactly:

$$\overline{C}^{11}(T) = \frac{\kappa\beta}{e^{\beta T} - \kappa\mathcal{I}_{11}}, \tag{62}$$

where the constant κ depends on the initial conditions. Observe that for $\beta > 0$, $\overline{C}^{11}(T)$ decays exponentially at large T, i.e., faster than

---

[8]This is again reminiscent of the splitting between fast and slow modes which one uses in the analysis of renormalization group flows.

$1/T$. We interpret this as driving information into the visible sector. Conversely, for $\beta < 0$, we observe that the solution asymptotes to $-\beta/\mathcal{I}_{11} > 0$, i.e., we are well above the Cramér–Rao bound (no falloff at large T at all). We interpret this as dissipation: we are continually losing information.

In the above, we made several simplifying assumptions in order to analytically approximate the solution to the observable flow equations. At a phenomenological level, the interpolation from a simple $1/T$ behavior to an exponential decay law can be accomplished by a more general power law of the form $1/T^{1+\nu}$ with $\nu > 0$, dependent on the particular inference scheme. This will be borne out by our numerical experiments, especially the ones in Section 5 involving inference in a neural network, where we study the loss function and its dependence on T.

It is interesting to note that the crossover between a power law and exponential decay is also implicitly tied to the accuracy of the underlying model. This suggests that at lower accuracy, there is more information left for the algorithm to draw into its estimates. As the accuracy improves, the available information decreases and hence the driven behavior is slowly deactivated, resulting in more approximately power-law-type behavior. Stated in this way, it is interesting to ponder what the precise nature of this crossover is, and whether it may be regarded as a kind of phase transition. We leave a more fundamental explanation of this crossover behavior to future work.

3. Dynamical Bayes for Gaussian Data

To give an analytic example of dynamical Bayesian updating, we now consider the illustrative case of sampling from a Gaussian distribution. An interesting special case is that of the Gaussian random process which can also be used to gain insight into the inference of neural networks (see, e.g., Ref. [23]).

3.1. *Analysis for multivariate Gaussian data*

A d-dimensional Gaussian random variable can be regarded as a random variable distributed according to a family of distributions governed by two parameters: a mean vector μ and a symmetric, positive semi-definite covariance matrix Σ. Explicitly,

$$f(y \mid \mu, \Sigma) = ((2\pi)^d \det(\Sigma))^{-1/2} \exp\left(-\frac{1}{2}(y - \mu)^\mathsf{T}\Sigma^{-1}(y - \mu)\right),$$
(63)

where Σ^{-1} is the matrix inverse of the covariance; $\Sigma\Sigma^{-1} = \mathbb{I}$. By a simple counting argument, the number of free parameters governing the distribution of a d-dimensional Gaussian random variable is $d + \frac{d(d+1)}{2}$.

Bayesian inference over Gaussian data consists in determining a posterior distribution in the space of parameters $\Theta = (\mu, \Sigma)$. We can be slightly more general by allowing for reparameterizations of the space of parameters in terms of some $\theta \in \mathcal{S} \subset \mathbb{R}^{(d+\frac{d(d+1)}{2})}$, that is,

$$\Theta = \Theta(\theta) = (\mu(\theta), \Sigma(\theta)).$$
(64)

Hence, the result of a Dynamical Bayesian inference procedure on Gaussian data is to determine a flow in the parameters, $\theta = \alpha(T)$, giving rise to a flow in the posterior distribution $\pi(\theta; T)$.

In the case of the Gaussian distribution, and many other standard distributions for that matter, we can say slightly more than what we could when the family governing data remains unspecified. In particular, we have an explicit form for the KL divergence between multivariate Gaussian distributions:

$$D_{KL}((\mu_0, \Sigma_0) \parallel (\mu_1, \Sigma_1)) = \frac{1}{2}\left(\text{tr}(\Sigma_1^{-1}\Sigma_0) + (\mu_1 - \mu_0)^\mathsf{T}\Sigma_1^{-1}(\mu_1 - \mu_0)\right.$$

$$\left. + \ln\left(\frac{\det(\Sigma_1)}{\det(\Sigma_0)}\right) - d\right).$$
(65)

This can be expressed in terms of θ_0 and θ_1 by composition with the reparameterization 64 provided $(\mu_a, \Sigma_a) = (\mu(\theta_a), \Sigma(\theta_a))$ for $a = 0, 1$:

$$D_{KL}(\theta_0 \parallel \theta_1) = \frac{1}{2}\left(\begin{array}{c}\text{tr}(\Sigma(\theta_1)^{-1}\Sigma(\theta_0)) + \ln(\frac{\det(\Sigma(\theta_1))}{\det(\Sigma(\theta_0))}) - d) \\ +(\mu(\theta_1) - \mu(\theta_0))^\mathsf{T}\Sigma(\theta_1)^{-1}(\mu(\theta_1) - \mu(\theta_0))\end{array}\right).$$
(66)

Given the flowing of the parameters, $\alpha(T)$, and the true underlying parameters, α_*, the posterior distribution is given by the solution to the Dynamical Bayesian updating equation:

$$\pi(\theta; T) = \exp\left(\int_0^T dT'(D_{KL}(\alpha_* \parallel \alpha(T')) - D_{KL}(\alpha_* \parallel \theta))\right). \quad (67)$$

This solution can be written in the form:

$$\pi(\theta; T) = \exp\left(-T D_{KL}(\alpha_* \parallel \theta)\right) \exp\left(N \int_0^T dT' \, D_{KL}(\alpha_* \parallel \alpha(T'))\right). \quad (68)$$

Note that the posterior distribution is proportional to the exponentiated KL divergence evaluated against the true underlying model parameter — a standard result from the theory of large deviations:

$$\pi(\theta; T) \propto \exp\left(-T D_{KL}(\alpha_* \parallel \theta)\right). \quad (69)$$

Using the explicit form of the KL divergence for the normal distribution, we find

$$\pi(\theta; T) \propto \det(\Sigma(\alpha_*)) \det(\Sigma(\theta))^{-1}$$
$$\exp\left(T\left\{-\frac{1}{2}\mathrm{tr}(\Sigma(\alpha_*)\Sigma(\theta)^{-1}) - \frac{1}{2}(\mu(\theta) - \mu(\alpha_*))\right.\right.$$
$$\left.\left. \Sigma(\theta)^{-1}(\mu(\theta) - \mu(\alpha_*))\right\}\right). \quad (70)$$

This distribution is of the form of a Normal-Inverse-Wishart with location parameter $\mu(\alpha_*)$ and inverse scale parameter $\Sigma(\alpha_*)$. This is precisely the expected result for the posterior of a normal data model whose conjugate prior distribution is Normal-Inverse-Wishart.

3.2. *Gaussian random processes*

Having addressed the Dynamical Bayesian inference of multivariate Gaussian data, it becomes natural to discuss the Dynamical Bayesian inference of data which is distributed according to a Gaussian Random Process (GRP).[9] A GRP may be interpreted as the functional

---

[9]For an introduction to GRPs in machine learning, see Ref. [26].

analog of a Gaussian distribution. That is, instead of considering random vectors, one considers random *functions*, and instead of specifying a mean vector and a covariance matrix, one specifies a mean *function* and a covariance *kernel*. Let us be more precise.

Suppose the data we are interested in consist of the space of random functions, $\phi : D \to \mathbb{R}$.[10] To specify a GRP on such a sample space, one must specify a mean function

$$\mu : D \to \mathbb{R} \tag{71}$$

and a covariance kernel

$$\Sigma : D \times D \to \mathbb{R}. \tag{72}$$

Then, the distribution over functions takes the symbolic form:

$$f(\phi \mid \mu, \Sigma) = \mathcal{N} \exp\left(-\frac{1}{2} \int_{D \times D} dx dy \, (\phi(x) - \mu(x)) \Sigma^{-1} \right.$$
$$\left. \times (x, y)(\phi(y) - \mu(y))\right), \tag{73}$$

where $\Sigma^{-1}(x, y)$ is the inverse of $\Sigma(x, y)$ in the functional sense

$$\int_D dy \, \Sigma^{-1}(x, y)\Sigma(y, z) = \delta(x - z) \tag{74}$$

and the prefactor $\mathcal{N}$ is formally infinite and can be identified with the partition function (path integral) of the unnormalized GRP.

Taken literally, distribution (73) is difficult to use. It should rather be viewed as a set of instructions for how to interpret the GRP. Formally, a GRP is defined by restricting our attention to a finite partition of the domain D: $P = \{x_1, \ldots, x_n\} \subset D$. A functional random variable $f : D \to \mathbb{R}$ follows a Gaussian Process with mean $\mu(x)$ and covariance $\Sigma(x, y)$ if, for any such partition, the n-vector $f_P = (f(x_1), \ldots, f(x_n))$ in a multivariate Gaussian random variable with mean $\mu = (\mu(x_1), \ldots, \mu(x_n))$ and covariance $\Sigma = \Sigma(x_i, x_j)$.

---

[10]Note that this construction can be straightforwardly generalized to functions with values in arbitrary spaces; we consider maps into $\mathbb{R}$ for the sake of clarity.

In this respect, the study of a GRP is precisely the same as the study of the multivariate Gaussian — we need only restrict our attention to some finite partition of the domain of the functional random variable and then perform Dynamical Bayesian inference over the resulting multivariate normal random variable.

4.   Inference in the Ising Model

We now turn to some numerical experiments to test the general framework of dynamical Bayesian updating. Along these lines, we consider the following basic physical question: Given a collection of experimental data, how well can an observer reconstruct the underlying model?[11] To make this tractable, we assume that the particular physical model is known, but the couplings are unknown. A tractable example of this sort is the statistical mechanics of the Ising model, as specified by a collection of spins $\sigma = \pm 1$ arranged on a graph. In this setting, the statistical mechanics provides us with a probability distribution over spin configurations $\{\sigma\}$ as specified by the Boltzmann factor:

$$P[\{\sigma\}|J] = \frac{1}{\mathcal{Z}(J)} \exp(-H_{\text{Ising}}[\{\sigma\}|J]), \qquad (75)$$

where $\mathcal{Z}(J)$ is a normalization constant (i.e., the partition function) introduced to ensure a normalized distribution and H_{Ising} is the Ising model Hamiltonian with coupling constant J:

$$H_{\text{Ising}}[\{\sigma\}|J] = -J\sum_{n.n.}\sigma\sigma'. \qquad (76)$$

In the above, the sum is over nearest neighbors on the graph. One can generalize this model in various ways, by changing the strength of any given bond in the graph, but for ease of analysis, we focus on the simplest non-trivial case as stated here. In this case, each draw from the distribution $P[\{\sigma\}|J]$ is specified by a collection of spins $\{\sigma\}$. We can bin all of these events, as we already explained in Section 2, and

---

[11]See also Refs. [14,22,27,28] for related discussions.

this specifies a posterior distribution $\pi_{\text{post}}(J;T)$. Using this, we can extract the T dependence of various observables, for example,

$$\langle J^m \rangle = \int dJ \, \pi_{\text{post}}(J;T) J^m. \tag{77}$$

We can also introduce the centralized moments:

$$\overline{C}^m = \langle (J - \langle J \rangle)^m \rangle. \tag{78}$$

4.1. *Numerical experiment: 1D Ising model*

As an explicit example, we now turn to the specific case of the 1D Ising model, i.e., a 1-dimensional periodic lattice of evenly spaced spin. The Hamiltonian in this case is

$$H_{\text{Ising}} = -J \sum_{1 \leq i \leq L} \sigma_i \sigma_{i+1}, \tag{79}$$

with $\sigma_{L+1} \equiv \sigma_1$. We have an analytic expression for the partition function (see, e.g., Ref. [29]) and can also explicitly extract the Fisher information metric:

$$\mathcal{I}(J) = (L-1)\text{sec h}^2(J). \tag{80}$$

We would like to understand the convergence of the model to the true value of the parameter. Since the main element of our analysis involves adjusting the posterior distribution, it is enough to work with a small number of spins, i.e., $L = 4$. We take a benchmark value of $J_* = 0.38$ (so the Fisher information metric is $\mathcal{I}(J_*) = 2.60533$) and track the dynamical Bayesian updating on the inference of this coupling. For a given trial, we performed a Bayesian update to track how well we could infer the value of the coupling constant. In each trial, we sampled from the Boltzmann distribution 100,000 distinct spin configurations. Starting from the initial prior $J = 0$ (uniform distribution), we performed an initial update using 10,000 events to get the first estimate for J. We then used the remaining 90,000 events to obtain a series of sequential updates. The posterior was updated after the inclusion of every additional set of 900 events. This then ran for a total of 1000 time steps.

For each trial, we observe some amount of random fluctuation, but after averaging over 1000 trials, we observe strikingly regular behavior, especially in the moments of the coupling J as computed

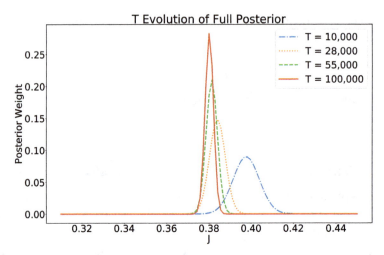

Figure 2.   Example of a trial in which the posterior distribution over couplings is inferred at different update "times" incremented in steps of 900 starting from an initial training at $T = 10,000$. We observe that the central value of the distribution converges to $J_* = 0.38$, and the width of the distribution narrows sharply. The match on higher-order moments is displayed in Table 3.

by the posterior distribution (see Equation (77)). The late T posterior distribution is Gaussian and can be seen for a sample run at progressively later times in Figure 2. The observable flow of the even centralized moments for the update dependent posterior distribution can be seen in the following. Assuming we saturate the Cramér–Rao bound, we find

$$\langle (J - \langle J \rangle)^{2l} \rangle = \overline{C}^{2l} = \frac{(2l - 1)!!}{(\mathcal{I}_*)^l} T^{-l}, \qquad (81)$$

where $n!! = \prod_{k=0}^{[\frac{n}{2}]-1} (n - 2k)$. This agrees very well with the numerical experiment, as can be seen in Figure 3 and summarized in Table 3.

Finally, we note there is some statistical variation present on the space of trajectories for the maximum likelihood estimate (MLE) (see Figure 4). This makes manifest that there is statistical variation in any individual inference scheme, but that on aggregate, the paths converge to the maximum likelihood estimate. This observation inspires a path integral interpretation of dynamical Bayesian updating that we leave for future work.

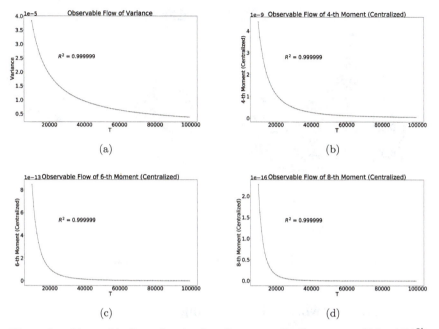

Figure 3. Observable flows for the first four centralized moments $\langle (J - \langle J \rangle)^{2l} \rangle$ for $l = 1, 2, 3, 4$ of the posterior distribution for the Ising Model Experiment. In all cases, we observe a power-law decay which is in close accord with the behavior saturated by the Cramér–Rao bound (see Equation (81)): (a) variance of posterior distribution; (b) fourth centralized moment; (c) sixth centralized moment; (d) eighth centralized moment.

Table 3. Comparison of predicted scaling for n-point functions from Dynamical Bayesian inference in the limit where the Cramér–Rao bound is saturated (see Equation (81)) and the observed scaling from the Ising Model Experiment. We have displayed additional significant figures to exhibit the extent of this match. Observe that in all cases, the experimentally determined power law is of the form $1/T^{1-\nu}$ for $\nu > 0$, i.e., it respects the lower limit expected from the Cramér–Rao bound.

Moment	C-R Limit	Experiment
$\langle (J - \langle J \rangle)^2 \rangle$	$0.38/T$	$0.38/T^{0.9997}$
$\langle (J - \langle J \rangle)^4 \rangle$	$0.44/T^2$	$0.44/T^{1.9996}$
$\langle (J - \langle J \rangle)^6 \rangle$	$0.84/T^3$	$0.84/T^{2.9993}$
$\langle (J - \langle J \rangle)^8 \rangle$	$2.28/T^4$	$2.26/T^{3.999}$

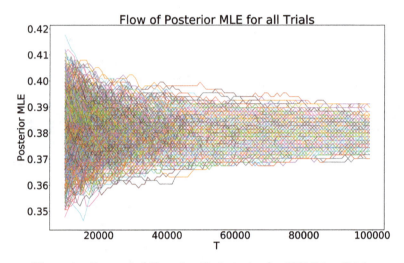

Figure 4.   Dynamical Bayesian Trajectories for 1000 Ising Trials.

5.   Neural Networks and Learning

The Bayesian approach to neural networks was pioneered by Neal in Ref. [23]. In what follows, we will examine whether the dynamical inference model described in this work can be applied to neural networks. We will take the viewpoint that a neural network is simply a model whose parameters are given by its weights and biases. Training a neural network using data infers the most likely set of weights given the training set (at least one hopes that this is true). As such, one may adopt the view that the training of neural networks is a Bayesian problem of inferring a posterior distribution over the weights given the data available and then one chooses a net with the most likely weights from the posterior distribution. Note that training a network is a stochastic process where the outcome depends on the initialization of weights and the path taken through training.

To apply the reasoning in the chapter, we will examine how the trained neural network is dependent on the quantity of data used in its training. In particular, we will measure how a trained neural network changes as we increment the amount of data used in the training process. We will certainly not be able to follow in a fully quantitative way the calculations in the previous sections because a neural network has far too many parameters (its weights) to carry out the Bayesian analysis explicitly. Instead, we will empirically investigate whether the neural network follows a similar qualitative dependence on data as indicated by dynamical Bayesian updating. Insofar as the loss function can be approximated near the final inference in terms of quantities which are quadratic in the underlying θ parameters, we expect a simple power-law behavior as we approach a high level of accuracy. We expect the loss function to exhibit an exponential decaying profile when the inference is only moderately successful. The fact that we empirically observe precisely this sort of behavior provides support for the general picture developed in Section 2.

Let us outline the experiment. For a helpful glossary of terms and additional background, see, e.g., Ref. [30]. The basic idea is that we will consider training a neural network using differing sample sizes from the same dataset and see how loss depends on the amount of data. (For comparison, we will repeat the whole experiment using the MNIST, Fashion-MNIST and CIFAR10 datasets.) The first neural network we use will have a very simple feedforward (FF) architecture. The input layer is a 28×28 layer, corresponding to the MNIST input data. Next is a simple 128 node dense layer followed by the final 10 node output layer with softmax activation. The cost function is taken to be the categorical cross-entropy.

We also consider some experiments involving more sophisticated convolutional neural networks, training on the MNIST dataset and the CIFAR10 dataset. In the case of the MNIST dataset, we consider a convolutional layer with kernel size 2 and filter size 64, followed by max pooling (with pool size 2), followed by a drop out layer (with drop out parameter 0.3) and then another convolution layer, kernel size 2 and filter size 32, then max pooling (with pool size 2), a dropout layer (parameter 0.3), followed by a dense layer with 256 neurons with rectified linear unit (ReLU) activation and a final dropout layer (parameter 0.5) and a final dense layer with 10 outputs and softmax activation.

For the CIFAR10 data, we used a convolutional neural network with three convolutional layers with respective filter sizes 32, 64, and 128, with kernel size 3 for each layer; a max pooling layer with 3×3 pool size was included after each convolutional layer. This set of convolution/pooling layers are then followed by a 128 node dense layer with ReLU activation followed by a dropout layer with dropout parameter 0.4 leading on to the final dense layer of 10 outputs with softmax activation.

The main difference between the convolutional neural networks used in the MNIST and CIFAR10 experiments, apart from having the larger input layer for CIFAR10, is the kernel size of the convolutions. In all cases, the hyperparameters such as for dropout were untuned. Given that such hyperparameter tuning tends to depend on the specifics of the data being learnt for the purposes of the questions in this chapter, we did not consider hyperparameter tuning as necessary.

Crucially, we wish to investigate the dependence of the loss on the amount of data and not the amount of training of the network. Usually, in training a neural network, these two become connected since in any given epoch the amount of training depends on the amount of data. But crucially, neural networks often learn by repeated training using the same data set over many epochs. We are interested in the final state of the neural network after we have completed training.

We wish to keep the amount of training fixed and only compare the loss with different amounts of data used to do the training. (By training, we really mean the attempt to minimize the cost through some form of repeated gradient flow.) To do this, we link the number of epochs to the size of the training set we use. We have chosen to train over four epochs if the dataset is maximal, i.e., 60,000 samples. This is a reasonable choice that produces good accuracy without overfitting. To demonstrate the reasoning behind this, consider training one neural net with N data samples and another with $2N$. One training epoch for the network trained with $2N$ samples will have effectively twice the amount of training as the network with just N samples. Thus, to compare the effect of the larger data set as opposed to the amount of training, we should train the network that uses the $2N$ data half the number of epochs as the one using the N dataset.

We train the networks using the Adam optimizer [31] with learning rate set to a standard 0.001. (For the full 60,000 samples and four epochs, this gives a healthy sparse categorical accuracy of around 0.97 for MNIST with the simple neural net.) After the network has been trained using the training set of N samples, it is tested on the full test set of 10,000 samples.

In what follows, we begin with a large sample size (e.g., 3,000) and then examine the loss after the training is complete as a function of the size of the training dataset. We will then increase the training set size N by some increment δN where typically we take δN to be around 500 and then repeat this until we reach a final dataset an order of magnitude bigger, e.g., 30,000 data points. We then fit the resulting curve to the power-law behavior as expected from the dynamical Bayesian updating analysis. We find that for MNIST with the convolutional net, the power law is close to one, but for Fashion-MNIST where the loss is higher, the power law is of the form $1/T^{1+\nu}$ for $\nu > 0$. This is compatible with the contribution from hidden variables for Bayesian flows given in Section 2.

We then repeat this with the CIFAR10 dataset and the even more involved convolutional network where we find the exponential decay is a better fit than power law indicating that the network has untrained parameters as in the hidden variable example discussed before.

The reader familiar with Stochastic and Batch gradient descent may feel that we are just doing the same thing in this experiment and these are just the traditional learning curves. This is *not* the case since we train for multiple epochs and the curves measure only the loss as a function of *total* data used in the training.

All the code is available to view in a Google Colab: https:// colab.research.google.com/drive/1zNxHj7qCoE1-WzawqRTbaa9Qh FWpQZqr?usp=sharing.

5.1. *Results*

Training neural nets is notoriously stochastic. To take this into account, we actually perform multiple trials of each experiment (with different initial conditions in each case). We plot loss against T and then fit to a power law in each case. Performing multiple trials, we also extract the mean and variance for these fitting parameters, in particular, the exponent appearing in the power-law fit. We also quote the root mean variance as an indicator of how robust the results are. For 10 trials, the root variance of the power law was between 8% and 10% depending on the dataset in question.

We display here some representative examples of this analysis, as in Figure 5 for the experiments with a feedforward neural network trained on the MNIST and Fashion-MNIST datasets, as well as Figure 6 for the convolutional neural network experiments trained on

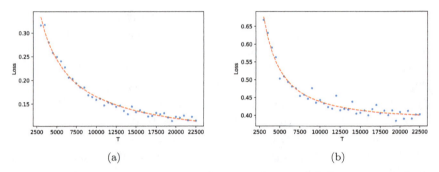

(a) (b)

Figure 5. Categorical cross-entropy loss as a function of T in a simple feed-forward neural network with varying amounts of trial data. Here, we display the results for a single complete run in the case of the MNIST and Fashion-MNIST datasets. In nearly all examples, we observe a highly accurate fit to a power-law behavior, with respective power laws $103T^{-0.74} + 0.05$ (R^2 of 0.98) and $16033T^{-1.36} + 0.38$ (R^2 of 0.96) for the MNIST and Fashion-MNIST and examples. See also Table 4. We collect the central values and variance of the decay law parameters for the different data sets in Table 5: (a) MNIST Trial; (b) Fashion-MNIST Trial.

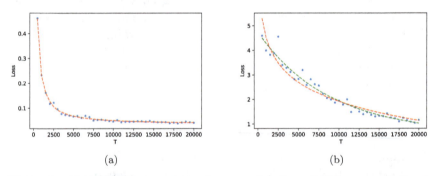

(a) (b)

Figure 6. Categorical cross-entropy loss as a function of T in a convolutional neural network with varying amounts of trial data. Here, we display the results for a single complete run in the case of the MNIST and CIFAR10 datasets. In this case, we obtain a good fit to a power-law decay in the case of the MNIST dataset, while in the case of the CIFAR10 data set, the lower accuracy is better fit by an exponential function (red curve) as opposed to a power law (green curve). See also Table 4. We collect the central values and variance of the decay law parameters for the different data sets in Table 5: (a) MNIST Trial; (b) CIFAR10 Trial.

the MNIST and CIFAR10 datasets. In these plots, we display the loss function (i.e., the categorical cross-entropy) on the vertical axis and the number of data samples used for training on the horizontal axis. In each case, we also display the corresponding fit for these particular examples, and the results are collected in Table 4. As discussed above, an important aspect of these individual fits is that the actual parameters deviate from trial to trial and so we also give the central values of the fitting parameters and their 1σ deviations. The mean values of the fitting parameters are displayed in Table 5.

5.1.1. *A simple feedforward network*

The first curve is with 3000 initial samples used as training data and then incremented in steps of 500. The fit to a power law has an R^2 value of 0.98, showing a very strong fit to the data with a power-law behavior $\sim 1/T^{0.74}$. We then repeated the experiment with the Fashion-MNIST dataset, which had an R^2 fit to power law of 0.96 with power-law behavior $\sim 1/T^{1.36}$. See Figure 5 for the plots of the loss function and the fitting curves, and Table 4 for a summary of the fitting functions for these particular examples. Table 5 also reports the mean and 1σ uncertainties for the power law fitting parameters.

Table 4. Fitting functions categorical cross-entropy loss as a function of T for the example trial runs displayed in Figures 5 and 6 for various datasets and neural network architectures (FF refers to feedforward and CNN refers to convolutional neural network). In most cases, we observe a rather good fit to a power-law behavior when the accuracy of inference is also high. For situations where there is a degraded performance as in the CIFAR10 dataset, we instead observe a better fit to an exponential decay function. Note also that in some cases, we obtain a power law with exponent above or below -1. Including hidden variables in the Bayesian flow equations can accommodate both phenomena. Comparing over multiple trial runs, we observe some variance in individual fits. We collect the central values and variance of the decay law parameters for the different datasets in Table 5.

Dataset	Network	Function Type	Loss (T)	R^2
MNIST	FF	Power Law	$103T^{-0.74} + 0.05$	0.98
Fashion-MNIST	FF	Power Law	$16033T^{-1.36} + 0.41$	0.96
MNIST	CNN	Power Law	$241T^{-1.03} + 0.03$	0.99
CIFAR10	CNN	Exponential	$4.1e^{-0.000113T} + 0.60$	0.96

Table 5.   Central values of the fitting parameters averaged over 10 different trials. Uncertainties are quoted at the 1σ level. For the MNIST and Fashion-MNIST datasets, these fit well to power-law behavior of the form $aT^{-b} + c$. For the CIFAR10 where the overall accuracy was lower, we instead find a better fit to an exponential decay law $ae^{-bT} + c$. While there is some variance in the overall value of these fitting parameters, each individual trial fits well to the expectations of the dynamical Bayesian evolution equations. The experiments thus reveal the sensitivity to initial conditions in the training of the neural networks.

Dataset	Network	Loss (T)	b
MNIST	FF	$aT^{-b} + c$	0.74 ± 0.06
Fashion-MNIST	FF	$aT^{-b} + c$	1.32 ± 0.12
MNIST	CNN	$aT^{-b} + c$	1.01 ± 0.06
CIFAR10	CNN	$ae^{-bT} + c$	$1.6 \times 10^{-4} \pm 2.4 \times 10^{-5}$

5.1.2.   *Convolutional neural networks*

We also performed a similar set of experiments using the convolutional neural networks as described above. We again repeated the experiments 10 times so as to take into account the stochastic nature of the training process and take mean values. We took the initial data size to be 500 and increment size 500 as before.

In the case of the MNIST dataset, we find the mean power-law fit has $R^2 = 0.99$ and mean decay coefficient 1.01. (The root of the variance of the decay constant was 0.06.) This network had a very low final loss 0.99 and captured well the properties of the full dataset. It is interesting that when this happened, the exponent of the power law approached the value for the Cramér–Rao bounded flow. Figure 6(a) displays one such trial. Averaging over all the trials, we also determined the exponent for the power-law decay; the results are displayed in Table 5.

Finally, for the CIFAR10 dataset with the three-layer convolutional network, we took an initial data size of 500 and increment size of 500. We repeated the experiment 10 times, and in each trial, we performed a best fit to the loss function, and in general, we observed the data was better fit by an exponential rather than a power law. In Figure 6(b), we present the data from one such trial, where the power-law fit (green curve) gave an R^2 of 0.92, while the exponential fit (red curve) gave an R^2 of 0.96. Averaging over all the trials, we also determined the decay constant for the exponential fit; the results are displayed in Table 5. Note that although it is better fit by an exponential decay, the actual decay constant is quite small.

6. Conclusion

In this note, we have presented an interpretation of Bayesian updating in terms of a dynamical system. In a given model of the world, each new piece of evidence provides us with an improved understanding of the underlying system, thus generating an effective flow in the space of parameters which is saturated by a simple $1/T$ power law, the analog of a "unitarity bound" in conformal field theory. This can be exceeded when additional information flows in via hidden variables. We have shown how this works in practice both in an analytic treatment of Gaussian distributions and Gaussian Random Processes and have also performed a number of numerical experiments, including inference on the value of the coupling constants in the 1D Ising Model and in training of neural networks. We find it remarkable that simple Bayesian considerations accurately capture the asymptotic behavior of so many phenomena.

The appearance of a $1/T^b$ power-law scaling for learning in neural networks is of course quite suggestive. In the context of statistical field theory, the onset of such a scaling law behavior is usually a clear indication of a phase transition. We have also seen that inference in the presence of hidden variables provides a simple qualitative explanation for some of this behavior. It would be very interesting to develop a more fundamental explanation.

A unifying thread of this work has centered on giving a physical interpretation of Bayesian updating. This equation shares a number of common features with the related question of renormalization group flow in a quantum field theory.[12] But whereas renormalization is usually interpreted as a flow from the ultraviolet to the infrared

---

[12]The notion of "renormalization" has been discussed in Refs. [30,32,33], though we should point out that in a quantum field theory, the utility of organizing by scale has a great deal to do with the fact that there is a clear notion of locality, something which is definitely *not* present in many inference problems! For additional discussion on connections between statistical/quantum field theory and machine learning, see, e.g., Refs. [34–38].

wherein we *lose* information about microscopic physics, the Bayesian updating procedure does precisely the opposite: we are *gaining* information as we evolve along a flow. We have also seen that new evidence in Bayesian updating can either perturb a trajectory or not impact it very much, and this again parallels similar notions of relevant and irrelevant perturbations. We have also taken some preliminary steps in developing a path integral interpretation of Bayesian flows in Appendix A. This in turn suggests that there should be a direct analog of Polchinski's exact renormalization group equation which would be exciting to develop.

One of the original motivations of this work was to better understand the sense in which the structure of quantum gravity might emerge from an observer performing local measurements in their immediate vicinity (see, e.g., Refs. [14,27,28,39–41] for related discussions). From this perspective, each new piece of data corresponds to this local observer making larger excursions in the spacetime, as well as the parameters of the theory. This is particularly well motivated in the specific context of the AdS/CFT correspondence [42], where the radial direction of the bulk anti-de Sitter space serves as a renormalization scale in the CFT with a cutoff. Given that we have a flow equation and that it shares many formal similarities to an RG equation; this suggests a natural starting point for directly visualizing radial evolution in terms of such an inference procedure.

At a more practical level, it would also be interesting to test how well an observer can infer such "spacetime locality". Along these lines, there is a natural class of numerical experiments involving a mild generalization of our Ising model analysis in which we continue to draw from the same Ising model with only nearest neighbor interactions, but in which the model involves additional contributions coupling neighbors which might be very far away.

Acknowledgments

We thank J.G. Bernstein, R. Fowler and R.A. Yang for helpful discussions and many of the members of the "Physics meets ML" group. DSB thanks Pierre Andurand for his generous donation supporting this work. The work of JJH is supported in part by the DOE (HEP) Award DE-SC0013528 and a generous donation by P. Kumar, as well as a generous donation by R.A. Yang and Google.

Appendix

A. Interpreting Dynamical Bayesian Updating

In the main text of our chapter, we implemented an approach to dynamical Bayesian Inference in which the posterior distribution is probed by observing the scaling of its various centralized moments as a function of update "time". In this appendix, we would like to draw attention to an alternative strategy for studying Dynamical Bayesian inference in which one solves the flow equation for the complete posterior, (20), directly. As was the case in the main text, we will find it more natural to consider our update in terms of a "time" parameter $T = N\tau$. One can think of T as corresponding to the number of data point utilized in the Bayesian Inference model up to a given iteration. In these terms, we can write the T-dependent posterior distribution which solves the flow equation as

$$\pi(\theta; T) = \exp(-TD_{KL}(\alpha_* \parallel \theta)) \exp\left(\int_0^T dT' D_{KL}(\alpha_* \parallel \alpha(T'))\right).$$
(A.1)

We will see that the structure of this solutions calls to mind many of the common approaches utilized in the analysis of physical systems, especially statistical ensembles.

To begin, observe that $\pi(\theta; T)$ is a *normalized* probability density function for each value of T:

$$1 = \int d\theta \pi(\theta; T) \ \forall \ T.$$
(A.2)

Performing the integration explicitly, we note that only the first factor in (A.1) depends on θ. Thus, we find

$$1 = \exp\left(\int_0^T dT' D_{KL}(\alpha_* \parallel \alpha(T'))\right) \int d\theta \exp(-TD_{KL}(\alpha_* \parallel \theta)).$$
(A.3)

It is natural to define the integral appearing in (A.3) as the Partition Function of an unnormalized density:

$$\mathcal{Z}(T) := \int d\theta e^{-TD_{KL}(\alpha_* \parallel \theta)}.$$
(A.4)

This gives the Dynamical Bayesian Posterior the complexion of a Boltzmann weight with "energy" $D_{KL}(\alpha_* \parallel \theta)$. It also suggests that we should regard T as an inverse temperature or imaginary time parameter as is typical in statistical field theory contexts.

Referring back to (A.3), we conclude that the role of the θ independent term in the posterior density (A.1) is explicitly to maintain the normalization of the posterior density at all T. Indeed, we can write

$$\mathcal{Z}(T) = \exp\left(-\int_0^T dT'\, D_{KL}(\alpha_* \parallel \alpha(T'))\right) \tag{A.5}$$

or equivalently

$$-\ln(\mathcal{Z}(T)) = \int_0^T dT'\, D_{KL}(\alpha_* \parallel \alpha(T')). \tag{A.6}$$

This equation relates the KL divergence of the T-dependent parameter estimate $\alpha(T)$ with the cumulant generating functional of the posterior distribution. Taking the first derivative of this equation with respect to T, we find

$$D_{KL}(\alpha_* \parallel \alpha(T)) = \langle D_{KL}(\alpha_* \parallel \theta)\rangle_{\pi(\theta;T)}, \tag{A.7}$$

which is precisely Equation (26)! More generally, note that

$$-\left(\frac{d}{dT}\right)^n \ln(\mathcal{Z}(T)) = (-1)^{n+1} \mathcal{C}^n_{\pi(\theta;T)}\left(D_{KL}(\alpha_* \parallel \theta)\right), \tag{A.8}$$

where $\mathcal{C}^n_{\pi(\theta;T)}(Q(\theta))$ denotes the nth cumulant of $Q(\theta)$ with respect to the time T posterior distribution, $\pi(\theta;T)$. We therefore obtain the expression

$$\left(\frac{d}{dT}\right)^{n-1} D_{KL}(\alpha_* \parallel \alpha(T)) = (-1)^{n+1} \mathcal{C}^n_{\pi(\theta;T)}\left(D_{KL}(\alpha_* \parallel \theta)\right). \tag{A.9}$$

One may interpret this equation as saying that all of the relevant connected correlation functions associated with the statistical inference are encoded in the path $\alpha(T)$. Once $\alpha(T)$ is known, these cumulants can extracted through Equation (A.9).

References

[1] T. Bayes, Rev., An essay toward solving a problem in the doctrine of chances, *Phil. Trans. Roy. Soc. Lond.* **53** (1764), 370–418.

[2] M. Gell-Mann and F. E. Low, Quantum electrodynamics at small distances, *Phys. Rev.* **95** (1954), 1300–1312.

[3] L. P. Kadanoff, Scaling laws for Ising models near T_c, *Phys. Phys. Fiz.* **2** (1966), 263–272.

[4] K. G. Wilson, Renormalization group and critical phenomena. 1. Renormalization group and the Kadanoff scaling picture, *Phys. Rev. B* **4** (1971), 3174–3183.

[5] K. G. Wilson, Renormalization group and critical phenomena. 2. Phase space cell analysis of critical behavior, *Phys. Rev. B* **4** (1971), 3184–3205.

[6] J. Polchinski, Renormalization and effective Lagrangians, *Nucl. Phys. B* **231** (1984), 269–295.

[7] V. Balasubramanian, Statistical inference, occam's razor and statistical mechanics on the space of probability distributions, arXiv:cond-mat/9601030.

[8] S. Kullback and R. A. Leibler, On information and sufficiency, *Ann. Math. Stat.* **22**(1) (1951), 79–86.

[9] C. R. Rao, Information and accuracy attainable in the estimation of statistical parameters, *Bull. Calcutta Math. Soc.* **37** (1945), 81–91.

[10] S. Amari, *Differential-Geometrical Methods in Statistics*. Lecture Notes in Statistics. Springer-Verlag (1985).

[11] W. Bialek, C. G. Callan, Jr. and S. P. Strong, Field theories for learning probability distributions, *Phys. Rev. Lett.* **77** (1996), 4693–4697, arXiv:cond-mat/9607180.

[12] M. Blau, K. S. Narain and G. Thompson, Instantons, the information metric, and the AdS / CFT correspondence, arXiv:hep-th/0108122.

[13] U. Miyamoto and S. Yahikozawa, Information metric from a linear sigma model, *Phys. Rev. E* **85** (2012), 051133, arXiv:1205.3211 [math-ph].

[14] J. J. Heckman, Statistical inference and string theory, *Int. J. Mod. Phys. A* **30**(26) (2015), 1550160, arXiv:1305.3621 [hep-th].

[15] J. J. Heckman, J. G. Bernstein and B. Vigoda, MCMC with Strings and Branes: The suburban algorithm (Extended Version), *Int. J. Mod. Phys. A* **32**(22) (2017), 1750133, arXiv:1605.05334 [physics.comp-ph].

[16] J. J. Heckman, J. G. Bernstein and B. Vigoda, MCMC with Strings and Branes: The suburban algorithm, arXiv:1605.06122 [stat.CO].

[17] T. Clingman, J. Murugan and J. P. Shock, Probability density functions from the Fisher information metric, arXiv:1504.03184 [cs.IT].

[18] E. Malek, J. Murugan and J. P. Shock, The Information Metric on the moduli space of instantons with global symmetries, *Phys. Lett. B* **753** (2016), 660–663, arXiv:1507.08894 [hep-th].

[19] H. Dimov, I. N. Iliev, M. Radomirov, R. C. Rashkov and T. Vetsov, Holographic Fisher information metric in Schrödinger spacetime, *Eur. Phys. J. Plus* **136**(11) (2021), 1128, arXiv:2009.01123 [hep-th].

[20] J. Erdmenger, K. T. Grosvenor and R. Jefferson, Information geometry in quantum field theory: Lessons from simple examples, *SciPost Phys.* **8**(5) (2020), 073, arXiv:2001.02683 [hep-th].

[21] A. Tsuchiya and K. Yamashiro, A geometrical representation of the quantum information metric in the gauge/gravity correspondence, *Phys. Lett. B* **824** (2022), 136830, arXiv:2110.13429 [hep-th].

[22] R. Fowler and J. J. Heckman, Misanthropic entropy and renormalization as a communication channel, arXiv:2108.02772 [hep-th].

[23] R. Neal, *Bayesian Learning for Neural Networks*. Lecture Notes in Statistics. Springer-Verlag (1996).

[24] P. Mehta, M. Bukov, C.-H. Wang, A. G. R. Day, C. Richardson, C. K. Fisher and D. J. Schwab, A high-bias, low-variance introduction to Machine Learning for physicists, *Phys. Rept.* **810** (2019), 1–124, arXiv:1803.08823 [physics.comp-ph].

[25] G. Mack, All unitary ray representations of the conformal group SU(2,2) with positive energy, *Commun. Math. Phys.* **55** (1977), 1.

[26] C. E. Rasmussen and C. K. I. Williams, *Gaussian Processes for Machine Learning*. The MIT Press (2006).

[27] V. Balasubramanian, J. J. Heckman and A. Maloney, Relative entropy and proximity of quantum field theories, *JHEP* **05** (2015), 104, arXiv:1410.6809 [hep-th].

[28] V. Balasubramanian, J. J. Heckman, E. Lipeles and A. P. Turner, Statistical coupling constants from hidden sector entanglement, *Phys. Rev. D* **103**(6) (2021), 066024, arXiv:2012.09182 [hep-th].

[29] R. K. Pathria, *Statistical Mechanics*. Butterworth-Heinemann (1996).

[30] D. A. Roberts, S. Yaida and B. Hanin, The principles of deep learning theory, arXiv:2106.10165 [cs.LG].

[31] D. P. Kingma and J. Ba, Adam: A method for stochastic optimization, *arXiv e-prints* (December, 2014), arXiv:1412.6980, arXiv:1412.6980 [cs.LG].

[32] J. Halverson, A. Maiti and K. Stoner, Neural networks and quantum field theory, *Mach. Learn. Sci. Tech.* **2**(3) (2021), 035002, arXiv:2008.08601 [cs.LG].

[33] J. Halverson, Building quantum field theories out of neurons, arXiv:2112.04527 [hep-th].

[34] D. Bachtis, G. Aarts and B. Lucini, Quantum field-theoretic machine learning, *Phys. Rev. D* **103**(7) (2021), 074510, arXiv:2102.09449 [hep--lat].

[35] D. Bachtis, G. Aarts and B. Lucini, Quantum field theories, Markov random fields and machine learning, in *32nd IUPAP Conference on Computational Physics*. 10, 2021. arXiv:2110.10928 [cs.LG].

[36] G. Aarts, D. Bachtis and B. Lucini, Interpreting machine learning functions as physical observables, in *38th International Symposium on Lattice Field Theory*. 9, 2021. arXiv:2109.08497 [hep-lat].

[37] D. Bachtis, G. Aarts and B. Lucini, Machine learning with quantum field theories, in *38th International Symposium on Lattice Field Theory*. 9, 2021. arXiv:2109.07730 [cs.LG].

[38] D. Bachtis, G. Aarts, F. Di Renzo and B. Lucini, Inverse renormalization group in quantum field theory, *Phys. Rev. Lett.* **128**(8) (2022), 081603, arXiv:2107.00466 [hep-lat].

[39] K. Hashimoto, S. Sugishita, A. Tanaka and A. Tomiya, Deep Learning and holographic QCD, *Phys. Rev. D* **98**(10) (2018), 106014, arXiv:1809.10536 [hep-th].

[40] K. Hashimoto, AdS/CFT correspondence as a deep Boltzmann machine, *Phys. Rev. D* **99**(10) (2019), 106017, arXiv:1903.04951 [hep-th].

[41] Y. Gal, V. Jejjala, D. K. Mayorga Pena and C. Mishra, Baryons from Mesons: A Machine Learning perspective, arXiv:2003.10445 [hep-ph].

[42] J. M. Maldacena, The Large N limit of superconformal field theories and supergravity, *Adv. Theor. Math. Phys.* **2** (1998), 231–252, arXiv:hep-th/9711200.

Chapter 3

Machine Learning: The Dimension of a Polytope

Tom Coates[*,‡], Johannes Hofscheier[†,§] and
Alexander M. Kasprzyk[†,¶]

*Department of Mathematics, Imperial College London,
180 Queen's Gate, London SW7 2AZ, UK
†School of Mathematical Sciences, University of Nottingham,
Nottingham NG7 2RD, UK

‡t.coates@imperial.ac.uk
§johannes.hofscheier@nottingham.ac.uk
¶a.m.kasprzyk@nottingham.ac.uk

Abstract

We use machine learning to predict the dimension of a lattice polytope directly from its Ehrhart series. This is highly effective, achieving almost 100% accuracy. We also use machine learning to recover the volume of a lattice polytope from its Ehrhart series and to recover the dimension, volume and quasi-period of a rational polytope from its Ehrhart series. In each case, we achieve very high accuracy, and we propose mathematical explanations for why this should be so.

1. Introduction

Let $P \subset \mathbb{Z}^d \otimes_{\mathbb{Z}} \mathbb{Q}$ be a convex lattice polytope of dimension d, that is, let P be the convex hull of finitely many points in $\mathbb{Z}^d$ whose

$\mathbb{Q}$-affine combinations generate $\mathbb{Q}^d$. A fundamental invariant of P is the number of lattice points that it contains, $|P \cap \mathbb{Z}^d|$. More generally, let $L_P(m) := |mP \cap \mathbb{Z}^d|$ count the lattice points in the mth dilation mP of P, where $m \in \mathbb{Z}_{\geq 0}$. Then, L_P is given by a polynomial of degree d called the *Ehrhart polynomial* [15]. The corresponding generating series, called the *Ehrhart series* and denoted by Ehr_P, can be expressed as a rational function with numerator a polynomial of degree at most d [29]:

$$\mathrm{Ehr}_P(t) := \sum_{m \geq 0} L_P(m) t^m = \frac{\delta_0 + \delta_1 t + \cdots + \delta_d t^d}{(1-t)^{d+1}}, \qquad \delta_i \in \mathbb{Z}.$$

The coefficients $(\delta_0, \delta_1, \ldots, \delta_d)$ of this numerator, called the δ-*vector* or h^*-*vector* of P, have combinatorial meaning [14]:

(1) $\delta_0 = 1$;
(2) $\delta_1 = |P \cap \mathbb{Z}^d| - d - 1$;
(3) $\delta_d = |P^\circ \cap \mathbb{Z}^d|$, where $P^\circ = P \setminus \partial P$ is the strict interior of P;
(4) $\delta_0 + \cdots + \delta_d = \mathrm{Vol}(P)$, where $\mathrm{Vol}(P) = d!\,\mathrm{vol}(P)$ is the lattice-normalized volume of P.

The polynomial L_P can be expressed in terms of the δ-vector:

$$L_P(m) = \sum_{i=0}^{d} \delta_i \binom{d+m-i}{d}.$$

From this, we can see that the leading coefficient of L_P is $\mathrm{vol}(P)$, the Euclidean volume of P.

Given $d + 1$ terms of the Ehrhart series, one can recover the δ-vector and hence the invariants $|P \cap \mathbb{Z}^d|$, $|P^\circ \cap \mathbb{Z}^d|$ and $\mathrm{Vol}(P)$. This, however, assumes knowledge of the dimension d.

Question 1. *Given a lattice polytope P, can machine learning recover the dimension d of P from sufficiently many terms of the Ehrhart series Ehr_P?*

There has been recent success using machine learning (ML) to predict invariants such as $\mathrm{Vol}(P)$ directly from the vertices of P [4] and to predict numerical invariants from a geometric analog of the Ehrhart series called the Hilbert series [5]. As we will see in Sections 2.1–2.3, ML is also extremely effective at answering Question 1. In Section 2.4, we propose a possible explanation for this.

1.1. *The quasi-period of a rational convex polytope*

Now, let P be a convex polytope with *rational* vertices, and let $k \in \mathbb{Z}_{>0}$ be the smallest positive dilation of P such that kP is a lattice polytope. One can define the Ehrhart series of P exactly as before:

$$L_P(m) := |mP \cap \mathbb{Z}^d|.$$

In general, L_P will no longer be a polynomial, but it is a *quasi-polynomial* of degree d and period k [15,27]. That is, there exist polynomials $f_0, \ldots, f_{k-1}$, each of degree d, such that

$$L_P(qk + r) = f_r(q), \quad \text{whenever } 0 \le r < k.$$

The leading coefficient of each f_r is $\text{vol}(kP)$, the Euclidean volume of the kth dilation of P.

It is sometimes possible to express L_P using a smaller number of polynomials. Let ρ be the minimum number of polynomials needed to express L_P as a quasi-polynomial; ρ is called the *quasi-period* of P and is a divisor of k. Each of these ρ polynomials is of degree d with leading coefficient $\text{vol}(\rho P)$. When $\rho < k$, we say that P exhibits *quasi-period collapse* [7,8,16,23,26]. The Ehrhart series of P can be expressed as a rational function:

$$\text{Ehr}_P(t) = \frac{\delta_0 + \delta_1 t + \cdots + \delta_{\rho(d+1)-1} t^{\rho(d+1)-1}}{(1 - t^\rho)^{d+1}}, \qquad \delta_i \in \mathbb{Z}.$$

As in the case of lattice polytopes, the δ-vector carries combinatorial information about P [6,7,20,21,25]. Given $\rho(d+1)$ terms of the Ehrhart series, one can recover the δ-vector. This, however, requires knowing both the dimension d and the quasi-period ρ of P.

Question 2. *Given a rational polytope P, can machine learning recover the dimension d and quasi-period ρ of P from sufficiently many terms of the Ehrhart series* Ehr_P?

ML again performs very well here — see Section 3. We propose a mathematical explanation for this, in terms of forward differences and affine hyperplanes, in Section 3.4.

1.2. *Some motivating examples*

Example 1.1. The 2-dimensional lattice polytope $P := $ conv $\{(-1,-1), (-1,2), (2,-1)\}$ has volume $\mathrm{Vol}(P) = 9$, $|P \cap \mathbb{Z}^2| = 10$ and $|P^\circ \cap \mathbb{Z}^2| = 1$. The Ehrhart polynomial of P is

$$L_P(m) = \frac{9}{2}m^2 + \frac{9}{2}m + 1,$$

and the Ehrhart series of P is generated by

$$\mathrm{Ehr}_P(t) = \frac{1 + 7t + t^2}{(1-t)^3} = 1 + 10t + 28t^2 + 55t^3 + 91t^4 + \cdots.$$

Example 1.2. The smallest dilation of the triangle $P := $ conv$\{(5,-1), (-1,-1), (-1,1/2)\}$ giving a lattice triangle is $2P$. Hence, L_P can be written as a quasi-polynomial of degree 2 and period 2:

$$f_0(q) = 18q^2 + 9q + 1, \quad f_1(q) = 18q^2 + 27q + 10.$$

This is not, however, the minimum possible period. As in Example 1.1,

$$L_P(m) = \frac{9}{2}m^2 + \frac{9}{2}m + 1$$

and thus P has quasi-period $\rho = 1$.

This striking example of quasi-period collapse is developed further in Example 4.1.

1.3. *Code and data availability*

The datasets used in this work were generated with V2.25-4 of Magma [9]. We performed our ML analysis with scikit-learn [28], a standard machine learning library for Python, using scikit-learn v0.24.1 and Python v3.8.8. All data, along with the code used to generate it and to perform the subsequent analysis, are available from Zenodo [10,11] under a permissive open-source license (MIT for the code and CC0 for the data).

2. Question 1: Dimension

In this section, we investigate whether machine learning can predict the dimension d of a lattice polytope P from sufficiently many terms of the Ehrhart series Ehr_P. We calculate terms $L_P(m)$ of the Ehrhart series, for $0 \leq m \leq 1100$, and encode these in a *logarithmic Ehrhart vector*:

$$(\log y_0, \log y_1, \ldots, \log y_{1100}), \quad \text{where } y_m := L_P(m).$$

We find that standard ML techniques are extremely effective, recovering the dimension of P with almost 100% accuracy from the logarithmic Ehrhart vector. We then ask whether ML can recover $\text{Vol}(P)$ from this Ehrhart data; again, this is achieved with near 100% success.

2.1. Data generation

A dataset [11] containing 2918 distinct entries, with $2 \leq d \leq 8$, was generated using Algorithm 2.1. The distribution of these data is summarized in Table 1.

Algorithm 2.1.

Input: A positive integer d.
Output: A vector

$$(\log y_0, \log y_1, \ldots, \log y_{1100}, d, \text{Vol}(P))$$

for a d-dimensional lattice polytope P, where $y_m := L_P(m)$.

(i) Choose $d + k$ lattice points $\{v_1, \ldots, v_{d+k}\}$ uniformly at random in a box $[-5, 5]^d$, where k is chosen uniformly at random in $\{1, \ldots, 5\}$.

Table 1. The distribution of the dimensions appearing in the dataset for Question 1.

Dimension	2	3	4	5	6	7	8
Total	431	787	812	399	181	195	113

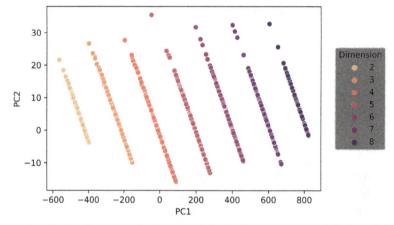

Figure 1.   Projection onto the first two principal components of the logarithmic Ehrhart vector colored by the dimension of P.

(ii) Set $P := \mathrm{conv}\{v_1, \ldots, v_{d+k}\}$. If $\dim(P) \neq d$, return to step (2.1).

(iii) Calculate the coefficients $y_m := L_P(m)$ of the Ehrhart series of P, for $0 \leq m \leq 1100$.

(iv) Return the vector $(\log y_0, \log y_1, \ldots, \log y_{1100}, d, \mathrm{Vol}(P))$.

We deduplicated on the vector $(\log y_0, \log y_1, \ldots, \log y_{1100}, d, \mathrm{Vol}(P))$ to get a dataset with distinct entries. In particular, two polytopes that are equivalent under the group of affine-linear transformations $\mathrm{GL}_d(\mathbb{Z}) \ltimes \mathbb{Z}^d$ give rise to the same point in the dataset.

2.2.   *Machine learning the dimension*

We reduced the dimensionality of the dataset by projecting onto the first two principal components of the logarithmic Ehrhart vector. As one would expect from Figure 1, a linear support vector machine (SVM) classifier trained on these features predicted the dimension of P with 100% accuracy. Here, we used a scikit-learn pipeline consisting of a **StandardScaler** followed by an **SVC** classifier with linear kernel and regularization hyperparameter $C = 0.1$, using 50% of the data for training the classifier and tuning the hyperparameter, and holding out the remaining 50% of the data for model validation.

In Section 2.4, we give a mathematical explanation for the structure observed in Figure 1 and hence for why ML is so effective at predicting the dimension of P. Note that the discussion in Section 3.4 suggests that one should also be able to extract the dimension using ML on the *Ehrhart vector*

$$(y_0, y_1, \ldots, y_{1100})$$

rather than the logarithmic Ehrhart vector

$$(\log y_0, \log y_1, \ldots, \log y_{1100}).$$

This is indeed the case, although here it is important not to reduce the dimensionality of the data too much.[1] A linear SVM classifier trained on the full Ehrhart vector predicts the dimension of P with 98.7% accuracy, with a pipeline exactly as above except that $C = 50{,}000$. A linear SVM classifier trained on the first 30 principal components of the Ehrhart vector (the same pipeline, but with $C = 20$) gives 93.7% accuracy, but projecting to the first two components reduces accuracy to 43.3%.

2.3. *Machine learning the volume*

To learn the normalized volume of a lattice polytope from its logarithmic Ehrhart vector, we used a scikit-learn pipeline consisting of a `StandardScaler` followed by an `SVR` regressor with linear kernel and regularization hyperparameter $C = 340$. We restricted attention to roughly 75% of the data with volume less than 10,000, thereby removing outliers. We used 50% of that data for training and hyperparameter tuning, selecting the training set using a shuffle stratified by volume; this corrects for the fact that the dataset contains a high proportion of polytopes with small volume. The regression had a coefficient of determination (R^2) of 0.432 and gave a strong hint

---

[1]This is consistent with the discussion in Section 3.4, which suggests that we should try to detect whether the Ehrhart vector lies in a union of linear subspaces that have fairly high codimension.

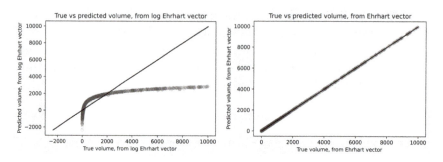

Figure 2.   Plotting the true versus the predicted normalized volume.

(see Figure 2) that we should repeat the analysis replacing the logarithmic Ehrhart vector with the Ehrhart vector.

Using the same pipeline (but with $C = 1000$) and the Ehrhart vector gives a regression with $R^2 = 1.000$; see Figure 2. This regressor performs well over the full dataset, with volumes ranging up to approximately 4.5 million: over the full dataset, we still find $R^2 = 1.000$. The fact that Support Vector Machine methods are so successful in recovering the volume of P from the Ehrhart vector is consistent with the discussion in Section 3.4.

2.4.   *Crude asymptotics for* $\log y_k$

Since

$$L_P(m) = \text{vol}(P)m^d + \text{lower order terms in } m,$$

we have that

$$\log y_m \sim d \log m + \log \text{vol}(P).$$

For $m \gg 0$, therefore, we see that the different components $\log y_m$ of the logarithmic Ehrhart vector depend approximately affine-linearly on each other as P varies. It seems intuitively plausible that the first two PCA components of the logarithmic Ehrhart vector should depend non-trivially on $\log y_m$ for $m \gg 0$, and in fact, this is the case — see Figure 3. Thus, the first two PCA components of the logarithmic Ehrhart vector should vary approximately affine-linearly as P varies, with constant slope and with a translation that depends only on the dimension of P.

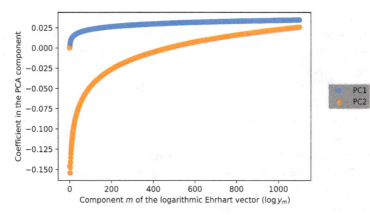

Figure 3.   Contribution of $\log y_m$ to the first two principal components of the logarithmic Ehrhart vector, as m varies.

3.   Question 2: Quasi-Period

Here, we investigate whether ML can predict the quasi-period ρ of a d-dimensional rational polytope P from sufficiently many terms of the Ehrhart vector of P. Once again, standard ML techniques based on Support Vector Machines are highly effective, achieving classification accuracies of up to 95.3%. We propose a potential mathematical explanation for this in Section 3.4.

3.1.   *Data generation*

In this section, we consider a dataset [10] containing 84,000 distinct entries. This was obtained by using Algorithm 3.1 to generate a larger dataset, followed by random downsampling to a subset with 2000 data points for each pair (d, ρ) with $d \in \{2, 3, 4\}$ and $\rho \in \{2, 3, \ldots, 15\}$.

Algorithm 3.1.

Input: A positive integer d.
Output: A vector

$$(\log y_0, \log y_1, \ldots, \log y_{1100}, d, \rho)$$

for a d-dimensional rational polytope P with quasi-period ρ, where $y_m := L_P(m)$.

(i) Choose $r \in \{2, 3, \ldots, 15\}$ uniformly at random.
(ii) Choose $d+k$ lattice points $\{v_1, \ldots, v_{d+k}\}$ uniformly at random in a box $[-5r, 5r]^d$, where k is chosen uniformly at random in $\{1, \ldots, 5\}$.
(iii) Set $P := \mathrm{conv}\{v_1, \ldots, v_{d+k}\}$. If $\dim(P) \neq d$, return to step (3.1).
(iv) Choose a lattice point $v \in P \cap \mathbb{Z}^d$ uniformly at random and replace P with the translation $P - v$. (We perform this step to ensure that the resulting rational polytope always contains a lattice point; this avoids complications when taking log in step (3.1).)
(v) Replace P with the dilation P/r.
(vi) Calculate the coefficients $y_m := L_P(m)$ of the Ehrhart series of P, for $0 \leq m \leq 1100$.
(vii) Calculate the quasi-period ρ.
(viii) Return the vector $(\log y_0, \log y_1, \ldots, \log y_{1100}, d, \rho)$.

As before, we deduplicated the dataset on the vector $(\log y_0, \log y_1, \ldots, \log y_{1100}, d, \rho)$.

3.2. *Recovering the dimension and volume*

Figure 4 shows the first two principal components of the logarithmic Ehrhart vector. As in Section 2.2, this falls into widely separated linear clusters according to the value of $\dim(P)$, and so the dimension of the rational polytope P can be recovered with high accuracy from its logarithmic Ehrhart vector. Furthermore, as in Section 2.3, applying a linear SVR regressor (with $C = 1000$) to the Ehrhart vector predicts the volume of a rational polytope P with high accuracy ($R^2 = 1.000$).

3.3. *Machine learning the quasi-period*

To learn the quasi-period of a rational polytope from its Ehrhart vector, we used a scikit-learn pipeline consisting of a StandardScaler followed by a LinearSVC classifier. We fixed a dimension $d \in \{2, 3, 4\}$, moved to PCA co-ordinates and used 50% of the data ($N = 14000$) for training the classifier and hyperparameter tuning, holding out the remaining 50% of the data for model validation. Results are summarized on the left-hand side of Table 2, with learning curves in the

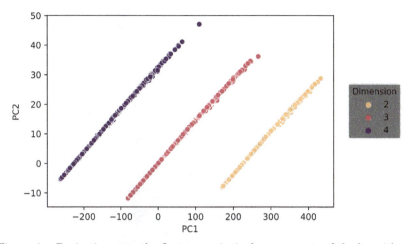

Figure 4. Projection onto the first two principal components of the logarithmic Ehrhart vector data colored by the dimension of P.

Table 2. The regularization hyperparameter C and accuracy for a `LinearSVC` classifier predicting the quasi-period from the Ehrhart vector and logarithmic Ehrhart vector of rational polytopes P.

Ehrhart Vector			log Ehrhart Vector		
Dimension	C	Accuracy (%)	Dimension	C	Accuracy (%)
2	0.01	80.6	2	1	79.7
3	0.001	94.0	3	1	85.2
4	0.001	95.3	4	1	83.2

left-hand column of Figure 5 and confusion matrices in the left-hand column of Figure 6. The confusion matrices hint at some structure in the misclassified data.

One could also use the same pipeline but applied to the logarithmic Ehrhart vector rather than the Ehrhart vector. Results are summarized on the right-hand side of Table 2, with learning curves in the right-hand column of Figure 5 and confusion matrices in the right-hand column of Figure 6. Using the logarithmic Ehrhart data resulted in a less accurate classifier, but the learning curves suggest that this might be improved by adding more training data. Again, there are hints of structure in the misclassified data.

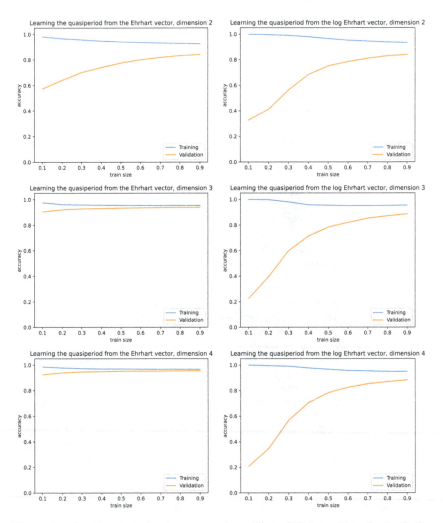

Figure 5.   Quasi-period learning curves for a linear SVM classifier, for both the Ehrhart vector (left-hand column) and the logarithmic Ehrhart vector (right-hand column).

3.4.   *Forward differences*

Let y denote the sequence $(y_m)_{m=0}^{\infty}$. Recall the forward difference operator Δ defined on the space of sequences:

$$\Delta y = (y_{m+1} - y_m)_{m=0}^{\infty}.$$

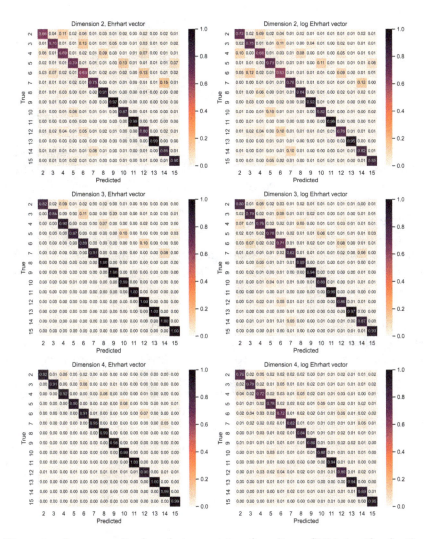

Figure 6.   Row-normalized confusion matrices for a linear SVM classifier for the quasi-period, for both the Ehrhart vector (left-hand column) and the logarithmic Ehrhart vector (right-hand column).

A sequence y depends polynomially on m, that is,

$$y_m = a_0 + a_1 m + \cdots + a_d m^d \quad \text{for some } a_0, \ldots, a_d \in \mathbb{R},$$

if and only if y lies in the kernel of Δ^{d+1}. Furthermore, in this case, $\Delta^d y$ is the constant sequence with value $d! \, a_d$.

Thus, a sequence $(y_m)_{m=0}^{\infty}$ is quasi-polynomial of degree d and period k, in the sense of Section 1.1, if and only if it lies in the kernel of Δ_k^{d+1}, where Δ_k is the k-step forward difference operator,

$$\Delta_k \left((y_m)_{m=0}^{\infty} \right) = (y_{m+k} - y_m)_{m=0}^{\infty},$$

and $(y_m)_{m=0}^{\infty}$ does not lie in the kernel of Δ_k^d. Furthermore, in this case, we can determine the leading coefficients of the polynomials $f_0, \ldots, f_{k-1}$ by examining the values of the k-periodic sequence $\Delta_k^d y$. When y arises as the Ehrhart series of a rational polytope P, all of these constant terms equal the volume of kP, and so the value of the constant sequence $\Delta_k^d y$ determines the normalized volume $\mathrm{Vol}(P)$.

This discussion suggests that an SVM classifier with linear kernel should be able to learn the quasi-period and volume with high accuracy from the Ehrhart vector of a rational polytope, at least if we consider only polytopes of a fixed dimension d. Having quasi-period k amounts to the Ehrhart vector lying in (a relatively open subset of) a certain subspace $\ker \Delta_k^{d+1}$; these subspaces, being linear objects, should be easily separable using hyperplanes. Similarly, having fixed normalized volume amounts to lying in a given affine subspace; such affine subspaces should be easily separable using affine hyperplanes.

From this point of view, it is interesting that an SVM classifier with linear kernel also learns the quasi-period with reasonably high accuracy from the logarithmic Ehrhart vector. Passing from the Ehrhart vector to the logarithmic Ehrhart vector replaces the linear subspaces $\ker \Delta_k^{d+1}$ by nonlinear submanifolds. But our experiments above suggest that these nonlinear submanifolds must nonetheless be close to being separable by appropriate collections of affine hyperplanes.

4.   A Remark on the Gorenstein Index

In this section, we discuss a geometric question where machine learning techniques failed. This involves a more subtle combinatorial invariant called the Gorenstein index and was the question that motivated the rest of the work in this chapter. We then suggest why in retrospect we should not have expected to be able to answer this question using machine learning (or at all).

4.1. *The Gorenstein index*

Fix a rank d lattice $N \cong \mathbb{Z}^d$, write $N_{\mathbb{Q}} := N \otimes_{\mathbb{Z}} \mathbb{Q}$ and let $P \subset N_{\mathbb{Q}}$ be a lattice polytope. The *polar polyhedron* of P is given by

$$P^* := \{u \in M \otimes_{\mathbb{Z}} \mathbb{Q} \mid u(v) \geq -1 \text{ for all } v \in P\},$$

where $M := \mathrm{Hom}(N, \mathbb{Z}) \cong \mathbb{Z}^d$ is the lattice dual to N. The polar polyhedron P^* is a convex polytope with rational vertices if and only if the origin lies in the strict interior of P. In this case, $(P^*)^* = P$. The smallest positive integer k_P such that $k_P P^*$ is a lattice polytope is called the *Gorenstein index* of P.

The Gorenstein index arises naturally in the context of *Fano toric varieties*, and we will restrict our discussion to this setting. Let $P \subset N_{\mathbb{Q}}$ be a lattice polytope such that the vertices of P are primitive lattice vectors and that the origin lies in the strict interior of P; such polytopes are called *Fano* [22]. The spanning fan Σ_P of P — that is, the complete fan whose cones are generated by the faces of P — gives rise to a Fano toric variety X_P [12,17]. This construction gives a one-to-one correspondence between $\mathrm{GL}_d(\mathbb{Z})$-equivalence classes of Fano polytopes and isomorphism classes of Fano toric varieties. Let $P \subset N_{\mathbb{Q}}$ be a Fano polytope that corresponds to a Fano toric variety $X := X_P$. The polar polytope $P^* \subset M_{\mathbb{Q}}$ then corresponds to a divisor on X called the *anticanonical divisor*, which is denoted by $-K_X$. In general, $-K_X$ is an ample $\mathbb{Q}$-Cartier divisor, and X is $\mathbb{Q}$-Gorenstein. The Gorenstein index k_P of P is equal to the smallest positive multiple k of the anticanonical divisor such that $-kK_X$ is Cartier.

Under the correspondence just discussed, the Ehrhart series Ehr_{P^*} of the polar polytope P^* coincides with the Hilbert series $\mathrm{Hilb}_X(-K_X)$. The Hilbert series is an important numerical invariant of X, and it makes sense to ask whether the Gorenstein index of X is determined by the Hilbert series. Put differently, we have the following.

Question 3. *Given a Fano polytope P, can ML recover the Gorenstein index k_P of P from sufficiently many terms of the Ehrhart series Ehr_{P^*} of the polar polytope P^*?*

There are good reasons, as we discuss in the following, to expect the answer to Question 3 to be 'no'. But part of the power of ML in mathematics is that it can detect or suggest structure that was not known or expected previously (see, e.g., Ref. [13]). That did not happen on this occasion: applying the techniques discussed in Sections 2 and 3 did not allow us to predict the Gorenstein index of P from the Ehrhart series of the polar polytope Ehr_{P^*}.

4.2. *Should we have expected this?*

The Hilbert series is preserved under an important class of deformations called *qG-deformations* [24]. But the process of *mutation* [2] can transform a Fano polytope P to a Fano polytope Q with $\mathrm{Ehr}_{P^*} = \mathrm{Ehr}_{Q^*}$. Mutation gives rise to a qG-deformation from X_P to X_Q [1] but need not preserve the Gorenstein index: k_P need not be equal to k_Q. Thus, the Gorenstein index is not invariant under qG-deformation. It might have been unrealistic to expect that a qG-deformation invariant quantity (the Hilbert series) could determine an invariant (the Gorenstein index) which can vary under qG-deformation.

4.3. *Quasi-period collapse*

Although the phenomenon of quasi-period collapse remains largely mysterious from a combinatorial viewpoint, in the context of toric geometry, one possible explanation arises from mutation and qG-deformation [23]. The following example revisits Examples 1.1 and 1.2 from this point of view and illustrates why Question 3 cannot have a meaningful positive answer.

Example 4.1. Let $P_{(a,b,c)} \subset N_{\mathbb{Q}}$ denote the 2-dimensional Fano polytope associated with weighted projective space $\mathbb{P}(a^2, b^2, c^2)$, where a, b, c are pairwise coprime positive integers. Then, $P_{(1,1,1)} :=$ conv$\{(1,0), (0,1), (-1,-1)\}$ is the Fano polygon associated with $\mathbb{P}^2$, with polar polygon $P^*_{(1,1,1)} \subset M_{\mathbb{Q}}$ the lattice triangle appearing in Example 1.1.

The graph of mutations of $P_{(1,1,1)}$ has been completely described [3,19]. Up to $\mathrm{GL}_2(\mathbb{Z})$-equivalence, there is exactly one mutation from $P_{(1,1,1)}$: this gives $P_{(1,1,2)}$ corresponding to $\mathbb{P}(1, 1, 4)$. The polar polygon $P^*_{(1,1,2)}$ is the rational triangle in Example 1.2. As Figure 7 illustrates, a mutation between polytopes gives rise to a

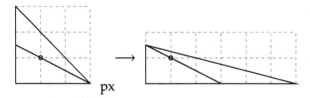

px

Figure 7. The mutation from $P_{(1,1,1)}$ to $P_{(1,1,2)}$ gives a scissors congruence between the polar polytopes.

scissors congruence [18] between polar polytopes. Mutation therefore preserves the Ehrhart series of the polar polytope, and this explains why we have quasi-period collapse in this example.

We can mutate $P_{(1,1,2)}$ in two ways that are distinct up to the action of $GL_2(\mathbb{Z})$: one returns us to $P_{(1,1,1)}$, while the other gives $P_{(1,2,5)}$. Continuing to mutate, we obtain an infinite graph of triangles $P_{(a,b,c)}$, where the (a, b, c) are the *Markov triples*, that is, the positive integral solutions to the Markov equation:

$$3xyz = x^2 + y^2 + z^2.$$

The Gorenstein index of $P_{(a,b,c)}$ is abc. In particular, the Gorenstein index can be made arbitrarily large while the Ehrhart series, and hence quasi-period, of $P^*_{(a,b,c)}$ is fixed. See Ref. [23] for details.

5.   Conclusion

We have seen that Support Vector Machine methods are very effective at extracting the dimension and volume of a lattice or rational polytope P, and the quasi-period of a rational polytope P, from the initial terms of its Ehrhart series. We have also seen that ML methods are unable to reliably determine the Gorenstein index of a Fano polytope P from the Ehrhart series of its polar polytope P^*. The discussions in Sections 2.4, 3.4, and 4.2 suggest that these results are as expected: that ML is detecting known and understood structure in the dimension, volume, and quasi-period cases and that there is probably no structure to detect in the Gorenstein index case. But there is a more useful higher-level conclusion to draw here too: when applying ML methods to questions in pure mathematics, one needs to think carefully about methods and results. Questions 2 and 3 are superficially similar, yet one is amenable to ML and the other is not. Furthermore, applying standard ML recipes in a naive way would have led to false negative results. For example, since the Ehrhart series grows so fast, it would have been typical to suppress the growth rate by taking logarithms and also to pass to principal components. Taking logarithms is a good idea for some of our questions but not for others; this reflects the mathematical realities underneath the data and not just whether the vector components y_m involved grow rapidly with m or not. Passing to principal components is certainly a useful tool, but naive feature extraction would have retained only the first principal component, which is responsible for more than 99.999% of the variation (in both the logarithmic Ehrhart vector and the Ehrhart vector). This would have left us unable to detect the positive answers to Questions 1 and 2 in the former case because projection to one dimension amalgamates clusters (see Figure 1) and in the latter case because we need to detect whether the Ehrhart vector lies in a certain high-codimension linear subspace and that structure is destroyed by projection to a low-dimensional space.

Acknowledgments

TC is supported by ERC Consolidator Grant 682603 and EPSRC Programme Grant EP/N03189X/1. JH is supported by a Nottingham Research Fellowship. AK is supported by EPSRC Fellowship EP/N022513/1.

References

[1] M. Akhtar, T. Coates, A. Corti, L. Heuberger, A. M. Kasprzyk, A. Oneto, A. Petracci, T. Prince and K. Tveiten, Mirror symmetry and the classification of orbifold del Pezzo surfaces, *Proc. Amer. Math. Soc.* **144**(2) (2016), 513–527. MR 3430830.

[2] M. Akhtar, T. Coates, S. Galkin and A. M. Kasprzyk, Minkowski polynomials and mutations, *SIGMA Symmetry Integrability Geom. Methods Appl.* **8**(Paper 094) (2012), 17. MR 3007265.

[3] M. E. Akhtar and A. M. Kasprzyk, Mutations of fake weighted projective planes, *Proc. Edinb. Math. Soc.* (2) **59**(2) (2016), 271–285. MR 3509229.

[4] J. Bao, Y.-H. He, E. Hirst, J. Hofscheier, A. M. Kasprzyk and S. Majumder, Polytopes and Machine Learning, arXiv:2109.09602 [math.CO] (2021).

[5] J. Bao, Y.-H. He, E. Hirst, J. Hofscheier, A. M. Kasprzyk and S. Majumder, Hilbert series, machine learning, and applications to physics, *Phys. Lett. B* **827** (2022), Paper No. 136966, 8.

[6] M. Beck, B. Braun and A. R. Vindas-Meléndez, Decompositions of Ehrhart h^*-polynomials for rational polytopes, *Discrete Comput. Geom.* **68**(1) (2022), 50–71.

[7] M. Beck, S. Elia and S. Rehberg, Rational Ehrhart theory, arXiv:2110.10204 [math.CO] (2022).

[8] M. Beck, S. V. Sam and K. M. Woods, Maximal periods of (Ehrhart) quasi-polynomials, *J. Combin. Theory Ser. A* **115**(3) (2008), 517–525.

[9] W. Bosma, J. Cannon and C. Playout, The Magma algebra system. I. The user language, *J. Symbolic Comput.* **24**(3–4) (1997), 235–265, Computational algebra and number theory (London, 1993).

[10] T. Coates, J. Hofscheier and A. M. Kasprzyk, *Ehrhart Series Coefficients and Quasi-period for Random Rational Polytopes.* Zenodo (2022). Doi: 10.5281/zenodo.6614829.

[11] T. Coates, J. Hofscheier and A. M. Kasprzyk, *Ehrhart Series Coefficients for Random Lattice Polytopes.* Zenodo (2022). Doi: 10.5281/zenodo.6614821.

[12] D. A. Cox, J. B. Little and H. K. Schenck, *Toric Varieties*, Graduate Studies in Mathematics, Vol. 124, Providence, RI: American Mathematical Society (2011).

[13] A. Davies, P. Veličković, L. Buesing, S. Blackwell, D. Zheng, N. Tomašev, R. Tanburn, P. Battaglia, C. Blundell, A. Juhász, M. Lackenby, G. Williamson, D. Hassabis and P. Kohli, Advancing mathematics by guiding human intuition with AI, *Nature* **600** (2021), 70–74.

[14] E. Ehrhart, Sur un problème de géométrie diophantienne linéaire. II. Systèmes diophantiens linéaires, *J. Reine Angew. Math.* **227** (1967), 25–49.

[15] E. Ehrhart, Sur les polyèdres homothétiques bordés à n dimensions, *C. R. Acad. Sci. Paris* **254** (1962), 988–990.

[16] M. H. J. Fiset and A. M. Kasprzyk, A note on palindromic δ-vectors for certain rational polytopes, *Electron. J. Combin.* **15**(1) (2008), Note 18, 4.

[17] W. Fulton, *Introduction to Toric Varieties*, Annals of Mathematics Studies, Vol. 131, Princeton, NJ: Princeton University Press (1993), The William H. Roever Lectures in Geometry.

[18] C. Haase and T. B. McAllister, *Quasi-period Collapse and* GL$_n(\mathbb{Z})$-*scissors Congruence in Rational Polytopes*, Integer points in polyhedra — geometry, number theory, representation theory, algebra, optimization, statistics, *Contemp. Math.*, Vol. 452, Amer. Math. Soc., Providence, RI, pp. 115–122 (2008).

[19] P. Hacking and Y. Prokhorov, Smoothable del Pezzo surfaces with quotient singularities, *Compos. Math.* **146**(1) (2010), 169–192.

[20] G. Hamm, J. Hofscheier and A. M. Kasprzyk, *Half-Integral Polygons with a Fixed Number of Lattice Points*, in Preparation.

[21] A. J. Herrmann, *Classification of Ehrhart Quasi-polynomials of Half-integral Polygons*, Master's thesis, San Francisco State University (2010).

[22] A. M. Kasprzyk and B. Nill, *Fano Polytopes*, Strings, gauge fields, and the geometry behind, World Sci. Publ., Hackensack, NJ, pp. 349–364 (2013).

[23] A. M. Kasprzyk and B. Wormleighton, Quasi-period collapse for duals to Fano polygons: An explanation arising from algebraic geometry, arXiv:1810.12472 [math.CO] (2018).

[24] J. Kollár and N. I. Shepherd-Barron, Threefolds and deformations of surface singularities, *Invent. Math.* **91**(2) (1988), 299–338.

[25] T. B. McAllister, Coefficient functions of the Ehrhart quasi-polynomials of rational polygons, *Proceedings of the 2008 International Conference on Information Theory and Statistical Learning, ITSL 2008, Las Vegas, Nevada, USA*, July 14–17, 2008 (Matthias Dehmer, Michael Drmota, and Frank Emmert-Streib, eds.), CSREA Press (2008).

[26] T. B. McAllister and K. M. Woods, The minimum period of the Ehrhart quasi-polynomial of a rational polytope, *J. Combin. Theory Ser. A* **109**(2) (2005), 345–352.

[27] P. McMullen, Lattice invariant valuations on rational polytopes, *Arch. Math. (Basel)* **31**(5) (1978/79), 509–516.

[28] F. Pedregosa, G. Varoquaux, A. Gramfort, V. Michel, B. Thirion, O. Grisel, M. Blondel, P. Prettenhofer, R. Weiss, V. Dubourg, J. Vanderplas, A. Passos, D. Cournapeau, M. Brucher, M. Perrot and E. Duchesnay, Scikit-learn: Machine learning in Python, *J. Mach. Learn. Res.* **12** (2011), 2825–2830.

[29] R. P. Stanley, Decompositions of rational convex polytopes, *Ann. Discrete Math.* **6** (1980), 333–342.

Chapter 4

Intelligent Explorations of the String Theory Landscape

Andrei Constantin

Rudolf Peierls Centre for Theoretical Physics,
University of Oxford, Parks Road, Oxford OX1 3PU, UK;
Wolfson College, Linton Road, Oxford, UK

andrei.constantin@physics.ox.ac.uk

Abstract

The goal of identifying the Standard Model of particle physics and its extensions within string theory has been one of the principal driving forces in string phenomenology. Recently, the incorporation of artificial intelligence in string theory and certain theoretical advancements have brought to light unexpected solutions to mathematical hurdles that have so far hindered progress in this direction. In this review, we focus on model-building efforts in the context of the $E_8 \times E_8$ heterotic string compactified on smooth Calabi–Yau threefolds and discuss several areas in which machine learning is expected to make a difference.

1. Introduction

Despite the wealth of settings available in string theory, it is currently not known how to embed the Standard Model of particle physics in any concrete string model. The primary reason for this is the sheer mathematical difficulty associated with the analysis of string compactifications. Numerous mathematical choices have to be made in order to specify a string compactification and the physical properties of the resulting four-dimensional quantum field theory depend on these choices in very intricate ways.

Ideally, one would start with the empirical properties of the Standard Model and derive in a bottom-up fashion the topology and geometry of the underlying string compactification. Unfortunately, such a direct bottom-up approach has never been a real option. The reasons are multiple. On the one hand, there are too many physical properties to account for in the Standard Model: the gauge group, the particle content, as well as a large number of free parameters, such as the masses of the elementary particles and the strengths of the interaction couplings. On the other hand, these physical properties are related in a complicated way to the underlying topology and geometry: the particle spectrum is often computed in terms of cohomology groups, while the free parameters, which in principle can be dynamically traced back to the string length scale, depend on geometrical quantities that are difficult to find explicitly, such as the Calabi–Yau metric. On top of these complications, there is the problem of moduli dependence: the compactification spaces come in infinite families, labeled by continuous parameters, which manifest as massless scalar fields in the low-energy theory. Finding mechanisms for dynamically fixing these parameters is non-trivial, and in the absence of such mechanisms, very little can be said about the quantitative properties of the low-energy theory.

The alternative top-down approach to string phenomenology has only met with limited success. In this approach, the internal topology and geometry are fixed at the start and the ensuing physical properties of the four-dimensional quantum field theory are subsequently derived. The difficulty here lies in the huge number of choices that can be made about the internal space — the model-building experience of the past few decades has taught us much about the magnitude of this problem and about how (and also about how not) to approach it. The first lesson is that the size of the string landscape is much larger than previously thought. The famous first estimate of $O(10^{500})$ consistent type IIB flux compactifications [1] seems rather conservative in comparison with the latest estimates. For instance, in Ref. [2], it was shown that a single elliptically fibered fourfold gives rise to $O(10^{272,000})$ F-theory flux compactifications. The second lesson is that the number of compactifications that match the symmetry group and the particle spectrum of the Standard Model is very large, despite representing only a tiny fraction of all consistent compactifications to four dimensions. In Ref. [3], it was argued that there are at least 10^{23} and very likely up to 10^{723} heterotic MSSMs, while the authors of Ref. [4] argued for the existence of a quadrillion standard models from F-theory. The third lesson is that these numbers are so large that traditional scanning methods cannot be used for systematic exploration. One can, of course, focus on small, accessible corners of the string landscape and this approach has been successful to some extent. For instance, in Refs. [3,5], some 10^7 pairs of Calabi–Yau threefolds and holomorphic bundles leading to $SU(5)$ heterotic string models that can accommodate the correct MSSM spectrum have been explicitly constructed.

Constructing effective field theories from string theory that agree with the Standard Model beyond the gauge group and the particle spectrum is non-trivial. On the one hand, the constraints that need to be imposed are mathematically and computationally challenging. On the other hand, even if these technical hurdles could somehow be resolved so as to include more constraints in the search algorithm, there is a high probability that no viable models would be found, unless the search space is considerably enlarged beyond the current possibilities. What is then needed is a tool set of tailored search methods that can quickly detect phenomenologically rich patches of the string landscape without systematically scanning over all compactifications and which can quickly implement a large number of checks that go beyond the usual spectrum considerations. The implementation of such methods is now being made possible through the emergence of new techniques of optimization and search, in particular, machine learning. In this sense, the exploration of the string landscape in the search of familiar Physics is akin to the search for new Physics in the vast experimental data generated by present-day particle colliders, which also relies heavily on machine learning techniques. Experiment and theory need to converge and machine learning is likely to play a key role in bridging the gap between them.

Machine learning essentially offers a mid-way alternative that avoids the difficulties inherent to both top-down and bottom-up approaches. While not solving directly for the ideal internal geometry and topology, methods such as reinforcement learning and genetic algorithms are capable of identifying many and possibly all the viable models available within certain classes of compactifications after exploring only a tiny fraction of the entire range of possibilities [6–15].

In the following discussion, we will focus on model-building efforts in the context of the $E_8 \times E_8$ heterotic string compactified on smooth Calabi–Yau threefolds with holomorphic vector bundles. This has been the earliest and arguably the most promising proposal for connecting string theory to particle physics but by no means the only one. Indeed, machine learning techniques have been successfully used in recent years in several other string theory contexts, starting with the early works of Refs. [16–20] (see also the reviews [21,22]). Our discussion will focus on three propositions:

(1) A much larger portion of the heterotic string landscape can now be accessed through the use of heuristic methods of search.
(2) The recent discovery of analytic formulae for bundle-valued cohomology has lead to a significant speed up in a number of checks that go beyond the net number of families.
(3) The computation of physical couplings from string theory has been advanced by the development of machine learning algorithms for the numerical computation of Calabi–Yau metrics and Hermitian Yang–Mills connections on holomorphic vector bundles.

In the following sections, I will expand on these ideas, identifying a number of subproblems where machine learning can make a difference.

2.   Heterotic String Model Building: An Overview

In the heterotic string context, the problem of constructing a low-energy limit that recovers the Standard Model can be phrased as a two-step mathematical problem encoded by a pair (X, V) consisting of a smooth, compact Calabi–Yau threefold X and a slope-stable holomorphic vector bundle V over X. The first step involves topology and algebraic geometry and concentrates on the identification of Calabi–Yau threefolds and holomorphic bundles with certain topological and quasi-topological properties. The second step involves differential geometry and concentrates on the problem of computing the Ricci-flat metric on the Calabi–Yau threefold, the Hermitian Yang–Mills connection on the holomorphic vector bundle, as well as the harmonic representatives of certain bundle-valued cohomology classes that are in one-to-one correspondence with the low-energy particles. If achievable, these two steps would produce for every pair (X, V) a class of four-dimensional effective field theories whose properties would be expressed in terms of the moduli determining the internal geometry. Fixing the moduli adds another layer of complication to the problem.

2.1. *Generalities*

The $E_8 \times E_8$ heterotic string theory has an in-built gauge symmetry, with each of the E_8 factors large enough to accommodate the Standard Model gauge group, as well as some of the standard GUT groups: $SU(5)$, $SO(10)$ and E_6. The two E_8 factors decouple at low energies: if the Standard Model gauge group is embedded in a single E_8, the other E_8 factor remains hidden and does not play a role in the initial construction of the low-energy theory and its particle spectrum. The hidden E_8 can, however, play an important role in moduli stabilization.

At low energies, the $E_8 \times E_8$ heterotic string theory in flat space can be consistently truncated to ten-dimensional $\mathcal{N} = 1$ supergravity coupled to $E_8 \times E_8$ super-Yang–Mills theory. The gauge group and the multiplets of the Standard Model are naturally contained in the super-Yang–Mills theory. In order to make contact with empirical particle physics, one needs to dimensionally reduce the theory to four dimensions and to specify a non-vanishing background for the gauge fields, which has the double effect of partially breaking one of the E_8 factors and generating a chiral spectrum in four dimensions. Mathematically, one needs to specify a six-dimensional manifold X for the compactification space and a vector bundle V over it whose connection specifies the background gauge fields. The gauge transformations available in four dimensions are the $E_8 \times E_8$ transformations which commute with the internal gauge transformations. This implies that the unbroken subgroup of $E_8 \times E_8$ is the commutant H of the structure group G of V. The quantum numbers of the four-dimensional multiplets are determined by decomposing the adjoint representation of $E_8 \times E_8$ under $G \times H$. The bundle V decomposes into two parts, called the visible bundle and the hidden bundle, corresponding to the two E_8 factors. In order to obtain the usual GUT groups $SU(5)$, $SO(10)$ and E_6, the structure group of the visible bundle has to be $SU(5)$, $SU(4)$ or $SU(3)$, respectively.

Often, the compactification data (X, V) are chosen such that they leave $\mathcal{N} = 1$ supersymmetry unbroken in four dimensions at the compactification scale. On the one hand, this choice simplifies the analysis, and on the other hand, it makes use of the advantages offered by $\mathcal{N} = 1$ supersymmetry for Physics beyond the Standard Model, especially in combination with grand unification ideas. The implications of retaining $\mathcal{N} = 1$ supersymmetry in four dimensions for the compactification data (X, V) were first analysed in Ref. [23]. If the structure of spacetime is assumed to be $\mathbb{R}^4 \times X$, where $\mathbb{R}^4$ is four-dimensional Minkowski space and X is a compact six-dimensional manifold, the vanishing of the supersymmetry variation of the four-dimensional fields requires, in the simplest setting, that X supports the existence of a covariantly constant spinor, which forces X to be a Ricci-flat Kähler manifold. Finding Ricci-flat metrics on Kähler manifolds is a notoriously difficult problem, however, as Calabi conjectured [24,25] and Yau later proved [26], a simple topological condition on a Kähler manifold X, namely the vanishing $c_1(X) = 0$ of its first Chern class, guarantees the existence of a unique Ricci-flat metric in each Kähler class. Such spaces are known as Calabi–Yau manifolds. The simple criterion offered by the Calabi–Yau theorem made possible the construction of large classes of examples, such as complete intersections in products of projective spaces [27,28] (CICY threefolds for short), as well as hypersurfaces and complete intersections in toric varieties [29].

The requirement of $\mathcal{N} = 1$ supersymmetry in four dimensions also implies that the field strength on the vector bundle $V \to X$ satisfies the Hermitian Yang–Mills equations, $F_{ab} = F_{\bar{a}\bar{b}} = 0$ and $g^{a\bar{b}} F_{a\bar{b}} = 0$. These equations are difficult to solve explicitly, not least because they involve the Ricci-flat metric g on X. Fortunately, there is a theorem due to Donaldson [32] (in complex dimension two) and Uhlenbeck and Yau [33] (in arbitrary dimension), which proves that on a Kähler manifold, the Hermitian Yang–Mills equations admit a unique solution if and only if V is holomorphic and slope-polystable. While in general it is non-trivial to check that a holomorphic bundle is polystable, for certain classes of bundles, there exist algebro-geometric methods that make such checks more tractable (see Ref. [34]). Finally, the theory is anomaly free if and only if V and the tangent bundle TX are related by the constraint $dH \sim tr(F \wedge F) - tr(R \wedge R)$, where H is the field strength associated with the Kalb–Ramond 2-form B-field and R is the curvature of X. The simplest solution to this constraint, known as the standard embedding, is to take the vector bundle V to be the holomorphic tangent bundle TX, to set the gauge connection equal to the spin connection and $H = 0$.

2.2. *Three generation models*

The initial heterotic model-building efforts focused on the standard embedding and produced a handful of three-generation supersymmetric E_6 GUTs [35–40]. A single multiplet in the fundamental **27** representation of E_6 or the anti-fundamental $\overline{\mathbf{27}}$ representation contains all the fermions in one family of the Standard Model. Since the number of **27** multiplets is counted by the Hodge number $h^{2,1}(X)$ and the number of $\overline{\mathbf{27}}$ multiplets is given by the other non-trivial Hodge number $h^{1,1}(X)$, in order to obtain three generations of quarks and leptons at low energies, the threefold X must satisfy

$$3 = |h^{2,1}(X) - h^{1,1}(X)| = \frac{1}{2}|\chi(X)|, \tag{1}$$

where $\chi(X)$ is the Euler characteristic of X and the matching numbers of generations and anti-generations are assumed to pair up and acquire mass at a high energy scale.

The paucity of three generation standard embedding models obtained over the years is not unexpected. In fact, what is remarkable is that any three-generation models at all could be found in this way. This is so because in order to break the E_6 symmetry down to $SU(3) \times SU(2) \times U(1)$, the manifold X needs to be non-simply connected and, unfortunately, the number of known examples of non-simply connected Calabi–Yau threefolds with Euler character-istic equal to ± 6 is very small (equal to 5 according to the slightly old tabulation of Ref. [41]). The requirement of non-simple connected-ness comes from the fact that the standard GUT symmetry breaking mechanism makes use of the existence of topologically non-trivial gauge fields with vanishing field strengths (Wilson lines) on mani-folds with non-trivial fundamental group. Note that since their field strengths vanishes, the Wilson lines do not contribute to the Hermi-tian Yang–Mills equations nor to the anomaly cancelation condition, so no additional complications arise.

The realization that more general vector bundles on Calabi–Yau threefolds provide true solutions of the heterotic string opened up a much wider class of compactifications in which one could also con-struct $SO(10)$ and $SU(5)$ GUTs [42,43]. While the number of avail-able choices for X remains relatively small due to the requirement of non-simply connectedness [41,44–49], the number of possibilities for V is virtually unbounded. Various constructions of holomorphic stable bundles have been used over the years, including the spec-tral cover construction over elliptically fibered Calabi–Yau threefolds [50–64], monad bundles [34,43,65–68], extension bundles [61,62,69], as well as direct sums of line bundles [5,49,61,62,70–80].

Each of these compactification settings has its own virtues: bun-dles obtained through the spectral cover construction can be directly used in the study of heterotic/F-theory duality, while monad and extension sequences provide an accessible construction of non-abelian bundles. The main virtue of line bundle sums resides in their 'split' nature: many of the consistency and phenomenological con-straints can be imposed line bundle by line bundle, making this class searchable by systematic methods, at least for manifolds with a relatively small Picard number. In this manner, in Ref. [5], an exhaustive search[1] for $SU(5)$ GUT models has been accomplished for Calabi–Yau threefolds with non-trivial fundamental group and a

---

[1]While the space of line bundle sums of a fixed rank over a given manifold is unbounded, it was noted that phenomenologically viable models correspond to line bundle sums where all entries are relatively small integers, an observa-tion which effectively renders the search space finite, though typically very large (e.g., the size of the search space involved in Ref. [5] was of order 10^{40} bundles).

Picard number smaller than 7, the search being extended in Ref. [3] to manifolds of Picard number equal to 7.

These searches resulted in the largest dataset of three generation $SU(5)$ GUT models derived from string theory to date, with some 10^7 explicitly constructed models [3,5]. One of the important empirical lessons of these searches was that, if extended to larger Picard number manifolds, this class of compactifications would produce at least 10^{23} and very likely up to 10^{723} three generation models [3]. This is certainly good news, as the string phenomenology experience accumulated over the last few decades suggests that it is staggeringly difficult to fine-tune any particular construction to simultaneously meet all the properties of the Standard Model. Having at hand a huge number of good starting points (three generation models) brings about much better prospects. However, in order to cope with the large exponents, the systematic scanning approach needs to be replaced with more effective methods of search.

2.3. *A model builder's to-do list*

What lies in front of the model builder is a list of non-trivial steps:

(1) Consider Calabi–Yau threefolds X from existing databases, such as the list of $\sim$8000 CICYs [27,81], the Kreuzer–Skarke dataset of Calabi–Yau hypersurfaces in four-dimensional toric varieties of around half a billion [29], as well as the more recently constructed generalized CICYs [28] and Gorenstein Calabi–Yau threefolds [82]. Most of these manifolds are simply connected which renders them unusable at Step 2, hence the need to look for discrete, freely acting groups $\Gamma : X \to X$ in order to construct smooth quotients X/Γ with fundamental group Γ. To date, there are a few hundred known examples of Calabi–Yau threefolds with non-trivial fundamental groups [41,44–49,83].

(2) Construct holomorphic stable bundles V over X such that the four-dimensional compactification contains the Standard Model gauge group $SU(3) \times SU(2) \times U(1)$. This step is usually realized in two stages,[2] by first breaking E_8 to one of the standard GUT

---

[2]In Ref. [78], it was shown that it is not feasible to directly break E_8 to the Standard Model group because the large number of conditions that have to be

groups and then breaking the latter to the Standard Model gauge group using Wilson lines. Since the final model is constructed on the quotient X/Γ, the bundle V needs to be Γ-equivariant in order to descend to a bundle on the quotient threefold, which is non-trivial to check. Checking stability is also a difficult step, in general [34]. The bundle V and the tangent bundle TX also have to satisfy the anomaly cancelation condition.

(3) Derive the matter spectrum of the four-dimensional theory and check that it matches the MSSM spectrum. The fermion fields in the low-energy theory correspond to massless modes of the Dirac operator on the internal space, counted by bundle-valued cohomology groups on X. This step involves checking the following: (a) the number of generations, which is relatively easy to compute as a topological index, and (b) the presence of a Higgs field and the absence of any exotic matter charged under the Standard Model gauge group, both of which requiring knowledge of cohomology, which can be computationally expensive, in general. Typically, only a small fraction of models have the exact MSSM spectrum.

(4) Constrain the resulting Lagrangian, in order to avoid well-known problems of supersymmetric GUTs, such as fast proton decay. For this purpose, additional discrete or continuous symmetries derived from the compactification set-up can be essential.

(5) Derive information about the detailed properties of the model, such as holomorphic Yukawa couplings, fermion mass-terms and μ-terms. In the first step, these quantities can be extracted from the holomorphic superpotential of the theory using techniques from algebraic and/or differential geometry.

(6) Compute physical Yukawa couplings. For this, the kinetic terms for the matter fields need to be rendered in canonical form, a computation that requires the explicit knowledge of the Calabi–Yau metric on X and the gauge connection on V. Except in very special cases, these quantities are not known analytically and are very hard to obtain numerically. As reviewed in the following, the recent use of machine learning techniques has significantly

---

imposed in order to obtain a correct physical spectrum in the absence of an underlying grand unified theory is incompatible with gauge coupling unification.

improved the efficiency of such computations, making feasible the calculation of physical couplings.

(7) Stabilize the unconstrained continuous parameters of the internal geometry (moduli fields). Spontaneously break supersymmetry and compute soft supersymmetry-breaking terms.

Every phenomenological requirement in this list leads to a substantial reduction in the number of viable models. As such, it is crucial to start with a large number of models or else the chances of retaining a realistic model in the end are extremely limited. Constructing a large number of models by hand is impractical. Systematic automated searches have their own limitations, despite substantial advancements in the computational power. Pushing further the boundaries of the explorable part of the string landscape requires a new approach, based on heuristic methods of search such as reinforcement learning and genetic algorithms, to the discussion of which we now turn.

3. Reinforcement Learning and Genetic Algorithms

3.1. *Reinforcement learning*

Reinforcement learning (RL) is a machine learning approach in which an artificial intelligence agent self-trains to make a sequence of decisions in order to achieve a specified goal within a large and potentially complex environment. The environment corresponds to the space of potential solutions for a given problem. The navigation is aided by a set of rewards and penalties, specified by the programmer, which guide the machine's learning process. The RL agent self-trains without any prior knowledge of the environment, a feature that distinguishes RL from supervised and unsupervised learning.

Every state of the environment, that is every potential solution to the given problem, is associated with a numerical value reflecting how well it fits the properties sought from target solutions. The learning process relies on this *intrinsic value function,* and such different functions can lead to very different kinds of performance. The search is then divided into multiple *episodes* involving a fixed number of maximal states. Typically, the initial state is randomly chosen and the episode ends either when a target state is found or when the maximal episode length is reached. The progression of states within an episode is dictated by the current *policy*, which is initially a random function that gets corrected using a neural network after each episode or periodically after a fixed number of episodes specified by the programmer during the self-training phase. Training is usually stopped once the agent is capable of reaching a target state from virtually any starting point. The typical maximal length of the episodes can be estimated in the following way. If the space of solutions is a d-dimensional hypercube of length l, then

$$\text{typical maximal episode length } \sim d^{1/2}l, \qquad (2)$$

which is the length of the diagonal, the idea being that within an episode the agent should have enough 'time' to travel between any two points of the search space. A longer episode length gives the agent more 'time' to find a good solution within any given episode, however it can also determine it to become fixated on a small number of terminal states. For this reason, it is customary to introduce a penalty on the episode length, giving the agent an incentive to find terminal states that are as close as possible to the original random starting point. On the other hand, if the search space contains sizeable 'gaps' with no target states, the episode length should be large enough so that the agent can move out of these regions within an episode. Often, the distribution of target states in the search space is not known, which makes the episode length an important hyperparameter that needs adjustment.

Ideally, after sufficiently many training episodes, the AI agent 'knows' enough about the landscape (the intrinsic value function) to (1) reach a terminal state for virtually any initial random point and (2) reach any specific target state within an episode provided that the initial random point is close enough. For the purpose of illustration, Figure 1 shows a situation where the target states (the red points) are uniformly distributed. If the initial random point of an episode falls within a blue ball (basin of attraction), the corresponding target state will be found within that episode. The basins of attraction cover the entire space, which means that the number of episodes needed to obtain all the target states is, in principle, comparable to the total number of target states available in the search space. Of course, in

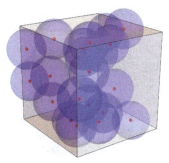

Figure 1.   An idealized picture of the search space and target states.

practice, the basins of attraction are not spheres; they roughly correspond to level hypersurfaces of the value function, though their exact shape depends very much on the training history. However, the main idea remains essentially the same: the target states get 'thickened', acting as attractor points within the corresponding attractor basins.

3.2.   *Fixed and dynamical elements of RL*

We review here some of the basic ideas and terminology used in RL referring the reader to Refs. [21,84] for more in-depth accounts. We divide the presentation into fixed and dynamical elements. The fixed (hard-wired) elements include the following:

(i) The *environment*, consisting of a set $\mathcal{S}$ of *states*, typically of very large size. Often the states are represented as numerical lists (vectors). At every instance, the agent (the computer programme) is in one of the states. The agent performs a sequence of steps, which leads to a notion of time.

(ii) The set of possible actions $\mathcal{A}(s)$ that can be taken from a state $s \in \mathcal{S}$ to move to other states. In the simplest situation, this set is the same for all states s and is denoted by $\mathcal{A}$.

(iii) At time step t, the agent moves from state s_t to a new state s_{t+1} by performing an action a_t. The choice of action is dictated (deterministically or probabilistically) by a *policy*. The policy is essentially dynamical, but its initialization is fixed by the programmer. Often, the initial policy consists of a random choice of actions at every step.

(iv) A characterization of *terminal states*, defining a subset $\mathcal{T} \subset \mathcal{S}$. Not every environment has terminal states, but when it has, these are the targets towards which the agent moves.

(v) The maximal length of an *episode*, l_{ep}. The search is divided into episodes $\mathcal{E}_i \subset \mathcal{S}$ which end either when a terminal state is reached or after a certain number of steps specified by the maximal length.

(vi) The method of *sampling* the initial states of episodes. This can be completely random or specified by a probability distribution.

(vii) The *reward function*. This is the essential tool in controlling the agent since the system of rewards and penalties is the only way to communicate with the learning process and to modify the existing policy. Typically, the reward is constructed as a real number $r(s, s')$ associated with each possible step $s \rightarrow s'$. Thus, at time step t, the agent receives a reward r_t associated with $s_t \rightarrow s_{t+1}$.

(viii) Often, it is appropriate to construct the reward function by first defining the *intrinsic value of states*, $V : \mathcal{S} \rightarrow \mathbb{R}$ as a measure of how badly a state s fails to achieve the properties expected from a terminal state. For instance, if V is semi-negative, the reward $r(s, s')$ can be chosen as $V(s') - V(s)$, giving an incentive to move towards states of higher value. To this reward function one can add, e.g., a fixed penalty for each step, a penalty for stepping outside of the environment, as well as a typically large bonus for reaching a terminal state.

(ix) In general, it is not wise to make judgments (update the policy) based on immediate rewards alone. In order to take into account delayed rewards, one defines a *return function* $G : \mathcal{S} \rightarrow \mathbb{R}$ as a weighted sum

$$G_t = \sum_{k \geq 0} \gamma^k r_{t+k}, \tag{3}$$

computed for a state s_t by following the trajectory dictated (deterministically or probabilistically) by the policy and adding the weighted rewards until the end of an episode. Of course, the numbers $\{G_t\}$ associated with the states $\{s_t \in \mathcal{E}_i\}$ can only be computed once the episode $\mathcal{E}_i$ ends. The number $\gamma \in [0, 1)$ is called *discount factor*. It is sub-unitary in order to give a greater weight to rewards in the immediate future, and typically very close to 1 in order to give some reasonable weight to rewards arising in the more distant future.

(x) The size of the *batch*. The agent collects data in the form of triplets (s_t, a_t, G_t) and communicates it in batches to the algorithm controlling the policy. The policy is then updated and a new batch is collected and communicated back. Thus, the learning process follows an iterative approach.

The learning curve is typically very sensitive to the architecture and some scanning is required to fix hyperparameters such as the maximal length of episodes l_{ep}, the discount factor γ and the batch size.

Learned (dynamical) elements. There are various flavors of RL and they differ in the quantities that are being learnt. In general, there are three learnt elements:

(i) The *policy*. In deterministic approaches, the policy is a map $\pi : \mathcal{S} \to \mathcal{A}$ specifying what action $a = \pi(s)$ needs to be taken if state s is reached. In stochastic approaches, the policy is a probability distribution $\pi : \mathcal{A} \times \mathcal{S} \to [0, 1]$, specifying the probability $\pi(a|s)$ for action a to be picked in state s. The aim of the game is to find a policy that brings a maximal return (in the deterministic case) or a maximal expected return (in the stochastic case). RL provides a method of obtaining an approximately optimal policy in this sense. The method is not guaranteed to work in all cases and the algorithm may often lead to policies that are only locally optimal, as they essentially rely on a local search. As already mentioned, even in the cases where the method eventually proves to be successful, a certain amount of fine tuning of the hyperparameters is usually required. In the stochastic setting described in the following, the policy is a function taking as input a state of the environment, represented by a numerical list, and outputting a list of probabilities, one for each possible action.

(ii) The *state-value function* under policy π is defined as the expected return when starting in state s and following the policy π thereafter, $v_\pi(s) = \mathbb{E}_\pi[G_t|s_t = s]$. The value of a terminal state is zero, since there are no future returns in this case.

(iii) The *action-value function* under policy π is the expected return starting from state s, taking the action a and thereafter following policy π, $q_\pi(s, a) = \mathbb{E}_\pi[G_t | s_t = s, a_t = a]$. The value of a state $v_\pi(s)$ depends on the values of the actions possible in that state and on how likely each action is to be taken under the current policy.

In the simplest setting, called REINFORCE, the aim is to learn a parameterized policy that can select actions without consulting a value function. A brute force optimization would run over all possible policies, sample returns while following them and then choose the policy with the largest expected return. Unfortunately, the number of possible policies is typically very large or infinite, making brute force optimisation unfeasible.

For this reason, in RL algorithms, the policy π is controlled by a neural network with internal parameters (weights and biases) collectively denoted by $\boldsymbol{\theta}$. The network takes as input a state $s \in \mathcal{S}$ and outputs a list of probabilities, denoted by $f_{\boldsymbol{\theta}}(s)$. Then, if the a-th action is represented by the a-th unit vector in $\mathbb{R}^{|\mathcal{A}|}$, the probability to choose action a in state s will be the dot product $\pi_{\boldsymbol{\theta}}(a|s) = a \cdot f_{\boldsymbol{\theta}}(s)$. The internal parameters $\boldsymbol{\theta}$ get corrected after the analysis of each batch, so as to minimize the loss function defined in the following. REINFORCE uses triplets of data (s_t, a_t, G_t) which include the complete return G_t from time t, that is, all future rewards up until the end of the episode. The internal parameters $\boldsymbol{\theta}$ get updated after the analysis of the (s_t, a_t, G_t) data triplet in the following way (see Chapter 13 of Ref. [84]):

$$\boldsymbol{\theta}_{t+1} = \boldsymbol{\theta}_t + \alpha \, G_t \frac{\nabla \pi_{\boldsymbol{\theta}_t}(a_t, s_t)}{\pi_{\boldsymbol{\theta}_t}(a_t, s_t)}, \tag{4}$$

where α is the learning rate specified by the programmer as a hyperparameter. Put differently, the neural network is trained on the loss function $L(\boldsymbol{\theta}_t) = G_t \ln(a_t \cdot f_{\boldsymbol{\theta}_t}(s_t))$.

There are many other flavors of RL. For instance, a version of RL called actor-critic introduces, apart from the policy network discussed above, a second network which controls the state-value function. The agent continues to follow π, but the performance of the policy is judged by the second network. Both networks are used to improve each other in this case.

3.3. Genetic algorithms

Genetic algorithms are a class of heuristic problem solving methods inspired by evolutionary biology. The idea is to encode the data specifying a solution attempt into a sequence of (binary) digits. A population of such solution attempts is created and evolved according to a fitness function which gives a measure for how close the attempt is to an actual solution. The fitness function corresponds to what we called intrinsic value function in the context of RL.

The optimal size of the population, N, depends logarithmically on the length of the sequence of digits encoding solution attempts. Typically, N is of order of a few hundred individuals. The initial population can be generated randomly or seeded around areas of the solution space where optimal solutions are likely to be found.

Evolution then proceeds by selection, breeding and mutation. A popular choice for the *selection* method is to start by ranking the solution attempts according to their fitness. An individual at rank k is then selected for breeding with a probability that depends linearly on its ranking such that the probability for the top individual P_1 is equal to a multiple α of the probability P_N of the least fit individual. Typically, α is chosen in the range $2 \leq \alpha \leq 5$. While the fittest individuals have a higher chance to reproduce, the scheme also ensures that the less fit individuals are also able to breed, which preserves a healthy variety of 'genes' throughout the evolutionary process.

The *breeding* is usually implemented as an M-point cross-over by which the two binary sequences are cut at the same M random points and the cut sections are alternatively swapped. This implementation is made possible by the fact that in the simplest setting all binary sequences have a fixed length. There exist other, more sophisticated versions of genetic algorithms, including genetic programming, where solution attempts are represented as bit strings of variable size or as trees/graphs. In these cases, the cross-over implementation is more complex. Often a single point cross-over turns out to perform well enough. Once a new generation is formed through cross-over, a small fraction (usually around one percent) of the binary digits, selected randomly, are flipped. These *mutations* ensure that the population does not stagnate and continues to evolve towards better solutions or towards different optimal solutions. For the applications envisaged here, the optimal solution is not unique; rather there are many optimal solutions sparsely scattered over a huge landscape. Finally, one can invoke an element of *elitism*: in order to ensure that the new generation has a greater or equal maximum fitness than the previous generation, the fittest individual(s) from the previous generation can be copied into the new one replacing the least fit next individual.

The process is then repeated over many generations and terminates after a pre-defined number of evolutionary cycles N_{gen}. This number can be chosen by trial and error. It needs to be large enough to allow the algorithm to find a sufficiently large number of optimal solutions. On the other hand, the typical situation is that beyond a certain number of cycles, very few new solutions are found, indicating that the search can stop and restart from a different random initialization.

Compared to Reinforcement Learning, Genetic Algorithms benefit from the advantage of a simpler implementation as well as from the absence of a training phase. On the other hand, the success or failure of each method very much depends on the problem in question, so having available several complementary methods can be crucial in tackling certain problems. For situations where both methods turn out to be successful, they can be used in conjunction in order to estimate the achieved degree of comprehensiveness in finding most of the solutions present in the environment.

In particle physics and string theory, genetic algorithms have not yet been widely used. The first application in string theory was undertaken in Ref. [6] for heterotic model building in the Free Fermionic formulation. More recently, RL has been used in Refs. [7,15] to generate type IIA intersecting brane configurations that lead to standard-like models and in Refs. [9,10] to construct $SU(5)$ and $SO(10)$ string GUT models. The landscape of type IIB flux vacua was explored in Ref. [8] using GAs and Markov chain Monte Carlo methods, while in Refs. [11,14], the same methods were used, as well as RL. Other applications of RL include the construction of quark mass models [85], solving the conformal bootstrap equations [86] and learning to unknot [87].

It is important to note that RL and GAs are qualitatively different from the more standard supervised and unsupervised learning techniques, which have also been recently used in the exploration of the heterotic string landscape [88–91].

4. Model Building with Monad Bundles and Line Bundle Sums

In this section, we look at the details of heterotic model building on smooth Calabi–Yau threefolds with holomorphic bundles constructed either as monad bundles or as sums of line bundles. These classes of compactifications have proven to include many phenomenologically attractive models [5,34,49,61,62,66–68,70–80,92–95], hence the motivation to explore them further. Our aim here will be to understand the extent to which the heuristic search methods discussed above can speed up the search for realistic models.

The discussion at the end of Section 3.1 suggested that after the initial self-training stage, RL networks have the capacity to guide the search towards a terminal state from virtually any starting point in the environment within a small number of steps, thus splitting the environment into basins of attractions. Finding all terminal states then amounts to finding one starting point in each basin of attraction. If basins of attraction are of roughly the same size, the computational time required to find most of the solutions scales linearly with the number of terminal states present in the environment. This has to be contrasted with the case of systematic scans where the computational time scales linearly with the total number of states contained in the environment.

The same (and, in fact a better) behavior in terms of computational time has been observed in the case of GAs [12,13]. As such, RL and GAs can be extremely efficient in exploring spaces that are too large and the desirable states too sparse to be found by systematic scans or by random searches. More interestingly, and somewhat counterintuitively, the fact that the computational time required to find most of the solutions scales with the number of optimal solutions, rather than the total size of the environment, implies that the search is more efficient when more constraints are being included. In any systematic scan, including more constraints comes with an inevitable computational cost, however with RL or GAs, this cost can be overcompensated by the (typically substantial) reduction in the number of basins of attraction corresponding to different solutions that satisfy all the constraints. Our focus in the following sections will fall on identifying which constraints can be currently implemented in automated searches or are susceptible of implementation in the near future given certain theoretical advancements, such as the discovery of explicit analytic formulae for cohomology dimensions.

For string theory model building, the reduction in computational time can be a real game changer. The size of the search spaces is typically very large. For a fixed Calabi–Yau threefold X, infinite classes of topologically distinct bundles can be considered. However, the experience of various systematic scans indicates that viable models can only be found in a finite search region whose size scales exponentially like $10^{\alpha h^{1,1}(X)}$ with a multiple α of the Picard number $h^{1,1}(X)$. The number α depends on the details of the class of bundles in question but is generally greater or equal to 5. The size of the solution space, on the other hand, is much smaller. To give an estimate figure, we refer to the comprehensive study of line bundle sums leading to $SU(5)$ models with three families undertaken in Refs. [3,5], which found a number of $10^{h^{1,1}(X)}$ solutions for a typical Calabi–Yau threefold X. The change in the exponent is significant, and by adding more physical constraints, the size of the solution space is bound to decrease further.

4.1. *Monad bundles*

A monad bundle V on a complex manifold X is constructed from two sums of holomorphic line bundles B and C, via the short exact sequence

$$0 \to V \to B \xrightarrow{f} C \to 0, \tag{5}$$

where f is a bundle morphism and, by exactness, $V = \ker(f)$. Each line bundle in B and C is specified by its first Chern class, which in a basis of the second cohomology of X corresponds to a list of $h^{1,1}(X)$ integers. This means that V is specified by $h^{1,1}(X)\,(\mathrm{rk}(B) + \mathrm{rk}(C))$ integers. V also depends on the monad map f, which encodes the bundle moduli. The map f can be assumed to be generic as long as the rank of V, given by the dimension of $\ker(f)$, is constant across X. This condition guarantees that V is a bundle rather than a more general type of sheaf. When V is a bundle, its rank is given by $\mathrm{rk}(V) = \mathrm{rk}(B) - \mathrm{rk}(C)$.

Provided that f is generic enough, the structure group of V is $U(\mathrm{rk}(V))$. In order to break the heterotic E_8 gauge symmetry to one of the standard GUT symmetry groups, $SU(5)$, $SO(10)$ or E_6, the structure group of V has to be of special type, which implies that $c_1(V) = 0$, and hence $c_1(B) = c_1(C)$. This condition reduced the number of integers specifying V to $h^{1,1}(X)\,(\mathrm{rk}(B) + \mathrm{rk}(C) - 1)$.

Since the line bundle integers specifying B and C can take arbitrary values, the search space is infinite. To make it finite, one can allow these integers to run in a finite range, for instance, between -4 and 5, which turns out to be the range where most of the good models lie. In this case, the size of the search space is of order $10^{h^{1,1}(X)(\mathrm{rk}(B)+\mathrm{rk}(C)-1)}$. Since $\mathrm{rk}(C) \geq 1$ and $\mathrm{rk}(V) = 4$ for $SO(10)$ models, while for $SU(5)$ models $\mathrm{rk}(V) = 5$, it follows that the size of the search space is

$$10^{\geq 5\, h^{1,1}(X)}. \tag{6}$$

The computational time required to perform even the most basic checks for a monad bundle being of order of a few milliseconds on a standard machine, this implies that for any manifold with $h^{1,1}(X) \geq 2$, a systematic and comprehensive search is not possible (or just about possible in the case $h^{1,1}(X) = 2$).

In Refs. [10,12,13], it was shown that, despite its gigantic size, this class of heterotic string compactifications is searchable by means of RL and GA methods. More specifically, the studies concentrated on monad bundles leading to $SO(10)$ supersymmetric GUT models. For group-theoretical reasons, the Wilson line breaking of $SO(10)$ to the Standard Model requires a discrete group Γ which is at least $\mathbb{Z}_3 \times \mathbb{Z}_3$. Unfortunately, there are not many known Calabi–Yau threefolds admitting a freely acting symmetry group of this size [10,41,45,47], so the choice of manifold in this case is rather constrained. As such, these studies focused on a few manifolds realized as complete intersections in products of projective spaces. The simplest of these is the bicubic threefold represented by the configuration matrix

$$X = \begin{bmatrix} \mathbb{P}^2 & 3 \\ \mathbb{P}^2 & 3 \end{bmatrix}^{2,83}_{-162}. \tag{7}$$

It is worth noting that the search space has a large degeneracy. For the bicubic, equivalent bundles arise from permuting the two $\mathbb{P}^2$-factors in the embedding, as well as from permuting the line bundles in B and C. This amounts to a group of order $2! \cdot 6! \cdot 2! = 2800$.

Both the RL and GA implementations turned out to be successful in identifying models, termed 'perfect states', that pass the following checks:

(a) a sufficient criterion for checking the bundleness of V;
(b) the anomaly cancelation condition;
(c) the Euler characteristic being equal to $-3|\Gamma|$, where Γ is a freely acting symmetry on X;
(d) a necessary condition for the equivariance of V with respect to the symmetry Γ;
(e) a number of necessary conditions for the stability of V relying on Hoppe's criterion and the availability of explicit line bundle cohomology formulae on X.

Including more checks in the search algorithm would require further theoretical progress. For instance, for properties such as the full spectrum or bundle stability, analytical formulae for cohomology dimensions of monad bundles would be a crucial ingredient.

The RL/GA explorations of monad bundles on the bicubic manifold accomplished a high degree of comprehensiveness in finding all the models satisfying the above criteria using relatively modest computational resources. Indirect evidence in support of this claim was obtained by exploiting the degeneracy of the environment. As shown in Figure 2, the number of inequivalent perfect models found in the search saturates as a function of the total number of perfect models found, suggesting that most of the inequivalent perfect models have been found. Moreover, comparing the results of the GA search with those obtained through RL, it turns out that the two datasets of inequivalent models have an overlap of over 90%, despite the great differences distinguishing the two methods. This also suggests that the details of the optimisation process are not really essential once the processes begin to saturate, provided that they share the same incentives.

Comparing the efficiencies of the two methods, it turns out that on this environment GA is, overall, more efficient by about an order of magnitude than RL in identifying models that pass all the above criteria. In general, such a comparison would be difficult to make due to the intrinsic differences between the two methods, however in this case, the comparison is legitimate as it refers to the time taken to accomplish a sufficiently high degree of comprehensiveness.

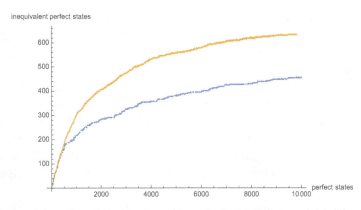

Figure 2.   Saturation of the number of inequivalent 'perfect models'. The orange curve corresponds to RL search and the blue curve to the GA search. The RL search took 35 core days, while the GA search took only 1 core day. A total of ~ 700 inequivalent models have been found, with an overlap of over 90% between the two methods.

The methods described above can be easily extended to other contexts, for instance, to rank 5 monad bundles leading to $SU(5)$ models. In this case, there are no group-theoretic restrictions on the freely acting symmetry Γ (e.g., Γ can be as small as $\mathbb{Z}_2$), so many more choices for X are available. As such, the expectation is that vastly larger numbers of $SU(5)$ models can be found using RL, GAs and monad bundles.

4.2.   *Line bundle sums*

There are several advantages to working with sums of line bundles, as opposed to irreducible vector bundles. First, such configurations are relatively simple to deal with from a computational point of view. Second, abelian models are characterized by the presence of additional $U(1)$ gauge symmetries, which are broken at a high-energy scale but remain in the low-energy theory as global symmetries, constraining the resulting Lagrangian and giving more information than is usually available in other constructions. Finally, although line bundle sums represent special loci in the moduli space of vector bundles of a given topology, these simple configurations provide a computationally accessible window into a bigger moduli space of heterotic compactifications: if a line bundle sum corresponds to a standard-like model, then usually it can be deformed into non-abelian bundles that also lead to standard-like models [74,75]. Moreover, the effect of the $U(1)$ symmetries persists even beyond the locus where the bundle splits into a direct sum [76].

In Ref. [5], a dataset of about 10^6 models with $SU(5)$ gauge group and the correct chiral asymmetry has been constructed on CICYs with Picard number < 7. In Ref. [3], this dataset expanded by an order of magnitude by considering CICYs with Picard number 7. It is expected that a significant number of these models will descend to standard-like models after dividing by the corresponding discrete symmetry. However, the detailed analysis of this wealth of models has so far been hindered by the difficulty of (equivariant) cohomology computations.

Cohomology computations indeed represent the main limiting factor in the analysis of heterotic compactifications on Calabi–Yau manifolds with holomorphic vector bundles. For instance, in the search algorithm for monad bundles described above, it was not possible to include criteria related to the full description of the low-energy spectrum, as these would rely on slow — if achievable at all — cohomology computations. The situation is different for line bundle sums, due to the recent discovery of analytic formulae for cohomology [96–104]. The new cohomology formulae allow for a quick check of the entire low-energy spectrum, which represents a significant improvement from the usual check on the number of chiral families, computed as a topological index. Concretely, cohomology constraints can be imposed to ensure the following:

(a) three families of quarks and leptons;
(b) the presence of a Higgs field and the absence of any exotic matter charged under the Standard Model gauge group;
(c) a hierarchy of Yukawa couplings compatible with a heavy third generation;
(d) the absence of operators inducing fast proton decay and R-parity violating operators;
(e) the presence of a μ-term and the existence of right-handed neutrinos;
(f) Yukawa unification, etc.

These constraints can be imposed along with the usual set of requirements:

(a) the anomaly cancelation condition;
(b) poly-stability of the line bundle sum, that is, checking the existence of a non-empty locus in Kähler moduli space where the slopes of all line bundles simultaneously vanish;
(c) equivariance with respect to the freely acting discrete symmetry.

We illustrate the implementation of the new constraints relying on line bundle cohomology formulae with the discussion of dimension four proton decay operators in $SU(5)$ GUT models. These operators are of the form $\mathbf{\bar 5\,\bar 5\,10}$, possibly with a number of singlet insertions, $\mathbf{11\ldots1\bar5\,\bar5\,10}$. In heterotic line bundle models, the $SU(5)$ multiplets come with additional $U(1)$ charges, in fact with $S\left(U(1)^5\right)$ charges. These can be represented by vectors $\mathbf{q} = (q_1,\ldots,q_5)$. The group $S\left(U(1)^5\right)$ consists of elements $\left(e^{i\theta_1},\ldots,e^{i\theta_5}\right)$, such that the sum of the phases $\theta_1 + \cdots + \theta_5 = 0$. Due to this determinant condition, two $S\left(U(1)^5\right)$ representations, labeled by $\mathbf{q}$ and $\mathbf{q'}$, have to be identified, if $\mathbf{q} - \mathbf{q'} \in \mathbb{Z}\mathbf{n}$, where $\mathbf{n} = (1,1,1,1,1)$. By working out the necessary branching rules, it turns out that each of the $\mathbf{10}$ multiplets is charged under a single $U(1)$. Thus, denoting by $\{\mathbf{e}_a\}_{a=1,\ldots,5}$ the standard basis in five dimensions, a multiplet $\mathbf{10}$ charged under the a-th $U(1)$ can be denoted by $\mathbf{10}_{\mathbf{e}_a}$. Similarly, the patterns of charge assignments for the other $SU(5)$ multiplets are $\mathbf{1}_{\mathbf{e}_a-\mathbf{e}_b}$, $\mathbf{5}_{-\mathbf{e}_a-\mathbf{e}_b}$, $\mathbf{\bar 5}_{\mathbf{e}_a+\mathbf{e}_b}$, $\mathbf{\overline{10}}_{-\mathbf{e}_a}$. In any concrete model, that is, for any specific sum of five line bundles over the Calabi–Yau manifold, determining the number of $SU(5)$ multiplets of each type and their charge assignments amounts to the computation of line bundle cohomology dimensions.

In the case of dimension four operators of the form $\mathbf{\bar 5}_{a,b}\,\mathbf{\bar 5}_{c,d}\,\mathbf{10}_e$, the $S\left(U(1)^5\right)$ charge is $\mathbf{e}_a + \mathbf{e}_b + \mathbf{e}_c + \mathbf{e}_d + \mathbf{e}_e$. In order for such operators to be allowed, a, b, c, d and e must all be different. Thus, a sufficient constraint for the absence of such operators is that for any triplet of $SU(5)$ multiplets present in the spectrum $(\mathbf{\bar 5}_{a,b}, \mathbf{\bar 5}_{c,d}, \mathbf{10}_e)$, the values of a, b, c, d and e must have some overlap. This is a combinatorial problem which can be easily decided provided that the full details of the spectrum (i.e., multiplets and $U(1)$-charges) are known, information which can be quickly gathered during the search using the analytic formulae for cohomology discussed in the following section. The large number of constraints listed above is expected to select a relatively small number of string compactifications that can accommodate the Standard Model.

5.   Line Bundle Cohomology Formulae

The standard methods for computing cohomology include algorithmic methods, based on Čech cohomology and spectral sequences [105–107]. However, these methods are computationally intensive and provide little insight into the origin of the results. The effect is that model-building efforts are typically limited to trial-and-error searches. The existence of simple analytic formulae for line bundle cohomology can dramatically change this situation. Initially, these formulae were discovered empirically, through a combination of direct observation [96,97,99] and machine learning techniques [98,102].

The main observation was that line bundle cohomology dimensions on many manifolds of interest in string theory, of complex dimensions two and three, appear to be described by formulae which are essentially piecewise polynomial. More precisely, the Picard group decomposes into a (possibly infinite) number of polyhedral chambers, in each of which the cohomology dimensions are captured by a closed form expression. This observation holds for both the zeroth cohomology and the higher cohomologies, with a different chamber structure emerging in each case. The mathematical origin of these formulae has been uncovered in Refs. [100,103] for the case of complex surfaces and partially uncovered in Ref. [104] for Calabi–Yau threefolds (see Ref. [108] for a recent review).

5.1.   *Algebraic results*

For complex surfaces, it suffices to understand the zeroth cohomology function $h^0(X, V)$. The formulae for the first and second cohomologies then follow by Serre duality and the Atiyah–Singer index theorem. The zeroth cohomology formulae can be traced back to the following: (i) the existence of a fundamental region (usually the nef cone) in which the zeroth cohomology can be equated to the

Euler characteristic due to the vanishing of all higher cohomologies and (ii) the existence of a projection map, constructed using Zariski decomposition, that preserves the zeroth cohomology and relates line bundles from the outside of the fundamental region to line bundles inside this region. In Ref. [103], it was shown that the nef cone data and the Mori cone data are sufficient to determine all line bundle cohomologies on several classes of complex surfaces, including compact toric surfaces, weak Fano surfaces (generalized del Pezzo surfaces) and K3 surfaces.

For Calabi–Yau threefolds qualitatively new phenomena arise. In Ref. [104], some of the mathematical structures underlying the empirical formulae for the zeroth line bundle cohomology dimensions on Calabi–Yau threefolds were identified. In particular, it was shown that the zeroth line bundle cohomology encodes a wealth of information about the flops connecting the birational models of the manifold, as well as about Gromov–Witten (GW) invariants. It was also noted that the effective cone (containing all the line bundles with global sections, i.e., with a non-trivial zeroth cohomology group) decomposes into cohomology chambers where the zeroth cohomology can be expressed as a topological index. The chambers were understood to be either (i) Kähler cones of birational models of X, inside which the zeroth cohomology can be equated to the Euler characteristic computed on the flopped manifold, or (ii) Zariski chambers, analogous to those arising in the two-dimensional case, where a cohomology-preserving projection operates. Moreover, it was understood that the vast majority of known Calabi–Yau threefolds admit flops, many of them flopping to manifolds isomorphic to themselves. In particular, many threefolds admit infinite sequences of flops (and hence an infinite number of zeroth cohomology chambers) and have an infinite number of contractible rational curves [109–111].

We illustrate the discussion of cohomology formulae with an example that has been previously studied in Refs. [74,96,97]. However, note that the earlier formulae were incomplete as they did not take into account the infinite number of chambers that arise in zeroth cohomology. Consider a generic hypersurface of multi-degree $(2,2,2,2)$ in $(\mathbb{P}^1)^{\times 4}$, corresponding to a smooth Calabi–Yau threefold X, known as the tetra-quadric. The manifold has $h^{1,1}(X) = 4$ and $h^{2,1}(X) = 68$. The Kähler cone $\mathcal{K}(X)$ descends from the Kähler cone of $(\mathbb{P}^1)^{\times 4}$ and we denote by $\{J_i\}_{i=1,\ldots,4}$ its generators, which are the pullbacks to X of the four $\mathbb{P}^1$ Kähler forms. A line bundle L over X is then specified by its first Chern class $c_1(L) = \sum_{i=1}^{4} k_i J_i$, where k_i are integers. The Euler characteristic of L is

$$\chi(X, L) = \int_X \text{ch}(L) \cdot \text{td}(X)$$

$$= 2(k_1 + k_2 + k_3 + k_4 + k_1 k_2 k_3$$

$$+ k_1 k_2 k_4 + k_1 k_3 k_4 + k_2 k_3 k_4). \tag{8}$$

The effective cone for this manifold consists of an infinite number of additional Kähler cones, neighboring the four boundaries of $\mathcal{K}(X)$, which corresponds to bi-rationally equivalent and isomorphic Calabi–Yau threefolds related to X by sequences of flops (see Refs. [109]). These additional cones are obtained from the Kähler cone by the action of a group generated by

$$M_1 = \begin{pmatrix} -1 & 0 & 0 & 0 \\ 2 & 1 & 0 & 0 \\ 2 & 0 & 1 & 0 \\ 2 & 0 & 0 & 1 \end{pmatrix}, \quad M_2 = \begin{pmatrix} 1 & 2 & 0 & 0 \\ 0 & -1 & 0 & 0 \\ 0 & 2 & 1 & 0 \\ 0 & 2 & 0 & 1 \end{pmatrix},$$

$$M_3 = \begin{pmatrix} 1 & 0 & 2 & 0 \\ 0 & 1 & 2 & 0 \\ 0 & 0 & -1 & 0 \\ 0 & 0 & 2 & 1 \end{pmatrix}, \quad M_4 = \begin{pmatrix} 1 & 0 & 0 & 2 \\ 0 & 1 & 0 & 2 \\ 0 & 0 & 1 & 2 \\ 0 & 0 & 0 & -1 \end{pmatrix}.$$

Consequently, any effective non-trivial line bundle L is related to a line bundle L' belonging to the closure of the Kähler cone by a finite number of transformations

$$c_1(L') = M_{i_1} M_{i_2} \dots M_{i_k} c_1(L) \in \overline{\mathcal{K}(X)}. \tag{9}$$

Since the number of global sections of a line bundle is invariant under flops, it follows that

$$h^0(X, L) = h^0(X, L') = \chi(X, L'), \tag{10}$$

where the Euler characteristic can be computed from Equation (8) and the second equality holds by Kodaira's vanishing theorem and the Kawamata–Viehweg vanishing theorem (needed on the walls separating the Kähler cone of X from the neighboring Kähler cones). In fact, there are a number of two-faces of $\overline{\mathcal{K}(X)}$ which do not belong to the interior of the extended Kähler cone and consequently are not covered by the Kawamata–Viehweg vanishing theorem. These correspond to two of the integers k_i vanishing and the other two being non-negative, which we denote by k_A and k_B. In these cases, the zeroth cohomology function is simply $(1 + k_A)(1 + k_B)$, which can be easily traced back to the zeroth cohomology of two line bundles on $\mathbb{P}^1 \times \mathbb{P}^1$.

This procedure gives an extremely efficient method for computing the zeroth cohomology of line bundles on the tetra-quadric threefold. Alternatively, one could write down an explicit formula containing an infinite number of case distinctions corresponding to the infinite number of Kähler cones obtained by flopping X. In practice, however, only a small number of such cohomology chambers matters, since the chambers are increasingly away from the original Kähler cone $\mathcal{K}(X)$ and contain line bundles where at least one of the integers k_i is very large.

Once the zeroth cohomology is known, the third cohomology follows by Serre duality,

$$h^3(X, L) = h^0(X, L^*). \tag{11}$$

Note that since the effective cone is convex, there are no line bundles, except for the trivial line bundle, that have both $h^0(X, L)$ and $h^3(X, L)$ non-vanishing.

The middle cohomologies are related to the zeroth and the third cohomologies by the formula

$$h^1(X, L) - h^2(X, L) = h^0(X, L) - h^3(X, L) - \chi(X, L). \tag{12}$$

On the tetra-quadric manifold, it turns out that almost all line bundles either have $h^1(X, L) = 0$ or $h^2(X, L) = 0$. In all these cases, Equation (12) provides a formula for the middle cohomologies. The exceptions correspond to line bundles for which two of the k_i integers are zero and the other two have opposite sign and are greater than 1 in modulus. If k_A and k_B denote the non-zero integers, it turns out that in all these exceptional cases, the following simple relation holds:

$$h^1(X, L) + h^2(X, L) = -2(1 + k_A k_B), \tag{13}$$

which together with Equation (12) fixes the middle cohomologies.

5.2. *The role of machine learning*

Machine learning played an important role in the initial identification of cohomology formulae [98,102] on complex surfaces and threefolds. It has also been used in the context of line bundles over complex curves in Ref. [112].

More concretely, in Ref. [102], it was shown that the standard black box approach based on simple fully connected networks is not of much use for the problem of finding analytic cohomology formulae, which requires the simultaneous learning of the chamber structure, as well as the polynomials describing the cohomology function in each chamber. Instead, a three-step procedure was shown to be successful. First, a neural network is set up for the purpose of learning the number of chambers and their approximate boundaries. For each so-obtained region, the corresponding cohomology polynomial can then be found by a simple fit. Finally, the polynomials are used to determine the exact boundaries of the cohomology chambers. The algorithm is capable of learning the piecewise polynomial cohomology formulae.

Conversely, and relying on the theoretical understanding of the structure of cohomology formulae [100,103,104], it was shown that machine learning of cohomology data can be used to derive information about the geometric properties of the manifold [102]. For instance, in the case of complex projective surfaces, the information about the nef cone and the Mori cone is sufficient to determine all line bundle cohomologies. However, it can be hard to obtain this information, in general. On the other hand, algorithmic methods for computing line bundle cohomology can be employed to obtain enough training input as needed to learn the cohomology formulae and then use these to extract the information about the nef cone and the Mori cone. In the case of Calabi–Yau threefolds, machine learning of cohomology formulae can be used to extract information about flops, rigid divisors and Gromov–Witten invariants.

For string theory applications, the cohomology formulae become useful if the entire chamber structure and the piecewise quasi-polynomial functions are known for both the zeroth and the higher cohomologies. This can be difficult since the number of cohomology chambers increases quickly with the Picard number of the manifold and in many cases is infinite. Finding the boundaries of the chambers and the cohomology functions can be non-trivial and machine learning may help where algebro-geometric methods become unmanageable. On the other hand, we are currently lacking a theoretical understanding of the higher line bundle cohomologies on Calabi–Yau threefolds and machine learning can provide important hints about the underlying structures. Finally, machine learning can be used to go beyond the case of abelian bundles to explore the existence of analytic formulae for the cohomology of non-abelian bundles.

6. ML Techniques for the Computation of Physical Couplings

The goal of deriving quantitative predictions from heterotic string models hinges on the resolution of the following three difficult problems:

(i) the computation of (moduli dependent) physical couplings, relying on the knowledge of the Calabi–Yau metric and the Hermitian Yang–Mills connection on the holomorphic vector bundle;

(ii) moduli stabilization, that is, the problem of fixing the free parameters of the internal geometry;

(iii) supersymmetry breaking and the derivation of the resulting properties at the electroweak scale via renormalization group analysis.

In the following discussion, we will mainly focus on the first problem, where machine learning is expected to make the strongest impact. Numerical computations of Calabi–Yau metrics and the Hermitian Yang–Mills connections for fixed values of the moduli have been performed in Refs. [113–120] and more recently in Refs. [121–127] using machine learning techniques. Most of these methods have been implemented on a case-by-case basis. However, in order to analyze a relatively large number of models, as expected to arise from the automated searches discussed above, a more systematic approach is needed.

6.1.   *Physical Yukawa couplings*

One of the key steps towards realistic particle physics from string theory is to find models with the correct Yukawa couplings. The calculation of four-dimensional physical Yukawa couplings from string theory is notoriously difficult and proceeds in three steps. First, the holomorphic Yukawa couplings, that is, the trilinear couplings in the superpotential of the form

$$\lambda_{IJK} \propto \int_X \bar{\Omega} \wedge \nu_I^a \wedge \nu_J^b \wedge \nu_K^c f_{abc}, \tag{14}$$

have to be determined. Here, Ω denotes the homomorphic $(3,0)$-form on the Calabi–Yau threefold X, while f_{abc} are structure constants descending from the structure constants of E_8. The 1-forms ν_I^a, ν_J^b and ν_K^c correspond to the matter fields and are harmonic. However, the integral in Equation (14) is quasi-topological and depends only on the cohomology classes of the 1-forms. This fact greatly simplifies the computation of the holomorphic Yukawa couplings, which can be accomplished either by algebraic methods [128–131] or by methods rooted in differential geometry [80,128,132,133]. Although non-trivial, these computations can in principle keep track analytically of the moduli dependence.

The second step is the calculation of the matter field Kähler metric which determines the field normalization and the re-scaling required to convert the holomorphic couplings into the physical Yukawa couplings. The matter field Kähler metric takes the form

$$G_{IJ} \propto \int_X \nu_I \wedge \bar{\star}_V(\nu_J), \tag{15}$$

where $\bar{\star}_V$ refers to a Hodge dual combined with a complex conjugation and an action of the Hermitian bundle metric on V. This quantity is non-holomorphic and requires not only the harmonic representatives for the 1-forms but also the knowledge of the Ricci-flat metric on X and the Hermitian Yang–Mills connection on V both of which enter in the definition of the Hodge dual $\bar{\star}_V$. The third step in the computation of physical Yukawa couplings involves the stabilization of the moduli. The existing methods are typically unable to fix all the moduli perturbatively, having to rely on difficult to handle non-perturbative arguments. A possible approach here could be to insert the values of the moduli stabilized at the perturbative level into the moduli-dependent numerical expressions for the physical Yukawa couplings and to use these values to infer in a bottom-up manner the required VEVs for the unstabilized moduli. This is a numerical optimization problem where machine learning can once again make a difference.

6.2. *Calabi–Yau metrics and Hermitian Yang–Mills connections*

The only class of heterotic Calabi–Yau models where an analytic expression for the matter field Kähler metric is known corresponds to standard embedding models. In this case, the matter field Kähler metrics for the $(1,1)$ and $(2,1)$ matter fields are essentially given by the metrics on the corresponding moduli spaces [128,134]. For non-standard embeddings, things are more complicated and, unfortunately, there are no known analytic expressions[3] for the Ricci-flat metric on X and the Hermitian Yang–Mills connection on V, except for certain approximations in a number of special cases [136]. One approach is to use Donaldson's numerical algorithm to determine the Ricci-flat Calabi–Yau metric [137–139] and the subsequent work applying this algorithm to various explicit examples and to the numerical calculation of the Hermitian Yang–Mills connection on vector bundles [113–119,140]. A significant drawback of this method is that it provides numerical expressions for the required quantities only at fixed values of the moduli; trying different points in the moduli space corresponds to re-running the algorithm from scratch which can be computationally very intensive.

6.2.1. *Ricci-flat metrics on Calabi–Yau threefolds*

Following the work of Calabi and Yau, we known that every compact Kähler manifold X with vanishing first Chern class has a unique Ricci-flat metric in every Kähler class. The problem of finding a

---

[3]Recently, analytic expressions for K3 metrics have been found in Ref. [135], however the methods used there do not have an immediate generalization to threefolds.

metric g_{CY} with vanishing Ricci curvature can be simplified to the problem of finding a metric with a prescribed volume form. Thus, if J_{CY} denotes the Kähler form associated with the unique Ricci-flat metric in a given class $[J_{CY}]$, it can be shown that J_{CY} must satisfy the equation

$$J_{CY} \wedge J_{CY} \wedge J_{CY} = \kappa \, \Omega \wedge \bar{\Omega}, \tag{16}$$

for a certain number $\kappa \in \mathbb{C}$ that only depends on the moduli. In order to find J_{CY}, one can start with a Kähler form J' in the same cohomology class, which must be related to J_{CY} by

$$J_{CY} = J' + \partial \bar{\partial} \phi, \tag{17}$$

for some smooth zero-form ϕ on X. Thus, the problem of finding the Ricci-flat metric boils down to finding the zero-form ϕ that satisfies Equation (16) — this is the Monge–Ampere equation for which Yau's non-constructive proof showed that a solution must exist [141]. The simplification brought by this reformulation is important, since the Ricci curvature depends on the second derivatives of the metric, while Equation (16) involves only the metric and not its derivatives.

There have been several proposals for how to train a neural network in order to learn the Calabi–Yau metric. Here, we outline a direct method of learning the metric, as used in Ref. [126] for the case of Calabi–Yau threefolds constructed as complete intersections in products of projective spaces. In this case, one can start with the Kähler form J' given by the pull back to X of the Fubini–Study form on the embedding space. The process of finding ϕ then proceeds in a self-supervised learning fashion by uniformly sampling points of X and minimizing a loss function that takes into account the following:

(i) how well the Monge–Ampere equation is satisfied;
(ii) the amount by which the form $J' + \partial \bar{\partial} \phi$ fails to be closed;
(iii) the amount by which different expressions fail to match on overlapping patches;
(iv) the amount by which the class of $J' + \partial \bar{\partial} \phi$ deviates from the original class of J', as measured by the corresponding overall volumes;
(v) the amount by which the Ricci curvature fails to vanish.

The computation of the Ricci-loss is expensive, as it involves derivatives of the metric. In fact, this loss is not needed, as it is already taken into account by the Monge–Ampere loss, however, it can be used as a cross-check. A key advantage of using neural networks is that numerical metrics can be computed relatively quickly (a few hours on a laptop) for any values of the moduli.

6.2.2. *Hermitian Yang–Mills connections on holomorphic line bundles*

Solving the Hermitian Yang–Mills equation $g^{a\bar{b}}F_{a\bar{b}} = 0$ requires the use of a previously trained network to compute the Ricci-flat metric $g^{a\bar{b}}$. Provided that such a neural network exists, the training of the connection network can proceed in a similar self-supervised fashion, by sampling a large number of points on the manifold and minimizing a loss function that takes into account the amount by which $g^{a\bar{b}}F_{a\bar{b}}$ fails to vanish as well as the gluing conditions between patches. Initial steps in this direction have been taken in Ref. [127].

The study of harmonic forms, needed for the computation of the matter field Kähler metric, also boils down to finding numerical solutions to PDEs, in this case, Laplace's equation on Calabi–Yau threefolds, and can be approached using similar self-supervised methods (see Refs. [142,143] for some recent work).

7. Conclusion

The primary message of this review is that the ongoing developments in string phenomenology and the new opportunities opened up by machine learning make the problem of embedding the Standard Model of particle physics into string theory much more likely to be resolved in the near future. If successful, this monumental effort would provide an ultraviolet completion of particle physics and a natural setting to address the physics beyond the Standard Model, including quantum gravity. The incorporation of AI tools into string theory make possible the implementation of an unprecedented scrutiny of the string landscape and facilitate the derivation of numerical values for the physical couplings in realistic string models.

The resolution of these long standing issues in string phenomenology would represent a major advancement in fundamental physics, with the prospect of deriving from first principles fundamental quantities in nature, such as the mass of the electron.

Acknowledgments

This work is supported by a Stephen Hawking Fellowship, EPSRC grant EP/T016280/1.

References

[1] M.R. Douglas, The Statistics of String/M Theory Vacua, *JHEP* **05** (2003), 046, available at hep-th/ 0303194.

[2] W. Taylor and Y.-N. Wang, The F-theory geometry with most flux vacua, *JHEP* **12** (2015), 164, available at 1511.03209.

[3] A. Constantin, Y.-H. He and A. Lukas, Counting string theory standard models, *Phys. Lett. B* **792** (2019), 258–262, available at 1810.00444.

[4] M. Cvetič, J. Halverson, L. Lin, M. Liu and J. Tian, Quadrillion *F*-theory compactifications with the exact chiral spectrum of the standard model, *Phys. Rev. Lett.* **123**(10) (2019), 101601, available at 1903.00009.

[5] L.B. Anderson, A. Constantin, J. Gray, A. Lukas and E. Palti, A comprehensive scan for heterotic SU(5) GUT models, *JHEP* **01** (2014), 047, available at 1307.4787.

[6] S. Abel and J. Rizos, Genetic algorithms and the search for viable string vacua, *JHEP* **08** (2014), 010, available at 1404.7359.

[7] J. Halverson, B. Nelson and F. Ruehle, Branes with brains: Exploring string vacua with deep reinforcement learning, *JHEP* **06** (2019), 003, available at 1903.11616.

[8] A. Cole, A. Schachner and G. Shiu, Searching the landscape of flux vacua with genetic algorithms, *JHEP* **11** (2019), 045, available at 1907.10072.

[9] M. Larfors and R. Schneider, Explore and exploit with heterotic line bundle models, *Fortsch. Phys.* **68**(5) (2020), 2000034, available at 2003.04817.

[10] A. Constantin, T.R. Harvey and A. Lukas, Heterotic string model building with Monad bundles and reinforcement learning (2021), available at 2108.07316.

[11] S. Krippendorf, R. Kroepsch and M. Syvaeri, Revealing systematics in phenomenologically viable flux vacua with reinforcement learning, (2021), available at 2107.04039.

[12] S. Abel, A. Constantin, T.R. Harvey and A. Lukas, Evolving heterotic gauge backgrounds: Genetic algorithms versus reinforcement learning (2021), available at 2110.14029.

[13] S. Abel, A. Constantin, T.R. Harvey and A. Lukas, String model building, reinforcement learning and genetic algorithms, *Nankai Symposium on Mathematical Dialogues: In Celebration of S.S.Chern's 110th Anniversary*, 2021, available at 2111.07333.

[14] A. Cole, S. Krippendorf, A. Schachner and G. Shiu, Probing the structure of string theory Vacua with genetic algorithms and reinforcement learning, *35th Conference on Neural Information Processing Systems*, 2021, available at 2111.11466.

[15] G.J. Loges and G. Shiu, Breeding realistic D-brane models (2021), available at 2112.08391.

[16] Y.-H. He, Machine-learning the string landscape, *Phys. Lett. B* **774** (2017), 564–568.

[17] Y.-H. He, Deep-learning the landscape (2017), available at 1706.02714.

[18] F. Ruehle, Evolving neural networks with genetic algorithms to study the String Landscape, *JHEP* **08** (2017), 038, available at 1706.07024.

[19] J. Carifio, J. Halverson, D. Krioukov and B.D. Nelson, Machine Learning in the String Landscape, *JHEP* **09** (2017), 157, available at 1707.00655.

[20] D. Krefl and R.-K. Seong, Machine Learning of Calabi-Yau volumes, *Phys. Rev. D* 96(6) (2017), 066014, available at 1706.03346.

[21] F. Ruehle, Data science applications to string theory, *Phys. Rept.* **839** (2020), 1–117.

[22] Y.-H. He, Universes as Big Data, *Int. J. Mod. Phys. A* **36**(29) (2021), 2130017, available at 2011.14442.

[23] P. Candelas, G.T. Horowitz, A. Strominger and E. Witten, Vacuum configurations for superstrings, *Nucl. Phys. B* **258** (1985), 46–74.

[24] E. Calabi, The space of Kähler metrics, *Proc. Internat. Congress Math. Amsterdam* **2** (1954), 206–207.

[25] E. Calabi, On Kähler manifolds with vanishing canonical class, *Algebraic Geom. Topol. Symp. Honor S. Lefschetz* **Princeton Mathematical Series 12** (1957), 78–89.

[26] S.-T. Yau, Calabi's conjecture and some new results in algebraic geometry, *Proc. Nat. Acad. Sci. USA* **74**(5) (1977), 1798–1799.

[27] P. Candelas, A.M. Dale, C.A. Lutken and R. Schimmrigk, Complete intersection Calabi-Yau manifolds, *Nucl. Phys. B* **298** (1988), 493.

[28] L.B. Anderson, F. Apruzzi, X. Gao, J. Gray and S.-J. Lee, A new construction of Calabi-Yau manifolds: Generalized CICYs, *Nucl. Phys. B* **906** (2016), 441–496, available at 1507.03235.

[29] M. Kreuzer and H. Skarke, Complete classification of reflexive polyhedra in four-dimensions, *Adv. Theor. Math. Phys.* **4** (2002), 1209–1230, available at hep-th/0002240.

[30] J. Bao, Y.-H. He, E. Hirst, J. Hofscheier, A. Kasprzyk and S. Majumder, Polytopes and Machine Learning (2021), available at 2109.09602.

[31] D.S. Berman, Y.-H. He and E. Hirst, Machine Learning Calabi-Yau hypersurfaces, *Phys. Rev. D* **105**(6) (2022) 066002, available at 2112.06350.

[32] S.K. Donaldson, Anti self-dual Yang-Mills connections over complex algebraic surfaces and stable vector bundles, *Proc. Lond. Math. Soc.* **50** (1985) 1–26.

[33] K. Uhlenbeck and S.-T. Yau, On the existence of Hermitian-Yang-Mills connections in stable vector bundles, *Comm. Pure App. Math.* **39**(S1) (1986).

[34] L.B. Anderson, Heterotic and M-theory compactifications for string phenomenology, Ph.D. Thesis, 2008.

[35] B.R. Greene, K.H. Kirklin, P.J. Miron and G.G. Ross, A three generation superstring model. 1. Compactification and discrete symmetries, *Nucl. Phys. B* **278** (1986), 667–693.

[36] B.R. Greene, K.H. Kirklin, P.J. Miron and G.G. Ross, A three generation superstring model. 2. Symmetry breaking and the low-energy theory, *Nucl. Phys. B* **292** (1987), 606–652.

[37] R. Schimmrigk, A new construction of a three generation Calabi-Yau manifold, *Phys. Lett. B* **193** (1987), 175.

[38] R. Schimmrigk, Heterotic (2,2) Vacua: Manifold theory and exact results, *Nucl. Phys. B* 342 (1990), 231–245.

[39] V. Braun, P. Candelas and R. Davies, A three-generation Calabi-Yau manifold with small Hodge numbers, *Fortsch. Phys.* **58** (2010), 467–502, available at 0910.5464.

[40] V. Braun, P. Candelas, R. Davies and R. Donagi, The MSSM spectrum from (0,2)-deformations of the heterotic standard embedding, *JHEP* **05** (2012), 127, available at 1112.1097.

[41] P. Candelas, A. Constantin and C. Mishra, Calabi-Yau threefolds with small Hodge numbers, *Fortsch. Phys.* **66**(6) (2018), 1800029, available at 1602.06303.

[42] J. Distler, Resurrecting (2,0) compactifications, *Phys. Lett. B* **188** (1987), 431–436.

[43] J. Distler and B.R. Greene, Aspects of (2,0) string compactifications, *Nucl. Phys. B* **304** (1988), 1–62.

[44] P. Candelas and R. Davies, New Calabi-Yau manifolds with small Hodge numbers, *Fortsch. Phys.* **58** (2010), 383–466, available at 0809.4681.

[45] V. Braun, On free quotients of complete intersection Calabi-Yau manifolds, *JHEP* **1104** (2011), 005, available at 1003.3235.

[46] P. Candelas and A. Constantin, Completing the Web of Z_3 – quotients of complete intersection Calabi-Yau manifolds, *Fortsch. Phys.* **60** (2012), 345–369, available at 1010.1878.

[47] A. Braun, A. Lukas and C. Sun, Discrete symmetries of Calabi-Yau hypersurfaces in toric four-folds, *Commun. Math. Phys.* **360**(3) (2018), 935–984, available at 1704.07812.

[48] P. Candelas, A. Constantin and C. Mishra, Hodge numbers for CICYs with symmetries of order divisible by 4, *Fortsch. Phys.* **64**(6–7) (2016), 463–509, available at 1511.01103.

[49] M. Larfors, D. Passaro and R. Schneider, Heterotic line bundle models on generalized complete intersection Calabi Yau manifolds, *JHEP* **05** (2021), 105, available at 2010.09763.

[50] R. Friedman, J. Morgan and E. Witten, Vector bundles and F theory, *Commun. Math. Phys.* **187** (1997), 679–743, available at hep-th/9701162.

[51] R. Friedman, J.W. Morgan and E. Witten, Vector bundles over elliptic fibrations (1997), available at alg-geom/9709029.

[52] R. Donagi, A. Lukas, B.A. Ovrut and D. Waldram, Nonperturbative vacua and particle physics in M theory, *JHEP* **05** (1999), 018, available at hep-th/9811168.

[53] B. Andreas, G. Curio and A. Klemm, Towards the standard model spectrum from elliptic Calabi-Yau, *Int. J. Mod. Phys.* **A19** (2004), 1987, available at hep-th/9903052.

[54] R. Donagi, A. Lukas, B.A. Ovrut and D.Waldram, Holomorphic vector bundles and nonperturbative vacua in M theory, *JHEP* **06** (1999), 034, available at hep-th/9901009.

[55] R. Donagi, B.A. Ovrut, T. Pantev and D. Waldram, Standard models from heterotic M theory, *Adv. Theor. Math. Phys.* **5** (2002), 93–137, available at hep-th/9912208.

[56] R. Donagi, B.A. Ovrut, T. Pantev and D. Waldram, Standard model bundles on nonsimply connected Calabi-Yau threefolds, *JHEP* **08** (2001), 053, available at hep-th/0008008.

[57] R. Donagi, B.A. Ovrut, T. Pantev and D. Waldram, Standard model bundles, *Adv. Theor. Math. Phys.* **5** (2002), 563–615, available at math/0008010.

[58] V. Braun, Y.-H. He, B.A. Ovrut and T. Pantev, A heterotic standard model, *Phys. Lett. B* **618** (2005), 252–258, available at hep-th/0501070.

[59] V. Braun, Y.-H. He, B.A. Ovrut and T. Pantev, A standard model from the E(8) x E(8) heterotic superstring, *JHEP* **0506** (2005), 039, available at hep-th/0502155.

[60] V. Braun, Y.-H. He, B.A. Ovrut and T. Pantev, The exact MSSM spectrum from string theory, *JHEP* **0605** (2006), 043, available at hep-th/0512177.

[61] R. Blumenhagen, S. Moster and T. Weigand, Heterotic GUT and standard model vacua from simply connected Calabi-Yau manifolds, *Nucl. Phys. B* **751** (2006), 186–221, available at hep-th/0603015.

[62] R. Blumenhagen, S. Moster, R. Reinbacher and T. Weigand, Massless spectra of three generation U(N) heterotic string vacua, JHEP 0705 (2007), 041, available at hep-th/0612039.

[63] M. Gabella, Y.-H. He and A. Lukas, An abundance of heterotic vacua, *JHEP* **12** (2008), 027, available at 0808.2142.

[64] L.B. Anderson, X. Gao and M. Karkheiran, Extending the geometry of heterotic spectral cover constructions, *Nucl. Phys. B* **956** (2020), 115003, available at 1912.00971.

[65] S. Kachru, Some three generation (0,2) Calabi-Yau models, *Phys. Lett. B* **349** (1995), 76–82, available at hep-th/9501131.

[66] L.B. Anderson, Y.-H. He and A. Lukas, Monad bundles in heterotic string compactifications, *JHEP* **07** (2008), 104, available at 0805.2875.

[67] L.B. Anderson, J. Gray, Y.-H. He and A. Lukas, Exploring positive Monad bundles and a new heterotic standard model, *JHEP* **02** (2010), 054, available at 0911.1569.

[68] Y.-H. He, S.-J. Lee and A. Lukas, Heterotic models from vector bundles on toric Calabi-Yau manifolds, *JHEP* **05** (2010), 071, available at 0911.0865.

[69] V. Bouchard and R. Donagi, An SU(5) heterotic standard model, *Phys. Lett. B* **633** (2006), 783–791, available at hep-th/0512149.

[70] R. Blumenhagen, G. Honecker and T. Weigand, Loop-corrected compactifications of the heterotic string with line bundles, **JHEP 0506** (2005), 020, available at hep-th/0504232.

[71] L.B. Anderson, J. Gray, A. Lukas and E. Palti, Two hundred heterotic standard models on smooth Calabi-Yau threefolds, *Phys. Rev. D* **84** (2011), 106005, available at 1106.4804.

[72] L.B. Anderson, J. Gray, A. Lukas and E. Palti, Heterotic line bundle standard models, *JHEP* **06** (2012), 113, available at 1202.1757.

[73] Y.-H. He, S.-J. Lee, A. Lukas and C. Sun, Heterotic model building: 16 Special manifolds, *JHEP* **06** (2014), 077, available at 1309.0223.

[74] E.I. Buchbinder, A. Constantin and A. Lukas, The Moduli space of heterotic line bundle models: A case study for the tetra-quadric, *JHEP* **03** (2014), 025, available at 1311.1941.

[75] E.I. Buchbinder, A. Constantin and A. Lukas, A heterotic standard model with $B - L$ symmetry and a stable proton, *JHEP* **06** (2014), 100, available at 1404.2767.

[76] E.I. Buchbinder, A. Constantin and A. Lukas, Non-generic couplings in supersymmetric standard models, *Phys. Lett. B* **748** (2015), 251–254, available at 1409.2412.

[77] E.I. Buchbinder, A. Constantin and A. Lukas, Heterotic QCD axion, *Phys. Rev. D* **91**(4) (2015), 046010, available at 1412.8696.

[78] L.B. Anderson, A. Constantin, S.-J. Lee and A. Lukas, Hypercharge flux in heterotic compactifications, *Phys. Rev. D* **91**(4), (2015), 046008, available at 1411.0034.

[79] A. Constantin, A. Lukas and C. Mishra, The family problem: Hints from heterotic line bundle models, *JHEP* **03** (2016), 173, available at 1509.02729.

[80] E.I. Buchbinder, A. Constantin, J. Gray and A. Lukas, Yukawa unification in heterotic string theory, *Phys. Rev. D* **94**(4) (2016), 046005, available at 1606.04032.

[81] P.S. Green, T. Hubsch and C.A. Lutken, All Hodge numbers of all complete intersection Calabi-Yau manifolds, *Class. Quant. Grav.* **6** (1989), 105–124.

[82] H. Schenck, M. Stillman and B. Yuan, Calabi-Yau threefolds in $\mathbb{P}^n$ and Gorenstein rings (2020), available at 2011.10871.

[83] A. Constantin, J. Gray and A. Lukas, Hodge numbers for all CICY quotients, *JHEP* **01** (2017), 001, available at 1607.01830.

[84] S.R. Sutton and A.G. Barto, *Reinforcement Learning: An Introduction*, 2nd ed., MIT Press (2018).

[85] T.R. Harvey and A. Lukas, Particle physics model building with reinforcement learning (2021), available at 2103.04759.

[86] G. Kántor, V. Niarchos and C. Papageorgakis, Conformal bootstrap with reinforcement learning, *Phys. Rev. D* **105**(2) (2022), 025018, available at 2108.09330.

[87] S. Gukov, J. Halverson, F. Ruehle and P. Sułkowski, Learning to unknot, *Mach. Learn. Sci. Tech.* **2**(2) (2021), 025035, available at 2010.16263.

[88] E. Parr and P.K.S. Vaudrevange, Contrast data mining for the MSSM from strings, *Nucl. Phys. B* **952** (2020), 114922, available at 1910.13473.

[89] A. Mütter, E. Parr and P.K.S. Vaudrevange, Deep learning in the heterotic orbifold landscape, *Nucl. Phys. B* **940** (2019), 113–129, available at 1811.05993.

[90] A.E. Faraggi, G. Harries, B. Percival and J. Rizos, Towards machine learning in the classification of $\mathbb{Z}_2 \times \mathbb{Z}_2$ orbifold compactifications, *J. Phys. Conf. Ser.* **1586**(1) (2020), 012032, available at 1901.04448.

[91] R. Deen, Y.-H. He, S.-J. Lee and A. Lukas, Machine Learning string standard models (2020), available at 2003.13339.

[92] A.P. Braun, C.R. Brodie and A. Lukas, Heterotic line bundle models on elliptically fibered Calabi-Yau three-folds, *JHEP* **04** (2018), 087, available at 1706.07688.

[93] A.P. Braun, C.R. Brodie, A. Lukas and F. Ruehle, NS5-Branes and line bundles in heterotic/F-theory duality, *Phys. Rev. D* **98**(12) (2018), 126004, available at 1803.06190.

[94] H. Otsuka, SO(32) heterotic line bundle models, *JHEP*, **05** (2018), 045, available at 1801.03684.

[95] H. Otsuka and K. Takemoto, SO(32) heterotic standard model vacua in general Calabi-Yau compactifications, *JHEP* **11** (2018), 034, available at 1809.00838.

[96] A. Constantin, Heterotic string models on smooth Calabi-Yau three-folds, Ph.D. Thesis, 2013, 1808.09993.

[97] A. Constantin and A. Lukas, Formulae for line bundle cohomology on Calabi-Yau threefolds, *Fortsch. Phys.* **67**(12) (2019), 1900084, available at 1808.09992.

[98] D. Klaewer and L. Schlechter, Machine Learning line bundle cohomologies of hypersurfaces in toric varieties, *Phys. Lett. B* **789** (2019), 438–443, available at 1809.02547.

[99] M. Larfors and R. Schneider, Line bundle cohomologies on CICYs with Picard number two, *Fortsch. Phys.* **67**(12) (2019), 1900083, available at 1906.00392.

[100] C.R. Brodie, A. Constantin, R. Deen and A. Lukas, Topological formulae for the zeroth cohomology of line bundles on surfaces (2019), available at 1906.08363.

[101] C.R. Brodie, A. Constantin, R. Deen and A. Lukas, Index formulae for line bundle cohomology on complex surfaces, *Fortsch. Phys.* **68**(2) (2020), 1900086, available at 1906.08769.

[102] C.R. Brodie, A. Constantin, R. Deen and A. Lukas, Machine Learning line bundle cohomology, *Fortsch. Phys.* **68**(1) (2020), 1900087, available at 1906.08730.

[103] C.R. Brodie and A. Constantin, Cohomology chambers on complex surfaces and elliptically fibered Calabi-Yau three-folds (2020), available at 2009.01275.

[104] C.R. Brodie, A. Constantin and A. Lukas, Flops, Gromov-Witten invariants and symmetries of line bundle cohomology on Calabi-Yau three-folds (2020), available at 2010.06597.

[105] L.B. Anderson, J. Gray, Y.-H. He, S.-J. Lee and A. Lukas, *CICY package, based on methods described in arXiv:0911.1569, arXiv:0911.0865, arXiv:0805.2875, hep-th/0703249, hep-th/0702210*.

[106] *Cohomcalg Package*, 2010. High-performance line bundle cohomology computation based on methods described in arXiv:1003.5217, arXiv:1006.2392, arXiv:1006.0780. Download link: http://wwwth. mppmu.mpg.de/members/blumenha/cohomcalg/.

[107] M. Larfors and R. Schneider, Pycicy - a Python Cicy Toolkit (2019). Doi: 10.5281/zenodo.3243914, [githublink].

[108] C. Brodie, A. Constantin, J. Gray, A. Lukas and F. Ruehle, Recent developments in line bundle cohomology and applications to string phenomenology, Nankai Symposium on Mathematical Dialogues: In celebration of S.S.Chern's 110th anniversary (2021), available at 2112.12107.

[109] C. Brodie, A. Constantin, A. Lukas and F. Ruehle, Flops for complete intersection Calabi-Yau threefolds (2021), available at 2112.12106.

[110] C.R. Brodie, A. Constantin, A. Lukas and F. Ruehle, Swampland conjectures and infinite flop chains (2021), available at 2104.03325.

[111] C.R. Brodie, A. Constantin, A. Lukas and F. Ruehle, Geodesics in the extended Kähler cone of Calabi-Yau threefolds, *JHEP* **03** (2022), 024, available at 2108.10323.

[112] M. Bies, M. Cvetič, R. Donagi, L. Lin, M. Liu and F. Ruehle, Machine Learning and algebraic approaches towards complete matter spectra in 4d F-theory, *JHEP* **01** (2021), 196, available at 2007.00009.

[113] M. Headrick and T. Wiseman, Numerical Ricci-flat metrics on K3, *Class. Quant. Grav.* **22** (2005), 4931–4960, available at hep-th/0506129.

[114] M.R. Douglas, R.L. Karp, S. Lukic and R. Reinbacher, Numerical solution to the hermitian Yang-Mills equation on the Fermat quintic, *JHEP* **0712** (2007), 083, available at hep-th/0606261.

[115] C. Doran, M. Headrick, C.P. Herzog, J. Kantor and T. Wiseman, Numerical Kahler-Einstein metric on the third del Pezzo, *Commun. Math. Phys.* **282** (2008), 357–393, available at hep-th/0703057.

[116] M. Headrick and A. Nassar, Energy functionals for Calabi-Yau metrics, *Adv. Theor. Math. Phys.* **17**(5) (2013), 867–902, available at 0908.2635.

[117] M.R. Douglas and S. Klevtsov, Black holes and balanced metrics (2008), available at 0811.0367.

[118] L.B. Anderson, V. Braun, R.L. Karp and B.A. Ovrut, Numerical Hermitian Yang-Mills connections and vector bundle stability in heterotic theories, *JHEP* **1006** (2010), 107, available at 1004.4399.

[119] L.B. Anderson, V. Braun and B.A. Ovrut, Numerical Hermitian Yang-Mills connections and Kahler Cone substructure, *JHEP* **1201** (2012), 014, available at 1103.3041.

[120] W. Cui and J. Gray, Numerical metrics, curvature expansions and Calabi-Yau manifolds, *JHEP* **05** (2020), 044, available at 1912.11068.

[121] A. Ashmore, Y.-H. He and B.A. Ovrut, Machine Learning Calabi-Yau metrics, *Fortsch. Phys.* **68**(9) (2020), 2000068, available at 1910.08605.

[122] M.R. Douglas, S. Lakshminarasimhan and Y. Qi, Numerical Calabi-Yau metrics from holomorphic networks (2020), available at 2012.04797.

[123] L.B. Anderson, M. Gerdes, J. Gray, S. Krippendorf, N. Raghuram and F. Ruehle, Moduli-dependent Calabi-Yau and $SU(3)$-structure metrics from Machine Learning (2020), available at 2012.04656.

[124] V. Jejjala, D.K.M. Pena and C. Mishra, Neural network approximations for Calabi-Yau metrics (2020), available at 2012.15821.

[125] A. Ashmore, L. Calmon, Y.-H. He and B.A. Ovrut, Calabi-Yau metrics, energy functionals and Machine-Learning (2021), available at 2112.10872.

[126] M. Larfors, A. Lukas, F. Ruehle and R. Schneider, Learning size and shape of Calabi-Yau spaces (2021), available at 2111.01436.

[127] A. Ashmore, R. Deen, Y.-H. He and B.A. Ovrut, Machine learning line bundle connections, *Phys. Lett. B* **827** (2022), 136972, available at 2110.12483.

[128] P. Candelas, Yukawa couplings between (2,1) forms, *Nucl. Phys. B* **298** (1988), 458.

[129] V. Braun, Y.-H. He and B.A. Ovrut, Yukawa couplings in heterotic standard models, *JHEP* **04** (2006), 019, available at hep-th/0601204.

[130] L.B. Anderson, J. Gray, D. Grayson, Y.-H. He and A. Lukas, Yukawa couplings in heterotic compactification, *Commun. Math. Phys.* **297** (2010), 95–127, available at 0904.2186.

[131] L.B. Anderson, J. Gray and B. Ovrut, Yukawa textures from heterotic stability walls, *JHEP* **1005** (2010), 086, available at 1001.2317.

[132] S. Blesneag, E.I. Buchbinder, P. Candelas and A. Lukas, Holomorphic Yukawa couplings in heterotic string theory, *JHEP* **01** (2016), 152, available at 1512.05322.

[133] S. Blesneag, E.I. Buchbinder and A. Lukas, Holomorphic Yukawa couplings for complete intersection Calabi-Yau manifolds, *JHEP* **01** (2017), 119, available at 1607.03461.

[134] P. Candelas and X. de la Ossa, Moduli space of Calabi-Yau manifolds, *Nucl. Phys. B* **355** (1991), 455–481.

[135] S. Kachru, A. Tripathy and M. Zimet, K3 metrics (2020), available at 2006.02435.

[136] S. Blesneag, E.I. Buchbinder, A. Constantin, A. Lukas and E. Palti, Matter field Kähler metric in heterotic string theory from localisation, *JHEP* **04** (2018), 139, available at 1801.09645.

[137] S.K. Donaldson, Scalar curvature and projective embeddings. I, *J. Differential Geom.* **59** (2001), 479–522.

[138] S.K. Donaldson, Scalar curvature and projective embeddings. II, *Q. J. Math.* **56** (2005), 345–356.

[139] S.K. Donaldson, Some numerical results in complex differential geometry (2005), available at math.DG/0512625.

[140] X. Wang, Canonical metrics on stable vector bundles, *Comm. Anal. Geom.* **13** (2005), 253–285.

[141] S.-T. Yau, On the Ricci curvature of a compact Kahler manifold and the complex Monge-Ampere equation. I, *Comm. Pure Appl. Math.* **31** (1978), 847–865.

[142] A. Ashmore, Eigenvalues and eigenforms on Calabi-Yau threefolds (2020), available at 2011.13929.

[143] A. Ashmore and F. Ruehle, Moduli-dependent KK towers and the swampland distance conjecture on the quintic Calabi-Yau manifold, *Phys. Rev. D* **103**(10) (2021), 106028, available at 2103.07472.

Chapter 5

Deep Learning: Complete Intersection Calabi–Yau Manifolds

Harold Erbin[*,†,‡,¶] **and Riccardo Finotello**[‡,§,‖]

*Center for Theoretical Physics, Massachusetts Institute of Technology,
Cambridge, MA 02139, USA*
†*NSF AI Institute for Artificial Intelligence and Fundamental Interactions*
‡*Université Paris Saclay, CEA, LIST, Palaiseau 91120, France*
§*Université Paris Saclay, CEA, Service d'Études Analytiques et de
Réactivité des Surfaces (SEARS), Gif-sur-Yvette 91191, France*

¶*erbin@mit.edu*
‖*riccardo.finotello@cea.fr*

Abstract

We review advancements in deep learning techniques for complete intersection Calabi–Yau (CICY) 3- and 4-folds, with the aim of understanding better how to handle algebraic topological data with machine learning. We first discuss methodological aspects and data analysis, before describing neural network architectures. Then, we describe the state-of-the-art accuracy in predicting Hodge numbers. We include new results on extrapolating predictions from low to high Hodge numbers, and conversely.

1. Introduction

In recent years, deep learning has become a relevant research theme in physics and mathematics. It is a very efficient method for data processing, and elaboration and exploration of patterns [23]. Though the basic building blocks are not new [49], the increase in computational capabilities and the creation of larger databases lead new deep learning techniques to thrive. Specifically, the understanding of the geometrical structures [9,10] and the representation learning [5] are of particular interest from a mathematical and theoretical physics points of view [33–35,52].

We are interested in applications of data science and deep learning techniques for algebraic topology, especially Hodge numbers, of complete intersection Calabi–Yau (CICY) manifolds [13,27,28]. Traditional methods from algebraic topology lead to complicated algorithms, without closed-form solutions in general. Hence, it is interesting to derive new computational methods: given its track record, deep learning is particularly promising as a path to the discovery of novel structures and analytic formulas but also to the classification of Calabi–Yau manifolds [2,30,32], which is still an important open mathematical problem. However, the first step is to be able to reproduce known results, which is non-trivial given that algebraic topology provides a genuinely new type of data compared to what is usually studied by computer scientists. The computation using deep learning has been studied in Refs. [11,12,31,38] (see Refs. [36,37,43,45,51] for other works related to CICY) before being almost completely solved by Refs. [19–21]: the objective of this paper is to review these state-of-the-art results.

CICYs are also relevant for string theory model building where CY manifolds are needed to describe the compactified dimensions. The general properties of the 4-dimensional effective field theories can be determined from the analysis of the topology [24]. Given the complexity of string vacua [18,29], deep learning techniques may enable faster computations and may grant a larger exploration of possibilities.

CICY 3- and 4-folds have already been entirely classified and all of their topological properties are known:

- in complex dimension 3, there are 7890 CICYs which have been represented in two different ways: the *original* dataset [13,27,28] contains the original list of CICYs, while a newer classification [1] uses the *favorable* representation whenever possible. We shall focus on the former, the first being the most difficult case from a machine learning point of view;

- in complex dimension 4, 921 497 distinct CICYs were classified [25,26].

In this sense, they represent the ideal benchmark to test learning algorithms in supervised tasks.

2.   Data Analysis of CICYs

CY N-folds are N-dimensional complex manifolds with $SU(N)$ holonomy or, equivalently, with a vanishing first Chern class [30]. They are characterized by their topological properties, such as the Hodge numbers and the Euler characteristic. These features directly translate into properties of the 4-dimensional effective action, such as the number of chiral multiplets in heterotic compactifications, and the number of hyper and vector multiplets in type II compactifications. Ultimately, these are connected to the number of fermion generations, which could be used to test the effectiveness of the models.

The simplest CYs are constructed as *complete intersections* of hypersurfaces in a product of complex projective spaces $\mathbb{P}^{n_1} \times \cdots \times \mathbb{P}^{n_m}$ [28]. They are defined by systems of homogeneous polynomial equations, whose solutions identify CY manifolds. As we are interested in classifying CYs as topological manifolds, it is sufficient to keep track only of the dimensions of the projective spaces and the degree of the equations. In the general case of m projective spaces and k equations, a CICY X is represented by a *configuration matrix* of integer entries:

$$
X = \left[\begin{array}{c|ccc}
\mathbb{P}^{n_1} & \alpha_1^1 & \cdots & \alpha_k^1 \\
\vdots & \vdots & \ddots & \vdots \\
\mathbb{P}^{n_m} & \alpha_1^m & \cdots & \alpha_k^m
\end{array} \right], \tag{1}
$$

where α_r^i are positive integers satisfying

$$
n_i + 1 = \sum_{r=1}^{k} \alpha_r^i, \tag{2}
$$

encoding the vanishing of the first Chern class, and

$$\dim_{\mathbb{C}} X = \sum_{i=1}^{m} n_i - k = N, \tag{3}$$

where, in the following, $N = 3, 4$. Note that different configuration matrices can describe the same topological manifold. First, any permutation of lines and columns does not modify the intersection of the hypersurfaces. Second, different intersections can define the same manifold. Such ambiguity is often fixed by imposing some ordering on the coefficients. Moreover, in some cases, an optimal representation of X is available: in its *favorable* representation, the configuration matrix enables easier computations of topological quantities.

The classification of CICY 3-folds has been dealt with in Ref. [13], which lead to a dataset of 7890 configuration matrices, 22 of which in block diagonal form. In this dataset, 62 % of the configuration matrices are in a favorable representation, in which $h^{(1,1)} = m$. More recently, a different dataset of CICY 3-folds has been produced [1]: in this case, 99 % of the manifolds are in favorable representation. In what follows, we focus on the first, original dataset as it represents a more challenging and fascinating scenario from a machine learning point of view. As such, we deal with configuration matrices whose maximal size is 12×15. CICY 4-folds have also been classified in Refs. [25,26], producing 921 497 distinct matrices, with 15 813 manifolds in block diagonal form, of maximal size 16×20. Here, 55 % of the matrices are in a favorable representation. In our analysis, we discard the block diagonal matrices, as they can be understood from lower-dimensional manifolds.

2.1. *Hodge number distributions*

The number of Hodge numbers depends on the complex dimension N of X. In the case most relevant to string theory, $\dim_{\mathbb{C}} X = 3$ implies the existence of only two non-trivial Hodge numbers, $h^{(1,1)}$ and $h^{(2,1)}$, whose distributions are shown in Figure 1. Their average, minimum and maximum values are

$$\langle h^{(1,1)} \rangle = 7.4_1^{19}, \quad \langle h^{(2,1)} \rangle = 29_{15}^{101}. \tag{4}$$

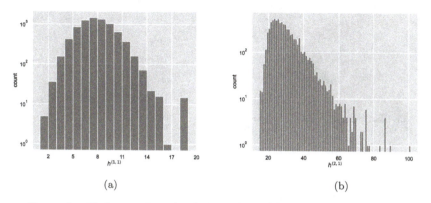

Figure 1.   Hodge numbers for CICY 3-folds. (a) $h(1,1)$ and (b) $h(2,1)$.

As visible in the figures, the two distributions greatly differ, with $h^{(1,1)}$ being almost normally distributed, contrary to $h^{(2,1)}$ which presents also several missing values towards the upper limit of its range.

CICY 4-folds are used for M- and F-theory compactifications: in this case, there are four non-trivial Hodge numbers whose distributions are shown in Figure 2. As for the previous case, their average values and ranges are

$$\langle h^{(1,1)} \rangle = 10_1^{24}, \quad \langle h^{(2,1)} \rangle = 0.8_0^{33},$$
$$\langle h^{(3,1)} \rangle = 40_{20}^{426}, \quad \langle h^{(2,2)} \rangle = 240_{204}^{1752}. \tag{5}$$

Note that, in this case, the distributions are highly unbalanced and defined on vastly different ranges. For instance, $h^{(2,1)}$ vanishes for 70 % of the configuration matrices in the dataset. Moreover, $h^{(2,1)}$ and $h^{(2,2)}$ look more similar to exponential distributions, which, in turn, may complicate the learning process. Note that the Hodge numbers are not independent [26]:

$$-4h^{(1,1)} + 2h^{(2,1)} - 4h^{(3,1)} + h^{(2,2)} = 44. \tag{6}$$

In each case, a linear combination of the Hodge numbers provides another topological number, the Euler characteristics, which is

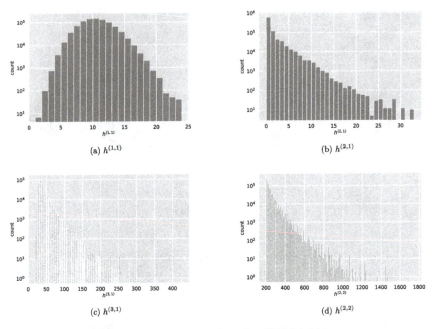

Figure 2. Hodge numbers for CICY 4-folds.

much simpler. For the 4-folds, we have

$$\chi = 4 + 2h^{(1,1)} - 4h^{(2,1)} + 2h^{(3,1)} + h^{(2,2)}, \tag{7}$$

while for the 3-folds, the formula reads

$$\chi = 2(h^{(1,1)} - h^{(2,1)}). \tag{8}$$

Note that they do not provide constraints on the Hodge numbers strictly speaking, since the Euler number is not a fixed number but depends on the CY.

2.2. Data engineering

In order to better understand patterns and characteristics of the data, first, we proceed to a phase of exploratory data analysis [20]. In turn, the in-depth study of the CICY datasets helps in designing the learning algorithms. As a reference, we adopt the machine learning dictionary and call *features* the input variables and *labels*

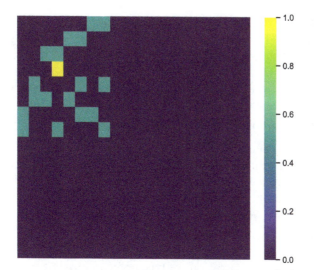

Figure 3. Configuration matrix of a CICY 4-folds ($h^{(1,1)} = 8$, $h^{(2,1)} = 0$, $h^{(3,1)} = 38$, $h^{(2,2)} = 228$) normalized by the highest possible entry in the training set.

the target predictions, for simplicity. Note that the following analysis should be performed on the subset of configuration matrices used for training the learning algorithms: in this case, we are authorized to access the full information on features and labels, which should not be touched in the case of the test set.

We start from a phase of *feature engineering* [59], in which new input features are derived from the raw input, that is the configuration matrix (see Figure 3). Engineered features are redundant variables, encoding information already present in the input data, under a different representation. They may help during the learning phase by providing an alternative formulation of salient characteristics. In the case of CICYs, useful quantities may be [30]

- the number of projective spaces m,
- the number of equations k,
- the number f of $\mathbb{P}^1$,
- the number of $\mathbb{P}^2$,
- the number F of $\mathbb{P}^n$, with $n \neq 1$,
- the excess number $N_{ex} = \sum_{r=1}^{F} (n_r + f + m - 2k)$,
- the dimension of the cohomology group $\mathrm{H}^{(0)}$ of the ambient space,
- the Frobenius norm of the matrix,

- the list of dimensions of the projective spaces and statistics (mean, min, max and median),
- the list of degree of the equations and statistics (mean, min, max and median),
- K-means clustering of the matrices (with a variable number of clusters),
- principal components of the configuration matrix.

The Principal Components Analysis (PCA), through the study of the singular value decomposition, may lead to clues for the learning algorithms. As shown in Figure 4 in the case of CICY 3-folds, the majority of the variance is contained in a smaller number of entries of the configuration matrices. Ultimately, this may help in finding the optimal learning algorithms: the information is contained in smaller portions of the configuration matrix, which can thus be analyzed in smaller patches.

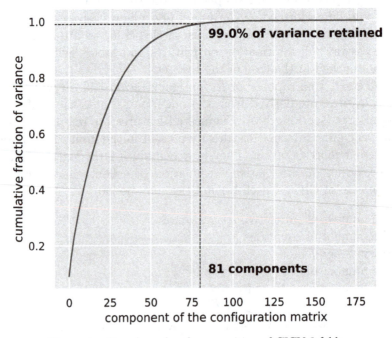

Figure 4.   Singular value decomposition of CICY 3-folds.

The next important step is the *feature selection*, that is, the extraction of a smaller number of features which may be more relevant to the determination of the labels. To get an idea, the correlations between engineered features may give an indication on the linear dependence of the features. Figure 5 shows the case of the CICY 3-folds: the number of projective spaces m, together with the rank and norm of the configuration matrix, seems to show a good correlation with the labels.

Other strategies for the selection of the features can also be used. For instance, decision trees [54] may return relevant information: as their binary structure is based on the optimal split of the variables to classify or predict the labels, the analysis of the choices made by the algorithm naturally selects the most important features. In Figure 6, we show the importance of the scalar engineered features: the number of projective spaces effectively seems to be relevant for predicting the labels. Figure 7 shows the cumulative importance of the vector-like engineered features: the dimensions of the projective spaces, together

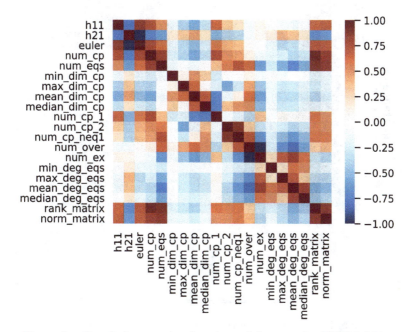

Figure 5. Correlation matrix of engineered features for CICY 3-folds.

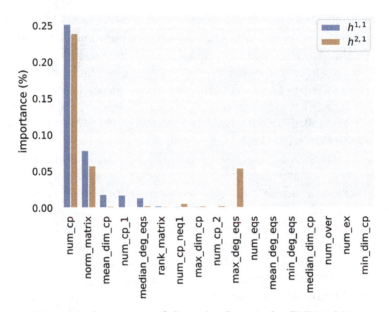

Figure 6.   Importance of the scalar features for CICY 3-folds.

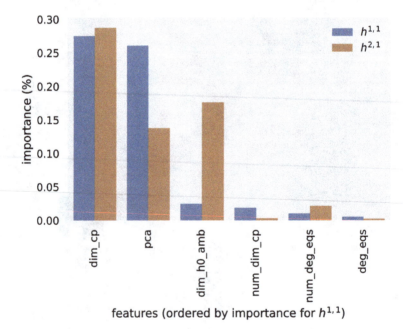

Figure 7.   Importance of the vector features for CICY 3-folds.

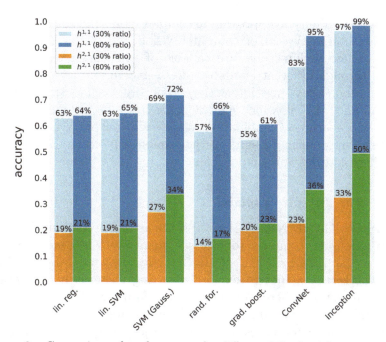

Figure 8. Comparison of performances for different ML algorithms to predict Hodge numbers in CICY 3-folds [20].

with the principal components of the configuration matrix, are by far the most important variables.

In conclusion, an accurate data analysis may recover relevant information hidden in the raw input. While this analysis suggests taking into consideration the information encoded separately in the rows and columns of the configuration matrix, the engineered features were not found to improve the results with neural networks [20]. Other ML algorithms do benefit from incorporating engineered features (Figure 8), but they are all outperformed by neural networks, on which we focus in the following sections.

3. Neural Networks for CICYs

In this section, we review the recently proposed neural network architectures to compute CICY Hodge numbers [19–21]. Recently, a novel interest in convolution-based architectures [46] sprouted in applications of deep learning techniques to physics [52]. Such architectures leverage the ability to approximate complex, nonlinear functions with the advantages typical of computer vision and object recognition tasks. These architectures are capable of exploring recurring patterns, through different learnable *filters*, and to extract meaningful information. They show interesting properties, such as translational equivariance [47,58], which may, in some cases, be beneficial to pick up specific features. Combinations of different convolution operations have shown promising results, as they enable exploration of the input at different scales and shapes [55].

3.1.   *The Inception module*

Inspired by GoogLeNet's [55] success, the ability to combine different convolutions to compute topological quantities has been explored for the first time in Refs. [19,21]. The *Inception* module combines different kernel shapes to explore recurring patterns in the input, which corresponds here to the configuration matrix (1).

In this case, the coefficients of a given row are associated with the degrees of the coordinates of a single projective space appearing in each equation, and correspondingly the coefficients of a given column are associated with the degrees of the coordinates of all projective spaces appearing in a single equation. This suggests that the optimal choice is using both maximal 1-dimensional kernel in parallel [19,20]. This choice may be motivated by relating the expression of Hodge numbers to the ambient space cohomology [21]: in the Koszul resolution, the projective spaces appear symmetrically in the ambient space. Moreover, the resolution contains antisymmetric products of the spaces describing the hypersurface equations. In both cases, the projective spaces and hypersurface equations appear in an equivalent way such that it makes sense to choose kernels which respect this property. Figure 9 shows the module used in Refs. [19–21] and in the current review. The ablation study performed in Ref. [19] displayed in a striking manner how both the use of Inception modules and $1d$ kernels together are necessary to reach the highest accuracy.

Note that the two concurrent convolutions are concatenated and followed by a batch normalization operation [40], which helps contain the values of the activations (rectified linear units [22]), using the running statistics of the training set.

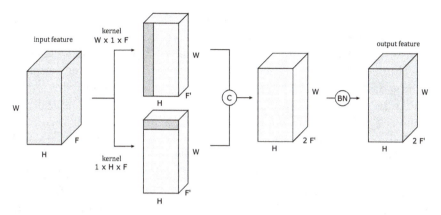

Figure 9. The Inception module. Concatenation (C) and batch normalization (BN) operations are indicated in the diagram.

3.2. *The Inception network*

In Refs. [19,20], we designed a neural network made by a succession of Inception modules to compute the Hodge numbers of the CICY 3-folds. With respect to previous attempts [11,31], the convolutional network profits from the parameter sharing, characteristic of the kernel operations, and it needs only few hidden layers to reach high accuracy. In the setup of 3-folds, we used two separate networks for the predictions of $h^{(1,1)}$ and $h^{(2,1)}$.

Though longer training time is needed for the operations, convolutions use less variables to compute the outputs. Namely, the Inception networks in Refs. [19,20] employ 2.5×10^5 parameters for the prediction of $h^{(1,1)}$ and 1.1×10^6 for $h^{(2,1)}$, to be compared to 1.6×10^6 for the fully connected network in Ref. [11]. The architectures allowed us to reach 99 % in accuracy for the prediction of $h^{(1,1)}$ and 50 % for $h^{(2,1)}$ [19,20].

The natural following step is to compute both Hodge numbers at the same time, using the natural generalization of the Inception network to a multi-task architecture with two output units. However, this network is not immediately suitable for multi-output inference, and accuracy remains higher when computing a single Hodge number at a time. This motivates us to test also for the 3-folds, the architecture introduced in Ref. [21] for the 4-folds, which we describe in the next section.

Nonetheless, we provide a baseline of the Inception network for CICY 4-folds, too. Basic hyperparameter optimization led to an architecture with three hidden layers and 32, 64 and 32 filters in the channel dimension and 0.2 as dropout rate. Larger architectures do not dramatically improve the accuracy on the predictions of the Hodge numbers, thus we choose the smaller architecture as the reference. The total number of parameters is thus 3.8×10^5. We use 0.05, 0.3, 0.25 and 0.35 as loss weights for $h^{(1,1)}$, $h^{(2,1)}$, $h^{(3,1)}$ and $h^{(2,2)}$, respectively. Training lasted 1500 epochs on a single NVIDIA V100 GPU, with a starting learning rate of 10^{-3} and the Adam [41] optimizer, and a mini-batch size of 64 configuration matrices. The learning rate is reduced by a factor of 0.3 after 450 epochs without improvement in the total validation loss.

3.3. *CICYMiner network*

CICYMiner is an architecture introduced in Ref. [21] to compute Hodge numbers of CICY 4-folds. In Figure 10, we show the original architecture used for simultaneous predictions of the four nontrivial Hodge numbers. The architecture enables multi-task learning via hard parameter sharing [50]: the output predictions are computed from a commonly shared representation of the input through differentiated branches. This approach has proven efficient in increasing the learning power of the network and in reducing the risk of overfitting [4,14]. The intermediate layers of the network replicate the same structure by introducing an auxiliary branch, which replicates the output predictions. In turn, this helps the stability of the learning process. It also enables the *mining* [6] of richer and diverse features from a shared feature map, that is, the computations of different characteristics at different levels and scales, in order to enrich the information extracted by each branch. CICYMiner is thus capable of leveraging the extraction of a larger number of features with the advantages of multi-task learning. Specifically, handling outliers is simpler in a multi-task architecture, as their presence for a specific output may help the prediction of a different task. We thus choose to keep the outliers in the training and validation sets for CICYMiner and, compared to Refs. [19,20], we find that they don't decrease the performance. The preprocessing of Hodge numbers in Ref. [19] becomes less impacting with this specific architecture. A simple dropout rate of 0.2 has been added before the dense layers

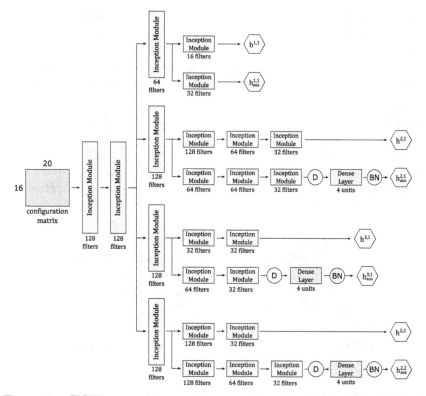

Figure 10. CICYMiner architecture. Dropout (D) and batch normalization (BN) operations are indicated.

to avoid a strong architecture dependence and to introduce a degree of randomness during training. The network in Figure 10 contains approximately 10^7 parameters.

Since the prediction of the Hodge numbers is a regression task, the output of CICYMiner are positive floating point numbers (ensured by adding a rectified linear unit to each output layer). As they need to be compared to integers, predictions are rounded to the next integer before computing the accuracy of the network. The learning process is complemented by the choice of the *Huber* loss function [39]:

$$
\mathcal{H}_{\delta}^{\{k\}}(x) =
\begin{cases}
\dfrac{1}{2} \displaystyle\sum_{n=1}^{k} \sum_{i=1}^{N_k} \omega_n \left(x^{(i)} \right)^2, & \left| x^{(i)} \right| \leq \delta, \\[2ex]
\delta \displaystyle\sum_{n=1}^{k} \sum_{i=1}^{N_k} \omega_n \left(\left| x^{(i)} \right| - \dfrac{\delta}{2} \right), & \left| x^{(i)} \right| > \delta.
\end{cases}
\tag{9}
$$

The choice of the learning objective is, again, dictated by the handling of outliers, through the introduction of a sparsity filter for largely diverging predictions. Robustness is implemented as an interpolation between the quadratic and linear behavior of the function. This solution has already been adopted in classification tasks [48], where different combinations of ℓ_1 norm, ℓ_2 norm and Frobenius norm are used for robustness. The parameter δ is an additional hyperparameter of the model. Regression metrics such as the mean squared error (MSE) and the mean absolute error (MAE) can also be used to get more indications on the learning process: in particular, they can show whether the network is actually capable of learning the discreteness of the Hodge numbers.

As mentioned in the previous section, we will test the same architecture in Figure 10 for predicting the Hodge numbers of the 3-folds, which is a new investigation. This is achieved by removing the legs for $h^{(2,2)}$ and $h^{(3,1)}$. In total, we have 3.3×10^6 parameters for the 3-folds, which is comparable to the two Inception networks in Ref. [20] combined (2.5×10^5 parameters for $h^{(1,1)}$ and 1.1×10^6 for $h^{(2,1)}$). Basic optimization of the hyperparameters enabled a reduction of the parameters by a factor of 3 without strongly impacting the accuracy. For simplicity, we will keep the same CICYMiner architecture of Ref. [21].

We preprocess the input data by simply rescaling the entries of the configuration matrices in the training set in the $[0, 1]$ range. Note that, even though the ranges of definition strongly differ among the Hodge numbers (see Figure 2), there is no need to rescale the labels, as the deep structure of CICYMiner is capable of handling such differences.

Training has been performed on a single NVIDIA V100 GPU over a fixed amount of 300 epochs for CICY 4-folds, while we use 1500 epochs in the 3-folds case, due to the limited cluster time. We use the Adam [41] optimizer with an initial learning rate of 10^{-3} and a mini-batch size of 64 (bs-64) configuration matrices. The learning rate is reduced by a factor of 0.3 after 75 epochs without improvements in the total loss of the validation set. Due to limited time, hyperparameter optimization is performed on the 4-folds dataset using a grid search over a reasonable portion of the hyperparameter space. The implementation uses $\delta = 1.5$ and loss weights of 0.05, 0.3, 0.25 and 0.35 for $h^{(1,1)}$, $h^{(2,1)}$, $h^{(3,1)}$ and $h^{(2,2)}$, respectively, in the 4-folds case.

In order to maintain the same ratio, we use 0.17 and 0.83 for $h^{(1,1)}$ and $h^{(2,1)}$ for the CICY 3-folds.

4. Applications

We provide three applications of the CICYMiner network. In Section 4.1, we reproduce the predictions for the Hodge numbers of the CICY 4-folds from Ref. [21] and generalize to the 3-folds. Next, in Sections 4.2 and 4.3, we study how CICYMiner can extrapolate its predictions after training only with low/high Hodge numbers. Except for the 4-fold predictions in Section 4.1, the results in Section 4 are new.

4.1. *Learning Hodge numbers*

As the first application, we are interested in predicting the Hodge numbers, using the configuration matrix as the input of the deep architecture. For both 3-folds and 4-folds, we select the training set via a stratifies approach on $h^{(2,1)}$ in order to preserve the distribution of the samples: the CICY 4-folds dataset is, in fact, highly peculiar, since $h^{(2,1)}$ vanishes for 70% of the configuration matrices. Though the effect is much less salient for the 3-folds, we adopt the same strategy for comparison. The validation set is chosen totally at random, using 10% of the samples. The remaining samples are included in the test set.

In Figure 11, we present the learning curve of the Inception network on the 4-folds dataset, used as baseline for comparisons with the CICYMiner architecture. In Figure 12, we show the learning curve of CICYMiner on the 4-folds dataset. As visible, with CICYMiner, $h^{(1,1)}$ reaches perfect accuracy with just 10% of the data. This behavior is partially due to the presence of several configuration matrices in the favorable representation (54.5%), for which $h^{(1,1)}$ is just the number of projective ambient space factors, $h^{(1,1)} = r$.

In Table 1, we briefly summarize the ablation study performed for the CICY 4-folds at 80% of training ratio. The CICYMiner network is also capable of learning accurately the discreteness of the Hodge numbers: for most of them, the regression metrics show values which can confidently indicate integer numbers (MAE $\ll 0.50$ and MSE $\ll 0.25$). As shown in Figure 13, the network is still underfitting

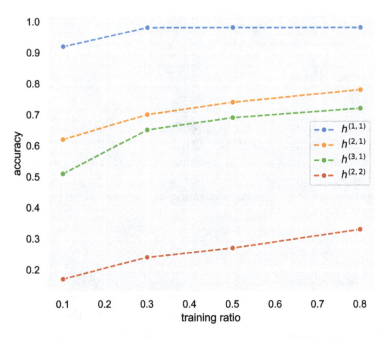

Figure 11.   Learning curve of Inception network on the CICY 4-folds dataset.

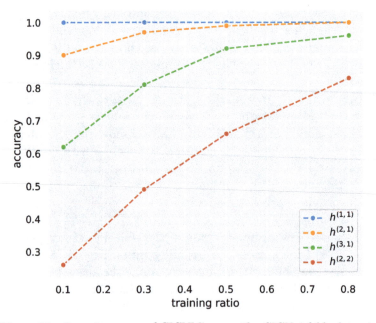

Figure 12.   Learning curve of CICYMiner on the CICY 4-folds dataset.

Table 1.   Ablation study at 80% training ratio for the CICY 4-folds. The metric displayed is the accuracy.

	$h^{(1,1)}$	$h^{(2,1)}$	$h^{(3,1)}$	$h^{(2,2)}$
+att	1.00	0.99	0.96	0.81
MSE loss	1.00	0.97	0.92	0.50
no aux	1.00	0.84	0.92	0.72
bs-256	1.00	0.99	0.94	0.65
layer norm	1.00	0.99	0.92	0.66
CICYMiner	1.00	1.00	0.96	0.83
MSE (10^{-4})	1.3	98	560	6800
MAE (10^{-3})	7.8	19	130	360
Inception	0.98	0.78	0.72	0.33

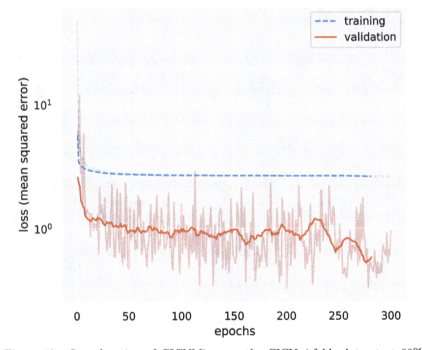

Figure 13.   Loss function of CICYMiner on the CICY 4-folds dataset at 80% training ratio.

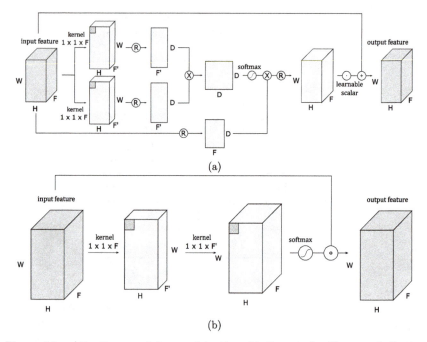

Figure 14. Attention modules used in the ablation study. Here, × indicates a matrix product along the appropriate axes, while ∘ is the Hadamard product. Reshape operations (R) are also indicated: (a) Spatial Attention Module; (b) Channel Attention Module.

the training set: longer training or different choices of the learning rate may be needed to investigate this aspect.

The ablation study was performed by exploring different architectures, such as the addition of attention modules used in Ref. [6] after each Inception module in the auxiliary branch, the use of the traditional ℓ_2 loss, the absence of the auxiliary branches, an increased mini-batch size (bs) and a different normalization strategy based on layer normalization [3]. The principal advantage of the introduction of an attention mechanism, made by the composition of a channel attention module (CHAM) and spatial attention module (SAM) shown in Figure 14, is the faster convergence of the loss function [21], but it does not lead to better results. On the contrary, the ℓ_2 loss shows a strong drop in accuracy in the presence of many outliers, as happens for instance for $h^{(2,2)}$. The ablation study also shows the function of the auxiliary branches, as their introduction is capable

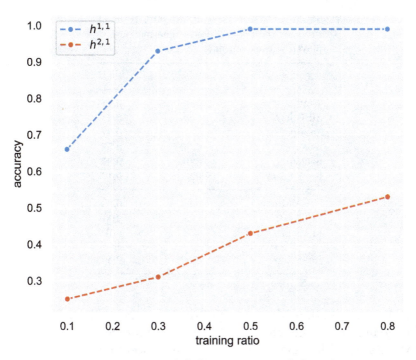

Figure 15.   Learning curve of CICYMiner on the CICY 3-folds dataset.

of mining richer information, which in turn is beneficial to $h^{(2,1)}$, as it boosts the prediction ability in the case of the "imbalanced class" (the term is used by extension, as this is not a classification task). The normalization strategies are also relevant, as the use of a non-trivial mini-batch size is capable of retaining partial information on the physics contained in the dataset. However, larger sizes can lead to a decrease in performance, as the large heterogeneity of the data may damage the stability of the predictions.

The same experiment can be run on CICY 3-folds. Since the dataset is vastly smaller than the 4-folds dataset, we opt for a longer training (1500 epochs) to test the convergence. In Figure 15, we show the learning curve associated with the training procedure: the architecture quickly reaches very high accuracy for $h^{(1,1)}$, while $h^{(2,1)}$ remains quite difficult to reproduce.

Table 2 shows the results of the ablation study performed on the CICY 3-folds. In this scenario, the reduced size of the training set (the full CICY 3-folds database is a factor of 10^2 smaller than the

Table 2. Ablation study at 80% training ratio for the CICY 3-folds. The metric displayed is the accuracy.

	$h^{(1,1)}$	$h^{(2,1)}$
+att	0.99	0.47
MSE loss	0.98	0.44
no aux	0.98	0.37
bs-8	0.99	0.52
bs-256	0.98	0.37
layer norm	0.98	0.17
CICYMiner	0.99	0.53
MSE (10^{-2})	5.3	100
MAE (10^{-2})	4.8	70
Inception	0.99	0.50

CICY 4-folds dataset) impacts negatively on the ability to learn the Hodge numbers. Though not fully optimized for the task, results are comparable with previous attempts using Inception-based architectures [19,20].

The regression metrics MAE and MSE show that only $h^{(1,1)}$ has been effectively learnt as an integer number, but the discreteness of $h^{(2,1)}$ is instead quite difficult to recover using a small dataset. Moreover, the use of a robust training loss makes up for the lack of hyperparameter optimization: using just a ℓ_2 loss shows a strong decrease in the accuracy of $h^{(2,1)}$. We also note that, in this case, the distribution of the configuration matrices seems to be non-homogeneous: larger mini-batch sizes seem to spoil the ability to provide good predictions for $h^{(2,1)}$, while the layer normalization strategy leads to worst results. In this case, given the smaller dataset, we also provide the ablation study with a small batch size, which shows results comparable with CICYMiner. The loss function shown in Figure 16 also shows a difficult training procedure: the loss on the validation set is unstable, due to the reduced number of configuration matrices. It also shows an increase towards the end of the training procedure.

Overall, the CICYMiner architecture shows good results in the presence of a large number of configuration matrices in the training

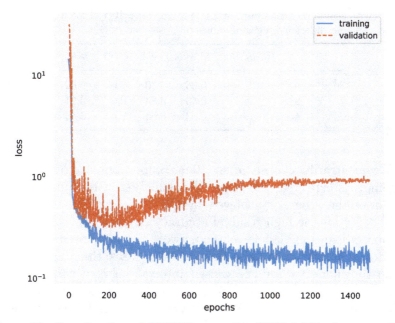

Figure 16. Loss function of CICYMiner on the CICY 3-folds dataset at 80% training ratio.

set. It also retains generalization capabilities, as no additional hyper-parameter optimization seems to be needed to switch from the 4-folds dataset to the 3-folds dataset.

4.2. *Training at low Hodge numbers*

Similar to the previous learning task, we focus on the CICY 4-folds dataset. Following Ref. [12], we test the ability to predict the entire range of Hodge numbers when using only a limited range for training. That is, we restrict the variability of the Hodge numbers, specifically $h^{(1,1)}$, by imposing an upper bound, in order to train only on small values. Then, we test how well the network performs in predicting Hodge numbers outside the training range. We reuse the same hyper-parameters as before but train CICYMiner on the reduced training set. Results are summarized in Table 3. Here, as in the following, the ratio of the training data refers to the full training data used in the previous section.

Table 3.   Accuracy of CICYMiner for CICY 4-folds
on different ranges of values of $h^{(1,1)}$.

	Ratio (%)	$h^{(1,1)}$	$h^{(2,1)}$	$h^{(3,1)}$	$h^{(2,2)}$
$h^{(1,1)} \leq 5$	2	0.06	0.70	0.07	0.02
$h^{(1,1)} \leq 8$	26	0.53	0.83	0.27	0.11
$h^{(1,1)} \leq 10$	59	0.93	0.95	0.62	0.40

We arbitrarily choose 5, 8, 10 as upper bounds of $h^{(1,1)}$ for training. As expected, the larger the reduction in training samples, the lower the accuracy achieved by CICYMiner. Note that in the $h^{(1,1)} \leq 5$ case, the high residual accuracy on $h^{(2,1)}$ reflects the large amount of vanishing labels, as the network is mostly predicting 0 for the Hodge number. Note also that, in these cases, the range of $h^{(2,2)}$ is mostly unaffected by the chosen intervals of $h^{(1,1)}$: its range of variation is constantly [204,1752], which shows a more complicated dependence of $h^{(2,2)}$ on $h^{(1,1)}$ with respect to other Hodge numbers. For the other Hodge numbers, the choice of the intervals of $h^{(1,1)}$ mostly impacts the lower bound of $h^{(3,1)}$ which varies as [35,426], [32, 426] and [30,426] in the three cases of Table 3. The upper bound of $h^{(2,1)}$ is also slightly concerned, as it is limited to [0,30].

In general, this experiment shows complicated relations between the Hodge numbers, particularly when referred to $h^{(1,1)}$. Nonetheless, good results can be obtained for some of them even when using smaller datasets. For instance, $h^{(1,1)}$ and $h^{(2,1)}$ gain quite good accuracy rapidly, even with 60% of the training ratio, dictated by a cut-off on $h^{(1,1)}$.

A similar approach can be used for CICY 3-folds. In Table 4, we show the results of the training at low Hodge numbers in the case of three complex dimensions. We see that the particular choice of the training set strongly impacts the ability of the network to reach high accuracy for both Hodge numbers: this is due to the hard cut-off imposed (compare with Figure 1, for instance), which does not allow the network to correctly predict the out-of-distribution samples. Note that, in general, the range of $h^{(2,1)}$ slightly changes under the different choices of $h^{(1,1)}$: for an upper bound on the first Hodge number of 3, 5,

Table 4. Accuracy of CICYMiner for CICY 3-folds on different ranges of values of $h^{(1,1)}$.

	Ratio (%)	$h^{(1,1)}$	$h^{(2,1)}$
$h^{(1,1)} \leq 3$	3	0.03	0.00
$h^{(1,1)} \leq 5$	20	0.04	0.18
$h^{(1,1)} \leq 7$	54	0.50	0.34
$h^{(1,1)} \leq 8$	70	0.81	0.42

7 and 8, the range of $h^{(2,1)}$ is modified into [27,101], [25,101], [23,101] and [22,101], respectively. With respect to Ref. [12], the accuracy reached by CICYMiner is in any case higher and increases consistently when the size of the training set is increased. Curiously, at very low training ratios, the accuracy on the prediction of the Hodge numbers can be greatly increased by flooring the predictions (rather than approximating to the nearest integer). For example, when considering $h^{(1,1)} \leq 5$, the accuracy for $h^{(1,1)}$ rises to 19%, contrary to what shown in Table 4 (the accuracy of $h^{(2,1)}$ drops to 16%, in this case). This may be an indication that the network is over-estimating the values of the Hodge numbers when smaller training sets are used.

4.3. *Training at high Hodge numbers*

The same experiment can be run in another interesting case, imposing a lower bound on $h^{(2,2)}$. Since the latter is the Hodge number with the largest number of outliers and the largest interval of variation, controlling its range may lead to some interesting relations. As previously, no hyperparameter optimization is run in this case. Results are shown in Table 5, where the ratio of the data refers to the size of the training set used in Section 4.1.

The upper bounds on $h^{(2,2)}$ were arbitrarily chosen as 225, 400, 700 and 900. These choices generally strongly impact the lower bound on $h^{(3,1)}$ whose range of variation is modified into [28,426], [79,426], [158,426] and [211,426], respectively. Moreover, the upper bound of $h^{(2,1)}$ is reduced from 33 to 0, as well as the upper bound on $h^{(1,1)}$

Table 5.   Accuracy of CICYMiner for CICY 4-folds on
different ranges of values of $h^{(2,2)}$.

	Ratio (%)	$h^{(1,1)}$	$h^{(2,1)}$	$h^{(3,1)}$	$h^{(2,2)}$
$h^{(2,2)} > 225$	50	1.00	0.88	0.39	0.04
$h^{(2,2)} > 250$	27	0.98	0.80	0.09	0.03
$h^{(2,2)} > 300$	8	0.95	0.72	0.05	0.03
$h^{(2,2)} > 400$	1.6	0.76	0.70	0.03	0.0

from 24 to 5. Good accuracy on $h^{(2,1)}$ are, again, due to the prevalence of vanishing labels.

As in the previous case, good results on $h^{(1,1)}$ and $h^{(2,1)}$ can be recovered starting from approximately 50% of the training samples. The same complicated relations between the Hodge numbers and the configuration matrices are, once again, evident.

5.   Conclusion

In our series of works [19–21], we have established the state of the art for the computations of Hodge numbers of CICY using machine learning. The Hodge number which has been the most studied is $h^{1,1}$, and we illustrate the improvement in predicting it over time and using different methods in Figure 17.

Computing accurately $h^{(2,1)}$ for the 3-folds is still an open problem. While the CICYMiner architecture performs slightly better than the pure Inception model, the drawback is a much slower training time and many more parameters. Moreover, while results are more precise for the 4-folds, it would be desirable to increase the accuracy of $h^{(2,2)}$. As suggested in Refs. [19,20], a possibility is to represent the configuration matrix by a graph [30,43].

Now that most Hodge numbers can be well computed using deep learning, it would be interesting to extract additional analytic information. One possibility is to use symbolic regression for neural networks as developed in Refs. [16,17] (noting that the authors point out that graph neural networks are much better in this context as they can encode substructure in a finer way), using algorithms such as eureqa [53] or AIFeynman [56,57]. In particular, eureqa can

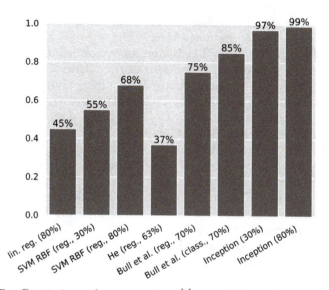

Figure 17. Comparison of accuracy for $h^{1,1}$ for CICY 3-folds using different methods [19,20]. "He" refers to the neural network in Ref. [31] (the accuracy is the one quoted in Ref. [11]) and "Bull *et al.*" to the one in Ref. [11].

learn piecewise functions [16], which is particularly relevant given the structure of the analytic expressions found for line bundle cohomologies [7,8,15,42,44].

Acknowledgments

We are grateful to Robin Schneider and Mohamed Tamaazousti for collaboration on Ref. [21]. This project has received funding from the European Union's Horizon 2020 research and innovation program under the Marie Sklodowska-Curie grant agreement No. 891169. This work is supported by the National Science Foundation under Cooperative Agreement PHY-2019786 (the NSF AI Institute for Artificial Intelligence and Fundamental Interactions, http://iaifi.org/).

References

[1] L.B. Anderson, X. Gao, J. Gray and S.-J. Lee, Fibrations in CICY threefolds, *J. High Energy Phys.* **2017**(10) (October 2017).

[2] L.B. Anderson and M. Karkheiran, TASI lectures on geometric tools for string compactifications (April 2018).

[3] J.L. Ba, J.R. Kiros and G.E. Hinton, Layer normalization (July 2016).

[4] J. Baxter, A Bayesian/information theoretic model of learning to learn via multiple task sampling, *Mach. Learn.* **28**(1) (July 1997), 7–39.

[5] Y. Bengio, A. Courville and P. Vincent, Representation learning: A review and new perspectives, *IEEE Trans. Pattern Anal. Mach. Intell.* **35**(8) (August 2013), 1798–1828.

[6] A. Benzine, M.E.A. Seddik and J. Desmarais, Deep miner: A deep and multi-branch network which mines rich and diverse features for Person re-identification (February 2021).

[7] C.R. Brodie, A. Constantin, R. Deen and A. Lukas, Index formulae for line bundle cohomology on complex surfaces, *Fortschritte der Physik* **68**(2) (February 2020), 1900086.

[8] C.R. Brodie, A. Constantin, R. Deen and A. Lukas, Machine Learning line bundle cohomology, *Fortschritte der Physik*, **68**(1) (January 2020), 1900087.

[9] M.M. Bronstein, J. Bruna, T. Cohen and P. Velickovic, Geometric Deep Learning: Grids, groups, graphs, geodesics, and gauges (May 2021).

[10] M.M. Bronstein, J. Bruna, Y. LeCun, A. Szlam and P. Vandergheynst, Geometric Deep Learning: Going beyond Euclidean data, *IEEE Signal Process. Mag.* **34**(4) (July 2017), 18–42.

[11] K. Bull, Y.-H. He, V. Jejjala and C. Mishra, Machine Learning CICY threefolds, *Phys. Lett. B* **785** (October 2018), 65–72.

[12] K. Bull, Y.-H. He, V. Jejjala and C. Mishra, Getting CICY high, *Phys. Lett. B* **795** (August 2019), 700–706.

[13] P. Candelas, A.M. Dale, C.A. Lütken and R. Schimmrigk, Complete intersection Calabi-Yau manifolds, *Nucl. Phys. B* **298**(3) (March 1988), 493–525.

[14] R. Caruana, Multitask learning, *Mach. Learn.* **28**(1) (July 1997), 41–75.

[15] A. Constantin and A. Lukas, Formulae for line bundle cohomology on Calabi-Yau threefolds, *Fortschritte der Physik* **67**(12) (December 2019), 1900084.

[16] M. Cranmer, A. Sanchez-Gonzalez, P. Battaglia, R. Xu, K. Cranmer, D. Spergel and S. Ho, Discovering symbolic models from Deep Learning with inductive biases (November 2020).

[17] M.D. Cranmer, R. Xu, P. Battaglia and S. Ho, Learning symbolic physics with graph networks (November 2019).

[18] F. Denef and M.R. Douglas, Computational complexity of the landscape I, *Ann. Phys.* **322**(5) (May 2007), 1096–1142.

[19] H. Erbin and R. Finotello, Inception neural network for complete intersection Calabi-Yau three-folds, *Mach. Learn.* **2**(2) (March 2021), 02LT03.

[20] H. Erbin and R. Finotello, Machine Learning for complete intersection Calabi-Yau manifolds: A methodological study, *Phys. Rev. D* **103**(12) (June 2021), 126014.

[21] H. Erbin, R. Finotello, R. Schneider and M. Tamaazousti, Deep multi-task mining Calabi-Yau four-folds, *Mach. Learn.* **3**(1) (November 2021), 015006.

[22] X. Glorot, A. Bordes and Y. Bengio, Deep sparse rectifier neural networks, in *Proceedings of the Fourteenth International Conference on Artificial Intelligence and Statistics*, pp. 315–323. JMLR Workshop and Conference Proceedings (June 2011).

[23] I. Goodfellow, Y. Bengio and A. Courville, *Deep Learning*. The MIT Press (November 2016). https://mitpress.mit.edu/9780262035613/.

[24] M. Graña, Flux compactifications in string theory: A comprehensive review, *Phys. Rep.* **423**(3) (January 2006), 91–158.

[25] J. Gray, A.S. Haupt and A. Lukas, All complete intersection Calabi-Yau four-folds, *J. High Energy Phys.* **2013**(7) (July 2013).

[26] J. Gray, A.S. Haupt and A. Lukas, Topological invariants and fibration structure of complete intersection Calabi-Yau four-folds, *J. High Energy Phys.* **2014**(9) (September 2014).

[27] P.S. Green, T. Hübsch and C.A. Lütken, All the Hodge numbers for all Calabi-Yau complete intersections, *Class. Quantum Gravity* **6**(2) (1989), 105.

[28] P. Green and T. Hübsch, Calabi-Yau manifolds as complete intersections in products of complex projective spaces, *Comm. Math. Phys.* **109**(1) (March 1987), 99–108.

[29] J. Halverson and F. Ruehle, Computational complexity of vacua and near-vacua in field and string theory, *Phys. Rev. D* **99**(4) (February 2019), 046015.

[30] T. Hübsch, *Calabi-Yau Manifolds: A Bestiary for Physicists*. World Scientific (March 1992). https://www.worldscientific.com/worldscibooks/10.1142/1410.

[31] Y.-H. He, Machine-Learning the string landscape, *Phys. Lett. B* **774** (November 2017), 564–568.

[32] Y.-H. He, Calabi-Yau spaces in the string landscape, *Oxford University Press*, Oxford Research Encyclopedia of Physics (June 2020).

[33] Y.-H. He, Machine-Learning mathematical structures (January 2021).

[34] Y.-H. He, *The Calabi–Yau Landscape: From Geometry, to Physics, to Machine Learning*. Springer, 1st edn. (August 2021).

[35] Y.-H. He, Universes as Big Data, *Int. J. Modern Phys. A* **36**(29) (October 2021), 2130017.

[36] Y.-H. He, S. Lal and M.Z. Zaz, The world in a grain of sand: Condensing the string vacuum degeneracy (November 2021).

[37] Y.-H. He and S.-J. Lee, Distinguishing elliptic fibrations with AI, *Phys. Lett. B* **798** (November 2019), 134889.

[38] Y.-H. He and A. Lukas, Machine Learning Calabi-Yau four-folds, *Phys. Lett. B* **815** (April 2021), 136139.

[39] P.J. Huber, Robust estimation of a location parameter, Vol. 35, pp. 73–101. Institute of Mathematical Statistics (March 1964).

[40] S. Ioffe and C. Szegedy, Batch normalization: Accelerating deep network training by reducing internal covariate shift (February 2015).

[41] D.P. Kingma and J. Ba, Adam: A method for stochastic optimization (January 2017).

[42] D. Klaewer and L. Schlechter, Machine Learning line bundle cohomologies of hypersurfaces in toric varieties, *Phys. Lett. B* **789** (February 2019), 438–443.

[43] S. Krippendorf and M. Syvaeri, Detecting symmetries with neural networks, *Mach. Learn.* **2**(1) (December 2020), 015010.

[44] M. Larfors and R. Schneider, Line bundle cohomologies on CICYs with Picard number two, *Fortschritte der Physik* **67**(12) (December 2019), 1900083.

[45] M. Larfors and R. Schneider, Explore and exploit with heterotic line bundle models, *Fortschritte der Physik* **68**(5) (May 2020), 2000034.

[46] Y. LeCun, B. Boser, J.S. Denker, D. Henderson, R.E. Howard, W. Hubbard and L.D. Jackel, Backpropagation applied to handwritten zip code recognition, *Neural Comput.* **1**(4) (1989), 541–551.

[47] C. Mouton, J.C. Myburgh and M.H. Davel, Stride and translation invariance in CNNs, *Artif. Intell. Res.* **1342** (2020), 267–281.

[48] S.J. Pan and Q. Yang, A survey on transfer learning, *IEEE Trans. Knowl. Data Eng.* **22**(10) (October 2010), 1345–1359.

[49] F. Rosenblatt, The perceptron: A probabilistic model for information storage and organization in the brain, *Psychol. Rev.* **65**(6) (1958), 386–408.

[50] S. Ruder, An overview of multi-task learning in deep neural networks (June 2017).

[51] F. Ruehle, Evolving neural networks with genetic algorithms to study the string landscape, *J. High Energy Phys.* **2017**(8) (August 2017).

[52] F. Ruehle, Data science applications to string theory, *Phys. Rep.* **839** (January 2020), 1–117.

[53] M. Schmidt and H. Lipson, Distilling free-form natural laws from experimental data, *Science* **324**(5923) (April 2009), 81–85.

[54] D. Steinberg, CART: Classification and regression trees, in *The Top Ten Algorithms in Data Mining*, pp. 193–216. Chapman and Hall/CRC (2009). http://www.taylorfrancis.com/chapters/edit/10.1201/9781420089653-17/cart-classi%EF%AC%81cation-regression-trees-dan-steinberg.

[55] C. Szegedy, W. Liu, Y. Jia, P. Sermanet, S. Reed, D. Anguelov, D. Erhan, V. Vanhoucke and A. Rabinovich, Going deeper with convolutions, in *2015 IEEE Conference on Computer Vision and Pattern Recognition (CVPR)*, pp. 1–9 (June 2015).

[56] S.-M. Udrescu, A. Tan, J. Feng, O. Neto, T. Wu and M. Tegmark, AI Feynman 2.0: Pareto-optimal symbolic degression exploiting graph modularity (December 2020).

[57] S.-M. Udrescu and M. Tegmark, AI Feynman: A physics-inspired method for symbolic regression (April 2020).

[58] W. Zhang *et al.*, Shift-invariant pattern recognition neural network and its optical architecture, in *Proceedings of Annual Conference of the Japan Society of Applied Physics* (1988).

[59] A. Zheng, *Feature Engineering for Machine Learning: Principles and Techniques for Data Scientists*. USA: O'Reilly Media, Inc. (2018).

https://doi.org/10.1142/9781800613706_0006

Chapter 6

Deep-Learning the Landscape

Yang-Hui He

London Institute for Mathematical Sciences,
Royal Institution of Great Britain, London, W1S 4BS, UK;
Merton College, University of Oxford, OX1 4JD, UK;
Department of Mathematics, City, University of London, EC1V0HB, UK;
School of Physics, Nankai University, Tianjin, 300071, P.R. China

hey@maths.ox.ac.uk

Abstract

We propose a paradigm to deep-learn the ever-expanding databases which have emerged in mathematical physics and particle phenomenology, as diverse as the statistics of string vacua or combinatorial and algebraic geometry. As concrete examples, we establish multi-layer neural networks as both classifiers and predictors and train them with a host of available data ranging from Calabi–Yau manifolds and vector bundles, to quiver representations for gauge theories. We find that even a relatively simple neural network can learn many significant quantities to astounding accuracy in a matter of minutes and can also predict hithertofore unencountered results. This paradigm should prove a valuable tool in various investigations in landscapes in physics as well as pure mathematics.

1. Introduction

Theoretical physics now firmly resides within an age wherein new physics, new mathematics and new data coexist in a symbiosis which transcends inter-disciplinary boundaries and wherein concepts and developments in one field are evermore rapidly enriching another. String theory has spearheaded this vision for the past few decades and has, perhaps consequently, become a paragon of the theoretical sciences. That she engenders the cross-fertilization between physics and mathematics is without dispute: interactions on an unprecedented scale have commingled fields as diverse as quantum field theory, general relativity, condensed matter physics, algebraic and differential geometry, number theory, representation theory, category theory, etc. With the advent of increasingly powerful computers, from this fruitful dialog has also arisen a plethora of data, ripe for mathematical experimentation.

This emergence of data in some sense began with the incipience of string phenomenology [1] where compactification of the heterotic string on Calabi–Yau threefolds (CY3) was widely believed to hold the ultimate geometric unification. A race, spanning the 1990s, to explicitly construct examples of Calabi–Yau (CY) manifolds ensued, beginning[1] with the so-called complete intersection CY manifolds (CICYs) [2], proceeding to the hypersurfaces in weighted projective space [3], to elliptic fibrations [4] and ultimately culminating in the impressive (at least some 10^{10}) list of CY3s from reflexive polytopes [5].

With the realization that the landscape of stringy vacua[2] might in fact exceed the number of inequivalent Calabi–Yau threefolds [6] by hundreds of orders of magnitude, there was a vering of direction toward a more multi-verse or anthropic philosophy. Nevertheless, hints have emerged that the vastness of the landscape might well be mostly infertile (cf. the swamp land of [7]) and that we could live in a very special universe [8–10], a "des res" corner within a barren vista.

Thus, undaunted by the seeming over-abundance of possible vacua, fortified by the rapid growth of computing power and inspirited by the omnipresence of big data, the first two decades of the new millennium saw a return to the earlier principle of creating and mining geometrical data; the notable fruits of this combined effort between pure and computational algebraic geometers as well

---

[1]The interested readers should find the opportunity to have Professor Philip Candelas FRS, relate to them the fascinating account of how this was achieved on the then CERN super-computer, involving dot matrix printers and magnetic tapes or, Professor Rolf Schimmrigk, on staring at VAX machines in Austin over long nights.

[2]The now-popular figure of some 10^{500} is a back-of-envelop estimate based on a generic number of cycles in a generic CY3 that could support fluxes.

as formally and phenomenologically inclined physicists have included (q.v. [11] for a review of the various databases) the following:

- Continuing with the Kreuzer–Skarke database, exemplified by the following:

  — finding quotients to reach small Hodge numbers [18];
  — improvement of PALP, the original KS computer programme [15] and incorporation into SAGE [19];
  — identifying refined structures [14,16,17];
  — interactive Calabi–Yau databases as websites [20,21];
  — building line bundles and monad bundles [22] for heterotic phenomenology in generalizing embedding;

- Generalizing the CICY construction, exemplified by the following:

  — porting the CICY database into Mathematica and establishing a catalog of stable bundles [24];
  — a database of MSSM and 3-generation models from heterotic compactification [25,26,28];
  — relaxing the ambient Fano requirement [23];
  — CICY 4-folds [27];

- Finding elliptic and K3 fibred CY for F-theory and string dualities [29,30], exemplified by the following:

  — identifying elliptic fibrations [13,14] from KS data;
  — establishing phenomenologically viable dataset of stable bundles using spectral covers [28,31];
  — studying finiteness in the elliptic landscape [32];

- D-brane world-volume theories as supersymmetric quiver gauge theories, exemplified by the following:

  — classifications of quivers from $\mathbb{C}^3$ and $\mathbb{C}^4$ orbifolds [33];
  — non-compact toric CY and brane tilings [34,35] and their databases [36–38,41];
  — specializing the toric CY to the reflexive polytopes, whereby linking with KS data [39,40].

All of the above cases are accompanied by typically accessible data of considerable size. To the collection of these databases, representing a concrete glimpse onto the string landscape, we shall refer as **landscape data**, for lack of better words. For instance, the heterotic line bundles on CICYs are on the order of 10^{10}, the spectral-cover bundles on the elliptically fibred Calabi–Yau, 10^6, the brane configurations in the Calabi–Yau volume studies, 10^5, type II intersecting brane models, 10^9, etc. Even by today's measure, these constitute a fertile playground of data, the likes of which Google and IBM are constantly analyzing. A natural course of action, therefore, is to do unto this landscape data what Google and others do each second of our lives: to machine-learn.

Let us be precise about what we mean by *deep machine-learning* this landscape. Much of the aforementioned data have been the brain child of the marriage between physicists and mathematicians, especially incarnated by applications of computational algebraic geometry, numerical algebraic geometry and combinatorial geometry to problems which arise from the classification in the physics and recast into a finite, algorithmic problem in the mathematics (cf. [12]). Obviously, computing power is a crucial limitation.

Unfortunately, in computational algebraic geometry — on which most of the data heavily rely, ranging from bundles stability in heterotic compactification to Hilbert series in brane gauge theories — the decisive step is finding a Groebner basis, which is notoriously known to be unparallelizable and double-exponential in running time. Thus, much of the challenge in establishing the landscape data had been to either circumvent the direct calculation of the Groebner bases by harnessing of the geometric configuration, e.g., using the combinatorics when dealing with toric varieties. Still, many of the combinatorial calculations, be they triangulation of polytopes or finding dual cones, are still exponentially expensive.

The good news for our present purpose is that, *much of the data have already been collected*. Oftentimes, as we shall find out in our forthcoming case studies, tremendous effort is needed for deceptively simple questions. Hence, to draw inferences from *actual* theoretical data by deep-learning therefrom would not only help identify undiscovered patterns but also aid in predicting results which would otherwise cost formidable computations. Subsequently, we propose the following:

> **Paradigm:** To set up neural networks to deep-learn the landscape data, to recognize unforeseeable patterns (as classifiers) and to extrapolate to new results (as predictors).

Of course, this paradigm is useful not only to physicists but to also to mathematicians. For instance, could our neural work be trained well enough to approximate bundle cohomology calculations? This, and a host of other examples, we will shortly examine. Indeed, such neural networks have recently been applied to data analyses in other fields of physics, such as high energy experiment [49], astrophysics/cosmology [50], energy landscapes [51] and holography [52]. Of note is a recent conference in the role of deep learning in fundamental physics [53,54]. It is therefore timely that we should employ this powerful tool to string theory/mathematical physics as well as to computational problems in pure mathematics.

The organization of this chapter is as follows. We begin in Section 2 with a bird's-eye view of the principles of machine deep learning and neural networks with emphasis on its implementations by the latest version of Mathematica so that the readers could familiarize themselves with this handy tool for their own entertainment.

Then, in Section 3, we establish various readily adapted and easily constructed neural networks of the multi-layer perceptron type for a host of examples from the above-mentioned databases, ranging from Calabi–Yau manifolds, to vector bundles, to quiver gauge theories, amply demonstrating the usefulness of our paradigm.

Throughout we shall be explicit about the layers and training as well as test data, adhering to Mathematica syntax for concreteness and familiarity, while keeping track of computation time and accuracy achieved. We beg the readers' indulgence in including code, which is perhaps uncustomary in a paper in mathematical physics; however, the nature of our investigations permits little alternative. We conclude with prospects, including a list of specific directions and issues, in Section 4.

This chapter is a detailed expansion of the brief companion letter [55] which summarizes the key results. Here, we will explain both the data and the methodology in detail, as well as give a pedagogical review of neural networks and machine learning to theoretical and mathematical physicists.

2. Neural Networks and Deep Learning

We begin with some rudiments of deep learning and neural networks; this by no means embodies an attempt to be a pedagogical introduction to this vast field but only serves to set some notations and concepts. Emphasis will be placed on their implementation in the newest versions of Mathematica [45,46] rather than on a general theory. We refer the reader to the classic texts [42–44] on the subject. Indeed, there are standard software available for the **Python** programming language which is standard among experts, such as **TensorFlow** [47], however, since Mathematica is the canonical software for theoretical physicists, we will adhere to tutorial using this familiar playground.

The prototypical problem which an artificial intelligence (AI) might encounter is one of text recognition. For example, how does a machine recognize the individual digits from

$1\ 2\ 3\ 4\ 5\ 6\ 7\ 8\ 9\ 0$? One could try to geometrically define the numbers by their homotopy and other invariants, but this is especially difficult given that handwriting has such huge variation.

In some sense, many problems in string theory and in algebraic geometry are of a similar nature. For example, to compute the cohomology of a vector bundle on an algebraic variety — which physically could encode the number of generations of particles in a gauge theory — is a highly non-trivial task of sequence-chasing but in the end produces a few non-negative integers, often rather small.

The premise of machine learning is to take a data-driven perspective by sampling over large quantities of handwritten digits and feeding them into an optimization routine, whose basic components are called *neurons* in analogy to the human brain. When there is a large collection — often organized in *layers* — of interconnected neurons, we have a **neural network**; the more the number of layers, or more generally, the greater the complexity of the inter-connectivity among the neurons, the "deeper" the learning.

2.1.   *The perceptron*

The archetypal neuron is the so-called *perceptron* (also called the single-layer perceptron (SLP) to emphasize its simplicity); this is a function $f(z_i)$ (called *activation function*) of some input vector z_i. The function f is usually taken to be binary, or some approximation thereof, such as by the hyperbolic tangent $f(z) = \tanh(z)$ or the logistic sigmoid function

$$f(z) = \sigma(z) := (1 + \exp(-z))^{-1}, \tag{1}$$

both of which we shall use liberally later. The activation function is set to contain real parameters, say of the form $f(\sum_i w_i z_i + b)$, where w_i are called weights and b the bias.

Suppose we are given *training data* $D = \{(x_i^{(j)}, d^{(j)})\}$, which is a collection, labeled by j, of inputs $x_i^{(j)}$ and *known* outputs $d^{(j)}$. We then consider minimizing on the parameters w_i and b, by some method of steepest descent, so that the error (standard deviation)

$$\text{SD} = \sum_j \left(f\left(\sum_i w_i x_i^{(j)} + b \right) - d^{(j)} \right)^2 \tag{2}$$

is minimized. We resort to numerical minimization because of the number of parameters could be very large in general, especially when there are many input channels and/or layers. Note that at this simple stage, the principle is very similar to a regression model in statistics, with the difference that the weight parameters w_i are updated with the introduction of each subsequent new data: this is the neuron "learning".

In Mathematica versions 11.0 and above, the **NeuroNetworks** package had been updated and integrated into the system functions; however, since it is still experimental and much of the documentation is rather skeletal, it behoves us to briefly describe the implementation (in all subsequently examples, we will adhere to Mathematica notation) as follows:

- We begin by defining the SLP with `NetChain[ ]`, with argument a list containing a single element (we will generalize this in the next section) specifying the activation function in the layer.
- The layer can be a linear layer specifying a linear transformation by a matrix of specified dimension, for example,

```
net = NetChain[{LinearLayer[5]}],
```

or by an appropriate activation function, for instance,
```
net = NetChain[{ElementwiseLayer[Ramp]}]
```
or `net = NetChain[{ElementwiseLayer[Tanh]}]`
or `net = NetChain[{ElementwiseLayer[LogisticSigmoid]}]`.

- We can initialize the SLP, now called **net**, with some random weights and bias via **net = NetInitialize[net]**.
- The neural network can now be trained with actual data. Since with a single layer not too much can be expected, we will discuss the training in the ensuing section, after introducing multi-layers.

We remark that in the above, the syntax for the linear layer can simply be abbreviated to **net = NetChain[{5}]**. Likewise, the word **ElementWiseLayer** can also be dropped, as in **net = NetChain[{Ramp}]**. Indeed, many other more sophisticated operations can also be chosen for the layer, such as **ConvulutionLayer[ ]** and **LongShortTermMemoryLayer[ ]**, and we refer the reader to Ref. [48] for some more pedagogical explanations as well as a useful lexicon of layers.

2.2.   *Neural networks*

An SLP can be chained together to a multiple layer perceptron (MLP). Sometimes, MLPs and neural networks are used interchangeably though it should be noted that MLPs are only a special type of neural networks, viz., feedforward, because it is a unidirectional chain. In other words, one joins a list of SLPs in a directed fashion to produce an MLP, while an neural work is a directed graph (with potential cycles to allow for feedback) each node of which is an SLP, analogous to the brain being a complex directed graph of neurons.

Nevertheless, with an MLP, we can already go quite far.[3] To return to our handwriting example, one could resort to many resources on the Internet, such as maintained by the Modified National Institute of Standards and Technology (MNIST) database, to which Mathematica can link. The data are simply a string of substitution rules of the form "writing sample" → "correct identification":

---

[3]We further remark that there are built-in functionalities in Mathematica such as Classify[ ] and Predict[ ] which perform similar tasks. However, because they are black box neural networks, we will adhere to our explicit MLP throughout this chapter for illustrative purposes.

$$\text{data} = \left\{ \text{6} \to 6, \ \text{2} \to 2, \ \text{5} \to 5, \ \text{6} \to 6, \ \text{/} \to 1, \ \text{4} \to 4 \ \ldots \right\}.$$

We now follow Wolfram's documentation for this example. The procedure, as will be throughout this chapter, will be in the following four steps:

(1) **Data acquisition:** First, the data can be obtained online directly, from which we take a sample of 100 of a total of some 60,000:

```
resource = ResourceObject["MNIST"];
data = ResourceData[resource, "TrainingData"];
sample = RandomSample[data, 100];
```

(2) **Establishing neural network:** Next, an MLP can then be set up as

```
net = NetChain[{ConvolutionLayer[20, 5], Ramp, PoolingLayer[2, 2],
        ConvolutionLayer[50, 5], Ramp, PoolingLayer[2, 2],
        FlattenLayer[], 500, Ramp, 10, SoftmaxLayer[]}];
```

(3) **Training neural network:** Finally, training the neural network is simply done with the command `NetTrain[ ]` as

```
net = NetTrain[net, sample].
```

Here is where one optimizes on all the parameters (weights and biases) in each layer, aiming to reduce error (standard deviation) as more data are encountered. One can check that even learning our relatively small sample gives us rather good results:

```
Table[{net[sample[[i, 1]]], sample[[i, 1]]}, {i, 1, 100}]
```

gives almost all correct answers.

(4) **Testing unseen data/validation:** A caveat of NNs is that because there are so many parameters over which we optimize that there is the danger of **over-fitting**. In the above example, we have seen 100 training data points and the NN has fitted to them completely. It is therefore crucial to let the trained NN test against data which is *not* part of the training set, i.e., data *unseen* by the NN.

In our example, the training set is of size 100. We now try against a validation set of size, say 1000, as follows:

```
validation = RandomSample[data, 1000];
Length[Select[Table[{net[validation[[i, 1]]], validation[[i, 2]]},
                    {i, 1, 1000}], #[[1]] == #[[2]]&]].
```

We find that the result is 808 (this is, of course, a typical value because we have randomized over samples), meaning that the NN has learnt, with a mere 100 data points, and managed to predict correct values to an accuracy of about 80%, on 1000 data points. This is quite impressive indeed!

There is obviously much flexibility in choosing the various layers and some experimentation may be required (q.v. Ref. [48]). What we have described above is usually called **supervised** learning because there is a definite input and output structure; we wish to train the NN so that it could be useful in predicting the output given unencountered input values. This is obvious usefulness to the problems in physics and mathematics at hand and now we will turn to a variety of case studies.

3. Case Studies

With the tool presented above, we now proceed to analyze our landscape data, a fertile ground constituting more than two decades of many international collaborations between physics and mathematicians. Our purpose is to first "learn" from the inherent structure and then "predict" unseen properties; considering how difficult some of the calculations involved had been in establishing the databases, such quick estimates, even if qualitative, would be highly useful indeed.

3.1. *Warm-up: Calabi–Yau hypersurfaces in* $W\mathbb{P}^4$

One of the first datasets [3] to experimentally illustrate mirror symmetry was that of hypersurfaces in weighted projective space $W\mathbb{P}^4$, which, though later subsumed by the Kreuzer–Skarke list [5] since $W\mathbb{P}^4$ is toric, is a good starting point because of the simplicity in definition. Given the ambient space $W\mathbb{P}^4_{[w_0:w_1:w_2:w_3:w_4]} \simeq (\mathbb{C}^5 - \{0\})/\sim$ where the equivalence relation is $(x_0, x_1, x_2, x_3, x_4) \sim$

$(\lambda^{w_0} x_0, \lambda^{w_1} x_1, \lambda^{w_2} x_2, \lambda^{w_3} x_3, \lambda^{w_4} x_4)$ for points $(x_0, x_1, x_2, x_3, x_4)$ in $\mathbb{C}^5$, $\lambda \in \mathbb{C}^*$ and weights $w_{i=0,\ldots,4} \in \mathbb{Z}_+$. This space is in general singular, but choosing a generic enough homogeneous polynomial of degree $\sum_{i=0}^4 w_i$ which misses the singularities, this polynomial defines a hypersurface therein which is a smooth Calabi–Yau threefold X.

There are 7555 inequivalent such configurations, each specified by a 5-vector $\vec{w}_{i=0,\ldots,4}$. The Euler characteristic χ of X is easily given in terms of the vector. However, as is usually the case, the individual Hodge numbers $(h^{1,1}, h^{2,1})$ are less amenable to a simple combinatorial formula (even though $\chi = 2(h^{1,1} - h^{2,1})$ is). In fact, the original computation had to resort to Landau–Ginzburg techniques from physics to obtain the full list of Hodge numbers [3]. One could in principle use a combination of the adjunction formula and Euler sequences, in addition to singularity resolution, but this is not an easy task to automate.

In Figure 1, we present some standard statistics of the data. In part (a), we plot the traditional $\chi = 2(h^{1,1} - h^{2,1})$ against the sum $(h^{1,1} + h^{2,1})$, exhibiting mirror symmetry; the histogram of χ is drawn in part (b). In parts (c) and (d), for reference, we draw the $h^{1,1}$ and $h^{2,1}$ values against the order as presented in the database of [20]; this is to illustrate that while $h^{1,1}$ has been organized more or less in an increasing order, $h^{2,1}$ appears rather random.

3.1.1. *Deep-learning complex structure*

Let us try to deep-learn the least suggestive set of data, i.e., $h^{2,1}$, which encodes the complex structure of the CY3 and is presented in Figure 1(d); the human eye cannot quite discern what patterns may exist therein. We let WPcy3 be the set of training data, being a list of

$$\{\text{configuration (5-vector)}, \chi, h^{1,1}, h^{2,1}\},$$

so that a typical element would be something like $\{\{1, 3, 5, 9, 13\}, -128, 14, 78\}$. Suppose we have a simple (qualitative) question: *How many such CY3s have a relatively large number of complex deformations?* We can, for instance, consider $h^{2,1} > 50$ to be "large" and set up our training data to be

```
ddd = Table[WPcy3[[i, 1]]    ->    If[(WPcy3[[i, 4]] > 50, 1, 0],
        {i, 1, Length[WPcy3]}].
```

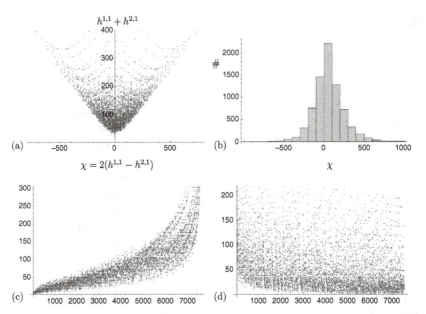

Figure 1.   From the set of 7555 Calabi–Yau threefold hypersurfaces in $W\mathbb{P}^4$, we plot (a) $\chi = 2(h^{1,1} - h^{2,1})$ against the sum $(h^{1,1} + h^{2,1})$, exhibiting mirror symmetry; (b) a histogram of χ, showing a concentration of self-mirror manifolds at $\chi = 0$; (c) an ordered list-plot of $h^{1,1}$ and (d) that of $h^{2,1}$.

Next, we set up a neural network (MLP) with the input being a 5-vector and the output a number and consisting of five total layers, three of which are intermediate (called "hidden layers" in the literature):

```
net = NetChain[
     {LinearLayer[100], ElementwiseLayer[LogisticSigmoid],
     ElementwiseLayer[Tanh], LinearLayer[100], SummationLayer[]},
     "Input" -> {5}].
```
$$(3)$$

The layers are self-explanatory. The input (first) layer is a linear function, essentially a 5×100 matrix, followed by a sigmoid function from (1), then by a hyperbolic tangent, both of which are elementary-wise operations, and another linear layer, here an 100×100 matrix, finishing with a weighted sum of the 100-vector into a number.

We now train, with say 500 iterations, our MLP by the data **ddd** as

```
net = NetTrain[net, ddd, MaxTrainingRounds -> 500],
```

and in under a minute on an ordinary laptop, the MLP is trained.

To appreciate the accuracy of the training, we can compare the predicted result of the network against the actual data. We do so by counting the number of cases where the net value for a given input *differs* from the correct value, for instance, by

```
Select[Table[{Round[net[ddd[[i, 1]]]], ddd[[i, 2]]}, {i, 1, 7555}],
    #[[1]] != #[[2]] &] // Length.
```

Note that while we have set the data to be binary, i.e., 1 if $h^{2,1} > 50$ and 0 otherwise, the neural network does not know this and has, especially with the use of the analytic functions in layers 2 and 3, optimized the weights and biases to give a (continuous) real output. Hence , we use round-off to do the comparison. The answer to the above is 282. In other words, our neural network has, in under one minute, learnt — from a seemingly random set of data — to answer the question of deciding whether a given CY3 has a large number of complex parameters, to an accuracy of $(7555 - 282)/7555 \simeq 96.2\%$. This is re-assuring, in the sense that this dataset seems to be "learnable" (we will see, in a later section, how certain problems seem intractable).

Learning curve: Having gained some confidence, we can now move to the crux of the problem: *How does our NN behave on unseen data?* This would give one an appreciation of the *predictive* power of the network. Suppose that we only had partial data. This is particularly relevant when, for instance, due to computational limitations, a classification is not yet complete or when the quantity in question, here $h^{2,1}$, has not been or could not be yet computed. Therefore, let us pretend that we have only data available for a random selection of 3000 out of the 7555 $(X, h^{2,1})$ pairs, i.e.,

```
net = NetTrain[net, RandomSample[ddd, 3000], MaxTrainingRounds -> 500].
```

This is less than a half of the total.

Suppose now we are given a new configuration, one which we have not encountered before, with what confidence could we predict that it would have a large number for $h^{2,1}$? We repeat the last two commands in the above, using **NetTrain[ ]** on the 3000 and then testing against the full 7555. We find that only 421 cases were actually wrong. Thus, with rather incomplete training data (about some 40% of the total number in the classification), the relatively simple neural network consisting of a feedforward five layer MLP has learnt, in under a minute, our question and predicted new results to 94.4% accuracy. One standard measure of the goodness of fit is the so-called **cosine distance**, where we take the normalized dot product between the predicted value, as a vector $v_N N$ (here of length 7555) with the correct values, also as a vector v_{data}:

$$d(v_{NN}, v_{data}) := \frac{v_{NN} \cdot v_{data}}{|v_{NN}| \, |v_{data}|} \in [-1, 1] \subset \mathbb{R}. \tag{4}$$

Therefore, a value close to $+1$ is a good fit. In the above example, we find $d = 0.91$.

This partial data paradigm, in splitting the data into (1) training set and (2) validation set, is an important one. An illustrative quantity is the so-called **learning curve**: we take random samples of increasing size and check the percentage discrepancy (or cosine distance) of the predicted data versus actual data. We do this for our example, in intervals of, say, size 200, starting from 500 and present this curve in Figure 2. The axis of abscissa is the percentage of total data size (here 7555) which is used to train the NN and the ordinate is the percentage of discrepancy. We see that even at a low percentage of trained data, we achieved around 90% accuracy, increasing to about 96% to the full set. We will see different shapes of curves later, but this problem is particularly well suited for prediction since with a relatively small available data one can achieve a good fit.

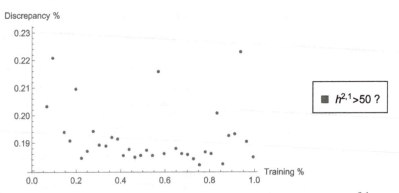

Figure 2. The learning curve for large complex structure (whether $h^{2,1} > 50$) for the hypersurface Calabi–Yau threefolds in weighted projective $\mathbb{P}^4$. We take, in increments of 200, and starting from 500 random samples, with which we train the NN (shown as percentage of the total data size of 7555 in the horizontal). We then check against the full data to see the percentage discrepancy, shown in the vertical.

3.1.2. *Deep-learning number of generations*

Emboldened, let us move onto another question, of importance here to string phenomenology: *Given a configuration, can one tell whether* χ *is a multiple of 3?* In the early days of heterotic string compactifications, using what has now come to be known as the standard embedding, this question was decisive on whether the model admitted three generation of particles in the low-energy effective gauge theory. Of course, we have an analytic formula for χ in terms of the input 5-vector w_i. However, testing divisibility is not an immediate task.

Again, we can define a binary function taking the value of 1 if $\chi \mod 3 \equiv 0$ and 0 otherwise. Training with the network in (3), we achieve 82% accuracy with 1000 training rounds, taking about 2 minutes; this means that such a divisibility problem is a bit less learnable than the previous problem (we will again address and contrast the class of problems later). With partial data, say taking a random sample of 3000 to train and validating against the full set give also about 80% correct results.

The astute reader might question at this stage why we have adhered to *binary queries*. Why not train the network to answer a direct query, i.e., to try for instance to learn and predict the value of $h^{2,1}$ itself? This is a matter of spread in the present dataset: we have only some 10^4 inputs but we can see that the values of $h^{1,1}$ range from 1 to almost 500; the neural network would have to learn from a relatively small sample in order to distinguish some 500 output channels. We simply do not have enough data here to make more accurate statements, though we will shortly proceed to multiple-channel output. One can check that net-training on the direct data

```
ddd=Table[WPcy3[[i, 1]]  -> WPcy3[[i, 4]], {i,1,Length[WPcy3]}]
```

would give the rough trend but not the precise value of the complex structure.

This is precisely in line with our philosophy: the power of deep-learning the landscape lies in rapid *estimates*. The computation of the exact values in the landscape data often takes tremendous efforts in algebraic geometry and quantum field theory, and we wish to learn and benefit from the fruits the labor from the last two decades. We aim to identify patterns and draw inferences and to avoid the intense computations.

3.2. *CICYs*

Having warmed up with the hypersurfaces in weighted projective $W\mathbb{P}^4$, let us move onto our next case, the CICY dataset, of complete intersection Calabi–Yau threefolds in products of (unweighted) projective spaces. This is both the first Calabi–Yau database (or, for that matter, the first database in algebraic geometry) [2] and the most heavily studied recently for phenomenology [23–26,28]. It has the obvious advantage that the ambient space is smooth by choice and no singularity resolution is needed. The reason we study this after the $W\mathbb{P}^4$ data is because, as we see shortly, the input is a configuration of non-negative integer matrices, one rank up in complexity from the 5-vector input in the previous section.

Briefly, CICYs embedded as K homogeneous polynomials in $\mathbb{P}^{n_1} \times \cdots \times \mathbb{P}^{n_m}$, of multi-degree q_j^r. Here, complete intersection means that the dimension of the ambient space exceeds the number K of defining equations by precisely 3, i.e., $K = \sum_{r=1}^{m} n_r - 3$. Moreover, the Calabi–Yau condition of vanishing first Chern class of TX translates to $\sum_{j=1}^{K} q_j^r = n_r + 1 \ \forall \ r = 1, \ldots, m$. Subsequently, each manifold can be written as an $m \times K$ configuration matrix (to which we may sometimes adjoin the first column, designating the ambient product of projective spaces, for clarity; we should bear in mind that this column is redundant because of the CY condition):

$$
X = \begin{bmatrix} \mathbb{P}^{n_1} & q_1^1 & q_2^1 & \cdots & q_K^1 \\ \mathbb{P}^{n_2} & q_1^2 & q_2^2 & \cdots & q_K^2 \\ \vdots & \vdots & \vdots & \ddots & \vdots \\ \mathbb{P}^{n_m} & q_1^m & q_2^m & \cdots & q_K^m \end{bmatrix}_{m \times K},
\qquad
\begin{aligned}
& q_j^r \in \mathbb{Z}_{\geq 0}, \\
& K = \sum_{r=1}^{m} n_r - 3, \\
& \sum_{j=1}^{K} q_j^r = n_r + 1, \\
& \forall \ r = 1, \ldots, m.
\end{aligned}
\tag{5}
$$

The most famous CICY is, of course, [4|5] or simply the matrix [5], denoting the quintic hypersurface in $\mathbb{P}^4$.

The construction of CICYs is thus reduced to a combinatorial problem of classifying the integer matrices in (5). It was shown that such configurations are finite in number and the best available computer at the time (1990's), viz., the super-computer at CERN [2],

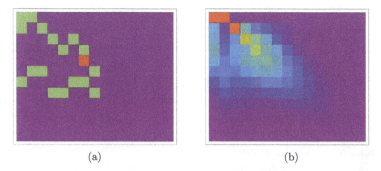

(a)   (b)

Figure 3. We realize the set of 7890 CICYs (Calabi–Yau threefolds as complete intersections in products of projective spaces) as 12×15 matrices, padding with zeros where necessary. Then, all CICY configurations are such matrices with entries in $\{0, 1, 2, 3, 4, 5\}$. We consider these as pixel colors and draw a typical CICY in (a), with 0 being purple. In (b), we average over all such matrices component-wise and draw the "average" CICY as a pixelated image.

was employed. A total of 7890 inequivalent manifolds were found, corresponding to matrices with entries $q_j^r \in [0, 5]$, of size ranging from 1×1 to maximum number of rows and columns being 12 and 15, respectively. In a way, this representation is much closer to our archetypal example of handwriting recognition in Section 2.2 than one might imagine. The standard way to represent an image is to pixelate it, into blocks of $m \times n$, each of which carrying a color info, for example, a 3-vector encapturing the RGB data.

Therefore, we can represent all the 7890 CICYs into 12×15 matrices over $\mathbb{Z}/6\mathbb{Z}$, embedded starting from the upper-left corner, say, and padding with zeros everywhere else. A typical configuration (say, number 2000 in the list) thus becomes an image using Mathematica's `ArrayPlot[ ]` which is shown in part (a) of Figure 3. Here, the purple backgrounds are the zeros, the greens are the ones and the one red block is 2. Indeed, the CICY configuration matrices are rather sparse, dominated by 0 and following that by 1. In part (b) of the figure, we try to show the "average" CICY by component-wise average over all the 12×15 matrices. Again, we see the largely purple (entry 0) background, with various shades mixed by the averaging process. It is rather aesthetically pleasing to see the average CICY as an image.

It should be emphasized that such a pixelated depiction of CICY is *only* for visualization purposes and nothing more. Usually, with graphic images, the best NN to use is the so-called *convolution* layer where each pixel is convolved with its neighbors. Our MLP does not have such a convolution layer, so strictly speaking, we are not taking advantage of the image-processing aspects of our data. Nevertheless, this representation is very visual and one can check that *not* representing the CICY in matrix form and simply flattening the entire matrix into a long vector also achieves the same nice results.[4] Throughout the rest of this writing, we will likewise use pixelation as a good visual guide for our geometries but will not be using any convolutional neural networks (CNNs).

Now, our input space is much larger than that of the $W\mathbb{P}^4$ case consider above: $7890 \times 12 \times 15$ is 2 orders of magnitude larger than 7555×5, thus let us indulge ourselves with a full rather than binary query. That is, can we deep-learn, say, the full list of Hodge numbers? As usual, the Euler number is relatively easy to obtain and there is a combinatorial formula in terms of the integers q_j^r, while the individual Hodge numbers $(h^{1,1}, h^{2,1})$ involve some non-trivial adjunction and sequence-chasing, which luckily had been performed for us and occupied a sizeable portion of the exposition in the Bestiary [2]. Our warm-up exercise is to machine-learn this result.

Again, we set up a list of training rules (padded configuration matrix $\rightarrow h^{1,1}$); a typical entry, adhering to our example in Figure 3(a), would be

$$
\left(\begin{array}{cccccccc|c}
1 & 1 & 0 & 0 & 0 & 0 & 0 & 0 & \\
1 & 0 & 1 & 0 & 0 & 0 & 0 & 0 & \\
0 & 0 & 0 & 1 & 0 & 1 & 0 & 0 & \\
0 & 0 & 0 & 0 & 1 & 0 & 1 & 0 & \\
0 & 0 & 0 & 0 & 0 & 0 & 2 & 0 & 0 \\
0 & 1 & 1 & 0 & 0 & 0 & 0 & 1 & \\
1 & 0 & 0 & 0 & 0 & 1 & 1 & 0 & \\
0 & 0 & 0 & 1 & 1 & 0 & 0 & 1 & \\
\hline
& & & 0 & & & & & 0
\end{array} \right)_{12 \times 15} \longrightarrow \quad 6, \qquad (6)
$$

[4]I would like to thank Wati Taylor and Sanjaye Arora for many conversations and their helpful comments in Ref. [54], especially to Sanjaye for checking that this vector representation for CICYs also works well.

this is a CY3 of Hodge numbers $(h^{1,1}, h^{2,1}) = (8, 22)$ and hence Euler characteristic $\chi = -28$. This training list we shall call dd.

We now set up the neural network as

```
net = NetChain[{LinearLayer[1000], ElementwiseLayer[LogisticSigmoid],
            LinearLayer[100], ElementwiseLayer[Tanh], SummationLayer[]},
        "Input" -> {12, 15}].
```

$$(7)$$

We specified the input as {12,15} and have allowed a quite large linear layer of 1000 weights at the input level to allow for parameters. Next, we train the network with the list dd, allowing for 1000 iterations to reduce error:

```
net = NetTrain[net, dd, MaxTrainingRounds -> 1000].
```

Despite these sumptuous choice of parameters, the training takes about a mere 8 minutes, associating an optimized real number to each configuration (image) and a simple check of the round-up against actual $h^{1,1}$

```
Select[Table[{Round[net[dd[[i, 1]]]], dd[[i, 2]]}, {i, 1, 7890}],
       #[[1]] != #[[2]] &] // Length
```

returns 7, meaning that our network has been trained to an accuracy of $(7890 - 7)/7890 \simeq 99.91\%$ in under 10 minutes. Thus, this is very much a "learnable" problem and the network functions well as a *classifier*, almost completely learning the Hodge data for CICYs.

Learning curve: What about the network as a predictor, which is obviously a more salient question? Let us repeat the methodology above, viz., to train with a portion of the input data, and see whether it could extrapolate to the full dataset. Suppose the neural network sees only a random sample of 4000 of dd, which is particularly pertinent were the classification not complete and which, though not here, would be the case with most problems in the business.

Using the above neural network takes about 6 minutes. Then, checking against the full dataset comprising of configurations/images the MLP has never before seen, we find 184 discrepancies. Considering (1) that we have only trained the network for a mere 6 minutes, (2) that it has seen less than half of the data, (3) that it is a rather elementary MLP with only five forward layers and (4) that the variation of the output is integral ranging from 0 to 19, with no room

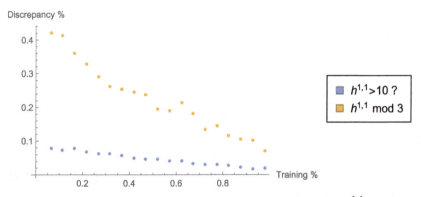

Figure 4. The learning curve for large Kähler structure (whether $h^{1,1} > 10$) and (in blue) divisibility of Kähler parametres modulo 3 (in orange), for the CICY manifolds. We take, in increments of 400, and starting from 500 random samples, with which we train the NN (shown as percentage of the total data size of 7890 in the horizontal). We then check against the full data to see the percentage discrepancy, shown in the vertical.

for continuous tuning, achieving 97.7% accuracy and cosine distance 0.99 with so little effort is quite amazing!

It is expedient to investigate the learning curve here, which is presented in Figure 4. The training data are taken as random samples, in increments of 400, and starting from 500 from the total 7890, shown as a percentage in the horizontal axis. We then validate against the total dataset of 7890 and see the percentage, drawn in the vertical, of discrepancies. We see that the question of whether $h^{1,1} > 10$ is extremely well behaved: where 10% discrepancy (90% accuracy) is achieved with only 10% training data, decreasingly steadily with increasing training data. Such a trend is even more dramatic for testing whether $h^{1,1}$ is divisible by 3: more than 40% discrepancy at 10% available data, decreasing to less than 10% at full data. Nevertheless, it is clear that testing whether a quantity exceeds a given value is better than testing its divisibility properties.

The general strategy when confronted with a difficult computation, especially in algebraic geometry, is therefore clear. Suppose we have a large or even unknown classification and we have handle only for a fraction of requisite geometrical/topological quantities. We can select, starting from a small percentage of known results, establish a NN and see the trend of the learning curve. If the discrepancies are obviously decreasing in a satisfactory manner, then we gain further confidence in predicting what the required quantity is over the entire dataset.

3.2.1. *Fourfolds*

The generalization from CICY threefolds to fourfolds, with (5) altered mutatis mutandis (e.g., making $K = \sum_{r=1}^{m} n_r - 4$), has more recently been accomplished [27] and the dataset is, understandably, much larger. Here, we have 921,497 configuration matrices of size 1×1 (corresponding to the sextic [5|6]) up to 16 rows and 20 columns, taking values in 0 to 6, with Euler characteristic ranging from 0 to 2610. The computation took an impressive 7487 CPU hours, almost 1 entire year if on a single core.

As before, we can consider each CICY4 as an 16×20 pixelated image, padding with zeros where necessary, with seven shades of color. We thus have about 1 million images to learn from. As above, the Euler characteristic has a simple combinatorial formula in terms of the q_j^r and it is also an alternating sum in the four non-trivial Hodge numbers $(h^{1,1}, h^{2,1}, h^{3,1}, h^{2,2})$. In Figure 5, we plot the average over all the images by component-wise arithmetic mean in part (a) and in part(b); for reference, we show the distribution of the

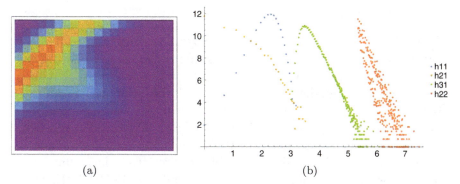

(a) (b)

Figure 5. We realize the set of 921,497 CICY4s as 16×20 matrices (bottom-right padding with zeros where necessary) with entries in $\{0, 1, 2, 3, 4, 5, 6\}$. Each is then a pixelated image with seven shades of color with 0 being, say, purple. In (a), we average over all such matrices component-wise and draw the "average" CICY4, in contrast to Figure 3(a). For reference, we include, in part (b), the histogram of the (now four) Hodge numbers: $(h^{1,1}, h^{2,1}, h^{3,1}, h^{2,2})$; because of the spread in values, we perform a log–log plot.

four Hodge numbers on a log–log plot. Let us try to deep-learn these Hodge numbers. With the same network as in (7) but with `"Input" -> {16,20}`, we purposefully take *incomplete* knowledge by using only the first 20,000 data points as training data. For $h^{1,1}$, which ranges between 1 and 24 in the training set, we achieve almost complete accuracy (22 discrepancies) within about an hour of deep-learning.

Encouraged, we try to extrapolate: testing against the first 30,000 of the full dataset, which takes about 30 minutes, we find 23,521 matches, meaning that we have achieved 78.4% accuracy within 2 hours, much less than the time to compute $h^{1,1}$ from the first principles. Similarly, for $h^{2,1}$, which ranges from 0 to 33, we achieve similar figures. The remaining Hodge numbers, $h^{3,1}$ and $h^{2,2}$, have a much wider spread, taking values in [21,426] and [204,1752], respectively, would require more than 20,000 to train to greater confidence.

There are many more properties of CICYs, and indeed of CY manifolds in general, comprising an ongoing industry, from identifying torus or K3 fibration structure for F-theory to adding orientifolds, which we could deep-learn. For now, let us move onto a closely related subject which has over the last two decades vastly generalized the computation of Hodge numbers.

3.3. *Bundle cohomology*

The subject of vector bundle cohomology has, since the so-named "generalized embedding" [1] of compactifying the heterotic string on smooth Calabi–Yau threefolds X endowed with a (poly-)stable holomorphic vector bundle V, become one of the most active dialogs between algebraic geometry and theoretical physics. The realization [9] that the theoretical possibility of Ref. [1] can be concretely achieved by a judicious choice of (X, V) to give the exact MSSM spectrum induced much activity in establishing relatively large datasets to see how often this might occur statistically [11,18,22,24,31], culminating in Refs. [25,26] which found some 200 out of a scan of 10^{10} bundles which have exact MSSM content.

Upon this vast landscape, let us take an insightful glimpse by taking the datasets of Ref. [31], which are $SU(n)$ vector bundles V on elliptically fibred CY3. By virtue of a spectral-cover construction [4,30], these bundles are guaranteed to be stable and hence preserves

$\mathcal{N} = 1$ supersymmetry in the low-effective action, together with GUT gauge groups E_6, $SO(10)$ and $SU(5)$ respectively for $n = 3, 4, 5$.

We take the base of the elliptic fibration — of which there is a finite list [29] — as the r-th Hirzebruch surface ($r = 0, 1, \ldots, 12$ denoting the inequivalent ways which $\mathbb{P}^1$ can itself fibre over $\mathbb{P}^1$ to give a complex surface), in which case, the stable $SU(n)$ bundle is described by five numbers (r, n, a, b, λ), with $(a, b) \in \mathbb{Z}_+$ and $\lambda \in \mathbb{Z}/2$ being coefficients which specify the bundle via the spectral cover. This ordered 5-vector will constitute our neural input. The database of viable models were set up in Ref. [31], viable meaning that the bundle-cohomology groups of V are such that

$$h^0(X, V) = h^3(X, V) = 0, \quad \left|h^1(X, V) - h^2(X, V)\right| \equiv 0 \ (\text{mod} \, 3),$$
$$(8)$$

where the first is a necessary condition for stability and the second, that the GUT theory has the potential to allow for three net generations of particles upon breaking to MSSM by Wilson lines. Over all the Hirzebruch-based CY3, 14,264 models were found, a sizeable play-ground.

Suppose we wish the output to be a 2-vector, indicating (I) what the gauge group is, as denoted by n, and (II) whether there are more generations than anti-generations, as denoted by the sign of the difference $h^1(X, V) - h^2(X, V)$; this is clearly a phenomenologically interesting question. The fact that the network needs to produce a vector output need not worry us; we replace the last summation layer of (7) by a linear layer of matrix size 2:

```
net = NetChain[{LinearLayer[1000], ElementwiseLayer[LogisticSigmoid],
         LinearLayer[100], ElementwiseLayer[Tanh], LinearLayer[2]},
      "Input" -> {5}].
```

With 1000 training rounds as before, and with the dataset consisting of replacements of the form

$$(r, n, a, b, \lambda) \to (n, \text{Sign}(h^1(X, V) - h^2(X, V)))$$

(note that we purposefully kept n common to both input and output as a cross-check and to see how the network responds to vector output), in about 10 minutes (the vector output and thus the last linear layer slow the network by a factor of 2 compared to previous trainings), we achieve 100% accuracy (i.e., the neural network has completely learnt the data). This seems like an extremely learnable problem. Indeed, training with partial data, say 100 points, less than 1% of the total data, achieves 99.9% predicative accuracy over the entire set!

Similarly, we could query whether $h^1(X, V) - h^2(X, V)$ is even or odd, which is also an important question because it dictates the parity of the size of the fundamental group (as a finite discrete symmetry group) of the CY3, which is a difficult issue to settle theoretically. Using the above network, a 67% accuracy can be attained in 10 minutes training on 8000 points This shows that the pattern here is indeed more difficult to recognize as compared to the sign, as is consistent with expectations. There are endless variations to this type of question and deep learning and we shall discuss some pertinent ones in the prospectus; for now, let us match onward to further available data.

3.4. *Aspects of the KS dataset*

The largest dataset in Calabi–Yau geometry, and indeed to our knowledge in pure mathematics, more than such online resources as modular forms or dessin d'enfants, is the Kreuzer–Skarke list of reflexive (convex lattice) polytopes [5]. There are 4319 in dimension 3 and 473,800,776 in dimension 4. Much work, still ongoing, has been focused on the latter because the anti-canonical divisor within the associated toric variety defines a smooth Calabi–Yau threefold [20,21]. We will leave explorations and deep learning of this formidable set to future work. For now, let us focus on the 4319 reflexive lattice polyhedra which has recently been harnessed for certain Sasaki–Einstein volume conjectures [40].

First, we can represent the data in a conducive way. Each polyhedron Δ consists of a list of integer vertices as 3-vectors (of which Δ is the convex hull); there is a single interior lattice point $(0, 0, 0)$ and we can record all the $n - 1$ lattice points on the boundary facets. Hence, each Δ is a $3 \times n$ integer matrix M, with one column being $(0, 0, 0)$. It turns out that n ranges from 5 to 39 (the 5 clearly including the lattice tetrahedron enclosing the origin), and the entries of M take values in $\{-21, -20, \ldots, 5, 6\}$.

Hence, each Δ is a 3×39 pixelated image (right padding where necessary), with 28 shades of color. We show a random sample

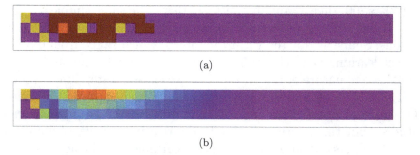

(a)

(b)

Figure 6.   We realize the set of 4319 reflexive polyhedra as 3×39 matrices (right padding with zeros where necessary) with entries in $\{-21, -20, \ldots, 5, 6\}$. Each is then a pixelated image with 28 shades of color with 0 being, say, purple. In (a), we show a typical sample; in part (b), we show the average by component-wise root mean square. Again, the image is purely for amusement; we are not using a CNN in this chapter.

(number 2000 in KS dataset) in parts (a) of Figure 6. In part (b), because we now have a mixture of positive and negative entries to the matrix, we compute the square root of the component-wise sum of the squares to the 4319 configurations, giving an idea of the "average" appearance of the reflexive polyhedra.

To each Δ, we can associate two different geometries:

- A compact smooth Calabi–Yau 2-fold, or K3-surface $\mathcal{K}$, being a hypersurface as the anti-canonical divisor in the Fano toric variety $X(\Delta)$ constructed from the polytope. These are algebraic K3 surfaces, so the Hodge numbers are all the same. The Picard number $Pic(\mathcal{K})$, one the other hand, is a non-trivial property and has been computed [5]. The reader is referred to Figure 16 of Ref. [17] for a distribution of these Picard numbers.
- A non-compact affine Calabi–Yau fourfold which is the total space of the anti-canonical bundle over $X(\Delta)$; this Calabi–Yau space is itself a real cone over a compact Sasaki–Einstein 7-manifold $\mathcal{Y}$. The various Z-minimized volumes $V(\mathcal{Y})$ of $\mathcal{Y}$, normalized with respect to S^7, are algebraic numbers computed in Ref. [40] (q.v. *ibid.*, Figure 10 for a distribution of these volumes).

We will now deep-learn $Pic(\mathcal{K})$ and $V(\mathcal{Y})$ with respect to our images. The data size here is relatively small compared to the previous, so once again we will use a binary function for the volume, say, if

$V(\mathcal{Y}) > 200$, then 1, and 0 otherwise. Using the same simple network as (5) but with input size 3×39, we achieve 57% accuracy in about 5 mins. Similarly, for the Picard numbers, which range from 0 to 19, direct learning can achieve 53% accuracy in equal time, and due to the discrete nature of the output, had we chosen a step function, say, 1 if $Pic(\mathcal{Y}) > 10$ and 0 otherwise, then a 59% accuracy is attained. Of course, these figures are not as impressive as the previous case studies, but this is precisely due to the relative paucity of data: less than 5000. As one would expect, deep learning must be accompanied by "big data".

A plethora of such big data we certainly have. The 473 million reflexive polytopes in dimension 4 is the *ne plus ultra* of our landscape data. In fact, because of the different possibilities of triangulations, the number of Calabi–Yau threefolds obtained therefrom is expected to be many orders of magnitude larger than this and is still very much work in progress. To deep-learn these data is *ipso facto* a significant endeavor which we shall leave for a major future undertaking.

For now, let us take a sample of 10,000 from the peak-distribution [17] of Euler characteristic zero, i.e., self-mirror, manifolds. Here, the configuration can be padded into 4×21 integer matrices taking integer values in $[-14, 9]$ and the individual Hodge numbers $h^{1,1} = h^{2,1} \in \{14, 15, 16, 17, 18\}$. This is therefore a well-suited classifier problem, with input pixelation of 4×21 with 24 shade and 5-channel output. Again, we train with partial data, say, the first 4000, and then test against the full 10,000 to see its predictive power. In under 5 minutes, the neural network (with modified input dimension) in (7) gives 61% accuracy in predicting the full set and 78% in fitting the 4000.

3.5.   *Quiver gauge theories*

As a parting example, having been emboldened by our venture, let us tackle affine varieties in the context of quiver representations. Physically, these correspond to world-volume gauge theories coming from D-brane probes of geometric singularities in string theory, as well as as the space of vacua for classes of supersymmetric gauge theories in various dimension; they have been data-mined since the early days of AdS/CFT (cf. [33,34]). When the geometry concerned is an affine toric Calabi–Yau variety, the realization of brane tiling

[35] has become the correct way to understand the gauge theory, and since then, databases have begun to be compiled [36,37].

As far as the input data are concerned, however, it is straight forward; it consists of a quiver (as a directed graph, with label 1 as dimension vector for simplicity) and a relation on the quiver imposed by the Jacobian of a polynomial super-potential (q.v. Ref. [11] for a rapid review). For example, the following is a typical quiver:

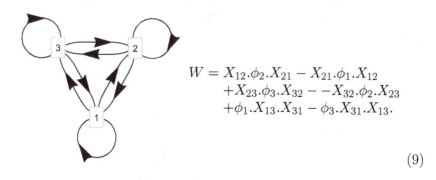

$$W = X_{12}.\phi_2.X_{21} - X_{21}.\phi_1.X_{12}$$
$$+X_{23}.\phi_3.X_{32} - -X_{32}.\phi_2.X_{23}$$
$$+\phi_1.X_{13}.X_{31} - \phi_3.X_{31}.X_{13}.$$

$$(9)$$

In the above, there are three nodes in the quiver and we have denoted arrows $a \to b$ as X_{ab} if $a \neq b$ and as ϕ_a if it is an arrow joining node a to itself (for $a, b = 1, 2, 3$). There are thus a total of nine arrows, which can be interpreted as spacetime fields in the gauge theory. The superpotential W is here a cubic polynomial in the 12 arrows, whose Jacobian ∂W imposes the set of relations. The representation variety is given as the GIT quotient of ∂W by the gauge-fixing conditions by the Eulerian cycles in the quiver and is here the affine variety $\mathbb{C} \times \mathbb{C}^2/(\mathbb{Z}/3\mathbb{Z})$ which is a local Calabi–Yau threefold, being a direct product of $\mathbb{C}$ and an orbifold surface singularity of type A.

We can succinctly encode the above information into two matrices:

1. D-term matrix Q_D, which comes from the kernel of the incidence matrix d of the quiver, a 3×12 matrix each column of which corresponds to an arrow with -1 as head and $+1$ as tail and 0 otherwise;
2. F-term matrix Q_F, a 2×12 matrix each column of which documents where and with what exponent the field corresponding to the arrow appears in ∂W.

Concatenating Q_D and Q_F gives the so-called total charge matrix Q_t of the moduli space as a toric variety (q.v. §2 of Ref. [34] for the precise procedure). For the above example, the incidence matrix d, the Jacobian of the superpotential and thence the total charge Q_t matrices are

$$d = \begin{pmatrix} 0 & -1 & -1 & 1 & 0 & 0 & 1 & 0 & 0 \\ 0 & 1 & 0 & -1 & 0 & -1 & 0 & 1 & 0 \\ 0 & 0 & 1 & 0 & 0 & 1 & -1 & -1 & 0 \end{pmatrix}$$

$$\partial W = \begin{cases} x_3 x_7 - x_2 x_4, \ x_4 x_5 - x_1 x_4, \\ x_2 x_5 - x_1 x_2, \ x_2 x_4 - x_6 x_8, \\ x_1 x_7 - x_7 x_9, \ x_1 x_3 - x_3 x_9, \\ x_8 x_9 - x_5 x_8, \ x_6 x_9 - x_5 x_6, \\ x_6 x_8 - x_3 x_7 \end{cases}$$

$$\rightsquigarrow Q_t = \left(\begin{array}{c|ccccccccc} Q_D & 4 & -1 & -2 & 0 & -1 & 0 & 0 & 0 & 0 \\ & 2 & -2 & -1 & 0 & 1 & 0 & 0 & 0 & 0 \\ \hline & 2 & -1 & -1 & 0 & -1 & 0 & 0 & 1 & 0 \\ & 1 & 0 & -1 & 0 & -1 & 0 & 1 & 0 & 0 \\ Q_F & 1 & -1 & 0 & 0 & -1 & 1 & 0 & 0 & 0 \\ & 1 & -1 & -1 & 1 & 0 & 0 & 0 & 0 & 0 \end{array} \right), \qquad (10)$$

where we have indexed the nine arrows, in accord with the columns of d, as $x_{i=1,\dots,9}$.

The combinatorics and geometry of the above are a long story spanning a lustrum of research to uncover followed by a decade of still-ongoing investigations. However, for our present purposes, we will only consider the theories to be data for the neural network to learn. In the first database of Ref. [36], a host of examples (albeit having many inconsistent theories as D-brane world-volume theories) were tabulated. A total of 375 quiver theories much like the above were cataloged (a catalog which has recently been vastly expanded in Ref. [37], which also took care of ensuring physicality). Though not very large, this gives us a playground to test some of our ideas. The input data are the total charge matrix Q_t, the maximal of whose number of rows and columns are, respectively, 33 and 36, and all taking values in $\{-3, -2, \dots, 3, 4\}$.

Now, suppose we wish to know the number of points of the toric diagram associated with the moduli space, which is clearly an importantly quantity. In principle, this can be computed: the integer kernel of Q_t should give a matrix whose columns are the coordinates of the toric diagram, with multiplicity. Such multiplicity had been realized, via the brane-tiling story, to be associated with the perfect matchings of the bipartite tiling. Nonetheless, one could train the network without any knowledge of this (where the functions pad[ ] and the list Tilings are self-explanatory):

```
data = Table[pad[("Qt" /. Tilings[[i]])] ->
                Length[Union["Points" /. ("Diag" /. Tilings[[i]])]],
      {i, 1, Length[Tilings]}];
ClearAll[net];
net = NetChain[{LinearLayer[1000], ElementwiseLayer[LogisticSigmoid],
            LinearLayer[100], ElementwiseLayer[Tanh], SummationLayer[]},
            "Input" -> {33, 36}];
net = NetTrain[net, data, MaxTrainingRounds -> 1000].
```

Training with our network with the full list achieves, in under 5 minutes, 99.5% accuracy. We now plot the learning curve, as shown in Figure 7. We see that the discrepancy decreases from 5% to less than 1% as we increase the percentage training data (taken as a random sample), validating against the full data. Thus, this problem

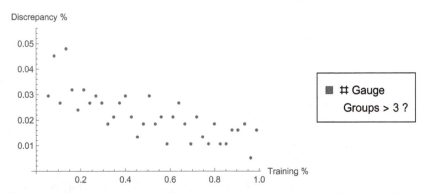

Figure 7. The learning curve for the number of gauge groups for brane tilings. We take, in increments of 10, and starting from 10 random tilings, with which we train the NN (shown as percentage of the total data size of 375 in the horizontal). We then check against the full data to see the percentage discrepancy, shown in the vertical.

is one perfectly adapted for the NN, with high accuracy achieved even for small training sample.

3.5.1. *A hypothetical input*

Now, let us attempt something more drastic. The step to go from d to Q_d is expensive and in fact constituted the major hurdle to understanding D-brane gauge theories before tiling/dimer technology; it involves finding Hilbert basis of lattice points and dual cones in very high dimensions. Even with the latest understanding and implementation of tilings, finding perfect matchings is still non-trivial [37]. Yet, we know that the input data d and Q_F, which can be written down rapidly from definition, *must* at some level determine the output. This is thus a perfect problem adapted to machine learning.

Let us create a matrix, of size 41×52, which will accommodate the stacking of d onto Q_F, right padding with 0 as necessary. It should again be emphasized that computationally, this matrix has no meaning with regard to the toric algorithms developed over the years. The entries of the matrix take integer values in $[-2, 3]$, and for us, this is formally a 41×52 pixelated image with six shades of color. Thus, a typical data would be of the form (say, for the $\mathbb{C} \times \mathbb{C}^2/(\mathbb{Z}/3\mathbb{Z})$ example above)

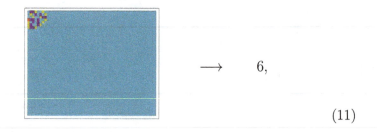

$$\longrightarrow \quad 6, \tag{11}$$

with magenta here denoting 0. Training with the above network still achieves 98.0% accuracy in learning the entire dataset in less than 5 minutes. Even with 200 random samples, the network can predict to an accuracy of 66.4% in minutes, which is expected to increase with training time as well as sample size.

3.6. *A reprobate*

Lest the readers' optimism be elevated to unreasonable heights by the string of successes with the neural networks, it is imperative that we be aware of deep learning's limitations. We therefore finish with a sanity check that a neural network is not some omnipotent magical device nor an oracle capable of predicting *any* pattern. An example which must be doomed to failure is the primes (or, for that matter, the zeros of the Riemann zeta function). Indeed, if a neural network could learn some unexpected pattern in the primes, this would be a rather frightening prospect for mathematics.

Let us thus take our reprobate example to be the following simple dataset:

```
dd = Table[ i -> Prime[i], {i, 1, 5000} ].
```

Training with our neural network (7) and counting discrepancies as always

```
Select[Table[Round[net[dd[[i, 1]]]]-dd[[i, 2]],
  {i, 1, 5000}],# == 0 &]//Length
```

gives 5 after some 10 minutes. That is, of the first 5000 primes, the network has learnt only 5.

Perhaps having more sophisticated input would help? We can attempt with a data structure like

```
dd = Table[   Table[If[j <= i, Prime[j], 0],
      {j, 1, 5000}] -> Prime[i + 1],
        {i, 1, 5000}]
```

so that the input is now a zero-right-padded vector associating the nth prime to the list of all its precedents. Again, we still achieve no better than a 0.1% accuracy.

Our neural network is utterly useless against this formidable challenge; we are better off trying a simple regression against some $n \log(n)$ curve, as dictated by the prime number theorem. This is a sobering exercise as well as a further justification of the various cases studied above, that it is indeed meaningful to deep-learn the landscape data and that our visual representation of geometrical configurations is an efficient methodology.

It is also interesting to find, through our experience, that NNs are good with algebraic geometry but not so much with number theory. This principle could be approximately understood. At the most basic level, every computation in algebraic geometry, be it a spectral sequence or a Gröbner basis, reduces to finding kernels and cokernels of sets of matrices (over $\mathbb{Z}$ or even over $\mathbb{C}$), albeit of quickly forbidding dimensions. Matrix/tensor manipulation is the heart of any NN. Number theory, on the other hand, ultimately involves patterns of prime numbers which, as is well known, remain elusive.

4.   Conclusion

There are many questions in theoretical physics, or even in pure mathematics, for which one would only desire a qualitative, approximate or partial answer and whose full solution would often either be beyond the current scope, conceptual or computational or would have taken considerable effort to attain. Typically, such questions could be "what is the likelihood of finding a universe with three generations of particles within the landscape of string vacua or inflationary scenarios", or "what percentage of elliptic curves have L-functions with prescribed poles"? Attempting to address these profound questions has, with the ever-increasing power of computers, engendered our community's version of "big data", which, though perhaps humble compared to some other fields, does comprise, especially considering the abstract nature of the problems at hand, of significant information often resulting from intense dialog between teams of physicists and mathematicians for many years.

On the still-ripening fruits of this labor, the philosophy of the last decade or so, particularly for the string phenomenology and computational geometry community, has been to (I) create larger and larger datasets and (II) scan through them to test the likelihood of certain salient features. Now that the data are augmenting in size and availability, it is only natural to follow the standard procedures of the data-mining community. In this chapter, we have proposed the paradigm of applying deep learning, via neural networks, to such data. The purpose is twofold; the neural network can act as follows:

Classifiers: by association of input configuration with a requisite quantity and pattern-match over a given dataset;

Predictors: by extrapolating to hithertofore unencountered configurations having deep-learnt a given (partial) dataset.

This is, of course, the archetypal means by which Google deep-learns
the Internet and handwriting recognition software adapts to the
reader's esoteric script. Indeed, this is why *neural networks are far
more sophisticated than usual logistic regression models* where a single
analytic function with a set of given parameters is used to "best-fit".
The network in general consists of a multitude of such functions, not
necessarily analytic but rather algorithmic, which mutually interact
and recursively optimize.

It is intriguing that by going through a wealth of concrete
examples from what we have dubbed **landscape data**, some of
whose creation the author had been a part, this philosophy remains
enlightening. Specifically, we have taken test cases from a range of
problems in mathematical physics, algebraic geometry and representation theory, such as Calabi–Yau datasets, classification of stable
vector bundles, and catalogs of quiver varieties and brane tilings. We
subsequently saw that even relatively simple neural networks like the
multi-layer perceptron can deep-learn with extraordinary accuracy.

In some sense, this is not surprising; there is underlying structure to any classification problem in our context, which may not be
manifest. Indeed, what is novel is to look at the likes of a complete
intersection Calabi–Yau manifold or an integer polytope as a pixelated image, no different from a handwritten digit, for whose analysis
machine-learning has become the *de facto* method and a blossoming
industry.

> *The landscape data, be they work of human hands, elements of
> Nature or conceptions of Mathematics, have inherent structure,
> sometimes more efficiently uncovered by AI via deep-learning.*

Thereby, one can rapidly obtain results, before embarking on finding a reductionist framework for a fundamental theory explaining
the results or proceed to intensive computations from the first principles. This paradigm is especially useful when classification problems become intractable, which is often the case; here, a pragmatic
approach would be to deep-learn partial classification results and predict the future outcome (for this, the predictive accuracy becomes
an important issue which we will address momentarily).

Under this rubric, the possibilities are endless. Several immediate and pertinent directions spring to mind.

- In this chapter, we have really only used NNs as predictors in the sense of *supervised training*. This addresses well the generic problems in, for instance, string phenomenology: we are given some classification of geometries through which we wish to sift in order to find a desired model (such as the MSSM); the classifications are large and we in principle know what we wish to compute though we have the computational power to perform only a fraction of the cases. Therefore, we train an NN in a supervised way, with a specific input and output in mind, in order to predict, with some confidence, the remaining intractable cases. To use neural networks in an unsupervised way, where they find patterns as classifiers, would be an entirely new direction to explore.
- The largest dataset in algebraic geometry/string theory is the Kreuzer–Skarke list [5,20,21] of reflexive polytopes in dimension 4 from each of which many Calabi–Yau manifolds (compact and non-compact) can be constructed. To discover hidden patterns is an ongoing enterprise [14,17] and the help of deep learning would be a most welcome one. Moreover, it is not known how many compact CYs can arise from inequivalent triangulations of the polytopes and a systematic scan had only been done to small Hodge numbers [21]; we could use the neural network's predictive power to extrapolate to the total number of triangulations and hence estimate the total number of Calabi–Yau threefolds.
- The issue of bundle stability and cohomology is a central problem in heterotic phenomenology as well as algebraic geometry. In many ways, this is a perfect problem for machine-learning: the input is usually encodable into an integer matrix or a list of matrices, representing the coefficients in an expansion into effective divisor classes, and the output is simply a vector of integers (in the case of cohomology) or a binary answer (with respective to a given Kähler class, the bundle is either stable or not).
  The brute-force way involves the usual spectral sequences and determining all coboundary maps or finding the lattices of sub-sheafs, expensive by any standards. In the case of stability checking, this is an enormous effort to arrive at a yes/no query. With increasing number of explicitly known examples of stable bundles

constructed from the first principles, to deep-learn this and then estimate the probability of a given bundle being stable would be tremendous time-saver.

- While we could continue to list more prospective projects, there are theoretical issues which have arisen in all the above. First, there is a matter of convergence: How does increasing the complexity of the neural network or its training time decrease the error? There are detailed asymptotic studies of this [42–44] which should be taken into consideration. Second, every prediction must be accompanied by a confidence. The built-in `Classify[ ]` command gives a probability for each extrapolated data point. For our neural networks, we have done a naive comparison to untrained data to get an idea but, especially when dealing the terra incognita of yet unclassified data, we need to specify and investigate the confidence level.

  For example, an ideal statement would be as follows: here is a newly constructed manifold; we barely know its properties and computing them from scratch would be difficult, however, based on similar manifolds classified before whose landscape we have deep-learnt, we can say with confidence a that its Betti numbers are $b_1, b_2, \ldots$

We hope the reader has been persuaded by not only the scope but also the feasibility of our proposed paradigm, a paradigm of increasing importance in an age where even the most abstruse of mathematics or the most theoretical of physics cannot avoid compilations of and investigations on perpetually growing datasets. The case studies of deep learning such landscape of data here presented are but a few nuggets in an unfathomably vast gold mine, rich with new science yet to be discovered.

Acknowledgments

Catharinae Sanctae Alexandriae adque Majorem Dei Gloriam. I am grateful to V. Jejjala, L. Motl (and his kind words), B. Nelson, G. Sankaran, R. Schimmrigk, R.-K. Seong and R. Thomas for comments on the first version of this chapter, as well as to S. Arora W. Taylor for the many helpful conversations at the String Data conference [54] which J. Halverson, C. Long and B. Nelson have brilliantly organized.

Indeed, I am indebted to the Science and Technology Facilities Council, UK, for grant ST/J00037X/1, the Chinese Ministry of Education, for a Chang-Jiang Chair Professorship at Nankai University, and the city of Tianjin for a Qian-Ren Award. Above all, I thank Merton College, Oxford, for continuing to provide a quiet corner of Paradise for musings and contemplations.

References

[1] P. Candelas, G. T. Horowitz, A. Strominger and E. Witten, Vacuum configurations for superstrings, *Nucl. Phys. B* **258** (1985), 46.

[2] P. Candelas, A. M. Dale, C. A. Lutken and R. Schimmrigk, Complete intersection Calabi-Yau manifolds, *Nucl. Phys. B* **298** (1988), 493; P. Candelas, C.A. Lutken and R. Schimmrigk, Complete intersection Calabi-Yau manifolds. *Nucl. Phys. B* **306** (1988), 113; M. Gagnon and Q. Ho-Kim, An exhaustive list of complete intersection Calabi-Yau manifolds, *Mod. Phys. Lett. A* **9** (1994), 2235; T. Hubsch, Calabi-Yau manifolds: A bestiary for physicists, *World Scientific* (1992).

[3] P. Candelas, M. Lynker and R. Schimmrigk, Calabi-Yau manifolds in weighted P(4), *Nucl. Phys. B* **341** (1990), 383.

[4] A. Grassi and D. R. Morrison, Group representations and the Euler characteristic of elliptically fibered Calabi-Yau threefolds, math/0005196 [math-ag]; R.Y. Donagi, Principal bundles on elliptic fibrations, *Asian J. Math.* **1** (1997), 214 [alg-geom/9702002].

[5] A. C. Avram, M. Kreuzer, M. Mandelberg and H. Skarke, The Web of Calabi-Yau hypersurfaces in toric varieties, *Nucl. Phys. B* **505** (1997), 625 [hep-th/9703003]; V.V. Batyrev and L.A. Borisov, On Calabi-Yau complete intersections in toric varieties, arXiv:alg-geom/9412017; M. Kreuzer and H. Skarke, Reflexive polyhedra, weights and toric Calabi-Yau fibrations, *Rev. Math. Phys.* **14** (2002), 343 [math/0001106 [math-ag]].

[6] S. Kachru, R. Kallosh, A. D. Linde and S. P. Trivedi, De Sitter vacua in string theory, *Phys. Rev. D* **68** (2003), 046005. Doi: 10.1103/PhysRevD.68.046005 [hep-th/0301240].

[7] C. Vafa, The String landscape and the swampland, hep-th/0509212.

[8] F. Gmeiner, R. Blumenhagen, G. Honecker, D. Lust and T. Weigand, One in a billion: MSSM-like D-brane statistics, *JHEP* **0601** (2006), 004 [hep-th/0510170].

[9] V. Braun, Y.-H. He, B. A. Ovrut and T. Pantev, The exact MSSM spectrum from string theory, *JHEP* **0605** (2006), 043 [hep-th/0512177].

[10] P. Candelas, X. de la Ossa, Y.-H. He and B. Szendroi, Triadophilia: A special corner in the landscape, *Adv. Theor. Math. Phys.* **12** (2008), 429 [arXiv:0706.3134 [hep-th]].

[11] Y. H. He, Calabi-Yau geometries: Algorithms, databases, and physics, *Int. J. Mod. Phys. A* **28** (2013), 1330032 [arXiv:1308.0186 [hep-th]].

[12] Y.-H. He, P. Candelas, A. Hanany, A. Lukas and B. Ovrut, Ed. *Computational Algebraic Geometry in String, Gauge Theory*. Special Issue, Advances in High Energy Physics, Hindawi Publishing (2012). Doi: 10.1155/2012/431898.

[13] V. Braun, Toric elliptic fibrations and F-theory compactifications, *JHEP* **1301**(2013), 016 [arXiv:1110.4883 [hep-th]].

[14] W. Taylor, On the Hodge structure of elliptically fibered Calabi-Yau threefolds, *JHEP* **1208** (2012), 032 [arXiv:1205.0952 [hep-th]].

[15] A. P. Braun, J. Knapp, E. Scheidegger, H. Skarke and N. O. Walliser, PALP — A user manual, arXiv:1205.4147 [math.AG].

[16] P. Candelas, A. Constantin and H. Skarke, An abundance of K3 fibrations from polyhedra with interchangeable parts, arXiv:1207.4792 [hep-th].

[17] Y. H. He, V. Jejjala and L. Pontiggia, Patterns in Calabi-Yau distributions, arXiv:1512.01579 [hep-th].

[18] P. Candelas and R. Davies, New Calabi-Yau manifolds with small Hodge numbers, *Fortsch. Phys.* **58** (2010), 383 [arXiv:0809.4681 [hep-th]].

[19] W. A. Stein *et al.*, *Sage Mathematics Software (Version)*. The Sage Development Team (2017) http://www.sagemath.org.

[20] Calabi Yau data, hep.itp.tuwien.ac.at/~kreuzer/CY/.

[21] R. Altman, J. Gray, Y. H. He, V. Jejjala and B. D. Nelson, A Calabi-Yau database: Threefolds constructed from the Kreuzer-Skarke list, *JHEP* **1502** (2015), 158 [arXiv:1411.1418 [hep-th]]. Toric Calabi-Yau Database: www.rossealtman.com.

[22] Y. H. He, S. J. Lee and A. Lukas, Heterotic models from vector bundles on Toric Calabi-Yau manifolds, *JHEP* **1005** (2010), 071 [arXiv:0911.0865 [hep-th]]; Y.H. He, M. Kreuzer, S.J. Lee and A. Lukas, Heterotic bundles on Calabi-Yau manifolds with small Picard number, *JHEP* **1112** (2011), 039 [arXiv:1108.1031 [hep-th]].

[23] L. B. Anderson, F. Apruzzi, X. Gao, J. Gray and S. J. Lee, A new construction of Calabi–Yau manifolds: Generalized CICYs, *Nucl. Phys. B* **906** (2016), 441 [arXiv:1507.03235 [hep-th]].

[24] L. B. Anderson, Y. H. He and A. Lukas, Heterotic compactification, an algorithmic approach, *JHEP* **0707** (2007), 049 [hep-th/0702210 [HEP-TH]].

[25] L. B. Anderson, J. Gray, A. Lukas and E. Palti, Heterotic line bundle standard models, *JHEP* **1206** (2012), 113 [arXiv:1202.1757 [hep-th]].

[26] L. B. Anderson, A. Constantin, J. Gray, A. Lukas and E. Palti, A comprehensive scan for heterotic SU(5) GUT models, *JHEP* **1401** (2014), 047 [arXiv:1307.4787 [hep-th]].

[27] J. Gray, A. S. Haupt and A. Lukas, All complete intersection Calabi-Yau four-folds, *JHEP* **1307** (2013), 070 [arXiv:1303.1832 [hep-th]].

[28] P. Gao, Y. H. He and S. T. Yau, Extremal bundles on Calabi–Yau threefolds, *Commun. Math. Phys.* **336**(3) (2015), 1167 [arXiv:1403.1268 [hep-th]].

[29] D. R. Morrison and C. Vafa, Compactifications of F theory on Calabi-Yau threefolds. 1 & 2, *Nucl. Phys.* B **473** (1996), 74 [hep-th/9602114]; *Nucl. Phys.* B **476** (1996), 437 [hep-th/9603161].

[30] R. Friedman, J. Morgan and E. Witten, Vector bundles and F theory, *Commun. Math. Phys.* **187** (1997), 679 [hep-th/9701162].

[31] M. Gabella, Y. H. He and A. Lukas, An abundance of heterotic vacua, *JHEP* **0812** (2008), 027 [arXiv:0808.2142 [hep-th]].

[32] M. Cvetič, J. Halverson, D. Klevers and P. Song, On finiteness of Type IIB compactifications: Magnetized branes on elliptic Calabi-Yau threefolds, *JHEP* **1406** (2014), 138 [arXiv:1403.4943 [hep-th]].

[33] A. Hanany and Y. H. He, NonAbelian finite gauge theories, *JHEP* **9902** (1999), 013 [hep-th/9811183]; A. Hanany and Y. H. He, A monograph on the classification of the discrete subgroups of SU(4), *JHEP* **0102** (2001), 027 [hep-th/9905212].

[34] B. Feng, A. Hanany and Y. H. He, D-brane gauge theories from toric singularities and toric duality, *Nucl. Phys.* B **595** (2001), 165 [hep-th/0003085].

[35] S. Franco, A. Hanany, D. Martelli, J. Sparks, D. Vegh and B. Wecht, Gauge theories from toric geometry and brane tilings, *JHEP* **0601** (2006), 128 [hep-th/0505211].

[36] J. Davey, A. Hanany and J. Pasukonis, On the classification of Brane Tilings, *JHEP* **1001** (2010), 078 [arXiv:0909.2868 [hep-th]].

[37] S. Franco, Y. H. He, C. Sun and Y. Xiao, A comprehensive survey of Brane Tilings, arXiv:1702.03958 [hep-th].

[38] J. Davey, A. Hanany, N. Mekareeya and G. Torri, M2-Branes and Fano 3-folds, *J. Phys.* A **44** (2011), 405401 [arXiv:1103.0553 [hep-th]].

[39] A. Hanany and R. K. Seong, Brane Tilings and reflexive polygons, *Fortsch. Phys.* **60** (2012), 695 [arXiv:1201.2614 [hep-th]].

[40] Y. H. He, R. K. Seong and S. T. Yau, Calabi-Yau volumes and reflexive polytopes, arXiv:1704.03462 [hep-th].

[41] S. Franco, S. Lee, R. K. Seong and C. Vafa, Brane Brick models in the mirror, *JHEP* **1702** (2017), 106 [arXiv:1609.01723 [hep-th]].

[42] J. Herz, A. Krough and R. G. Palmer, *Introduction to the Theory of Neural Computation.* Addison-Wesley (1991). https://doi.org/10. 1201/9780429499661.

[43] M. H. Hassoun, *Fundamentals of Artificial Neural Networks.* MIT Press (1995).

[44] S. Haykin, *Neural Networks: A Comprehensive Foundation.* 2nd edn. New York: Macmillan (1999).

[45] J. A. Freeman, *Simulating Neural Networks with Mathematica.* Addison-Wesley (1994). https://library.wolfram.com/infocenter/ Books/3485.

[46] Wolfram Research, Inc., *Mathematica*, Version 11.1, Champaign, IL (2017).

[47] TensorFlow, An open-source software library for Machine Intelligence. https://www.tensorflow.org/.

[48] Mathematica v11: Neural Networks. https://mathematica. stackexchange.com/questions/124977/.

[49] K. J. C. Leney [ATLAS Collaboration], A neural-network clusterisation algorithm for the ATLAS silicon pixel detector, *J. Phys. Conf. Ser.* **523** (2014), 012023.

[50] C. P. Novaes, A. Bernui, I. S. Ferreira and C. A. Wuensche, A neural-network based estimator to search for primordial non-Gaussianity in Planck CMB maps, *JCAP* **1509**(09) (2015), 064 [arXiv:1409.3876 [astro-ph.CO]].

[51] A. J. Ballard, R. Das, S. Martiniani, D. Mehta, L. Sagun, J. Stevenson and D. Wales, Perspective: Energy landscapes for Machine Learning, arXiv:1703.07915.

[52] W. C. Gan and F. W. Shu, Holography as deep-learning, arXiv:1705.05750 [gr-qc].

[53] Deep-Learning and Physics Conference. http://kabuto.phys.sci. osaka-u.ac.jp/~koji/workshop/tsrp/Deep_Lerning.html.

[54] String Data, *A 2017 Workshop on Data Science and String Theory*, Northeastern University, Nov 30–Dec 2 (2017). https://web. northeastern.edu/het/string_data/.

[55] Y. H. He, Machine-learning the string landscape, *Phys. Lett. B* **774** (2017), 564. Doi: 10.1016/j.physletb.2017.10.024.

Chapter 7

hep-th

Yang-Hui He[*,§]**, Vishnu Jejjala**[†,¶]**, and Brent D. Nelson**[‡,∥]

*London Institute for Mathematical Sciences, Royal Institution of
Great Britain, London, W1S 4BS, UK;
Merton College, University of Oxford, OX1 4JD, UK;
Department of Mathematics, City, University of London, EC1V0HB, UK;
School of Physics, Nankai University, Tianjin, 300071, P.R. China
†Mandelstam Institute for Theoretical Physics, NITheP, CoE-MaSS, and
School of Physics, University of the Witwatersrand,
Johannesburg WITS 2050, South Africa
‡Department of Physics, College of Science, Northeastern University,
Dana Research Center, 110 Forsyth Street, Boston, MA 02115, USA

§hey@maths.ox.ac.uk
¶vishnu@neo.phys.wits.ac.za
∥b.nelson@neu.edu

Abstract

We apply techniques in natural language processing, computational
linguistics and machine-learning to investigate papers in hep-th and
four related sections of the arXiv: hep-ph, hep-lat, gr-qc and math-ph.
All of the titles of papers in each of these sections, from the inception of the arXiv until the end of 2017, are extracted and treated as
a corpus which we use to train the neural network Word2Vec. A comparative study of common n-grams, linear syntactical identities, word
cloud and word similarities is carried out. We find notable scientific
and sociological differences between the fields. In conjunction with support vector machines, we also show that the syntactic structures of the
titles in different subfields of high energy and mathematical physics are

sufficiently different that a neural network can perform a binary classification of formal versus phenomenological sections with 87.1% accuracy and can perform a finer fivefold classification across all sections with 65.1% accuracy.

1. Introduction

The `arXiv` [1], introduced by Paul Ginsparg to communicate preprints in high energy theoretical physics in 1991 and democratize science [2], has since expanded to encompass areas of physics, mathematics, computer science, quantitative biology, quantitative finance, statistics, electrical engineering and systems science, and economics and now hosts nearly 1.4 million preprints. In comparison with 123,523 preprints archived and distributed in 2017 [3], around 2.4 million scholarly articles across all fields of academic enquiry are published every year [4]. As a practitioner in science, keeping up with the literature in order to invent new knowledge from old is itself a formidable labor that technology may simplify.

In this chapter, we apply the latest methods in computational linguistics, natural language processing and machine learning to preprints in high energy theoretical physics and mathematical physics to demonstrate important proofs of concept: by mapping words to vectors, algorithms can automatically sort preprints into their appropriate disciplines with over 65% accuracy, and these vectors capture the relationships between scientific concepts. In due course, many interesting properties of the word vectors emerge and we make comparative studies across the different sub-fields. Developing this technology will facilitate the use of computers as idea generating machines [5]. This is complementary to the role of computers in mathematics as proof assistants [6] and problem solvers [7].

The *zeitgeist* of the moment has seen computers envelop our scientific lives. In particular, in the last few years, we have seen an explosion of activity in applying artificial intelligence to various aspects of theoretical physics (cf. [8] for a growing repository of papers). In high energy theoretical physics, there have been attempts to understand the string landscape using deep neural networks [9], with genetic algorithms [10], with network theory [11,12], for computing Calabi–Yau volumes [13], for F-theory [14], for CICY manifolds [15], etc.

Inspired by a recent effort by Evert van Nieuwenburg [16] to study the language of condensed matter theory, we are naturally led to wonder what the latest technology in language-processing using machine learning, utilized by the likes of `Google` and `Facebook`, would tell us about the language of theoretical physics.

As members of the high energy theoretical physics community, we focus on particular fields related to our own expertise: hep-th (high energy physics — theory), hep-ph (high energy physics — phenomenology), hep-lat (high energy physics — lattice), gr-qc (general relativity and quantum cosmology) and math-ph (mathematical physics). In December 2017, we downloaded the titles and abstracts of the preprints thus far posted to `arXiv` in these disciplines. In total, we analyze a collection of some $395,000$ preprints. Upon cleaning the data, we use `Word2vec` [17,18] to map the words that appear in this corpus of text to vectors in $\mathbb{R}^{400}$. We then proceed to investigate this using the standard `Python` package `gensim` [19]. In parallel, a comparative study of the linguistic structure of the titles in the different fields is carried out.

It should be noted that there have been investigations of the `arXiv` using textual analyses [20–22] (We thank Paul Ginsparg for kindly pointing out the relevant references and discussions.). In this chapter, we focus on the five sections of theory/phenomenology in the high-energy/mathematical physics community as well as their comparisons with titles outside of academia. Moreover, we will focus on the syntactical identities which are generated from the contextual studies. Finally, where possible, we attempt to provide explanations why certain features in the data emerge, features which are indicative of the socio-scientific nature of the various sub-disciplines of the community.

We hope this chapter will have readers in two widely separated fields: our colleagues in the high energy theory community and those who study natural language processing in academia or in industry. As such, some guidance to the structure of what follows is warranted. For physicists, the introductory material in Section 2 will serve as a very brief summary and introduction to the vocabulary and techniques of computational textual analysis. Experts in this area can skip this entirely. Section 3 begins in Section 3.1 with an introduction to the five `arXiv` sections we will be studying. Our colleagues in physics will know this well and may skip this. Data scientists will want to understand our methods for preparing the data for analysis, which is described in Section 3.2, followed by some general descriptive properties of the hep-th vocabulary in Section 3.3. The analyses of hep-th using the results of Word2vec's neural network are presented in Section 4 and those of the other four arXiv sections in Section 5. These two sections will be of greatest interest and amusement for authors who regularly contribute to the arXiv, but we would direct data scientists to Section 4.1, in which the peculiar geometrical properties of our vector space word embedding are studied, in a manner similar to that of the recent work by Mimno and Thompson [24]. Our work culminates with a demonstration of the power of Word2vec, coupled with a support vector machine classifier, to accurately sort arXiv titles into the appropriate sub-categories. We summarize our results and speculate about future directions in Section 7.

2. Computational Textual Analysis

2.1. *Distributed representation of words*

We begin by reviewing some terminology and definitions (the reader is referred to Refs. [25,26] for more pedagogical material). A **dictionary** is a finite set whose elements are **words**, each of which is an ordered finite sequence of letters. An n-**gram** is an ordered sequence of n words. A sentence can be considered an n-gram. Moreover, since we will not worry about punctuation, we shall use these two concepts interchangeably. Continuing in a familiar manner, an ordered collection of sentences is a **document** and a collection (ordered if necessary) of documents is a **corpus**:

$$\text{word} \in n\text{-gram} \subset \text{document} \subset \text{corpus}. \tag{1}$$

Note that for our purposes, the smallest unit is "word" rather than "letters" and we will also not make many distinctions among the three set inclusions, *i.e.*, after all, we can string the entire corpus of documents into a single n-gram for some very large n. As we shall be studying abstracts and titles of scientific papers, n will typically be no more than $\mathcal{O}(10)$ for titles and $\mathcal{O}(100)$ for abstracts.

In order to perform any analysis, one needs a numerical representation of words and n-grams; this representation is often called a **word embedding**. Suppose we have a dictionary of N words. We can lexicographically order them, for instance, giving us a natural vector of length N. Each word is a vector containing precisely a single 1, corresponding to its position in the dictionary and 0 everywhere else. The entire dictionary is thus the $N \times N$ identity matrix and the ith word is simply the elementary basis vector e_i. This representation is sometimes called the **one-hot** form of a vector representation of words (the hot being the single 1-entry). This representation of words is not particularly powerful because not much more than equality-testing can be performed.

The insight of Ref. [27] is to have a weighted vectorial representation $\vec{v}_w$, constructed so as to reflect the *meaning* of the word w. For instance, $\vec{v}_{\text{"car"}} - \vec{v}_{\text{"cars"}}$ should give a close value to $\vec{v}_{\text{"apple"}} - \vec{v}_{\text{"apples"}}$. Note that, for the sake of brevity, we will be rather lax about the notation on words: i.e., $\vec{v}_{\text{"word"}}$ and "word" will be used interchangeably. Indeed, we wish to take advantage of the algebraic structure of a vector space over $\mathbb{R}$ to allow for addition and subtraction of vectors. An archetypal example in the literature is that

$$\text{"king"} - \text{"man"} + \text{"woman"} = \text{"queen"}. \tag{2}$$

In order to arrive at a result such as (2), we need a few non-trivial definitions.

Definition 1. A **context window** with respect to a word W, or specifically, a *k-around context window* with respect to W, is a subsequence within a sentence or n-gram containing the word W, containing all words a distance k away from W, in both directions. Similarly, a k context window, without reference to a specific word, is simply a subsequence of length k.

For example, consider the following 46-gram, taken from the abstract of Ref. [28], which is one of the first papers to appear on hep-th in 1991:

> String theories with two dimensional space-time target spaces are characterized by the existence of a ground ring of operators of spin (0,0). By understanding this ring, one can understand the symmetries of the theory and illuminate the relation of the critical string theory to matrix models.

In this case, a 2-around context window for the word "spaces" is the 5-gram "spacetime target spaces are characterized". Meanwhile, 2-context windows are 2-grams such as "ground ring" or "(0,0)". Note that we have considered hyphenated words as a single word and that the n-gram has crossed between two sentences.

The above example immediately reveals one distinction of scientific and mathematical writing that does not often appear in other forms of writing: the presence of mathematical symbols and expressions in otherwise ordinary prose. Our procedure will be to ignore all punctuation marks in the titles and abstracts. Thus, "(0,0)" becomes the 'word' "00". Fortunately, such mathematical symbols are generally rare in the abstracts of papers (though, of course, they are quite common in the body of the works themselves) and even more uncommon in the titles of papers.

The correlation between words in the sense of context, reflecting their likely proximity in a document, can be captured by a matrix:

Definition 2. The k **co-occurrence matrix** for an n-gram is a symmetric, 0-diagonal square matrix (of dimension equaling the number of unique words) which encodes the adjacency of the words within a k context window.

Continuing with the above example of the 46-gram, we list all the unique words horizontally and vertically, giving a 37×37 matrix for this sentence (of course, one could consider the entire corpus as a single n-gram and construct a much larger matrix). The words can be ordered lexicographically, { "a", "and", "are", ... }. One can check that in a 2-context-window (testing whether two words are immediate neighbors), for instance, "a" and "and" are never adjacent; thus, the $(i, j) = (1, 2)$ entry of the 2 co-occurrence matrix is 0.

2.2.   *Neural networks*

The subject of neural networks is vast and into its full introduction we certainly shall not delve. Since this section is aimed primarily at theoretical physicists and mathematicians, it is expedient only to remind the reader of the most rudimentary definitions, enough to prepare for the ensuing section. We recall first the following definition.

Definition 3. A **neuron** is a (typically analytic) function $f(\sum_{i=1}^{k} w_i \cdot x_i + b)$ whose argument x_i is the *input*, typically some real tensor with multi-index i. The value of f is called the *output*, the parameter w_i is some real tensor called *weights* with "·" appropriate contraction of the indices and the parameter $b \in \mathbb{R}$ is called the *off-set* or *bias*.

The function f is called an activation function and often takes the nonlinear forms of a hyperbolic tangent or a sigmoid. The parameters w_i and b are to be determined empirically as follows:

- Let there be a set of input values x_i^j labeled by $j = 1, \ldots, T$ such that the output y^j is known: $\{x_i^j, y^j\}$ is called the **training set**;
- Define an appropriate measure of goodness-of-fit, typically one uses the standard deviation (mean square error)

$$Z(w_i, b) := \sum_{j=1}^{T} \left(f\left(\sum_{i=1}^{k} w_i \cdot x_i^j + b \right) - y^j \right)^2 ;$$

- minimize $Z(w_i, b)$ as a function of the parameters (often numerically by steepest descent methods), whereby determining the parameters (w_i, b);
- test the now-fixed neuron on unseen input data.

At this level, we are doing no more than (nonlinear) regression by best fit. We remark that in the above definition, we have made f a real-valued function for simplicity. In general, f will be itself tensor-valued.

The power of the neural network comes from establishing a network structure of neurons — much like the complexity of the brain comes from the myriad inter-connectivities among biological neurons:

Definition 4. A **neural network** is a finite directed graph, with possible cycles, each node of which is a neuron, such that the input for the neuron at tail of an arrow is the output of the neuron at the head of the arrow. We organize the neural network into *layers* so that

(1) the collection of nodes with arguments explicitly involving the actual input data is called the *input layer*;

(2) likewise, the collection of nodes with arguments explicitly involving the actual output of data is called the *output layer*;
(3) the collection of all other nodes are called *hidden layers*.

Training the neural network proceeds as the algorithm above, with the input and output layers interacting with the training data and each neuron giving its own set of weight/off-set parameters. The measure Z will thus be a function in many variables over which we optimize.

One might imagine the design of a neural network — with its many possible hidden layers, neuron types and internal architecture — would be a complicated affair and highly dependent on the problem at hand. But in this, we can take advantage of the powerful theorem by Cybenko and Hornik [29]:

Theorem 1. Universal Approximation Theorem [Cybenko–Hornik]. *A neural network with a single hidden layer with a finite number of neurons can approximate any neural network in the sense of prescribing a dense set within the set of continuous functions on $\mathbb{R}^n$.*

2.3.   *Word2Vec*

We now combine the concepts in the previous two sections to use a neural network to establish a *predictive* embedding of words. In particular, we will be dealing with Word2Vec [27], which has emerged as one of the most sophisticated models for natural language processing (NLP). The Word2Vec software can utilize one of two related neural network models: (1) the **continuous bag of words [CBOW]** model or (2) the **skip-gram [SG]** model, both consisting of only a single hidden layer, which we will shortly define in the following in detail.

The CBOW approach is perhaps the most straight forward: given an n-gram, form the multiset ('bag') of all words found in the n-gram, retaining multiplicity information. One might also consider including the set of all m-grams ($m \leq n$) in the multiset. A collection of such 'bags', all associated with a certain classifier (say, 'titles of hep-th papers'), then becomes the input upon which the neural network trains.

The SG model attempts to retain contextual information by utilizing context windows in the form of k-**skip**-n-**grams**, which are n grams in which each of the components of the n-gram occur at a distance k from one another. That is, length-k gaps exist in the n-grams extracted from a piece of text. The fundamental object of study is thus a k-skip-n-gram, together with the set of elided words. It is the collection of these objects that becomes the input upon which the neural network trains.

The two neural network approaches are complementary to one another. Coarsely speaking, CBOW is trained to predict a word given context, while SG is trained to predict context given a word. To be more concrete, a CBOW model develops a vector space of word embeddings in such a way as to maximize the likelihood that, given a collection of words, it will return a single word that best matches the context of the collection. By contrast, the vector space of word embeddings constructed by the SG model is best suited to give a collection of words likely to be found in context with a particular word.

While CBOW and SG have specific roles, the default method for generating word embeddings in a large corpus is to use the CBOW model. This is because it is clearly more deterministic to have more input than output, i.e., a single-valued function is easier to handle than a multi-valued one. This will be our choice going forward. Note that our ultimate interest is in the information contained in the word embedding itself and not in the ability of the model to make predictions on particular words. When we attack the document classification problem via machine learning, in Section 6, we will use the distributed representation generated by Word2Vec as training data for a simple support vector machine classifier.

With the CBOW model in mind, therefore, let us consider the structure of the underlying neural network, depicted schematically in Figure 1. Let V denote the vocabulary size so that any word can be *ab initio* trivially represented by a one-hot vector in $\mathbb{R}^V$. The dimension V could be rather large, and we will see how a reduction to an N-dimensional representation is achieved. The overall structure has three layers:

(1) The input layer is a list of C context words. Thus, this is a list of C vectors $\vec{x}_{c=1,\ldots,C}$ each of dimension V. We denote these component-wise as $x_{c=1,\ldots,C}^{i=1,\ldots,V}$. This list is the "bag of words" of

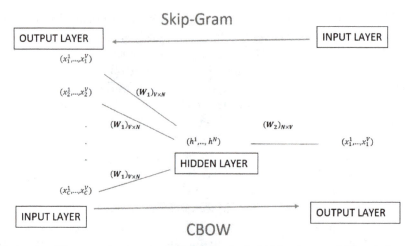

Figure 1.   The neural network consists of a single hidden layer, which constructs a mapping from $\mathbb{R}^V$ to $\mathbb{R}^V$. The parameters to be fit by the neural network are the transformation matrices W_1 and W_2, with the entries of W_1 constituting the word embedding into the space $\mathbb{R}^N$. After training, a CBOW model takes multiple $\vec{x}$ inputs, associated with a particular context C and maps them to a single output vector. Conversely, after training, a SG model takes a single word $\vec{x}$ as an input and returns the set of vectors $\vec{x}_C$ associated with the appropriate context.

CBOW, and in our case, each such list will represent a single, contextually closed object, such as a paper title or paper abstract.

(2) The output layer is a single vector $\vec{y}$ of dimension V. We will train the neural network with a large number of examples where y is known, given the words $\vec{x}$ within a context C, so that one could thence *predict* the output. Continuing with our example of Ref. [28], the title of this paper provides a specific context C: "Ground ring of two-dimensional string theory". Thus, for an input of {"ring", "of", "string", "theory"}, we ideally wish to return the vector associated with "two-dimensional" when the window size is set to two. Of course, we expect words like "theory" to appear in many other titles. The neural network will therefore optimize over many such titles (contexts) to give the "best" vector representation of words.

(3) There is a single hidden layer consisting of N neural nodes. The function from the input layer to the hidden layer is taken to be linear map, i.e., a $V \times N$ matrix W_1 of weights. Likewise, the map from the hidden layer to the output layer is an $N \times V$ weight

matrix W_2. Thus, in total, we have $2V \times N$ weights which will be optimized by training. Note that N is a fixed parameter (or hyper-parameter) and is a choice. Typically, $N \sim 300 - 500$ has been shown to be a good range [25,26,30]; in this paper, we take $N = 400$.

To find the optimal word embedding, or most faithful representation of the words in $\mathbb{R}^N$, each input vector $\vec{x}_c$, in a particular context (or bag), is mapped by W_1 to an N vector (the actual word vector after the neural network is trained) $\vec{h} = [\vec{x}_c]^T \cdot W_1$. Of course, because $\vec{x}$ is a Kronecker delta, $\vec{h}$ is just the k-th row of W_1 where k is the only component equal to 1 in $\vec{x}_c$. A measure of the proximity between an input and output word vector is the weighted inner product

$$\langle \vec{x}_c, \vec{y} \rangle := [\vec{x}_c]^T \cdot W_1 \cdot W_2 \cdot \vec{y}. \tag{3}$$

Hence, for each given context C_α, where α might label contextually distinct objects (such as paper titles) in our training set, we can define a score for each component i (thus in the one-hot representation, each word) $u_c^{j=1,\ldots,V}$ in the vocabulary as

$$u_c^j := [\vec{x}_c]^T \cdot W_1 \cdot W_2. \tag{4}$$

As always with a list, one can convert this to a probability (for each c and each component j) via the *softmax function*:

$$p(u_c^j | x_c) := \frac{\exp(u_c^j)}{\sum_{j=1}^V \exp(u_c^j)}. \tag{5}$$

Finally, the components of the output vector $\vec{y}$ are the product over the context words of these probabilities

$$y^j = \prod_{c=1}^C \frac{\exp(u_c^j)}{\sum_{j=1}^V \exp(u_c^j)}. \tag{6}$$

The neural network is trained by maximizing the log-likelihood of the probabilities across all of our training contexts

$$Z(W_1, W_2) := \frac{1}{|D|} \sum_{\alpha=1}^{|D|} \log \prod_{c=1}^{C_\alpha} \frac{\exp([\vec{x}_c]^T \cdot W_1 \cdot W_2)}{\sum_{j=1}^V \exp([\vec{x}_c]^T \cdot W_1 \cdot W_2)}, \tag{7}$$

where we have written the functional dependence in terms of the $2V \times N$ variables of W_1 and W_2 because we need to extremize over these. In (7), the symbol $|D|$ represents the number of independent contexts in the training set (i.e., $\alpha = 1, \ldots, |D|$).

We will perform a vector embedding study as discussed above and perform various contextual analyses using the bag-of-words model. Fortunately, many of the requisite algorithms have been implemented into **python** with the **gensim** package [19].

2.4. *Distance measures*

Once we have represented all words in a corpus as vectors in $\mathbb{R}^N$, we will loosely use the "=" sign to denote that two words are "close" in the sense that the Euclidean distance between the two vectors is small. In practice, this is measured by computing the cosine of the angle between the vectors representing the words. That is, given words w_1 and w_2, and their associated word vectors $\vec{v}_{w_1}$ and $\vec{v}_{w_2}$, we can define distance as

$$d(w_1, w_2) := \frac{\vec{v}_{w_1} \cdot \vec{v}_{w_2}}{|\vec{v}_{w_1}| |\vec{v}_{w_2}|}. \tag{8}$$

Generically, we expect $d(w_1, w_2)$ will be close to zero, meaning that two words are not related. However, if $d(w_1, w_2)$ is close to $+1$, the words are similar. Indeed, for the same word w, tautologically $d(w, w) = 1$. If $d(w_1, w_2)$ is close to -1, then the words are dissimilar in the sense that they tend to be far apart in any context window. We will adopt, for clarity, the following notation:

Definition 5. Two words w_1 and w_2 are

similar in the sense of $d(w_1, w_2) \sim 1$ (including the trivial case of equality) and are denoted as $w_1 = w_2$ and
dissimilar in the sense of $d(w_1, w_2) \sim -1$ and are denoted as

$$w_1 \neq w_2.$$

Vector addition generates signed relations such as $w_1 + w_2 = w_3$ and $w_1 + w_2 - w_3 = w_4$. We will call these relations **linear syntactic identities**.

For instance, our earlier example of (2) is one such identity involving four words. Henceforth, we will bear in mind that "=" denotes the *closest* word within context windows inside the corpus. Finding such identities in the hep-th arXiv and its sister repositories will be one of the goals of our investigation.

As a technical point, it should be noted that word vectors *do not span a vector space V* in the proper sense. First, there is no real sense of closure; one cannot guarantee the sum of vectors is still in V, only the closest to it by distance. Second, there is no sense of scaling by elements of the ground field, here $\mathbb{R}$. In other words, though the components of word vectors are real numbers, it is not clear what $aw_1 + bw_2$ for arbitrary $a, b \in \mathbb{R}$ means. The only operation we can perform is the one discussed above by adding two and subtracting two vectors in the sense of a syntactic identity.

2.5. *Term frequency and document frequency*

Following our model of treating the set of titles/abstracts of each section as a single document, one could thus consider the arXiv as a corpus. The standard method of cross-documentary comparisons is the so-called **term frequency-inverse document frequency (tf-idf)**, which attempts to quantify the importance of a particular word in the corpus overall:

Definition 6. Let D be a corpus of documents, $d \in D$ a document and $t \in d$ be a word (sometimes also called a term) in d. Let $f(t, d) := |x \in d : x = t|$ represent the raw count of the number of appearances of the word t in the document d, where the notation $|X|$ means the cardinality of the set represented by X.

- The **term frequency** $\mathrm{tf}(t, d)$ is a choice of function of the count of occurrences $f(t, d) := |x \in d : x = t|$ of t in d.
- The **inverse document frequency** $\mathrm{idf}(t, D)$ is the minus logarithm of the fraction of documents containing t:

$$\mathrm{idf}(t, D) := -\log \frac{|d \in D : t \in d|}{|D|} = \log \frac{|D|}{|d \in D : t \in d|}.$$

- The **tf-idf** is the product of the above two: $\mathrm{tfidf}(t, d, D) := \mathrm{tf}(t, d) \cdot \mathrm{idf}(t, D)$.

In the context of our discussion in Section 2.3, D might represent the sum of all titles, and each d might represent a distinct title (or "context").

The simplest tf is, of course, to just take $f(t,d)$ itself. Another commonly employed tf is a logarithmically scaled frequency $\text{tf}(t,d) = \log(1 + f(t,d))$, which we shall utilize in our analysis. This is used because heuristics such as Benford's law and Zipf's law suggest that word (and indeed letter) distributions tend to follow inverse power laws, and the logarithm tends to extract the critical exponent. Thus, we will have

$$\text{tfidf}(t, d, D) = \log(1 + |x \in d : x = t|) \log \frac{|D|}{|d \in D : t \in d|} \in \mathbb{R}_{\geq 0}, \quad (9)$$

where d might represent the string of words in all titles in a given arXiv section, labeled by D. The concept of weighting by the inverse document frequency is to penalize those words which appear in virtually all documents. Thus, a tf-idf score of zero means that the word either does not appear at all in a document or it appears in *all* documents.

3.   Data Preparation

3.1. *Datasets*

As mentioned in the introduction, we will be concerned primarily with the language of hep-th, but we will be comparing this section of the arXiv with closely related sections. The five categories that will be of greatest interest to us will be as follows:

hep-th: Begun in the summer of 1991, hep-th was the original preprint listserv for theoretical physics. Traditionally, the content has focused on formal theory, including (but not limited to) formal results in supersymmetric field theory, string theory and string model building, and conformal field theory.

hep-ph: Established in March of 1992, hep-ph was the bulletin board designed to host papers in phenomenology — a term used in high energy theory to refer to model-building, constraining known models with experimental data, and theoretical simulation of current or planned particle physics experiments.

hep-lat: Launched in April of 1992, **hep-lat** is the `arXiv` section dedicated to numerical calculations of quantum field theory observables using a discretization of spacetime ("lattice") that allows for direct computation of correlation functions that cannot be computed by standard perturbative (Feynman diagram) techniques. While closely related to the topics studied by authors in **hep-th** and **hep-ph**, scientists posting research to **hep-lat** tend to be highly specialized and tend to utilize high performance computing to perform their calculations at a level that is uncommon in the other `arXiv` sections.

gr-qc: The bulletin board for general relativity and quantum cosmology, **gr-qc**, was established in July of 1992. Publications submitted to this section of `arXiv` tend to involve topics such as black hole solutions to general relativity in various dimensions, treatment of spacetime singularities, information theory in general relativity and early universe physics. Explicit models of inflation, and their experimental consequences, may appear in **gr-qc**, as well as in **hep-th** and (to a lesser extent) **hep-ph**. Preprints exploring non-string theory approaches to quantum gravity typically appear here.

math-ph: The youngest of the sections we consider, **math-ph**, was born in March of 1998 by re-purposing a section of the general physics `arXiv` then called "Mathematical Methods in Physics". As the original notification email advised, "If you are not sure whether or not your submission is physics, then it should be sent to math-ph." Today, papers submitted to **math-ph** are typically the work of mathematicians, whose intended audience is other mathematicians, but the content of which tends to be of relevance to certain areas of string theory and formal gauge theory research.

Given that part of the motivation for this work is to use language as a marker for understanding the social dynamics — and overlapping interests — of our community, it is relevant to mention a few important facts about the evolution of the `arXiv`. The `arXiv` repository began originally as a listserv, which sent daily lists of titles and abstracts of preprints to its subscribers. The more technically savvy of these recipients could then seek to obtain these preprints via anonymous **ftp** or **gopher**. A true Web interface arrived at the end of 1993.

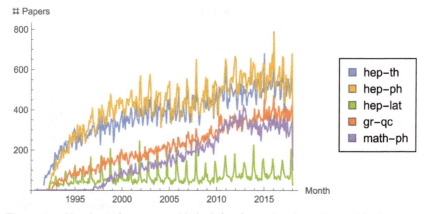

Figure 2.   Number of papers published for five related sections of high energy physics, since the beginning of the **arXiv** in 1991, until the end of December, 2017.

New sections of the **arXiv** proliferated rapidly in the early 1990s, at the request of practicing physicists. Given the limited bandwidth — both literal and metaphorical — of most university professors, it seemed optimal to sub-divide the **arXiv** into ever smaller and more focused units. Thus, research was pigeonholed into "silos" by design. As a result, individual faculty often came to identify strongly with the section of **arXiv** to which they regularly posted. While cross-listing from a primary section to a secondary (and even a tertiary) section began in May of 1992, such cross-listing was generally rare throughout much of the early years of the **arXiv**. The total number of publications per month, in these five sections of **arXiv**, is shown in Figure 2. The reader is also referred to **arXiv** itself for a detailed analysis of such statistics.

We extracted metadata from the **arXiv** website, in the form of titles and abstracts for all submissions, using techniques described in Ref. [16]. The number of publications represented by this dataset is given in Table 1. Also given is the mean number of words in the typical title and abstract of publications in each of the five sections, as well as the count of unique words in each of the sections.

Titles and abstracts are, of course, different categories serving different functions. To take a very obvious example, titles do not necessarily need to obey the grammatical rules which govern standard prose. Nevertheless, we can consider each title in **hep-th**, or any

Table 1. Gross properties of the five `arXiv` sections studied in this chapter. Numbers include all papers through the end of 2017. The count of unique words does not distinguish upper and lower-case forms of a word. "Length" here means the number of words in a given title or in a given sentence in the abstract. As anticipated, there is remarkable similarity across these five sections of `arXiv` for the mean lengths.

arXiv Section	No. of Papers	Titles		Abstracts	
		Mean Length	Unique Words	Mean Length	Unique Words
hep-th	120,249	8.29	37,550	111.2	276,361
hep-ph	133,346	9.34	46,011	113.4	349,859
hep-lat	21,123	9.31	10,639	105.7	78,175
gr-qc	69,386	8.74	26,222	124.4	194,368
math-ph	51,747	9.19	28,559	106.1	194,149

other section of the `arXiv`, as a sentence. For `hep-th`, this gives us the **raw data** of $120,249$ sentences.

Abstracts are inherently different. They represent a collection of sentences which cluster around particular semantic content. Grammatically, they are quite different from the titles. As an example, being comprised of full sentences suggests that punctuation is meaningful in the abstract while generally irrelevant in titles. Finally, whereas each of the 120,249 titles in `hep-th` can be though of as semantically distinct sentences in a single document (the entirety of `hep-th`), the abstracts must be thought of as individual documents within a larger corpus. This notion of "grouping" sentences into semantic units can make the word embedding process more difficult.

While variants of **Word2Vec** exist which can take this nuance into account, we will simply aggregate *all* abstracts on each section of the `arXiv` and then separate them only by full sentences. For `hep-th`, the abstracts produce 608,000 sentences over all 120,249 papers, comprising 13,347,051 words, of which 276,361 are unique.

3.2. Data cleaning: Raw, processed and cleaned

As any practicing data scientist will attest, cleaning and pre-processing raw data are crucial steps in any analysis in which machine learning is to be utilized. The current dataset is no exception. Indeed, some data preparation issues in this paper are likely to be unique in the natural language processing literature. In this section, we describe the steps we took to prepare the data for neural network analysis.

Our procedure for pre-processing data proceeded along the following order of operations:

(1) Put everything into lower case;

(2) Convert all key words, typically nouns, to singular case. Indeed, it typically does not make sense to consider the words "`equation`" and "`equations`" as different concepts;

(3) Spellings of non-English names, including LaTeX commands, are converted to standard English spelling. For example, "`schroedinger`", "`schr\"odinger`" and "`schr"odinger`" will all be replaced by simply "`schrodinger`" (note that at this stage, we already do not have any further upper case letters, so the "s" is not capitalized);

(4) At this stage, we can replace punctuation marks such as periods, commas and colons as well as LaTeX backslash commands such as `\c{}` which do appear (though not often) in borrowed words such as "aperçu" as well as `\cal` for calligraphic symbols (which do appear rather often), such as in "$\mathcal{N} = 4$ susy". Note that we keep parentheses intact because words such as `su(n)` appear often; so too we will keep such LaTeX commands as `^` and `_` because superscripts and subscripts, when they appear in a title, are significant;

(5) Now, we reach a highly non-trivial part of the replacements: including important technical acronyms. Though rarely used directly in titles, acronyms are common in our field. All acronyms serve the purpose of converting an n-gram into a single monogram. So, for example, "`quantum field theory`" should appear together as a single unit to be replaced by "`qft`". This is a special case of bi-gram and tri-gram grouping which is to be discussed in the following. In other cases, shorthand notation allows for a certain blurring between subject and adjective forms of a word. Thus, "`supersymmetry`" and "`supersymmetric`" will become "`susy`". Note that such synonym studies were carried out in Ref. [23].

At this stage, we use the term **processed data** to refer to the set of words. One could now construct a meaningful word embedding and use that embedding to study many interesting properties of the dataset. However, for some purposes, it is useful to do further preparation, so as to address the aspects of `arXiv` that are particularly scientific in nature. We thus performed two further stages of preparation on the datasets of paper titles, only.

First, we remove any conjunctions, definite articles, indefinite articles, common prepositions, conjugations of the verb "to be", etc. because they add no scientific content to the titles. We note, however, that one could argue that they add some grammatical content and could constitute a separate linguistic study. Indeed, we will restore such words as part of our analysis in Section 5.

In step #5, certain words were manually replaced with acronyms commonly used in the high energy physics community. However, there are certain bi-grams and tri-grams that — while sometimes shortened to acronyms — are clearly intended to represent a single concept. One can clearly see the advantage of merging certain word pairs into compound mono-grams for the sake of textual analysis. For example, one would never expect to see the word "Carlo" in a title which was not preceded by the word "Monte". Indeed, the vast majority of n-grams involving proper nouns (such as "de Sitter" and "Higgs boson") come in such rigid combinations such that further textual analysis can only benefit from representing them as compound mono-grams.

Thus, we will further process the data by listing all the most common 2-grams and then automatically hyphenating them into compound words, up to some cutoff in frequency. For example, as "`magnetic`" and "`field`" appear together frequently, we will replace this combination with "`magnetic-field`", which is subsequently treated as a single unit. We note that even with all of the above, it is inevitable that some hyphenations or removals will be missed. However, since we are doing largely a statistical analysis, such small deviations should not matter compared to the most commonly used words and concepts. The final output of this we will call **cleaned data**. This process of iterative cleaning of the titles is itself illustrative; we leave further discussion to Appendix A.

As an example, our set of **hep-th** titles (cleaned) thus becomes a list of about 120,000 entries, each being a list of words (both the mean and median are five words, down from the mean of eight in the raw titles). A typical entry, in **Python** format, would be (with our running example of Ref. [28])

['ground', 'ring', '2dimensional', 'string-theory'].

Note that the word "of" has been dropped because it is a trivial preposition, and the words "two" and "dimensional" have become joined to be "2dimensional". Both of these are done within the first steps of processing. Finally, the words "string" and "theory" have been recognized to be consistently appearing together by the computer in the final stages of cleaning the raw data, and the bi-gram has been replaced by a single hyphenated word.

We conclude this section by noting that steps #4 and #5 in the first stage of processing, and even the semi-automated merging of words that occurs in the cleaning of titles, require a fair amount of field expertise to carry out successfully. This is not simply because the data contain LATEX markup language and an abundance of acronyms; it also requires a wide knowledge of the mathematical nomenclature of high energy physics and the physical concepts contained therein. While it is possible, at least in principle, to imagine using machine learning algorithms to train a computer to recognize such compound n-grams as "**electric dipole moment**", in practice, this requires a fair amount of field expertise. To take another example, a computer will quickly learn that "**supersymmetry**" is a noun, while "**supersymmetric**" is an adjective. Yet, the acronym "**susy**" is used for both parts of speech in our community — a bending of the rules that would complicate computational language processing. *Thus, it is crucial that this approach to computational textual analysis in high energy physics and mathematical physics be carried out by practitioners in the field, who also happen to have a rudimentary grasp of machine learning, computational linguistics and neural networks.* The reader is also referred to an interesting recent work [31] which uses matrix models to study linguistics as well as the classic works by Refs. [20–22].

Table 2. The 15 most common words in hep-th titles, in raw and clean data. A graphical representation of this table, in terms of "word-clouds", is shown in Figure 3.

Raw Data			Cleaned Data		
Rank	Word	Count	Rank	Word	Count
1	of	46,766	1	model	5,605
2	the	43,713	2	theory	4,385
3	and	42,332	3	black-hole	4,231
4	in	39,515	4	quantum	4,007
5	a	17,805	5	gravity	3,548
6	on	16,382	6	string	3,392
7	theory	13,066	7	susy	3,135
8	for	12,636	8	solution	2,596
9	quantum	11,344	9	field	2,247
10	with	10,003	10	equation	2,245
11	field	8,750	11	symmetry	2,221
12	from	8,690	12	spacetime	2,075
13	gravity	7,347	13	brane	2,073
14	model	6,942	14	inflation	2,031
15	gauge	6,694	15	gauge-theory	2,014

3.3. *Frequency analysis of* hep-th

Having raw and cleaned data at hand, we can begin our analysis with a simple frequency analysis of mono-grams and certain n-grams. For simplicity, we will here only discuss our primary focus, hep-th, leaving other sections of the arXiv to Section 5. The 15 most common words in hep-th titles are given in Table 2. To understand the effect of our data cleaning process, we provide the counts for both the **raw** data and the **cleaned** data. Note, for example, that the count for a word such as "theory" drops significantly after cleaning. In the clean data, the count on the word "theory" excludes all bi-grams involving this word that appear at least 50 times in hep-th titles, such as "gauge-theory", which appears 2,014 times.

The standard method to present common words in natural language processing is called a **word cloud**, where words are presented in aggregate, sized according to the frequency of their appearance. We present the word clouds for the raw and cleaned titles in Figure 3.

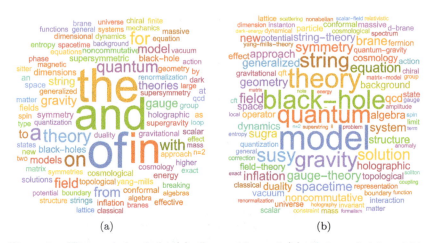

(a)   (b)

Figure 3.   The word clouds for (a) all raw titles and (b) all cleaned titles within hep-th. There is a total of 120,249 papers as of the end of 2017. In the raw titles, there are 37,550 unique words, and in the cleaned titles, 34,425.

In the above, we encounter a first non-trivial observation. In the raw data, the word "theory" outnumbers the word "model" at nearly two-to-one. After the cleaning process, however, the order is reversed, and the word "model" emerges as the most common word. The explanation involves the grouping of individual words into bi-grams and tri-grams. In particular, the word "theory" ends up in common n-grams at a rate that is far larger than the word "model", which will turn out to be a major discriminatory observation that separates hep-th from other sections of the arXiv.

Clearly, there is more discipline-specific contextual information in the cleaned data. For example, the most common technical word in all hep-th titles is "black-hole". The most common bi-gram involving the word "theory" is "gauge-theory", while "string-theory" appears with much lower frequency and is not one of the top 15 words, after cleaning. Note that not every instance of the word "string" appears in a common n-gram. Indeed, the word is more often used as an adjective in hep-th titles, as in "string derived models" or "string inspired scenarios".

For the abstracts of hep-th, we have only the raw data. Given the larger dataset, and the prevalence of common, trivial words, we here give the top 50 words in hep-th abstracts, together with their frequencies:

{the,1174435}, {of,639511}, {in,340841}, {a,340279},
{and,293982}, {we,255299}, {to,252490}, {is,209541},
{for,151641}, {that,144766}, {with,126022}, {are,104298},
{this,98678}, {on,97956}, {by,96032}, {theory,86041},
{as,78890}, {which,71242}, {an,68961}, {be,66262},
{field,65968}, {model,50401}, {from,49531}, {at,46747},
{it,46320}, {can,46107}, {quantum,44887}, {gauge,44855},
{these,39477}, {also,36944}, {show,35811}, {theories,32035},
{string,31314}, {two,30651}, {space,29222}, {models,28639},
{solutions,28022}, {energy,27895},
{one,27782}, {study,26889}, {gravity,25945}, {fields,25941},
{our,24760}, {scalar,24184}, {find,23957}, {between,23895},
{not,23273}, {case,22913}, {symmetry,22888}, {results,22760}.

The first technical words which appear are "theory", "field", "model", "quantum" and "gauge". As mentioned earlier, we have chosen not to "clean" the abstract data. It is interesting to note, however, that if the singular and plural forms of words were combined, we would find "theory" and "theories" appearing 118,076 times, or almost once per abstract, with "field"/"fields" appearing in 91,909 abstracts, or just over 76% of the total.

In addition to word frequency in the titles and abstracts, one could also study the n-grams. As it is clearly meaningless here to have n-grams cross different titles, we will therefore construct n-grams within each title and then count and list all n-grams together. The 15 most common bi-grams in hep-th titles are given in Table 3, again for raw and cleaned data.

There is little scientific content to be gleaned from the raw bi-grams, though we will find these data to be useful in Section 5. In the cleaned bi-grams, many authors reference "separation of variables", "tree amplitudes", "dark sectors", "quantum chromodynamics", "constrained systems", "Clifford algebras", "cosmological constraints", "black hole information", "black rings", "the accelerating universe", etc. in their titles. It is clear to the readers in the hep-th community that in the cleaned dataset, many of the bi-grams would themselves be collective nouns if we imposed more rounds of automatic concatenation in the cleaning process.

For completeness, we conclude by giving the 50 most common bi-grams in the raw data for hep-th abstracts:

{{of,the},224990}, {{in,the},115804}, {{to,the},64481},
{{for,the},49847}, {{on,the},46444}, {{that,the},44565},

Table 3.　The 15 most common bi-grams in hep-th titles, in raw and clean data.

	Raw Data		Cleaned Data	
Rank	Bi-gram	Count	Bi-gram	Count
1	of the	9,287	separation variable	53
2	in the	6,418	tree amplitude	53
3	on the	5,342	dark sector	53
4	and the	5,118	quantum chromodynamics	53
5	field theory	3,592	constrained system	53
6	in a	2,452	clifford algebra	53
7	of a	2,111	cosmological constraint	53
8	for the	2,051	black-hole information	53
9	gauge theories	1,789	black ring	53
10	string theory	1,779	accelerating universe	53
11	field theories	1,468	electroweak symmetry-breaking	53
12	to the	1,431	qcd string	53
13	quantum gravity	1,412	gravitational instanton	52
14	gauge theory	1,350	discrete torsion	52
15	quantum field	1,242	electric-magnetic duality	52

$\{\{of,a\},39334\}$,　　$\{\{and,the\},38891\}$,　　$\{\{can,be\},29672\}$, $\{\{with,the\},29085\}$, $\{\{show,that\},27964\}$, $\{\{we,show\},24774\}$, $\{\{in,a\},24298\}$,　　　$\{\{in,this\},23740\}$,　　　$\{\{it,is\},22326\}$, $\{\{from,the\},20924\}$,　$\{\{by,the\},20634\}$,　　$\{\{to,a\},18852\}$, $\{\{as,a\},18620\}$,　　　　　　　　　　　　$\{\{we,find\},17352\}$, $\{\{we,study\},17113\}$, $\{\{with,a\},16588\}$, $\{\{field,theory\},16270\}$, $\{\{we,also\},16184\}$,　　　$\{\{to,be\},15512\}$,　　　$\{\{is,a\},14125\}$, $\{\{at,the\},13722\}$,　　$\{\{terms,of\},13216\}$,　　$\{\{for,a\},13112\}$, $\{\{in,terms\},12573\}$,　　　　　　　　　　$\{\{as,the\},12233\}$, $\{\{study,the\},11638\}$, $\{\{we,consider\},11481\}$, $\{\{by,a\},11384\}$, $\{\{of,this\},11372\}$,　　$\{\{find,that\},11288\}$,　　$\{\{on,a\},11272\}$, $\{\{is,the\},11070\}$, $\{\{in,particular\},10479\}$, $\{\{which,is\},10478\}$, $\{\{based,on\},10123\}$, $\{\{we,discuss\},10051\}$, $\{\{is,shown\},9965\}$, $\{\{this,paper\},9871\}$, $\{\{of,these\},9529\}$, $\{\{between,the\},9480\}$, $\{\{number,of\},9169\}$, $\{\{string,theory\},8930\}$, $\{\{the,case\},8889\}$, $\{\{scalar,field\},8831\}$.

Again, the most common bi-grams are trivial grammatical conjunctions. The first non-trivial combination is "field theory" and then, a while later, "string theory" and "scalar field". Indeed, one would expect these to be the top concepts in abstracts in hep-th. We remark that the current computer moderation of arXiv uses full text, as it

Table 4. Number of unique words appearing at least N times in hep-th titles. The 16,105 words with at least two appearances were utilized as a training set for Word2vecfor the purposes of this section.

Number of Unique Words Appearing at Least N Times									
$N=1$	$N=2$	$N=3$	$N=4$	$N=5$	$N=6$	$N=7$	$N=8$	$N=9$	$N=10$
34,425	16,105	11,642	9,516	8,275	7,365	6,696	6,179	5,747	5,380

is richer and more accurate than titles and abstracts and establishes a classifier which is continuously updated and uses adaptive length n-grams (typically up to $n = 4$).[1]

4. Machine-Learning hep-th

Having suitably prepared a clean dataset, we then trained Word2vec on the collection of titles in hep-th. Given the typically small size of titles in academic papers, we chose a context window of length 5. To minimize the tendency of the neural network to focus on outliers, such as words that very rarely appear, we dropped all words that appear less than twice in the dataset for the purpose of training. As Table 4 indicates, that meant that a little over half of the unique words in the hep-th titles were not employed in the training.[2] Finally, we follow standard practice in the literature by setting $N = 400$ neurons for the hidden layer, using the CBOW model. The result is that each of the non-trivial words is assigned a vector in $\mathbb{R}^{400}$ so that the partition function (7) is maximized.

4.1. *Word similarity*

Once the word embedding has been established, we can form cosine distances in light of our definition of similarity and dissimilarity in Definition 5. This is our first glimpse into the ability of the neural network to truly capture the essence of syntax within the high energy

---

[1]We thank Paul Ginsparg for informing us of this.

[2]Later, when we attack the classification problem in Section 6, we will use all unique words in the training set.

theory community: to view which pairs of words the neural network has deemed "similar" across the entire corpus of hep-th titles.

Overall, we find that the neural network in Word2vec does an admirable job in a very challenging area of context. Consider the bi-gram "**super Yang–Mills**", often followed by the word "theory". In step #5 of the initial processing of the data, described in Section 3.2, we would have manually replaced this tri-gram with the acronym "sym" since "SYM" would be immediately recognized by most practitioners in our field as "super Yang-Mills". Thus, the tri-gram "**supersymmetric Yang–Mills theory**", a quantum field theory described by a non-abelian gauge group, will be denoted as '**sym**'. Some representative word similarity measurements are as follows:

$$d(\text{'sym'}, \text{'sym'}) = 1.0,$$
$$d(\text{'sym'}, \text{'n=4'}) = 0.9763,$$
$$d(\text{'sym'}, \text{'matrix-model'}) = 0.9569,$$
$$d(\text{'sym'}, \text{'duality'}) = 0.9486,$$
$$d(\text{'sym'}, \text{'black-hole'}) = 0.1567,$$
$$d(\text{'sym'}, \text{'dark-energy'}) = -0.0188,$$
$$d(\text{'sym'}, \text{'dark-matter'}) = -0.0370. \tag{10}$$

The above means that, for example, "sym" is identical to itself (a useful consistency check), close to "duality" and not so close to "dark-matter", within our context windows. To practitioners in our field, these relative similarities would seem highly plausible.

We computed the similarity distance (8) for all possible pairs of the 9,516 words in hep-th titles which appear at least four times in the set. The 20 most frequent words are given in Table 5, along with the word for which $d(w_1, w_2)$ is maximized and where it is minimized. We refer to these words as the 'most' and 'least' similar words in the set.

Some care should be taken in interpreting these results. First, authors clearly use a different type of syntax when constructing a paper title than they would when writing an abstract, the latter being most likely to approximate normal human speaking styles. The semi-formalized rules that govern typical practice in crafting titles will actually be of interest to us in Section 5, when we compare these rules across different sections of arXiv.

The second caveat is that for two words to be considered similar, it will be necessary that the two words (1) appear sufficiently often

Table 5. The 20 most frequent words in hep-th titles. Included is the word with the largest and smallest values of the word-distance $d(w_1, w_2)$ (from Equation (8)), as computed by `Word2vec`.

Word	Most Similar	$d(w_1, w_2)$	Least Similar	$d(w_1, w_2)$
model	theory	0.7775	entropy	−0.0110
theory	action	0.7864	holographic	0.0079
black-hole	rotating	0.9277	lattice	0.1332
quantum	entanglement	0.8645	sugra	0.1880
gravity	massive-gravity	0.8315	g^4	0.0618
string	string-theory	0.9016	approach	0.0277
susy	gauged	0.9402	energy	0.0262
solution	massive-gravity	0.6900	holographic	0.0836
field	massless	0.8715	instanton	0.0903
equation	bethe-ansatz	0.8271	matter	0.0580
symmetry	transformations	0.9286	gravitational	0.0095
spacetime	metric	0.8560	amplitude	0.2502
brane	warped	0.9504	method	0.1706
inflation	primordial	0.9200	cft	0.1137
gauge-theory	sym	0.8993	universe	0.1507
system	oscillator	0.8729	compactification	0.1026
geometry	manifold	0.8862	qcd	0.1513
sugra	gauged-sugra	0.8941	relativistic	0.1939
new	type	0.8807	state	−0.1240
generalized	class	0.9495	effect	0.0658

to make our list and (2) appear *together* in titles, within five words of one another, with high regularity. Thus, we expect words like "black hole" and "rotating", or "spacetime" and "metric", to be naturally similar in this sense. How then should we interpret the antipodal word, which we designate as the "least similar"? And what of the vast number of words whose cosine distance vanishes with respect to a particular word?

Recall the discussion in Section 2.3. The neural network establishes the vector representation of each word by attempting to optimize contextual relations. Thus, two words will appear in the same region of the vector space if they tend to share many common words within their respective content windows. Inverting this notion, two words will be more likely to appear in antipodal regions of the vector space if the words they commonly appear with in titles are fully disjoint from one another. Thus, "sym" (supersymmetric Yang–Mills theory) is not necessarily the "opposite" of "dark matter" or "dark energy" in any real sense but rather the word "sym" tends to appear in titles surrounded by words like "duality" or "matrix model", which themselves rarely appear in titles involving the words "dark matter" or "dark energy". Thus, the neural network located these vectors in antipodal regions of the vector space.

The results of Table 5 also indicate that strictly negative values of $d(w_1, w_2)$ are, in fact, quite rare. So, for example, the word that is "least similar" to "spacetime" is "amplitude", with $d(\text{'spacetime'}, \text{'amplitude'}) = 0.25$. Part of the reason for this behavior is that Table 5 is presenting the 20 most frequent words in hep-th titles. Thus, a word like "spacetime" appears in many titles and develops a contextual affinity with a great many of the 9,516 words in our dataset. As a consequence, no word in the hep-th title corpus is truly 'far' from the word "spacetime".

The relative lack of negative similarity distances and the lopsided nature of the vector space embedding produced by Word2vec are striking for the hep-th titles. However, such behavior was noted in recent work by Mimno and Thompson on natural language processing with the skip-gram method [24]. The authors observed that datasets tended to cluster in a cone around certain dominant words that appear frequently in context windows, such as the words like "model" and "theory" in our case. This is certainly the case with our data. A histogram of the $d(w_1, w_2)$ values for the 9,516 words in hep-th titles which appear at least four times is given in the left panel of Figure 4. The overwhelming majority of word pairs have similarity distances satisfying $d(w_1, w_2) \geq 0.9$, with a mean value given by

$$d(w_1, w_2)|_{\text{hepth}} = 0.9257 \pm 0.0889. \tag{11}$$

It might be thought that this extreme clustering is an artifact of the small size of the dataset or the restriction to words that appear at least four times. But *relaxing the cut-off to include all pairs of words that appear two or more times changes neither the average similarity distance nor the shape of the histogram.* As a control sample, we also trained Word2vec to produce a word embedding for the 22,950 unique words contained in 20,000 titles for news articles appearing in the *Times of India* [32]. The same clustering effect occurs in this data sample, as can be seen by the histogram in the right panel of Figure 4, but to a much more moderate extent. In fact, this dataset

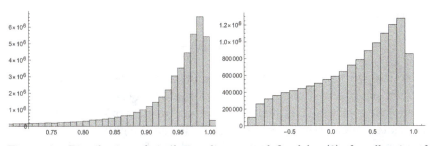

Figure 4. Distribution of similarity distances, defined by (8), for all pairs of words with at least four appearances in the corpus. The left panel gives the distribution for titles in hep-th. The right panel is the distribution for a similarly sized collection of news headlines from *Times of India*. While both distributions show a clustering effect of words around certain dominant words, the shape of the distribution for hep-th shows a much tighter 'conical' cluster than the hews headlines. In particular, we note the vertical scale in the two panels, in which negative similarity distances are essentially absent in hep-th titles but reasonably frequent in the *Times of India* headlines.

contains a significant number of negative $d(w_1, w_2)$ values, with a mean value given by

$$d(w_1, w_2)|_{\text{headlines}} = 0.2642 \pm 0.5171. \qquad (12)$$

We will return to this *Times of India* dataset in Section 6.

4.2. *Linear syntactic identities*

With a measure of similarity, we can now seek examples of meaningful syntactic identities, analogous to (2). This is done by finding the nearest vector to the vector sum/difference among word vectors. For example, we find that

$$\text{'holography'} + \text{'quantum'} + \text{'string'} + \text{'ads'} = \text{'extremal-black-hole'}. \qquad (13)$$

This is a correct expression, in that a hypothetical title containing the four words on the left-hand side could plausibly contain the one on the right-hand side. This is very interesting because by *context* alone, we are uncovering the *syntax* of hep-th, where likely concepts appear together. This is exactly the purpose of Word2vec, to attempt to study natural language through the proximity of context.

Another good example is

$$\text{`bosonic'} + \text{`string-theory'} = \text{`open-string'}. \tag{14}$$

Of course, we need to take heed. It is *not* that the neural network has learned physics well enough to realize that the bosonic string has an open string sector; it is just that the neural network has learned to associate "open-string" as a *likely* contextual neighbor of "bosonic" and "string theory". One could also add word vectors to themselves (subtracting would simply give the word closest to the 0-vector), such as (dropping the quotation marks for convenience) the following:

```
gravity   +   gravity = massive-gravity
string    +   string = string-theory
quantum   +   quantum = quantum-mechanics
holography +  holography = microscopic.
```

We will note that there is not much content to these identities. It is not at all clear what scaling means in this vector space.

We can systematically construct countless more "linear syntactic identities" from, say, our most common words. For instance, those of the form 'a' + 'b' = 'c' include the following:

```
symmetry     + black-hole    =  killing
spacetime    + inflation     =  cosmological-constant
string-theory + spacetime    =  near-horizon
black-hole   + holographic   =  thermodynamics
string-theory + noncommutative =  open-string
duality      + gravity       =  'd=5'
black-hole   + qcd           =  plasma
symmetry     + algebra       =  group.
```

The physical meaning of all of these statements are clear to a hep-th reader.

One can as well generate higher-order examples of the form 'a' + 'b' = 'c' + 'd', such as

```
field      + symmetry  =  particle + duality
system     + equation  =  classical + model
generalized + approach =  canonical + model
equation   + field     =  general + system
space      + black-hole =  geometry + gravity
```

```
duality  +  holographic  =  finite + string
string-theory + calabi-yau = m-theory + g2
```

as well as even longer ones:

```
string-theory + calabi-yau + f-theory = orientifold
quiver + gauge-theory + calabi-yau = scft
brane + near-horizon - worldvolume = warped.
```

It is amusing that we can find many such suggestive identities. On the other hand, we also find many statements which are simply nonsensical.

5. Comparisons with Other arXiv Sections

In the previous section, we performed some basic descriptive analyses of the vocabulary of the hep-th community, demonstrated the power of Word2vec in performing textual analysis, illuminated the nature of the vector space created by the neural network output and used this space to study word correlations and linear syntactic identities within the space generated by the corpus of all hep-th titles. We find these items interesting (or at least amusing) in their own right and expect that there is much more that can be extracted by expert linguists or computer scientists.

As an application, in this section, we would like to use the tools introduced above to perform an affinity analysis between the sociolinguistics of the hep-th community and sister communities that span theoretical high energy physics. There are many sections on arXiv to which a great number of papers on hep-th are cross-listed. Similarly, authors who post primarily to hep-th often also post to other sections, and vice versa. This was particularly relevant prior to mid-2007, when each individual manuscript was referred to by its repository and unique number and not solely by a unique number alone. As described in Section 3.1, the most pertinent physics sections besides hep-th are

- hep-ph (high energy phenomenology);
- hep-lat (high energy lattice theory);
- math-ph (mathematical physics);
- gr-qc (general relativity and quantum cosmology).

Table 6.   Gross properties of the collection of titles of the five `arXiv` sections studied in this chapter, now after the cleaning process (described in Section 3.2) has been performed. The final column gives the number of unique words divided by the total number of words, after cleaning.

arXiv Section	No. of Papers	Median Length	Mean Length	Number of Unique Words	Unique Word Fraction(%)
hep-th	120,249	5	5.08	34,425	4.66
hep-ph	133,346	5	5.58	39,611	4.59
hep-lat	21,123	5	5.58	9,431	6.96
gr-qc	69,386	5	5.34	22,357	5.32
math-ph	51,747	6	6.01	25,516	7.62

It is therefore potentially interesting to perform a cross-sectional comparative study.[3]

What sorts of phenomena might we hope to identify by such a study? Loosely speaking, we might ask where authors in hep-th lie in the spectrum between pure mathematics and pure observation. Can we quantify such a notion by looking at the language used by the authors in these various sections? The answer will turn out to be, in large part, affirmative. Intriguingly, we will see that the distinctions between the sub-fields are not merely one of *subject matter*, as there is a great deal of overlap here, but often it is encoded in the *manner* in which these subjects are described.

5.1.   *Word frequencies*

As in the previous sections, we first **clean** the data to retain only relevant physics-concept-related words. We again focus on the titles of papers in the five repositories. Some statistics for the datasets, in raw

---

[3]Note that of all the high-energy sections, we have not included hep-ex. This is because the language and symbols, especially the style of titles, of high-energy experimental physics are highly regimented and markedly different from the theoretical sections. This would render it an outlier in a comparative study of high-energy related `arXiv` sections.

form, were given in Table 1. After the cleaning process, titles are typically shortened, and the number of unique words diminishes somewhat, as is shown in Table 6. Again, the five repositories are roughly equal in their gross properties. We present the word clouds for the four new repositories, after the cleaning procedure, in Table B.1, found in B.

At this point, one could pursue an analysis for each repository along the lines of that in Section 4. However, we will be less detailed in our study of the other four sections of arXiv, as our focus in this section is twofold: (1) to begin to understand similarities and differences between the authors in these five groupings, as revealed by their use of language, and (2) lay the groundwork for the classification problem that is the focus of Section 6.

We therefore begin with a focus on the most common 'key' words in each section of arXiv. In Table 7, we list the 10 most common words in the titles of papers in each repository. We also give the overall word frequency for each word, normalized by the total number of words. Thus, for example, 1.91% of all the words used in hep-lat titles is the specific word "lattice", which is perhaps unsurprising. Indeed, the word frequencies in Table 7 are as one might expect if one is familiar with the field of theoretical high energy physics.

Many words appear often in several sections of arXiv; others are common in only one section. Can this be the beginning of a classification procedure? To some extent, it can. For example, the word "model" is a very common word in all five sections, while "theory" fails to appear in the top 10 words only for hep-ph. However, this is deceptive, since it would be ranked number 11 if we were to extend the table. Despite such obvious cautions, there is still some comparative information which can be extracted from Table 7.

Consider Table 8 in which we present only those words in Table 7 which appear in two or more sections of the arXiv. We again see the universal importance of words like "model" and "theory", but we also begin to see the centrality of hep-th emerge. Indeed, it was for this reason that we chose to focus on this section of the arXiv in the first place. Note that the words which are frequently found in hep-th tend to be frequent in other sections. Perhaps this represents some aspect of generality in the subject matter of hep-th, or perhaps it is related to the fact that among the other four sections, hep-th is

Table 7. Top 10 most frequent words in the titles of the five arXiv sections, after cleaning. The percentage is the number of appearances of the particular word divided by the total of all words (including multiplicities).

hep-th		hep-ph		hep-lat		gr-qc		math-ph	
Word	%	Word	%	Word	%	Word	%	Word	%
model	0.80	model	0.84	lattice	1.91	black-hole	1.17	model	1.06
theory	0.62	qcd	0.58	qcd	1.43	gravity	0.96	equation	0.93
black-hole	0.60	decay	0.53	lattice-qcd	1.39	spacetime	0.75	quantum	0.92
quantum	0.57	effect	0.53	model	0.95	model	0.70	system	0.75
gravity	0.51	lhc	0.51	quark	0.58	quantum	0.58	solution	0.59
string	0.48	dark-matter	0.46	theory	0.54	cosmology	0.58	theory	0.49
susy	0.45	neutrino	0.41	mass	0.53	universe	0.55	operator	0.48
solution	0.37	mass	0.38	fermion	0.53	theory	0.52	algebra	0.45
field	0.32	production	0.38	chiral	0.51	gravitational-wave	0.50	potential	0.44
equation	0.32	susy	0.37	meson	0.41	inflation	0.46	symmetry	0.42

Table 8. Words which are among the top 10 most frequent for more than one `arXiv` section, with the rank of the word in those sections. The dashes '-' mean that the particular words has not made it into the top 10 of the specified `arXiv` section.

Top Word	hep-th	hep-ph	hep-lat	gr-qc	math-ph
black-hole	3	—	—	1	—
equation	10	—	—	—	2
gravity	5	—	—	2	—
mass	—	8	7	—	—
model	1	1	4	4	1
quantum	4	—	—	5	3
solution	8	—	—	—	5
susy	7	10	—	—	—
theory	2	—	6	8	6

far more likely to be the place where a paper is cross-listed than any of the remaining three sections.

What is more, even at this very coarse level, we already begin to see a separation between the more mathematical sections (hep-th, gr-qc and math-ph) and the more phenomenological sections (hep-ph and hep-lat). Such a divide is a very palpable fact of the sociology of our field, and it is something we will see illustrated in the data analysis throughout this section.

From the point of view of document classification, the simple frequency with which a word appears is a poor marker for the section of `arXiv` in which it resides. In other words, if a paper contains the word "gravity" in its title, it may very likely be a gr-qc paper, but the certainty with which a classifying agent — be it a machine or a theoretical physicist — would make this assertion would be low. As mentioned in Section 2.5, term frequency-inverse document frequency (tf-idf) is a more nuanced quantity which captures the relative importance of a word of n-gram.

Recall that there are three important concepts when computing tf-idf values. First, there are the words themselves and then there are the individual *documents* which, collectively, form the *corpus*. If our goal is to uncover distinctions between the five `arXiv` sections using tf-idf values, it might make sense to take each paper as a document, with the total of all documents in a given section being the corpus.

If we were studying the abstracts, or even the full text of the papers themselves, this would be the best approach. But as we are studying only the titles here, a problem immediately presents itself.

After the cleaning process, in which small words are removed and common bi-grams are conjoined, a typical title is quite a small "document". As Table 6 indicates, the typical length of the document is five or six words. Thus, it is very unlikely that the *term frequency* across all titles will deviate greatly from the *document frequency* across the titles. This is borne out in the data. Taking the union of all words which rank in the top 100 in frequency across the five sections, we obtain 263 unique words. Of these, 42.3% never appear more than once in any title, in *any* of the five sections. For 63.5% of the cases, the term frequency and document frequency deviate by no more than two instances, across *all five* arXiv sections. Thus, tf-idf computed on a title-by-title basis is unlikely to provide much differentiation, as common words will have very similar tf-idf values.

Therefore, we will instead consider an alternative approach. We let the corpus be all titles for all five sections of the arXiv; in other words, we treat the entire (theoretical high energy) arXiv as a single corpus. The collections of five titles form the five "documents" in this corpus. While this clearly implies some blurring of context, it gives a sufficiently large dataset, document-by-document, to make tf-idf meaningful.

We provide the tf-idf values for a representative set of words in the five arXiv sections in Table 9. Recall that words that are extremely common in individual contexts (here, specifically, paper titles), across an entire arXiv section, will have very low values of tf-idf. For example, words such as "theory" and "model" appears in all sections and would therefore receive a vanishing value of tf-idf. Therefore, it is only illustrative to include words which do not trivially have a score of zero for all sections. Our collection of titles is sufficiently large in all cases that there are no words which appear in *all* paper titles, even prior to the cleaning step, which removes small words like "a" and "the". Therefore, entries which are precisely zero in Table 9 are cases in which the word appears in *none* of the paper titles for that section of arXiv.

So, for example, we see that, interestingly, the word "schrodinger-operator" appears only in **math-ph** but not in any of the others. This is, in fact, the word with the highest tf-idf score by far. Of course,

Table 9. Term frequency-inverse document frequency (tf-idf) for certain key words. The corpus here is the set of all titles for all papers in all five sections of the arXiv. These sections become the five documents of the corpus.

Word	hep-th	hep-ph	hep-lat	gr-qc	math-ph
chiral-perturbation-theory	0.71	1.45	1.24	0	0.15
cmb	1.36	1.43	0	1.4	0.49
cosmological-model	4.73	0	0	5.86	0
finite-volume	0.95	1.08	1.2	0	0.46
ising-model	2.82	0	2.74	0	2.78
landau-gauge	2.35	2.5	2.72	0	0
lattice-gauge-theory	2.66	2.39	2.97	0	0
lhc	1.19	1.87	0.69	0.9	0
modified-gravity	2.89	2.42	0	3.22	0
mssm	1.05	1.58	0.31	0.55	0
neutrino-mass	2.24	3.54	0	0.35	0
new-physics	0.92	1.57	0.31	0.15	0
nucleon	0.78	1.65	1.35	0.15	0
quantum-mechanics	1.49	1.15	0.	1.28	1.37
quark-mass	2.07	3.07	2.72	0.	0
scalar-field	1.51	1.34	0	1.56	1.12
schrodinger-operator	0	0	0	0	10.08
string-theory	1.67	1.28	0.	1.28	0.97
wilson-fermion	0	0	8.87	0	0

the Schrödinger equation is ubiquitous in all fields of physics, but only in math-ph — and not even in hep-th — is its operator nature being studied intensively. Likewise, the Wilson fermion is particular to hep-lat. The word "string-theory" is mentioned in all titles except, understandably, in hep-lat.

Using machine learning techniques to classify arXiv titles will be the focus of our next section, but we can take a moment to see how such an approach could potentially improve over a human classifier — even one with expertise in the field. A full-blown tf-idf analysis would not be necessary for a theoretical physicist to surmise that a paper whose title included the bi-gram "Wilson fermion" is very likely from hep-lat. But, surprisingly, having "lattice gauge theory" in the title is **not** a very good indicator of belonging to hep-lat nor is it sufficient to assign gr-qc to all papers with "modified gravity" in its title.

5.2. *Common bi-grams*

As before, from mono-grams (individual words), we proceed to common *n*-grams. In this section, we will concentrate on bi-grams for simplicity. Common 3-grams and 4-grams for the various sections can be found in Appendix B. It is enlightening to do this analysis for both the cleaned data (for which we will extract subject content information) as well as for the raw data, which retains the conjunctions and other grammatically interesting words. The latter should give us an idea of the syntax of the language of high energy and mathematical physics across the disciplines.

5.2.1. *Raw data*

The top 15 most commonly encountered bi-grams in the raw data, for each of the five sections of `arXiv`, are presented in Table 10, in descending order of frequency. At first glance, the table may seem to contain very little distinguishing information. Clearly, certain linguistic constructions, such as "on the" and "on a", are commonly found in the titles of academic works across many disciplines. One might be tempted to immediately remove such "trivial" bi-grams and proceed to more substantive bi-grams. But, in fact, there is more subtlety here than is immediately apparent. Let us consider the 12 unique, trivial bi-grams in the table above. They are given in Table 11 for each repository, with their ranking in the list of all bi-grams for that repository.

Three things immediately stand out. The first is the universal supremacy of the bi-gram "of the". The second is the presence of "at the" in hep-ph at a high frequency, yet largely absent from the other repositories. But this is clearly understood as the likelihood of hep-ph titles to include phrases like "at the Fermilab Tevatron" or "at the LHC", in their titles. This is unique to hep-ph among the five categories studied here. Finally, there is the construction "on a", which appears significantly only in hep-th and math-phand is very rare in hep-ph titles.

Again, this is easily understood, as the phrase "on a" generally precedes a noun upon which objects may reside. That is, plainly speaking, a surface. And the study of physics on surfaces of various sorts is among the most mathematical of the physical pursuits. So, this meta-analysis of physics language syntax would seem to indicate

Table 10. The top 15 most commonly encountered bi-grams in the raw data, for each of the five sections of arXiv. Bi-grams are listed from most frequent (top) to least frequent (bottom).

hep-th	hep-ph	hep-lat	gr-qc	math-ph
of the	of the	of the	of the	of the
in the	in the	lattice qcd	in the	on the
on the	dark matter	in the	on the	for the
and the	and the	on the	and the	in the
field theory	at the	the lattice	of a	and the
in a	on the	gauge theory	quantum gravity	of a
of a	in a	and the	dark energy	in a
for the	the lhc	in lattice	in a	to the
gauge theories	to the	from lattice	gravitational waves	for a
string theory	for the	lattice gauge	general relativity	on a
field theories	standard model	qcd with	for the	solutions of
to the	corrections to	at finite	scalar field	field theory
quantum gravity	production in	gauge theories	black-holes in	of quantum
gauge theory	production at	study of	gravitational wave	approach to
quantum field	from the	for the	with a	quantum mechanics

Table 11.   Contextually "trivial" bi-grams across five **arXiv** sections. The entry gives the rank of the bi-gram, in terms of the bi-gram frequency, after only removing capitalization.

Bi-gram	arXiv Repository Rank				
	hep-th	hep-ph	hep-lat	gr-qc	math-ph
of the	1	1	1	1	1
in the	2	2	3	2	4
on the	3	6	4	3	2
and the	4	4	7	4	5
in a	6	7	19	8	7
of a	7	16	35	5	6
for the	8	10	15	11	3
to the	12	9	21	16	8
on a	17	152	28	38	10
from the	19	15	27	27	74
with a	21	27	57	15	16
at the	87	5	97	114	224

Table 12.   Treating the columns of Table 11 as vectors in $\mathbb{R}^{12}$, the cosine of the angles between the various vectors is given.

	hep-th	hep-ph	hep-lat	gr-qc	math-ph
hep-th	1	0.29	0.94	0.99	0.96
hep-ph	0.29	1	0.39	0.38	0.12
hep-lat	0.94	0.39	1	0.90	0.84
gr-qc	0.99	0.38	0.90	1	0.95
math-ph	0.96	0.12	0.84	0.95	1

a close affinity between **hep-th** and **math-ph**, and a clear distinction between **hep-ph** and all the other theoretical categories. While this may confirm prejudices within our own fields, a closer inspection of these trivial bi-grams is warranted.

Considering Table 11 more seriously, we can treat the columns as vectors in a certain space of trivial bi-grams (not to be confused with word vectors which we have been discussing). A measure of affinity between the authors of the various **arXiv** sections would then be the cosine of the angle between these vectors. The value of these cosines is presented in Table 12.

What emerges from Table 12 is quite informative. It seems that the simplest of our community's verbal constructs reveal a great deal about how our colleagues organize into groups. Our central focus is the community of hep-th, and it is somewhat reassuring to see that the trivial bi-gram analysis reveals that this section has relatively strong affinity with all of the arXiv sections studied. Yet, there is clearly a break between hep-th and hep-ph, a distinction we will comment upon later. Clearly, some of this is driven by the "at the" bi-gram, suggesting (quite rightly) that hep-ph is the most experimentally minded of the arXiv sections studied here. But even if this particular bi-gram is excluded from the analysis, hep-ph would still have the smallest cosine measure with hep-th.

Clearly, the trivial bi-gram analysis suggests that our group of five sections fragments into one section (hep-ph), and the other four, which cluster rather tightly together. Among these remaining four, hep-lat is slightly the outlier, being more closely aligned with hep-th than the other sections. Most of these relations would probably not come as a surprise to the authors in the field, but the fact that the computer can make distinctions in such a specialized sub-field, in which even current practitioners would have a difficult time making such subtle differentiation, is intriguing.

5.2.2. *Cleaned data*

After the cleaning process, which includes the two rounds of computer-generated word concatenations, described in Appendix A, the majority of the most common bi-grams in each section of the arXiv will have been formed into single words. What remains reveals something of the specific content areas unique to each branch of theoretical particle physics. The 15 most frequent bi-grams after cleaning are given in Table 13.

While these bi-grams certainly capture important areas of theoretical physics research in each section of the arXiv, they are somewhat deceiving. For example, the "chiral magnetic effect" — a phenomenon of induced chiral behavior in a quark-gluon plasma — has been the subject of study of roughly five papers per year in hep-ph over the last decade. But it would be wrong to suppose that it is more commonly studied than "searches (at the) lhc" or "extensions

Table 13.   Most common bi-grams in cleaned data, after two rounds of automated concatenation.

hep-th	{separation,variable}, {tree,amplitude}, {dark,sector}, {quantum,chromodynamics}, {constrained,system}, {clifford,algebra}, {cosmological,constraint}, {black-hole,information}, {black,ring}, {accelerating,universe}, {electroweak,symmetry-breaking}, {qcd,string}, {gravitational,instanton}, {discrete,torsion}, {electric-magnetic,duality}
hep-ph	{first-order,phase-transition}, {chiral-magnetic,effect}, {double-parton,scattering}, {littlest-higgs-model,t-parity}, {momentum,transfer}, {extensions,sm}, {magnetic,catalysis}, {jet,substructure}, {matter,effect}, {energy,spectrum}, {spin-structure,function}, {equivalence,principle}, {light-scalar,meson}, {au+au,collision}, {searches,lhc}
hep-lat	{flux,tube}, {perturbative,renormalization}, {imaginary,chemical-potential}, {ground,state}, {gluon,ghost}, {electroweak,phase-transition}, {string,breaking}, {physical,point}, {2+1-flavor,lattice-qcd}, {lattice,action}, {2+1-flavor,qcd}, {random-matrix,theory}, {effective,action}, {screening,mass}, {chiral,transition}
gr-qc	{fine-structure,constant}, {extreme-mass-ratio,inspirals}, {closed-timelike,curves}, {bulk,viscosity}, {born-infeld,gravity}, {dirac,particle}, {ds,universe}, {einstein-field,equation}, {fundamental,constant}, {topologically-massive,gravity}, {bose-einstein,condensate}, {higher-dimensional,black-hole}, {hamiltonian,formulation}, {static,black-hole}, {generalized-second,law}
math-ph	{time,dependent}, {external,field}, {thermodynamic,limit}, {long,range}, {variational,principle}, {loop,model}, {minkowski,space}, {fokker-planck,equation}, {characteristic,polynomials}, {hamiltonian,dynamics}, {integral,equation}, {configuration,space}, {lattice,model}, {constant,curvature}, {gaussian,free-field}

(to the) sm", where the acronyms stand for Large Hadron Collider and Standard Model, respectively.

In this case, we see a potential drawback of the automated concatenation described in Appendix A: whereas tightly related topics will naturally be grouped together, some of the diversity of subject matter in each section of the arXiv will be obscured. So, for example, in step #5 in Section 3.2, we turn common compound expressions like "operator product expansion" into the acronym "ope". In addition, a handful of very common bi-grams were hyphenated, such as "dark matter" becoming "dark-matter". Cosmological dark matter is a topic of investigation in hep-ph which appears to be totally missing in Table 13! However, what has happened is that various sub-categories of postulated dark matter candidates have been concatenated in the automated steps which follow, producing "cold-dark-matter", "warm-dark-matter", "fuzzy-dark-matter", etc. The total frequency of appearance for "dark matter" itself is thus distributed across many "words" in the total corpus.

To take another example, particle physicists of a certain age will remember the flurry of papers appearing (primarily) in hep-ph in the early 2000s with the bi-gram "little Higgs" in the title. Indeed, for a certain period of time, it seemed that *every* paper in hep-ph concerned this alternative to the traditional Higgs mechanism of the Standard Model. From this were spun many off-shoots with their ever-more creative names: "littler Higgs", "littlest Higgs" (a hint of which appears in Table 13), "fat Higgs", "thin Higgs", etc. Where are all the "little Higgs" papers in our study?

The answer, as Table 14 shows, is that they are still there — only hidden. In the table, we work with **processed** data, which (as described in Section 3.2) are data in which the first five steps of the cleaning process — through the removal of small words — are performed but *prior* to the automated concatenation of common bi-grams. What is given in Table 14 is the number of unique bi-grams constructed with seven very common key words, for each of the five sections. To construct the Table above, we only considered the top 6000 bi-grams in each section, ranked by frequency of appearance.

First, we remark on the sheer number of bi-grams formed with "theory" and "model". Prior to automated concatenation, "model" far outstrips "theory" in hep-ph and to a lesser extent in math-ph. After the automated concatenation (i.e., in the cleaned data),

Table 14.   Number of unique bi-grams formed with seven key words, across the five `arXiv` sections. Frequencies are computed from **processed** data (small words are removed but automated concatenation is not performed).

Key Word	hep-th	hep-ph	hep-lat	gr-qc	math-ph
theory	290	72	144	141	131
model	259	251	185	178	228
Higgs	21	123	24	11	5
dark	3	8	—	8	1
black	6	1	—	9	3
natural	2	2	—	1	—
conformal	33	5	14	27	25

"model" will be one of the most common, or nearly most common, words in all five sections, as shown in Table 7. As we remarked in Section 3.3, it is this automated concatenation that will eventually reduce the frequency of the stand-alone word "theory" in hep-th.

The other five words reveal a great deal about the subject matter of the five `arXiv` sections, as well as demonstrating the creativity of the high energy theory community in creating new bi-grams. This is particularly so, as expected, in hep-ph's treatment of the word "Higgs", in which an astounding 123 bi-grams are identified involving this word, including everything from "abelian Higgs" to "Higgs vacuum". The distinction between the phenomenological (hep-ph and hep-lat) and more formal sections is evident in the number of bi-grams involving "conformal", with hep-th leading the group. It seems hep-ph concerns itself more with "dark" objects ("atoms", "forces", "gauge", "photon", "radiation", "sector", "side") than "black" ones; it is vice versa for hep-th ("black" plus "brane", "hole", "objects", "p-brane", "ring", "string"); and gr-qc is concerned with both in equal measure. Finally, despite the frequent use of "natural" in our community — and its ubiquitous adjectival noun form, "naturalness" — this word appears paired in a bi-gram with only two words with any great regularity: "inflation" and "susy (supersymmetry)".

5.3.   *Comparative syntactic identities*

We conclude this amusing bit of navel-gazing with a comparison of the five `arXiv` sections using the vector space word embeddings produced by Word2vec. As in Section 4, we train Word2vec on the five lists of words formed from the titles of the five sections, after the full cleaning procedure is performed. What we are seeking are differences in the way certain common words are represented in the five constructed vector spaces.

It is intriguing to consider how linear syntactic identities, such as those identified in Section 4.2, are modified when we map words from one vector space embedding to another. It would be particularly interesting to see if, in different sections of the arXiv, the same left-hand side of a linear syntactic identity 'a' + 'b' = 'c' leads to completely different 'c' in different spaces. This would be indicative of the very nature of the terminologies of the fields.

Many possible 'a' + 'b' pairs can be constructed, though very frequently one of the members of the ('a','b') pair happens to be seldom used in at least one of the five arXiv sections. One word which appears frequently with many partners is the word 'spin'. Some syntactic identities using this word include the following:

```
hep-th:   spin  +  system  =  free
hep-ph:   spin  +  system  =  1/2
hep-lat:  spin  +  system  =  ising
gr-qc:    spin  +  system  =  initial-data
math-ph:  spin  +  system  =  charged

hep-th:   spin  +  dynamics  =  point
hep-ph:   spin  +  dynamics  =  chromofield
hep-lat:  spin  +  dynamics  =  geometry
gr-qc:    spin  +  dynamics  =  orbiting
math-ph:  spin  +  dynamics  =  interacting

hep-th:   spin  +  effect  =  electron
hep-ph:   spin  +  effect  =  role
hep-lat:  spin  +  effect  =  bound-state
gr-qc:    spin  +  effect  =  detector
math-ph:  spin  +  effect  =  glass.
```

What these identities reveal is that 'spin' is used in very general contexts in both hep-th and hep-ph but in rather more specific contexts in the other three sections. So, for example, in gr-qc, a topic of inquiry may be the dynamics of spinning objects orbiting a black hole, whereas the thermodynamics and stability properties of spin glasses have been a common topic of research in **math-ph.**

We conclude this section with the syntactic identity formed from perhaps the two most fundamental concepts in theoretical particle physics: "field theory" (the tool with which all of our calculations are performed) and "scattering" (the primary observable we labor to compute). Across the five disciplines, these two concepts generate the following:

```
hep-th:  scattering + field-theory = green-function
hep-ph:  scattering + field-theory = dispersion-
                                      relation
hep-lat: scattering + field-theory = wave-function
gr-qc:   scattering + field-theory = bms
math-ph: scattering + field-theory = internal.
```

Note that "bms" here refers to the Bondi–Metzner–Sachs (BMS) group, a symmetry property of asymptotically flat Lorentzian spacetimes, which was shown by Strominger to be a symmetry of the S-matrix in perturbative quantum gravity [33].

6. Title Classification

The previous sections would be of some mild interest to theoretical particle physicists who routinely publish in the areas covered by our five **arXiv** sections. But for practicing data scientists, what is of interest is the ability of the word embeddings to generate a classification algorithm that accurately and efficiently assigns the proper **arXiv** section to a given paper title. In our context, the question is naturally as follows:

> *Question: Given a random title (not even necessarily a legitimate physics title), can a neural network decide to which section on the arXiv is it likely to belong?*

It turns out that one of the most powerful uses for **Word2vec** is classification of texts [34]. Indeed, document classification is one of the key tasks a neural network is asked to perform in natural language processing generally.

Classification is the canonical problem in supervised machine learning, and there are many possible approaches. The preceding sections have provided us with insights that will prove of value. In particular, 'cleaning' the data allowed us to examine certain contextual relations and make more meaningful frequency statements about certain concepts. Nevertheless, it eliminated some information that may be useful, such as the pattern of small words like conjunctions, and it tended to bury certain key descriptors (like 'dark') by embedding them in multiple hyphenated words. We will therefore train our classifier with **raw** data, with the only processing being the removal of upper-case letters.

The algorithm we will choose is the *mean word-vector* method [34], and it proceeds as follows:

- Combine all titles from all the relevant sections from `arXiv`; establish a word vector for each word using `Word2vec`'s CBOW neural network model. This gives a single vector space V consisting of many 400-vectors (recall that our convention is such that each word vector is an element of $\mathbb{R}^{400}$).
- Subsequently, for each title, considered as a list of words, take the component-wise mean of the list of word vectors; thus each title is associated with a single vector in V.
- Establish *labelled data* D consisting of entries (Title$_1$, i), (Title$_2$, i), ..., (Title$_k$, j), (Title$_{k+1}$, j), ... over all `arXiv` sections under consideration, where $i, j, \ldots \in \{1, 2, 3, 4, 5\}$ specifies the 5 sections, respectively, hep-th, hep-ph, hep-lat, gr-qc and math-ph.
- Construct a "training set", say 7,000 random samples from D, and use one's favorite classifier to train this sample.
- Construct a "validation set", a complementary set of, say 13,000 samples from D, to ensure that the classifier has *not seen* these before.
- Predict to which `arXiv` section each title in the validation set should belong and check the veracity of that prediction.

A few remarks are in order. First, we emphasize: for the input titles, we did *not* perform any cleaning of the data, and the only processing that was done was to put all letters to lower case. This is important because we wish to keep all grammatical and syntactical information, including conjunctions and (in)definite articles, etc., which could be indicative of the stylist choice in different sections of the arXiv. Moreover, that during the training of Word2vec we keep all words (instead of a cut-off of at least frequency four, as was done in Section 4 for the cleaned data). This is because we will establish as large a vocabulary as possible in order to (1) ensure the labeling of each title and (2) accommodate new unencountered titles.

Now, in the labeling of the titles, it may at first appear that by averaging over the word vectors in a title, one loses precious information such as the ordering of words. However, from similar studies in the literature [34], such a seemingly crude method (or variants such as taking component-wise max/min) is actually extremely effective. Furthermore, an often-used method is to *weight* the words in different documents (here, arXiv sections) with tf-idf, but we will not do so here since, as was described in Section 5.1, the vast majority of tf-idf values will be vanishing for the five "documents" crafted from the bag of all titles.

Finally, of the choices of classifiers, we use a support vector machine (SVM). Of course, other classifiers and neural networks can also be used, but SVMs are known to be efficient in discrete categorization (cf. [35]), thus we will adhere to this for this paper.

6.1. *Prediction results*

Following the above algorithm, and applying it to our five arXiv sections, we can establish the so-called **confusion matrix** $\mathcal{M}$, the (i, j)-th entry of which is established in the following way. Comparing to a title coming from section i, suppose the SVM predicted section j, then we add 1 to $\mathcal{M}_{ij}$. By construction, $\mathcal{M}$ is not necessarily symmetric. Furthermore, each row sum is equal to the validation size, since the SVM is trained to slot the result into one of the categories; column sums, on the other hand, need not have any constraints — for instance, everything could be (mis-)classified into a single category. In an ideal situation of perfect prediction by the SVM, $\mathcal{M}$ would, of course, be a diagonal matrix, meaning there are no mismatches at all (if we normalize to percentage correct per category, this would be the identity matrix).

Using the ordering of the sections as $(1, 2, 3, 4, 5)$ = (hep-th, hep-ph, hep-lat, gr-qc, math-ph), we find the confusion matrix to be as follows:

Word2vec + SVM Actual	1	2	3	4	5
1	5223	844	1132	3122	2679
2	1016	8554	1679	1179	572
3	977	1466	9411	188	958
4	1610	566	128	9374	1322
5	1423	279	521	1010	9767

$$\begin{cases} 1 : \text{hep-th} \\ 2 : \text{hep-ph} \\ 3 : \text{hep-lat} \\ 4 : \text{gr-qc} \\ 5 : \text{math-ph} . \end{cases} \tag{15}$$

We see that the classification is actually quite good, with confusion largely diagonal, especially in the last four sections, achieving around 70% accuracy. The overall **accuracy** is defined as the sum of the true positives (diagonal entries) divided by the total number of entries in the matrix (65,000), which yields 65.1%. Let us take a moment to put this accuracy rate into perspective. In the years since the arrival of Word2vec, in 2013, a number of papers have appeared that aim to improve upon the original technique. In this literature, the goal is generally to classify documents into categories that are well defined and highly distinct. For example, one might ask the classifier to distinguish whether a Wikipedia article [36] is about an office-holder or an athlete, or whether a thread on Yahoo! Answers [37] is about "science & math" or "business & finance" (c.f. the discussion in Zhang *et al.* [38]). Such trials have become somewhat standardized into benchmark tests in the NLP community. For example, Zhang *et al.* demonstrated that Word2vec was able to accomplish the above-mentioned tasks of sorting DBPedia articles and Yahoo! Answers threads, with an accuracy of 89% and 56%, respectively. In those cases, the classifier is generally given a much larger sample of words to address, and the task at hand is such that one expects a human classifier to perform the task with very high fidelity. In our test, however, it would be difficult for active researchers in high energy theory — frequent contributors to the `arXiv` — to achieve even 65% accuracy in sorting papers solely by title alone. One expects even better classification results can be achieved if one were to consider full abstracts or even the entire text of papers.[4]

The misclassifications are, themselves, very indicative of the nature of the sub-fields. For example, hep-th (1st entry) is more confused with gr-qc (4th entry) and math-ph (5th entry) than any other misclassifications. Indeed, this reflects that high energy theory is closer to these two fields than any other field is close to another. The asymmetry is also relevant: hep-th is more frequently confused (24.0%) with gr-qc than vice versa (12.4%). This is because the string theory community that populates hep-th derives from both a particle physics and a gravity tradition, whereas the gr-qc community has different historical roots. This is similarly true for hep-th and math-ph. The cultural origins of the communities can already be deduced from this analysis.

Similarly, the two more phenomenological sections, hep-ph and hep-lat, form a connected and isolated 2×2 block, more often confused with one another than any of the other three sections. And again, of the remaining three sections, hep-th stands out for misclassification. As mentioned earlier, this suggests the centrality of hep-th in the organization of this community of particle physicists. One can make this analysis more precise by reducing the 5×5 confusion matrix in (15) to a binary 2×2 form, in which we group hep-th, gr-qc and math-ph as "formal" sections and group hep-ph and hep-lat as "phenomenological" sections. In this form, the binary classification matrix is

$$\mathcal{M} = \begin{pmatrix} 35530 & 3470 \\ 4890 & 21120 \end{pmatrix}, \tag{16}$$

which corresponds to an accuracy, in executing this binary classification, of 87.1%, which is a remarkable success rate for such a subtle classification task.

Regular contributors to these sections of the `arXiv` may be curious to see, among those which have been misclassified, what sorts of titles

---

[4]Physicists distinguish titles of genuine papers posted on hep-th from fake titles generated using a context-free grammar [39] successfully only 59% of the time [40].

Table 15. Examples of titles that were misclassified by the support vector classifier.

True	Predicted	Title
hep-th	gr-qc	'string dynamics in cosmological and black-hole backgrounds: the null string expansion'
hep-ph	hep-th	'(inverse) magnetic catalysis in (2+1)-dimensional gauge theories from holographic models'
hep-ph	hep-lat	'combining infrared and low-temperature asymptotes in yang-mills theories'
hep-th	math-ph	'a generalized scaling function for ads/cft'
hep-lat	math-ph	'green's functions from quantum cluster algorithms'
hep-th	gr-qc	'quasiparticle universes in bose-einstein condensates'
hep-ph	hep-th	'on axionic dark matter in type iia string theory'
math-ph	gr-qc	'fluids in weyl geometries'
hep-lat	hep-ph	'vacuum stability and the higgs boson'
hep-th	hep-lat	'renormalization in coulomb-gauge qcd within the lagrangian formalism'

they are. We exhibit a few of the misclassified cases in Table 15. It is not hard to see why these titles were mismatched. For example, the words 'cosmological and black-hole' have made the first title more like gr-qc and 'coulomb-gauge qcd' in the last title more like hep-lat.

6.2. *Cross-checking results*

We now make a few remarks about the robustness of our methodology. First, it is important that we established a *single* word vector space V. As a sanity check, we established *separate* vector spaces, one for each section, used the SVM to classify and obtained, rather trivially, almost a diagonal matrix for $\mathcal{M}$. The typical false-positive rate was of order 0.3%. This means that the vector spaces created by the vector embeddings for the five sections are highly disjoint, with almost no overlap in the embedding space of $\mathbb{R}^{400}$, despite the similar vocabulary employed. Of course, establishing different vector spaces *a priori* is useless for a classification problem since categorizing into different section is precisely the problem to be solved.

Next, we can check that titles *within* the same section can be consistently classified. To test this, we train 20,000 titles from hep-th into a single vector space but separate into two random, non-overlapping groups, labeled as 1 and 2. Repeating the same procedure as above, we obtained a 2×2 confusion matrix

$$\mathcal{M} = \begin{pmatrix} 54.8 & 45.3 \\ 54.7 & 45.0 \end{pmatrix}, \tag{17}$$

where we will report percentages, as opposed to raw numbers, in the remaining confusion matrices. The fact that this matrix is almost perfectly divided into the four blocks is very reassuring. It strongly shows that titles coming from the same section, when translated into word vectors, are indistinguishable for the SVM.

Finally, we comment on the importance of the Word2vec neural network. One might imagine that in the classification algorithm, one could bypass Word2vec completely and use, instead, something much more straightforward. Consider the following alternative mechanism. The set of all titles in each of the five arXiv sections is already a labeled dataset. One could simply establish a vocabulary of words for each section and lexicographically order them. Then, each title in a section is a list of words which can be labeled by an integer vector, where each word is replaced by its position in the vocabulary. This is essentially replacing the Word2vec-generated vector embedding with a trivial (one-hot) embedding (in a single vector space). This collection of vectors, together with the section label, can then form the training data for a standard application of supervised machine learning.

We performed this straightforward exercise, using our same SVM architecture to attempt to classify titles, with a validation set of 50,000 titles. We find that the result of the predictor is rather random across the sections, as shown by the percentage confusion matrix

Word2vec + SVM Actual	1	2	3	4	5	
1	42.	3.7	20.	27.	6.9	
2	36.	5.2	28.	23.	8.3	(18)
3	36.	4.3	32.	20.	8.5	
4	30.	3.3	17.	20.	30.	
5	37.	4.2	29.	22.	8.1	

which is far from diagonal (and interestingly, mostly being misclassified as hep-th). We conclude that simply knowing the typical vocabulary of an author in hep-th, versus one in, say, gr-qc, is insufficient to sort papers into arXiv sections. In contrast, Word2vec not only knows the words but also has learnt the context of words by knowing their nearby neighbors. Knowing this context is crucial to our analysis, i.e., SVM without Word2vec is ineffectual.

6.3. *Beyond physics*

To further reassure ourselves of the validity and power of Word2vec in conjunction with SVM, we can perform a number of interesting cross-checks. Suppose we took all titles from a completely different section of the arXiv which, *a priori*, should not be related at all to any of our five physics sections. What about beyond the arXiv? How well does the neural network perform? To answer, let us take the following titles:

(1–5) as thus far studied: hep-th, hep-ph, hep-lat, gr-qc, math-ph.

(6) cond-mat: This is the condensed matter physics section. Beginning in April of 1992, it consists of research related to material science, superconductivity, statistical mechanics, etc.; there are many papers cross-listed between hep-th and cond-mat, especially after the AdS/CMT correspondence.

(7) q-fin: The quantitative finance section, beginning in December of 2008, is one of the newest sections to the arXiv.

(8) stat: Another newcomer to the arXiv, the statistics section began in April of 2007 and consists of such topical fields as machine learning.

(9) q-bio: Receiving contributions since September of 2003, quantitative biology is an important section of the arXiv consisting of the latest research in mathematical biology and bio-physics.

(10) Times-India: This is our control sample. The *Times of India* headlines [32] are available online, a compilation of 2.7 million news headlines published by *Times of India* from 2001 to 2017, from which we extract 20,000 random samples. These present a reasonably good analog to arXiv titles in terms of length and syntax.

(11) viXra-hep: An alternative to arXiv is the so-called viXra (which is arXiv spelt backwards) [41]. Set up by independent physicist Philip Gibbs as an alternative to arXiv in 2007, it aims to cover topics across the whole scientific community, accepting submissions without requiring authors to have an academic affiliation, and does not have the quality control which arXiv has. In fact, it typically consists of papers rejected by arXiv and has not been accepted by any of the major peer-reviewed journals.[5] So far, viXra has around 20,000 total titles across all disciplines in science, though dominated by physics and mathematics.

  viXra-hep is the high energy physics section of viXra and, up to the end of 2017, consists of 1,233 titles.

(12) viXra-qgst: Likewise, this is the Quantum Gravity and String Theory section of viXra and, up to the end of 2017, consists of 1494 titles. Both viXra-hep and viXra-qgst are relatively small in size but we will nevertheless study them as a curiosity.

We remark that we have specifically included the above three sections of (7–9) because many practitioners of the high energy theory and mathematical physics community, who once posted to Sections (1–5), have at various points of their careers switched to these three fields. It would be interesting to see whether any linguistic idiosyncrasies are carried over.

Now, it is obvious that both viXra sections have, unfortunately, much smaller sample size than the rest, so while we will include them when constructing the conglomerate word-vector embedding by Word2vec, it is sensible to single them out for the classification stage. We find that **no** title from categories (1–10) is misclassified into either of the two sections viXra-hep and viXra-qgst, and these two sections are almost randomly classified into the others. To some extent, this represents the disproportionately small size of the two viXra sections. But it also suggests that these particular sections do

---

[5]To give an example, one single contributor to viXra has submitted 2572 manuscripts since December of 2011 — a publication rate that exceeds one per calendar day. It seems clear that such output cannot be compatible with the normal standards of rigor and novelty that is standard in the academic community.

not even have a self-consistent linguistic structure. The classification probabilities for the two viXra sections into other categories are

NN Actual	1	2	3	4	5	6	7	8	9	10
viXra-hep	11.5	47.4	6.8	13.	11.	4.5	0.2	0.3	2.2	3.1
viXra-qgst	13.3	14.5	1.5	54.	8.4	1.8	0.1	1.1	2.8	3.

$$(19)$$

suggesting that titles in viXra-hep are most like titles in hep-ph while those in viXra-qgst are most like gr-qc. If one were to peruse the titles in viXra, this correspondence would become readily apparent.

For the remaining 10 sections, we find the percentage confusion matrix to be as follows:

NN + SVM Actual	1	2	3	4	5	6	7	8	9	10
1	39.	5.6	9.4	25.	15.8	4.1	0.02	0.4	0.5	0.2
2	7.9	61.	14.9	8.6	2.9	3.4	0.02	0.8	0.4	0.4
3	6.2	9.2	72.	1.2	4.6	4.5	0.03	1.2	0.6	0.2
4	11.5	3.7	0.7	72.	8.5	1.8	0.03	0.9	0.8	0.4
5	11.3	0.9	2.9	7.1	63.	9.8	0.09	2.6	2.2	0.2
6	2.4	1.2	4.1	1.4	8.5	73.	0.5	1.7	6.7	0.1
7	0.6	0.5	0.3	0.7	5.9	1.4	60.	18.3	11.4	1.4
8	0.3	0.5	0.5	0.6	5.4	0.5	1.7	81.	9.2	0.7
9	0.4	1.	0.5	0.7	3.9	7.3	0.4	12.6	72.	0.9
10	0.5	1.5	0.1	1.3	0.5	0.8	0.5	0.3	2.2	92.

$$(20)$$

where we present the results in percentage terms because some of the title sets studied have different numbers of samples. Reassuringly, $\mathcal{M}$ is very much diagonal. Even more significant is the fact that the greatest percentage correct (92%) is (10), corresponding to the newspaper headline: the syntax and word choice of the world of journalism is indeed very different from that of science. The next higher score is 81%, for (8), stat, while, interestingly, q-fin is not that markedly different from the physics sections.

To be more quantitative, we can reduce this dataset to a number of binary "X" versus "not-X" classifications and reduce the confusion matrix accordingly. For example, singling out only row/column 10, *Times of India* headlines, we find a confusion matrix of

$$
\begin{array}{l|cc}
\text{Word2vec + SVM} & & \\
\quad \text{Actual} & \text{Times not} - \text{Times} \\
\hline
\quad \text{Times} & 3176 & 263 \\
\text{not} - \text{Times} & 353 & 85040
\end{array}
\tag{21}
$$

corresponding to an overall accuracy of 99.3% for this particular classification. That scholarly publication titles can be separated from newspaper headlines with less than 0.7% inaccuracy may seem trivial, but this level of fidelity of Word2vec is generally not seen in canonical classification challenges.

It is also instructive to see how well our neural network was able to distinguish natural science (physics + biology) from everything else (statistics, quantitative finance and newspaper headlines) and how well it can distinguish high energy physics from everything else. In the latter case, we are asking for the separation between titles in the five high energy physics (HEP) sections and those in the condensed-matter section cond-mat. The separation of natural science gives a confusion matrix of

$$
\begin{array}{l|cc}
\text{Word2vec + SVM} & & \\
\quad \text{Actual} & \text{NaturalScience not} - \text{NaturalScience} \\
\hline
\quad \text{NaturalScience} & 69223 & 2137 \\
\text{not} - \text{NaturalScience} & 2584 & 13733
\end{array}
\tag{22}
$$

which corresponds to an accuracy of 94.6%, whereas the separation between HEP sections and non-HEP sections is only slightly less accurate

$$
\begin{array}{l|cc}
\text{Word2vec + SVM} & & \\
\quad \text{Actual} & \text{HEP not} - \text{HEP} \\
\hline
\quad \text{HEP} & 50882 & 3825 \\
\text{not} - \text{HEP} & 3325 & 30799
\end{array}
\tag{23}
$$

corresponding to an accuracy of 92.0%.

7. Conclusion

In this chapter, we have performed a systematic textual analysis of theoretical particle physics papers using natural language processing and machine learning techniques. Focusing specifically on titles of hep-th papers, and then later on the titles of papers in four related sections of the arXiv, we have demonstrated the ability of a classifying agent, informed by vector word embeddings generated by the continuous bag-of-words neural network model of Word2vec, to accurately classify papers into five arXiv sections, using only paper titles, with an accuracy of just over 65%. For the slightly easier task of separating high energy physics titles from those of other scientific pursuits — even other branches of theoretical physics — the classification accuracy was 92%.

We have demonstrated that this classification accuracy is not adequately explained by distinctions between the words themselves that are employed by the authors in the various sections. Rather, the contextual windows, captured by the vector space embeddings constructed by Word2vec, are clearly important to the ability to distinguish titles. A practitioner of theoretical particle physics, such as the authors, could hardly be expected to achieve such accuracy, which is, of course, why machine learning is so powerful in these sorts of problems. In fact, the use of natural language processing to classify documents is well established in the data analysis community. We would like to suggest the performance in classifying papers in arXiv be used as a benchmark test for classification algorithms generally, as the differences between the sections are subtle, even to long-time contributors to the field.

Along the way to demonstrating the classification ability of Word2vec, we discovered a number of interesting properties of arXiv authors, and hep-th specifically. Many of these observations belong to a growing field of meta-analysis in the sciences that has come to be known as *scientometrics* [42]. In particular, the contextual analysis revealed strong ties between hep-th and the more formal branches of the larger high energy theory community: math-ph and gr-qc. The connection between the syntax used by hep-th authors had close affinity to hep-ph but not to hep-lat, though the latter two sections of arXiv were themselves very similar in syntax and subject content.

As those who have been in the theoretical high energy community for some time can attest, there has long been a perception of a rather wide chasm between "formal theorists" and "phenomenologists", and that this sociological chasm is born out in the bifurcation of our field in terms of conference/workshop attendance, citation, co-authorship, etc.[6] Such compartmentalization of the high energy community can even be seen visually, in a representation of the citation network across various branches of high energy physics [43].

Finally, this work has a contribution to make to the more formal study of vector space word embeddings and natural language processing more generally. As mentioned earlier in the text, the "strange geometry" of vector space word embeddings is an interesting area of study. The tendency of word vectors to cluster in the positive orthant, and the highly conical nature of the assigned vectors, has been studied in other contexts [24]. Typically, these datasets are of a more general nature, like the *Times of India* headlines, whose affinity distances were shown in Section 4.1. For the highly technical and specific papers that form the corpus of hep-th, however, these geometrical properties are even more pronounced. Indeed, we suggest that the degree of conical clustering in a particular word embedding may serve as a marker for the degree of specificity of a particular corpus. Thus, we might expect more clustering in headlines drawn strictly from the finance section of the newspaper than from newspaper headlines generally. On a more mathematical note, it would be of interest to explore the true dimensionality of our vector space word embedding (undoubtedly far smaller than the 400-dimensional embedding space we have chosen) and to study the properties of the space orthogonal to any particular word vector. We leave such issues to a future work.

Ultimately, it would be of interest to devote more attention to the abstracts of arXiv papers and eventually to the text of those papers themselves. The decision to restrict ourselves primarily to titles was mainly made on the basis of limited computational resources, though there are technical issues to consider as well. In dealing with

---

[6]The relatively small string phenomenology community has a negligible effect on this division.

abstracts (and eventually whole documents), two methods of attack immediately present themselves: (a) we could to take *each* abstract as a document and then study cross-document word embeddings and (b) we could take the full list of abstracts as a single document, each sentence being a proper sentence in the English language, separated by the full stop. It is clear that (b) is more amenable to `Word2vec`, though it would clearly obscure the contextual differences between one paper and the next if context windows were to cross abstracts. We hope to return to this issue, perhaps employing variants of `Word2vec` such as `Doc2vec` [44], which takes not a list of list of words, but rather a triple layer of a list of list of list of words, and which is obviously more suited for method (a).

Acknowledgments

We are indebted to Paul Ginsparg for his many suggestions and helpful comments. YHH would like to thank the Science and Technology Facilities Council, UK, for grant ST/J00037X/1, the Chinese Ministry of Education, for a Chang-Jiang Chair Professorship at Nankai University and the City of Tianjin for a Qian-Ren Scholarship. VJ is supported by the South African Research Chairs Initiative of the DST/NRF.

Appendix A.   From Raw Titles to Cleaned Titles

In this appendix, we describe the process and consequences of cleaning. We work with 120,249 titles from **hep-th**, with a total of 996,485 words, of which 48,984 are unique. First, we convert the text to lower case and remove punctuation. Next, after replacing plurals, foreign spellings and some technical acronyms (such as "ramond ramond" → "rr"), we are left with 701,794 words of which 32,693 are unique.

Now, we can let the computer find the most common 2-grams (words which appear adjacent to each other). The top hits are "gauge theory", "field theory", "scalar field", etc. These terms are collective nouns. They clearly need to be hyphenated and considered as single words. Plotting the frequency of the top 300 2-grams, one can see that there is a tailing off at around 50 or so (cf. Figure A.1). This

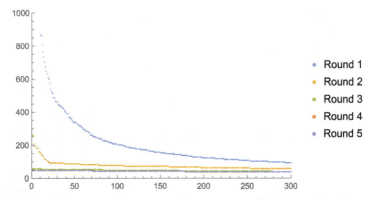

Figure A.1. Histogram of frequency of appearance of 2-grams after five rounds of hyphenating the 2-grams with frequencies exceeding 50. We see that after two iterations, the distribution is essentially flat, signifying that words which should be hyphenated have been.

means that we should simply hyphenate 2-grams that appear more than 50 times.

We repeat this process, hyphenating on each iteration those 2-grams that appear with a frequency exceeding 50. This can concatenate strings to form 3-grams, such as the word "quantum-field-theory". Figure A.1 shows that the histogram becomes essentially flat after two iterations. This is quite interesting as it signifies that technical words which should be hyphenated can be detected automatically. We will use the flatness of the curve to stop the automatic replacements after two rounds of hyphenation. For reference, we record the most common 10 words at each round of replacements, as well as the number of times that they appear.

Round 1	{{{gauge, theory}, 3232}, {{field, theory}, 2937}, {{string, theory}, 2025}, {{quantum, gravity}, 1552}, {{yang-mills, theory}, 1207}, {{scalar, field}, 1174}, {{quantum, mechanics}, 1117}, {{dark, energy}, 1084}, {{matrix, model}, 1040}, {{cosmological, constant}, 869}}
Round 2	{{{string-field, theory}, 260}, {{susy-gauge, theory}, 255}, {{loop-quantum, gravity}, 209}, {{scalar-field, theory}, 191}, {{chiral-symmetry, breaking}, 191}, {{n=4-sym, theory}, 182}, {{lattice-gauge, theory}, 182}, {{topological-field, theory}, 162}, {{noncommutative-gauge, theory}, 158}, {{susy-quantum, mechanics}, 155}}

Round 3	{{{pair, creation}, 56}, {{cosmic, censorship}, 56}, {{holographic, principle}, 56}, {{three, dimensional}, 56}, {{logarithmic, correction}, 56}, {{dimensional, regularization}, 56}, {{nonlinear, susy}, 56}, {{susy, standard-model}, 56}, {{stochastic, quantization}, 56}, {{density, perturbation}, 56}}
Round 4	{{{heavy-ion, collisions}, 52}, {{new, massive-gravity}, 49}, {{conformal, algebra}, 49}, {{warped, compactification}, 49}, {{group, manifold}, 49}, {{weak, gravity}, 49}, {{stress-energy, tensor}, 49}, {{elementary, particle}, 49}, {{bose, gas}, 49}, {{new, results}, 49}}
Round 5	{{{new, massive-gravity}, 49}, {{conformal, algebra}, 49}, {{warped, compactification}, 49}, {{group, manifold}, 49}, {{weak, gravity}, 49}, {{stress-energy, tensor}, 49}, {{elementary, particle}, 49}, {{bose, gas}, 49}, {{new, results}, 49}, {{brownian, motion}, 49}}

B.   Higher n-Grams Across the Sections

In this appendix, we will present some statistic of the higher n-grams for the various arXiv sections, extending the 1-gram (words) and 2-gram analyses in Sections 5.1 and 5.2. The 15 most common 3-grams in hep-th titles are as follows:

Raw	{{quantum,field,theory},826}, {{a,note,on},620}, {{conformal,field,theory},477}, {{in,string,theory},475}, {{string,field,theory},399}, {{the,cosmological,constant},395}, {{at,finite,temperature},390}, {{the,presence,of},353}, {{in,the,presence},346}, {{the,standard,model},329}, {{conformal,field,theories},324}, {{field,theory,and},284}, {{in,de,sitter},281}, {{approach,to,the},273}, {{corrections,to,the},263}
Cleaned	{{weak,gravity,conjecture},41}, {{causal,dynamical,triangulations},37}, {{strong,cp,problem},30}, {{string,gas,cosmology},29}, {{van,der,waals},28}, {{ads_5,times,s^5},25}, {{shape,invariant,potential},24}, {{chern-simons,matter,theory},24}, {{ads/cft,integrability,chapter},23}, {{review,ads/cft,integrability,},23}, {{type,0,string-theory},23}, {{closed,timelike,curves},22}, {{hard,thermal,loop},22}, {{lowest,landau,level},22}, {{varying,speed,light},21}

Once again, more information is to be found in the cleaned 3-grams. We conclude here as well that the most common terms such as "weak gravity conjecture", "causal dynamical triangulations" or "the strong CP problem" should be collective nouns with more stringent cleaning.

Finally, the 15 most common 4-grams in hep-th titles are as follows:

Raw	{{in,the,presence,of},345}, {{in,quantum,field,theory},201}, {{a,note,on,the},181}, {{and,the,cosmological,constant},145}, {{the,cosmological,constant,problem},120}, {{in,de,sitter,space},111}, {{of,the,standard,model},94}, {{open,string,field,theory},89}, {{the,presence,of,a},89}, {{in,conformal,field,theory},82}, {{chiral,symmetry,breaking,in},81}, {{in,a,magnetic,field},81}, {{of,the,cosmological,constant},80}, {{effective,field,theory,of},80}, {{the,moduli,space,of},77}
Cleaned	{{review,ads/cft,integrability,chapter},23}, {{solution,strong,cp,problem},12}, {{chiral,de,rham,complex},9}, {{superstring,derived,standard-like,model},8}, {{bundle,formulation,nonrelativistic-quantum,mechanics},7}, {{fibre,bundle,formulation,nonrelativistic-quantum},7}, {{radiatively,induced,lorentz,cpt-violation},7}, {{vortex,model,ir,sector},7}, {{center,vortex,model,ir},7}, {{ultra,high-energy,cosmic,rays},7}, {{radiation,d-dimensional,collision,shock-wave},7}, {{5d,standing,wave,braneworld},7}, {{logarithmic,tensor,category,theory,},7}, {{five-dimensional,tangent,vector,spacetime},7}, {{shear-viscosity,entropy,density,ratio},7}

The most common cleaned 4-gram is a reference to the Beisert *et al.* review on the integrable structure of $\mathcal{N} = 4$ super-Yang–Mills theory [45]. While again certain 4-grams obviously point to "a solution to the strong CP problem" or "the chiral de Rham complex", the prevalence of these terms is sufficiently scarce in the database that finding these collective terms automatically is somewhat difficult. What is striking as a member of the hep-th community is that these collective nouns tie in nicely to an expert's conception of what it is that hep-th people do.

In analogy to Figure 3, we consider in Table B.1 word clouds based on cleaned data for the subjects hep-ph, hep-lat, gr-qc and math-ph.

Table B.1. Some simple statistics of all titles of the various sections of the high energy `arXiv`, from the beginning in 1990 until 2017. The titles are *cleaned* according do the discussions in Section 3.2. The word cloud is sized according to frequency of relevant words. The number of papers and associated number of total unique words were compiled in December 2017.

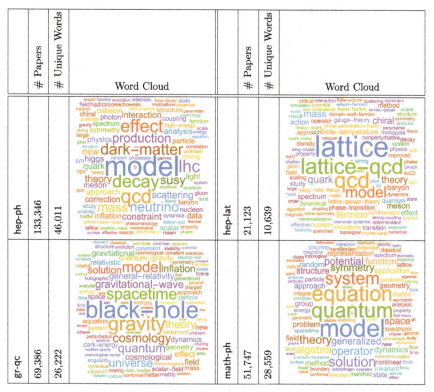

An expert can associate any of these word clouds with the label of the corresponding subject area. Thus, it is not entirely surprising that machine learning algorithms can discriminate titles between these areas as well.

A paper may be of interest to the readers of the `arXiv` in more than one subject area and indeed can reasonably be posted in either of hep-th or hep-ph, for example. Cross-listing on the `arXiv` enlarges the readership of a paper and enables the expression of a diversity of scientific interests. For these reasons, there is a significant overlap between the terms that appear in the word clouds. The emphasis of certain themes, however, renders the identification unambiguous.

The most common 15 3-grams in the other **arXiv** sections based on cleaned data are as follows:

hep-ph	{hidden,local,symmetry}, {hadron,resonance,gas}, {hard,thermal,loop}, {fine,structure,constant}, {higgs,triplet,model}, {t,bar,t}, {hadronic,light-by-light,scattering}, {resonance,gas,model}, {delta,i=1/2,rule}, {inverse,magnetic,catalysis}, {large,momentum,transfer}, {active,galactic,nuclei}, {susy,flavor,problem}, {q,bar,q}, {future,lepton,colliders}
hep-lat	{gluon,ghost,propagators}, {electric,dipole,moment}, {hadronic,vacuum,polarization}, {numerical,stochastic,perturbation-theory}, {mass,anomalous,dimension}, {first,order,phase-transition}, {maximum,entropy,method}, {causal,dynamical,triangulations}, {matrix,product,state}, {hadron,resonance,gas}, {chiral,magnetic,effect}, {delta,i=1/2,rule}, {physical,pion,mass}, {neutron,electric,dipole}, {nucleon,axial,charge}
gr-qc	{matters,gravity,newsletter}, {einstein,static,universe}, {causal,dynamical,triangulations}, {initial,value,problem}, {modified,newtonian,dynamics}, {topical,group,gravitation}, {van,der,waals}, {eddington-inspired,born-infeld,gravity}, {crossing,phantom,divide}, {baryon,acoustic,oscillation}, {physical,society,volume}, {american,physical,society,}, {newsletter,topical,group}, {gravity,newsletter,topical}, {lunar,laser,ranging}

math-ph	{asymmetric,simple-exclusion,process}, {spectruml,shift,function}, {alternating,sign,matrix}, {mutually,unbiased,bases}, {shape,invariant,potential}, {space,constant,curvature}, {quantum,affine,algebra}, {quantum,dynamical,semigroup}, {density,functional,theory}, {position,dependent,mass}, {inverse-scattering,fixed,energy}, {random,band,matrix}, {random,energy,model}, {asymptotic,iteration,method}, {spin,glass,model}

Finally, the 15 most common 4-grams in the other arXiv sections based on cleaned data are as follows:

hep-ph	{hadron,resonance,gas,model}, {variation,fine,structure,constant}, {35,kev,x-ray,line}, {au+au,collision,sqrts_nn=200,gev}, {130,gev,gamma-ray,line}, {hadronic,light-by-light,scattering,muon-g-2}, {hadronic,light-by-light,scattering,contribution}, {weak,radiative,hyperon,decay}, {after,lhc,run,1}, {nambu,-,jona-lasinio,model}, {variable,flavor,number,scheme}, {large,hadron,electron,collider}, {fermi,large,area,telescope}, {flavor,asymmetry,nucleon,sea}, {mu,->,e,gamma}
hep-lat	{neutron,electric,dipole,moment}, {ground,state,entropy,potts}, {center-vortex,model,ir,sector}, {hadron,resonance,gas,model}, {i=2,pion,scattering,length}, {gluon,ghost,propagators,landau-gauge}, {higgs,boson,mass,bound}, {international,lattice,data,grid}, {landau-gauge,gluon,ghost,propagators}, {color,confinement,dual,superconductivity}, {state,entropy,potts,antiferromagnets},

	{hadronic,contribution,muon,g-2},
	{nearly,physical,pion,mass}, {weinberg,-,salam,model},
	{kaon,mixing,beyond,sm}
gr-qc	{american,physical,society,volume},
	{newsletter,topical,group,gravitation},
	{gravity,newsletter,topical,group},
	{matters,gravity,newsletter,topical},
	{group,gravitation,american,physical},
	{topical,group,gravitation,american},
	{gravitation,american,physical,society,},
	{matters,gravity,newsletter,aps},
	{innermost,stable,circular,orbit},
	{stability,einstein,static,universe},
	{newsletter,aps,topical,group},
	{gravity,newsletter,aps,topical},
	{space,affine,connection,metric},
	{instanton,representation,plebanski,gravity},
	{laser,astrometric,test,relativity}
math-ph	{mean-field,spin,glass,model},
	{long,range,scattering,modified},
	{deformation,expression,elements,algebra},
	{totally,asymmetric,simple-exclusion,process},
	{nonlinear,accelerator,problems,wavelets},
	{scattering,modified,wave,operator},
	{range,scattering,modified,wave},
	{spectruml,parameter,power,series},
	{matrix,schrodinger-operator,half,line},
	{five-dimensional,tangent,vector,spacetime},
	{causal,signal,transmission,quantum-field},
	{master,constraint,programme,lqg},
	{set,spin,values,cayley-tree},
	{uncountable,set,spin,values},
	{model,uncountable,set,spin}

References

[1] https://arxiv.org.

[2] P. Ginsparg, It was twenty years ago today..., https://arxiv.org/abs/1108.2700 (2011).

[3] https://arxiv.org/help/stats/2017_by_area/index (2018).

[4] A. Plume and D. Van Weijen, Publish or perish? The rise of the fractional author? *Research Trends* **38** (2014), 16.

[5] F. Denef, Thoughts on future landscapes, Northeastern lecture (2017).

[6] V. Voevodsky, Type systems and proof assistant, IAS lecture (2012).

[7] M. Ganesalingam and W. T. Gowers, A fully automatic problem solver with human-style output, arXiv:1309.4501 (2013).

[8] Machine Learning in Physics, https://physicsml.github.io/pages/papers.html.

[9] Y. H. He, Deep learning the landscape, arXiv:1706.02714 [hep-th].
Y. H. He, Machine learning the string landscape, *Phys. Lett. B* **774** (2017), 564. Doi: 10.1016/j.physletb.2017.10.024.

[10] F. Ruehle, Evolving neural networks with genetic algorithms to study the string landscape, *JHEP* **1708** (2017), 038 [arXiv:1706.07024 [hep-th]].

[11] J. Carifio, J. Halverson, D. Krioukov and B. D. Nelson, Machine learning in the string landscape, *JHEP* **1709** (2017), 157 [arXiv:1707.00655 [hep-th]].

[12] J. Carifio, W. J. Cunningham, J. Halverson, D. Krioukov, C. Long and B. D. Nelson, Vacuum selection from cosmology on networks of string geometries, arXiv:1711.06685 [hep-th].

[13] D. Krefl and R. K. Seong, Machine Learning of Calabi–Yau volumes, *Phys. Rev. D* **96**(6) (2017), 066014 [arXiv:1706.03346 [hep-th]].

[14] Y. N. Wang and Z. Zhang, Learning non-Higgsable gauge groups in 4D F-theory, arXiv:1804.07296 [hep-th].

[15] K. Bull, Y. H. He, V. Jejjala and C. Mishra, arXiv:1806.03121 [hep-th].

[16] Evert van Nieuwenburg, Machine Learning the arXiv, https://quantumfrontiers.com/2017/11/29/machine-learning-the-arxiv/ cf. Physics2Vec: http://everthemore.pythonanywhere.com/.

[17] T. Mikolov, K. Chen, G. Corrado and J. Dean, Efficient estimation of word representations in vector space, arXiv:1301.3781 (2013).

[18] T. Mikolov, I. Sutskever, K. Chen, G. Corrado and J. Dean, Distributed representations of words and phrases and their compositionality, arXiv:1301.3781 (2013).

[19] R. Řehůřek and P. Sojka, Software framework for topic modelling with large corpora, *Proceedings of the LREC 2010 Workshop on New Challenges for NLP Frameworks*, ELRA (2010). https://radimrehurek.com/gensim/index.html.

[20] P. Ginsparg, P. Houle, T. Joachims and J.-H. Su, Mapping subsets of scholarly information, arXiv:cs/0312018 [cs.IR].

[21] H. M. Collins, P. Ginsparg and L. Reyes-Galindo, A note concerning Primary Source Knowledge, arXiv:1605.07228 [physics.soc-ph].

[22] P. Ginsparg, Preprint Déjà Vu: An FAQ, arXiv:1706.04188 [cs.DL].

[23] A. Alemi, Zombies reading segmented graphene articles on the Arxiv, https://ecommons.cornell.edu/handle/1813/40878.

[24] D. Mimno and L. Thompson, The strange geometry of skip-gram with negative sampling, *Proceedings of the 2017 Conference on Empirical Methods in Natural Language Processing*, pp. 2873–2878 (2017).

[25] P. D. Turney and P. Pantel, From frequency to meaning: Vector space models of semantics, *J. Artif. Intell. Res.* **37** (2010), 141–188. http://www.jair.org/media/2934/live-2934-4846-jair.pdf.

[26] K. Jain, An intuitive understanding of word embeddings: From count vectors to Word2Vec, https://www.analyticsvidhya.com/blog/2017/06/word-embeddings-count-word2veec/deeplearning4Jteam, "Word2Vec", https://deeplearning4j.org/word2vec.

[27] T. Mikolov, K. Chen, G. Corrado and J. Dean, Efficient estimation of word representations in vector space, arXiv:1301.3781[cs.CL]; T. Mikolov, K. Chen, G. Corrado and J. Dean, Distributed representations of words and phrases and their compositionality, arXiv:1310.4546 [cs.CL]; Y. Goldberg and O. Levy, word2vec Explained: deriving Mikolov *et al.*'s negative-sampling word-embedding method, arXiv:1402.3722 [cs.CL].

[28] E. Witten, Ground ring of two-dimensional string theory, *Nucl. Phys. B* **373** (1992), 187. Doi: 10.1016/0550-3213(92)90454-J [hep-th/9108004].

[29] G. Cybenko, Approximations by superpositions of sigmoidal functions, *Math. Control Signals Syst.* **2**(4) (1989), 303–314; K. Hornik, Approximation capabilities of multilayer feedforward networks, *Neural Networks* **4**(2) (1991), 251–257.

[30] Stanford CS Course, CS224d: Deep learning for natural language processing. http://cs224d.stanford.edu/syllabus.html.

[31] D. Kartsaklis, S. Ramgoolam and M. Sadrzadeh, Linguistic matrix theory, arXiv:1703.10252 [cs.CL].

[32] News Headlines of India, 16 years of categorized headlines focusing on India. https://www.kaggle.com/therohk/india-headlines-news-dataset.

[33] A. Strominger, On BMS invariance of gravitational scattering, *JHEP* **1407** (2014), 152 [arXiv:1312.2229 [hep-th]].

[34] G. Balikas and M.-R. Amini, An empirical study on large scale text classification with skip-gram embeddings, arXiv:1606.06623 [cs.CL];

M. Taddy, Document classification by inversion of distributed language representations, in *Proceedings of the 2015 Conference of the Association of Computational Linguistics* cf. also http://www.davidsbatista. net/blog/2017/04/01/document`classification/, https://stackoverflow. com/questions/47563821/how-can-i-use-word2vec-to-train-a-classifier http://nadbordrozd.github.io/blog/2016/05/20/text-classification-with-word2vec/ https://datawarrior.wordpress.com/2016/10/12/.

[35] I. Goodfellow, Y. Bengio and A. Courville, *Deep Learning*. MIT Press (2016). http://www.deeplearningbook.org.

[36] Wikipedia, https://www.wikipedia.org.

[37] Yahoo! Answers, https://answers.yahoo.com.

[38] X. Zhang and Y. LeCun, Text understanding from scratch, arXiv:1502.01710; X. Zhang, J. J. Zhao and Y. LeCun, Character-level convolutional networks for text classification, arXiv:1509.01626.

[39] The snarxiv, http://snarxiv.org/.

[40] D. Simmons-Duffin, The arXiv according to arXiv vs. snarXiv, http:// davidsd.org/2010/09/the-arxiv-according-to-arxiv-vs-snarxiv/.

[41] An alternative archive e-prints in Science and Mathematics serving the whole scientific community, http://vixra.org/.

[42] L. Leydesdorff and S. Milojevic, Scientometrics, arXiv:1208.4566 [cs.CL].

[43] Big Data Visualization of the Week: Paperscape, Inside BIGDATA (October 22, 2013), http://blog.paperscape.org.

[44] Q. Le and T. Mikolov, Distributed representations of sentences and documents, https://cs.stanford.edu/~quocle/paragraph_vector.pdf.

[45] N. Beisert *et al.*, Review of AdS/CFT integrability: An overview, *Lett. Math. Phys.* **99**(3) (2012), 3–32 [arXiv:1012.3982 [hep-th]].

Chapter 8

Symmetry-via-Duality: Invariant Neural Network Densities from Parameter-Space Correlators[*]

Anindita Maiti[†], Keegan Stoner[‡], and James Halverson[§]

The NSF AI Institute for Artificial Intelligence
and Fundamental Interactions,
Department of Physics, Northeastern University, Boston, MA 02115, USA
[†] maiti.a@northeastern.edu
[‡] stoner.ke@northeastern.edu
[§] j.halverson@northeastern.edu

Abstract

Parameter space and function space provide two different duality frames in which to study neural networks. We demonstrate that symmetries of network densities may be determined via dual computations of network correlation functions, even when the density is unknown and the network is not equivariant. Symmetry-via-duality relies on invariance properties of the correlation functions, which stem from the choice of network parameter distributions. Input and output symmetries of neural network densities are determined, which recover known Gaussian process results in the infinite width limit. The mechanism may also be utilized to determine symmetries during training, when parameters are correlated, as well as symmetries of the Neural Tangent Kernel. We demonstrate that the

---

[*] Equal contributions by Maiti and Stoner.

amount of symmetry in the initialization density affects the accuracy of networks trained on Fashion-MNIST and that symmetry breaking helps only when it is in the direction of ground truth.

1. Introduction

Many systems in Nature, mathematics, and deep learning are described by densities over functions. In physics, it is central in quantum field theory (QFT) via the Feynman path integral, whereas in deep learning, it explicitly arises via a correspondence between infinite networks and Gaussian processes.

More broadly, the density associated with a network architecture is itself of foundational importance. Though only a small collection of networks is trained in practice, due to computational limitations, a priori there is no reason to prefer one randomly initialized network over another (of the same architecture). In that case, ideally one would control the flow of the initialization density to the trained density, compute the trained mean $\mu(x)$, and use it to make predictions. Remarkably, $\mu(x)$ may be analytically computed for infinite networks trained via gradient flow or Bayesian inference [1–3].

In systems governed by densities over functions, observables are strongly constrained by symmetry, which is usually determined via experiments. Examples include the Standard Model of Particle Physics, which has gauge symmetry $SU(3) \times SU(2) \times U(1)$ (possibly with a discrete quotient), as well as certain multi-dimensional Gaussian processes. In the absence of good experimental data or an explicit form for the density, it seems difficult to deduce much about its symmetries.

We introduce a mechanism for determining the symmetries of a neural network density via duality, even for an unknown density. A physical system is said to exhibit a duality when it admits two different, but equally fundamental, descriptions, called duality frames. Hallmarks of duality include the utility of one frame in understanding a feature of the system that is difficult to understand in the other, as well as limits of the system where one description is more tractable than the other. In neural networks, one sharp duality is Parameter-Space/Function-Space duality: networks may be thought of as instantiations of a network architecture with fixed parameter densities or alternatively as draws from a function-space density. In

GP limits where a discrete hyperparameter $N \to \infty$ (e.g., the width), the number of parameters is infinite and the parameter description unwieldy, but the function space density is Gaussian and therefore tractable. Conversely, when $N = 1$, the function space density is generally non-perturbative due to large non-Gaussianities, yet the network has few parameters.

We demonstrate that symmetries of network densities may be determined via the invariance of correlation functions computed in parameter space. We call this mechanism symmetry-via-duality, and it is utilized to demonstrate numerous cases in which transformations of neural networks (or layers) at input or output leave the correlation functions invariant, implying the invariance of the functional density. It also has implications for learning, which we test experimentally. For a summary of our contributions and results, see Section 5.

1.1. *Symmetries, equivariance and invariant generative models densities*

Symmetries of neural networks are a major topic of study in recent years. Generalizing beyond mere invariance of networks, equivariant networks [4–20] have aided learning in a variety of contexts, including gauge-equivariant networks [21,22] and their their utilization in generative models [23–26], for instance in applications to Lattice QCD [27,28]. See also Refs. [29,30] for symmetries and duality in ML and physics.

Of closest relation to our work is the appearance of symmetries in generative models, where invariance of a generative model density is often desired. It may be achieved via draws from a simple symmetric input density ρ on V and an equivariant network $f_\theta : V \to V$, which ensures that the induced output density ρ_{f_θ} is invariant. In Lattice QCD applications, this is used to ensure that gauge fields are sampled from the correct G-invariant density ρ_{f_θ}, due to the G-equivariance of a trained network f_θ.

In contrast, in our work, it is the network f_θ itself that is sampled from an invariant density over functions. That is, if one were to cast our work into a lattice field theory context, it is the networks themselves that are the fields, and symmetry arises from symmetries in the density over networks. Notably, nowhere in our paper do we utilize equivariance.

1.2. *Modeling densities for non-Gaussian processes*

One motivation for understanding symmetries of network densities is that it constrains the modeling of neural network non-Gaussian process densities using techniques from QFT [31] (see also Ref. [32]), as well as exact non-Gaussian network priors [33] on individual inputs. Such finite-N densities arise for network architectures admitting a GP limit [2,34–41] as $N \to \infty$, and they admit a perturbative description when N is large-but-finite. These functional symmetry considerations should also place constraints on NTK scaling laws [42] and preactivation distribution flows [43] studied in parameter space for large-but-finite N networks.

2.   **Symmetry Invariant Densities via Duality**

Consider a neural network f_θ with continuous learnable parameters θ. The architecture of f_θ and parameter density P_θ induce a density over functions P_f. Let Z_θ and Z_f be the associated partition functions. Expectation values may be computed using either P_θ or P_f, denoted as $\mathbb{E}_\theta$ and $\mathbb{E}_f$, respectively, or simply just $\mathbb{E}$ when we wish to be agnostic as to the computation technique.

The n-point correlation functions (or correlators) of neural network outputs are then

$$G^{(n)}(x_1, \ldots, x_n) = \mathbb{E}[f(x_1) \ldots f(x_n)], \tag{1}$$

and (if the corresponding densities are known) they may be computed in either parameter or function space. These functions are the moments of the density over functions. When the output dimension $D > 1$, we may write output indices explicitly, e.g., $f_i(x)$, in which case the correlators are written as $G^{(n)}_{i_1,\ldots,i_n}(x_1, \ldots, x_n)$.

Neural network symmetries are a focus of this work. Consider a continuous transformation

$$f'(x) = \Phi(f(x')), \tag{2}$$

i.e., the transformed network f' at x is a function Φ of the old network f at x'. We say there is a classical symmetry if P_f is invariant under the transformation, which in physics is usually phrased in terms of the action $S_f = -\log P_f$. If the functional measure Df is also invariant, it is said that there is a quantum symmetry and the correlation functions are constrained by

$$G^{(n)}(x_1, \ldots, x_n) = \mathbb{E}[f(x_1) \ldots f(x_n)]$$
$$= \mathbb{E}[\Phi(f(x'_1)) \ldots \Phi(f(x'_n))] =: G'^{(n)}(x'_1, \ldots, x'_n).$$
$$(3)$$

See appendix for the elementary proof. In physics, if $x = x'$ but Φ is non-trivial, the symmetry is called internal, and if Φ is trivial but $x \neq x'$, it is called a spacetime symmetry. Instead, we will call them output and input symmetries to identify the part of the neural network that is transformed; examples include rotations of outputs and translations of inputs. Of course, if f_θ is composed with other functions to form a larger neural network, then input and output refer to those of the layer f.

Our goal in this chapter is to determine symmetries of network densities via the constraint 3. For a discussion of functional densities, see Appendix A.6.

2.1. *A glimpse of symmetry from Gaussian processes*

Further study in this direction is motivated by first deriving a result for one of the simplest function-space densities: a Gaussian process.

Consider a neural network Gaussian process (NNGP): a real-valued neural network $f_{\theta,N}$ where N is a discrete hyperparameter such that in the asymptotic limit $N \to \infty$, $f_{\theta,\infty}$ is drawn from a Gaussian process. The simplest example is [2] a fully connected single-layer network of width N. Suppressing θ, N subscripts and assuming the $N \to \infty$ limit, a NNGP f can be stacked to obtain a vector-valued neural network $f_i : \mathbb{R}^d \to \mathbb{R}^D$. The associated two-point function $G^{(2)}_{i_1 i_2}(x_1, x_2) = \delta_{i_1 i_2} K(x_1, x_2)$, $K(x_1, x_2)$ is the NNGP kernel (2-pt function) associated with f; i.e., stacking adds tensor structure to the kernel in the form of a Kronecker delta.

If the NNGP has zero mean, then $G^{(2n+1)}(x_1, \ldots, x_n) = 0$ for all n and the even-point functions may be computed in terms of the kernel via Wick's theorem,

$$G^{(2n)}_{i_1,\ldots,i_{2n}}(x_1,\ldots,x_{2n}) = \sum_{P \in \text{Wick}(2n)} \delta_{i_{a_1} i_{b_1}} \cdots \delta_{i_{a_n} i_{b_n}} K(x_{a_1},x_{b_1}) \cdots$$

$$\times \, K(x_{a_n},x_{b_n}), \tag{4}$$

where the Wick contractions are defined by the set

$$\text{Wick}(n) = \{P \in \text{Partitions}(1,\ldots,n) \,||\, p| = 2 \,\forall p \in P\}. \tag{5}$$

We write $P \in \text{Wick}(2n)$ as $P = \{(a_1,b_1),\ldots,(a_n,b_n)\}$. A network transformation $f_i \mapsto R_{ij} f_j$ induces an action on each index of each Kronecker delta in (4). For instance, as $\delta_{ik} \mapsto R_{ij} R_{kl} \delta_{jl} = (R\,R^T)_{ik} = \delta_{ik}$ where the last equality holds for $R \in SO(D)$. By this phenomenon, the even-point correlation functions (4) are $SO(D)$ invariant. Conversely, if the NNGP has a mean $\mu(x) = G^1_{i_1}(x_1) \neq 0$, it transforms with a single R and is not invariant. From the NNGP correlation functions, the GP density has $SO(D)$ symmetry iff it has zero mean. This is not surprising and could be shown directly by inverting the kernel to get the GP density and then checking its symmetry.

However, we see correlation functions contain symmetry information, which becomes particularly powerful when the correlation functions are known, but the network density is not.

2.2. *Parameter-Space/Function-Space duality*

To determine the symmetries of an unknown net work density via correlation functions, we need a way to compute them. For this, we utilize duality.

A physical system is said to exhibit a duality if there are two different descriptions of the system, often with different degrees of freedom, that exhibit the same predictions either exactly (an exact duality) or in a limit, e.g., at long distances (an infrared duality); see Ref. [44] for a review. Duality is useful precisely when one perspective, a.k.a. a duality frame, allows you to determine something about the system that would be difficult from the other perspective. Examples in physics include electric-magnetic duality, which in some cases allows a strongly interacting theory of electrons to be reinterpreted in terms of a weakly coupled theory of monopoles [45] and gauge-gravity duality [46], which relates gravitational and non-gravitational quantum theories via the holographic principle.

In the context of neural networks, the relevant duality frames are provided by parameter-space and function space, yielding a Parameter-Space/Function-Space duality. In the parameter frame, a neural network is considered to be compositions of functions which themselves have parameters drawn from P_θ, whereas in the function frame, the neural network is considered as an entire function drawn from a function-space density P_f. Of course, the choice of network architecture and densities P_θ determine P_f, but they do not appear explicitly in it, giving two different descriptions of the system.

2.3. *Symmetry-via-duality*

Our central point is that symmetries of function-space densities may be determined from correlation functions computed in the parameter-space description, even if the function-space density is not known. That is, it is possible to check (3) via correlators computed in parameter space; if so, then the product DfP_f is invariant. Barring an appearance of the Green–Schwarz mechanism [47] in neural networks, by which DfP_f is invariant but Df and P_f are not, this implies that P_f is invariant. This leads to our main result.

Theorem 1. *Consider a neural network or layer*

$$f_\theta : \mathbb{R}^d \to \mathbb{R}^D \tag{6}$$

with associated function-space measure Df and density P_f, as well as a transformation $f'(x) = \Phi(f(x'))$ satisfying

$$\mathbb{E}_\theta[f(x_1)\ldots f(x_n)] = \mathbb{E}_\theta[\Phi(f(x'_1))\ldots\Phi(f(x'_n))]. \tag{7}$$

Then, DfP_f is invariant, and P_f is itself invariant if a Green–Schwarz mechanism is not effective.

The proof of the theorem follows from the proof of (3) in Appendix and the fact that correlators may also be computed in parameter space. Additionally, there may be multiple such transformations that generate a group G of invariant transformations, in which case P_f is G-invariant.

The schematic for each calculation is to transform the correlators by transforming some part of the network, such as the input or output, absorb the transformation into a transformation of parameters $\theta_T \subset \theta$ (which could be all θ), and then show invariance of the correlation functions via invariance of P_{θ_T}. Thus,

Corollary 1. *Symmetries of P_f derived via duality rely on symmetry properties of P_{θ_T}.*

In what follows, we will show that (7) holds in numerous well-studied neural networks for a variety of transformations, without requiring equivariance of the neural network. Throughout, we use Z_θ to denote the parameter space partition function of all parameters θ of the network.

Example

$SO(D)$ Output Symmetry: We now demonstrate in detail that a linear output layer leads to $SO(D)$ invariant network densities provided that its weight and bias distributions are invariant. The network is defined by $f_i(x) = W_{ij}g_j(x) + b_i$, where $i = 1, \ldots, D$ and g_j is an N-dimension post-activation with parameters θ_g. Consider an invertible matrix transformation R acting as $f_i \mapsto R_{ij}f_j$; we use Einstein summation convention here and throughout. The transformed correlation functions are

$$G'^{(n)}_{i_1 \ldots i_n}(x'_1, \ldots, x'_n) = \mathbb{E}[R_{i_1 j_1} f_{j_1}(x_1) \ldots R_{i_n j_n} f_{j_n}(x_n)]$$

$$= \frac{1}{Z_\theta} \int DW\, Db\, D\theta_g\, R_{i_1 j_1}(W_{j_1 k_1}g_{k_1}(x_1) + b_{j_1}) \ldots$$

$$\times R_{i_n j_n}(W_{j_n k_n}g_{k_n}(x_n) + b_{j_n}) P_W P_b P_{\theta_g}$$

$$= \frac{1}{Z_\theta} \int |R^{-1}|^2 D\tilde{W}\, D\tilde{b}\, D\theta_g(\tilde{W}_{i_1 k_1}g_{k_1}(x_1) + \tilde{b}_{i_1}) \ldots$$

$$\times (\tilde{W}_{i_n k_n}g_{k_n}(x_n) + \tilde{b}_{i_n}) P_{R^{-1}\tilde{W}} P_{R^{-1}\tilde{b}} P_{\theta_g}$$

$$= \mathbb{E}[f_{i_1}(x_1) \ldots f_{i_n}(x_n)] = G^{(n)}(x_1, \ldots, x_n), \tag{8}$$

where, e.g., DW denotes the standard measure for all W-parameters in the last layer, and the crucial second-to-last equality holds when $|R| = 1$, $P_W = P_{R^{-1}\tilde{W}} = P_{\tilde{W}}$, and $P_b = P_{R^{-1}\tilde{b}} = P_{\tilde{b}}$. These stipulations hold in the well-studied case of $W \sim \mathcal{N}(0, \sigma_W^2)$, $W \sim \mathcal{N}(0, \sigma_b^2)$

when $R \in SO(D)$, due to the invariance of the $b_j b_j$ in $P_b = \exp(-b_j b_j / 2\sigma_b^2)$, and similarly for Gaussian P_W.

The result holds more generally, for any invariant P_W and P_b, which as we will discuss in Section 3 includes the case of correlated parameters, as is relevant for learning.

Example

$SO(d)$ Input Symmetry: We now demonstrate an example of neural networks with density invariant under $SO(d)$ input rotations, provided that the input layer parameters are drawn from an invariant distribution.

We will take a linear input layer and turn off the bias for simplicity, since it may be trivially included as in the $SO(D)$ output symmetry above. The network function is $f_i(x) = g_{ij}(W_{jk} x_k)$, $W \sim P_W$, and the input rotation $R \in SO(d)$ acts as $x_i \mapsto x_i' = R_{ij} x_j$. The output of the input layer is the preactivation for the rest of the network g, which has parameters θ_g. The transformed correlators are

$$
\begin{aligned}
G'^{(n)}_{i_1 \dots i_n}(x_1', \dots, x_n') &= \mathbb{E}[f_{i_1}(R_{k_1 l_1} x_{l_1}^1) \dots f_{i_n}(R_{k_n l_n} x_{l_n}^n)] \\
&= \frac{1}{Z_\theta} \int DW \, D\theta_g \, g_{i_1 j_1}(W_{j_1 k_1} R_{k_1 l_1} x_{l_1}^1) \dots g_{i_n j_n} \\
&\quad \times (W_{j_n k_n} R_{k_n l_n} x_{l_n}^n) P_W P_{\theta_g} \\
&= \frac{1}{Z_\theta} \int |R^{-1}| D\tilde{W} \, D\theta_g \, g_{i_1 j_1}(\tilde{W}_{j_1 l_1} x_{l_1}^1) \dots g_{i_n j_n} \\
&\quad \times (\tilde{W}_{j_n l_n} x_{l_n}^n) P_{R^{-1} \tilde{W}} P_{\theta_g} \\
&= \mathbb{E}[f_{i_1}(x_1) \dots f_{i_n}(x_n)] = G^{(n)}(x_1, \dots, x_n),
\end{aligned}
$$

$$(9)$$

where we have changed the x subscript label to a superscript to make room for indices, and again the important second-to-last equality holds when P_W is invariant under $R \in SO(D)$. This again holds for $W_{ij} \sim \mathcal{N}(0, \sigma_W^2)$, but also for any distribution P_W constructed from $SO(D)$ invariants. See Ref. [32] for $SO(d)$ input symmetry of the NNGP kernel.

$SU(D)$ Output Symmetry: We also demonstrate that a linear complex-valued output layer, given in detail in Appendix (A.2), leads to $SU(D)$ invariant network densities provided that the last linear layer weight and bias distributions are invariant. For clarity, we leave off the bias term; it may be added trivially similar to Equation (8). This network is defined by $\mathbf{f}_i = \mathbf{W}_{ij}g_j(x, \theta_g)$, and transforms as $\mathbf{f}_i \mapsto S_{ij}\mathbf{f}_j$, $\mathbf{f}_k^\dagger \mapsto \mathbf{f}_l^\dagger S_{lk}^\dagger$ under an invertible matrix transformation by $SU(D)$ group element S. A necessary condition for symmetry is that the only non-zero correlation functions have an equal number of f and $f^\dagger$s, as in (A.14), which transform as

$$
\begin{aligned}
G'^{(2n)}_{i_1\ldots i_{2n}}(x'_1,\ldots,x'_{2n}) &= \mathbb{E}\bigg[S_{i_1 j_1}\mathbf{f}_{j_1}(x_{p_1}) \cdots S_{i_n j_n}\mathbf{f}_{j_n}(x_{p_n})\mathbf{f}_{j_n}^\dagger(x_{p_{n+1}}) \\
&\quad \times S_{j_{n+1} i_{n+1}}^\dagger \cdots \mathbf{f}_{j_{2n}}^\dagger(x_{p_{2n}})S_{j_{2n} i_{2n}}^\dagger \bigg] \\
&= \frac{1}{4Z_\theta}\int D\mathbf{W}D\mathbf{W}^\dagger D\theta_g S_{i_1 j_1}(\mathbf{W}_{j_1 k_1}g_{k_1}(x_{p_1},\theta_g)) \\
&\quad \times \cdots S_{i_n j_n}(\mathbf{W}_{j_n k_n}g_{k_n}(x_{p_n},\theta_g)) \\
&\quad (g_{k_{n+1}}^\dagger(x_{p_{n+1}},\theta_g) \\
&\quad \times \mathbf{W}_{k_{n+1} j_{n+1}}^\dagger)S_{j_{n+1} i_{n+1}}^\dagger \cdots (g_{k_{2n}}^\dagger(x_{p_{2n}},\theta_g) \\
&\quad \times \mathbf{W}_{k_{2n} j_{2n}}^\dagger)S_{j_{2n} i_{2n}}^\dagger P_{\mathbf{W}},
\end{aligned}
$$

$$
\begin{aligned}
\mathbf{W}^\dagger P_{\theta_g} &= \frac{1}{4Z_\theta}\int |(S^\dagger)^{-1}||S^{-1}|D\tilde{\mathbf{W}}D\tilde{\mathbf{W}}^\dagger D\theta_g \\
&\quad \times (\tilde{\mathbf{W}}_{i_1 k_1}g_{k_1}(x_{p_1},\theta_g)) \cdots (\tilde{\mathbf{W}}_{i_n k_n}g_{k_n}(x_{p_n},\theta_g)) \\
&\quad \times (g_{k_{n+1}}^\dagger(x_{p_{n+1}},\theta_g)\tilde{\mathbf{W}}_{k_{n+1} i_{n+1}}^\dagger) \cdots \\
&\quad \times (g_{k_{2n}}^\dagger(x_{p_{2n}},\theta_g)\tilde{\mathbf{W}}_{k_{2n} i_{2n}}^\dagger)P_{S^{-1}\tilde{\mathbf{W}},\tilde{\mathbf{W}}^\dagger S^{\dagger -1}}P_{\theta_g} \\
&= \mathbb{E}\bigg[\mathbf{f}_{i_1}(x_{p_1}) \cdots \mathbf{f}_{i_n}(x_{p_n})\mathbf{f}_{i_{n+1}}^\dagger(x_{p_{n+1}}) \cdots \\
&\quad \times \mathbf{f}_{i_{2n}}^\dagger(x_{p_{2n}}) \bigg] = G^{(2n)}_{i_1\ldots i_{2n}}(x_1,\ldots,x_{2n}), \quad (10)
\end{aligned}
$$

where $\{p_1,\ldots,p_{2n}\}$ is any permutation of $\{1,\ldots,2n\}$ as in (A.2), and the crucial second-to-last equality holds when $|S|^{-1} = 1$, and $P_{\mathbf{W},\mathbf{W}^\dagger} = P_{\tilde{\mathbf{W}},\tilde{\mathbf{W}}^\dagger}$. This stipulation holds true, for example, when

$S \in SU(D)$, and $\mathrm{Re}(\mathbf{W}), \mathrm{Im}(\mathbf{W}) \sim \mathcal{N}(0, \sigma_W^2)$, due to the $SU(D)$ invariance of $\mathrm{Tr}(\mathbf{W}^\dagger \mathbf{W})$ in $P_{\mathbf{W},\mathbf{W}^\dagger} = \exp(-\mathrm{Tr}(\mathbf{W}^\dagger \mathbf{W})/2\sigma_W^2)$. For more details, please see Appendix (A.2).

Example
Translation Input Symmetry and T-layers: We now study architectures with translation (T) invariant network densities, which arise when the correlation functions are invariant under input translations $x \mapsto x+c, \forall c \in \mathbb{R}^d$, the usual notion of translations in physics. Our translations are more general than the pixel translations often studied in computer vision; for instance, in one dimension, a pixel shift to the right is induced by the choice $c_i = -x_i + x_{(i+1)\%d}$.

To arrive at T-invariant network densities via correlation functions, we first define the T-*layer*, a standard linear layer with deterministic weight matrix W and uniform bias on the circle, $b_i \sim \mathcal{U}(S^1)$, where we also map the Wx term to the circle by taking its mod 1 (written as $\% 1$) before adding the already S^1-valued bias. Since such a layer is defined by the hyperparameter weight matrix W, we label it T_W, with parameters b. Suppressing obvious indices, we write the T-layer as $T_W(x) = (Wx\%1) + b$. Under translations of the input to the T-layer, we have $T_W(x + c) = (Wx)\%1 + (Wc)\%1 + b =: (Wx)\%1 + b'$, where b' and b are equally probable bias draws and the periodic boundary condition of the S^1 solves problems that arise in the presence of boundaries of a uniform distribution on a subset of $\mathbb{R}$.

The T-layer may be prepended to any neural network to arrive at a new one with T-invariant density. Consider any neural network $g_\varphi : \mathbb{R}^N \to \mathbb{R}^D$, to which we prepend $T_W : \mathbb{R}^d \to \mathbb{R}^N$ to form a new network $f_\theta(x) = g_\varphi(T_W(x))$, where $\theta = \{\varphi, b\}$. The transformed correlation functions are translation invariant,

$$G_{i_1,\ldots,i_n}^{(n)}(x_1 + c, \ldots, x_n + c) = G_{i_1,\ldots,i_n}^{(n)}(x_1, \ldots, x_n) \qquad \forall n, \quad (11)$$

which follows by absorbing the shift via $b' = (Wc\%1) + b$, using $db' = db$, and renaming variables. See Appendix (A.4) for details. Thus, the density P_f is translation invariant.

The T-layer is compatible with training since it is differentiable everywhere except when the layer input is $\equiv 0 \mod 1$, i.e., an integer. When doing gradient descent, the mod operation is treated as the identity, which gives the correct gradient at all non-integer inputs to the layer, and thus training performs well on typical real-world datasets.

3. Symmetry-via-Duality and Deep Learning

We will now look at various aspects of relating symmetry, deduced via duality, and learning.

3.1. *Preserving symmetry during training via duality*

It may sometimes be useful to preserve a symmetry (deduced via duality) during training that is present in the network density at initialization. Corollary 1 allows symmetry-via-duality to be utilized at any time, relying on the invariance properties of P_{θ_T} (and therefore P_θ). The initialization symmetry is preserved if the invariance properties of P_θ that ensured symmetry at $t = 0$ persist at all times.

While this interesting matter deserves a systematic study of its own, here we study it in the simple case of continuous time gradient descent. The parameter update $d\theta_i/dt = -\partial\mathcal{L}/\partial\theta_i$, where $\mathcal{L}$ is the loss function, induces a flow in P_θ governed by

$$\frac{\partial P_\theta(t)}{\partial t} = \left(\frac{\partial}{\partial\theta_i}\frac{\partial}{\partial\theta_i}\mathcal{L}\right)P_\theta(t) + \frac{\partial P_\theta(t)}{\partial\theta_i}\frac{\partial\mathcal{L}}{\partial\theta_i}, \tag{12}$$

the update equation for $P_\theta(t)$. If $P_\theta(t)$ is invariant at initialization ($t = 0$), then the update is invariant provided that $\partial^2\mathcal{L}/(\partial\theta_i)^2$ is invariant and the second term is invariant.

When these conditions are satisfied, the symmetry of the network initialization density is preserved throughout training. However, they must be checked on a case-by-case basis. As a simple example, consider again the $SO(D)$ output symmetry from Section 2. Absorbing the action on output into parameters as before, the $(\partial/\partial\theta_i)(\partial/\partial\theta_i)$ is itself invariant, and therefore the first term in (12) is invariant when $\mathcal{L}$ is invariant. If additionally

$$\frac{\partial P_\theta(t)}{\partial\theta_i} = I_P\,\theta_i \quad \frac{\partial\mathcal{L}}{\partial\theta_i} = I_{\mathcal{L}}\,\theta_i \tag{13}$$

for θ-dependent invariants I_P and $I_{\mathcal{L}}$, then the second term is invariant as well, yielding an invariant symmetry-preserving update. See Appendix (A.6) for a detailed example realizing these conditions.

3.2. Supervised learning, symmetry breaking and the one-point function

A priori, it is natural to expect that symmetry breaking helps training: a non-zero one-point function or mean $G_i^{(1)}(x) = \mathbb{E}[f_i(x)]$ of a trained network density is crucial to making non-zero predictions in supervised learning, and if a network density at initialization exhibits symmetry, developing a one-point function during supervised learning usually breaks it. Contrary to this intuition, we will see in experiments that symmetry in the network density at initialization can help training.

To develop these ideas and prepare for experiments, we frame the discussion in terms of an architecture with symmetry properties that are easily determined via duality: a network with a linear no-bias output layer from an N-dimensional hidden layer to D-dimensional network output. The network function is $f_i(x) = W_{ij}^l g_j(x)$, $i = 1, \ldots, D$, where $g_j(x)$ is the post-activation of the last hidden layer, with parameters θ_g. Output weights in the final (l^{th}) layer are initialized as

$$W_{ij}^l \sim \mathcal{N}(\mu_{W^l}, 1/\sqrt{N}), \ \forall i < k+1$$

$$W_{ij}^l \sim \mathcal{N}(0, 1/\sqrt{N}), \ \forall i \geq k+1, \tag{14}$$

where k is a hyperparameter that will be varied in the experiments. By a simple extension of our $SO(D)$ output symmetry result, this network density has $SO(D-k)$ symmetry. The symmetry breaking is measured by the one-point function

$$G_i^{(1)}(x) = \mathbb{E}[f_i(x)] = N\mu_{W^l} \, \mathbb{E}_{\theta_g}[g_i(x)] \neq 0, \ \forall i < k, \tag{15}$$

and zero otherwise. Here, $\neq 0$ means as a function; for some x, $G_i^{(1)}(x)$ may evaluate to 0. This non-zero mean breaks symmetry in the first k network components, and since $SO(D)$ symmetry is restored in the $\mu_{W^l} \to 0$ limit, μ_{W^l} and k together control the amount of symmetry breaking.

3.3. Symmetry and correlated parameters

Learning-induced flows in neural network densities lead to correlations between parameters, breaking any independence that might exist in the parameter priors. Since symmetry-via-duality relies only on an invariant P_θ, it can apply in the case of correlations, when P_θ does not factorize. In fact, this is the generic case: a density P_θ which is symmetric due to being constructed from group invariants is not, in general, factorizable. For instance, the multivariate Gaussian $P_\theta = \exp(-x_i x_i / 2\sigma^2)$ with $i = 1, \ldots, m$ is constructed from the $SO(m)$ invariant $x_i x_i$ and leads to independent parameters due to factorization. However, provided a density normalization condition is satisfied, additional $SO(l)$-invariant terms $c_n (x_i x_i)^n$ (or any other Casimir invariant) may be added to the exponent which preserve symmetry but break independence for $n > 1$.

As an example, consider again the case with $SO(D)$ output symmetry with network function $f(x) = L(g(x, \theta_g))$ where $L : \mathbb{R}^N \to \mathbb{R}^D$ is a linear layer, but now draw its weights and biases from symmetric parameter distributions with quartic non-Gaussianities,

$$W_{ij} \sim P_W = e^{-\frac{\mathrm{Tr}(W^T W)}{2\sigma_W^2} - \lambda \, (\mathrm{Tr}\,(W^T W))^2} \qquad b_i \sim P_b = e^{-\frac{b \cdot b}{2\sigma_b^2} - \lambda \, (b \cdot b)^2}. \tag{16}$$

By construction, these distributions are invariant under $SO(D)$, and therefore the function-space density is as well. However, independence is broken for $\lambda \neq 0$. Training could also mix in parameters from other layers, yielding a non-trivial joint distribution which is nevertheless invariant provided that the final layer parameter dependence arises only through $SO(D)$ invariants.

Such independence-breaking networks provide another perspective on neural networks and GPs. Since the NNGP correspondence relies crucially on the central limit theorem and therefore independence of an infinite number of parameters as $N \to \infty$, we may break the GP to a non-Gaussian process not only by taking finite-N, but also by breaking independence, as with $\lambda \neq 0$ above. In this example, symmetry-via-duality requires neither the asymptotic $N \to \infty$ limit nor the independence limit.

Independence breaking introduces potentially interesting non-Gaussianities into function-space densities, which likely admit an effective field theory (EFT) akin to the finite-N EFT treatment developed in Ref. [31]. We leave this treatment for future work.

3.4.   *Symmetry and the Neural Tangent Kernel*

Gradient descent training of a neural network f_θ is governed by the Neural Tangent Kernel (NTK) [1], $\hat{\Theta}(x, x') = \partial_{\theta_i} f_\theta(x) \partial_{\theta_i} f_\theta(x')$. Since $\hat{\Theta}(x, x')$ depends on concrete parameters associated with a fixed neural network draw, it is not invariant. However, the NTK converges in appropriate large-N limits to a kernel Θ that is deterministic, due to the appearance of ensemble averages, allowing for the study of symmetries of $\Theta(x, x')$ via duality.

As an example, consider a neural network with a linear output layer (mapping from $\mathbb{R}^N \to \mathbb{R}^D$), $f_i(x) = W^l_{ij} g_j(x)/\sqrt{N}$, $W^l \sim \mathcal{N}(0, \sigma^2_W)$, where $g_j(x)$ is the post-activation of the last hidden layer and we have turned off bias for clarity; it may be added trivially. The corresponding NTK is

$$\hat{\Theta}_{i_1 i_2}(x, x') = \frac{1}{N}(g_j(x, \theta_g)\, g_j(x', \theta_g)\, \delta_{i_1 i_2}$$

$$+\, W^l_{i_1 j_1} W^l_{i_2 j_2} \frac{\partial g_{j_1}(x, \theta_g)}{\partial \theta^k_g} \frac{\partial g_{j_2}(x', \theta_g)}{\partial \theta^k_g}\Big). \qquad (17)$$

This depends on the concrete draw f and is not invariant. However, as $N \to \infty$, $\hat{\Theta}$ at initialization becomes the deterministic NTK

$$\Theta_{i_1 i_2}(x, x') = \delta_{i_1 i_2}\, \mathbb{E}[g^j(x, \theta_g)g^j(x', \theta_g)]$$

$$+\, \mathbb{E}[W^l_{i_1 j_1} W^l_{i_2 j_2}]\mathbb{E}\left[\frac{\partial g_{j_1}(x, \theta_g)}{\partial \theta^k_g} \frac{\partial g_{j_2}(x', \theta_g)}{\partial \theta^k_g}\right].$$

The transformation $f_i \to R_{ij} f_j$ for $R \in SO(D)$ acts only on the first factor in each term, which themselves may be shown to be invariant, rendering $\Theta_{i_1 i_2}(x, x')$ invariant under $SO(D)$. Alternatively, a related calculation shows that $\mathbb{E}[\Theta_{i_1 i_2}(x, x')]$ is also $SO(D)$ invariant.

Such results are more general, arising similarly in other architectures according to Corollary 1. Though the deterministic NTK at $t = 0$ is crucial in the linearized regime, invariance of Θ may also hold during training, as may be studied in examples via invariance of P_θ. See Ref. [32] for $SO(D)$ input symmetry of the deterministic NTK Θ.

4. Experiments

We carry out two classes of experiments[1] testing symmetry-via-duality. In the first, we demonstrate that the amount of symmetry in the network density at initialization affects training accuracy. In the second, presented in Appendix A.6, we demonstrate how symmetry may be tested via numerically computed correlators.

4.1. *Does symmetry affect training?*

We now wish to test the ideas from Section 3 on how the amount of symmetry at initialization affects test accuracy after training, as controlled by the hyperparameters μ_{W^1} and k; see Ref. [48] for another analysis of symmetry breaking and learning. We further specify the networks discussed there by choosing a single-layer network ($l = 1$, $d = 1$) with ReLU non-linearities (i.e., g_j is the post-activation of a linear layer), $N = 50$, weights of the first linear layer $W^0 \sim \mathcal{N}(0, 1/\sqrt{d})$, and weights of the output initialized as in (14). All networks were trained on the Fashion-MNIST dataset [49] for 20 epochs with MSE loss, with one-hot (or one-cold) encoded class labels, leading to network outputs with dimension $D = 10$ and, therefore symmetry $SO(10 - k)$ at initialization.

In the first experiment, we study how the amount of rotational symmetry breaking at initialization affects test accuracy on Fashion-MNIST with one-hot encoded class labels. We vary the amount of symmetry breaking by taking $k \in \{0, 2, 4, 6, 10\}$ and $\mu_{W^1} \in \{0.0, \dots, 0.2\}$ with 0.01 increment. Each experiment is repeated 20 times with learning rate $\eta = .001$. For each (k, μ_{W^1}) pair, the mean of the maximum test accuracy across all 20 experiments is plotted in Figure 1 (LHS). We see that performance is highest for networks initialized with $\mu_{W^1} = 0$ or $k = 0$, i.e., with an $SO(D)$ symmetric initialization density, and decreases significantly with increasing amounts of symmetry breaking (increasing μ_{W^1} and k), contrary to the intuition discussed in Section 3. See Appendix (A.6) for more details about the experiments.

---

[1]We provide an implementation of our code at https://github.com/keeganstoner/nn-symmetry.

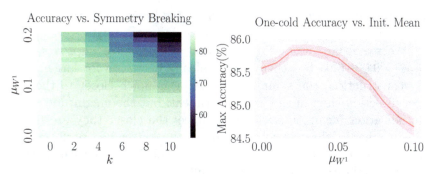

Figure 1. Test accuracy % on Fashion-MNIST. Left: Dependence on symmetry breaking parameters μ_W and k for one-hot encoded labels. The error is presented in Appendix (A.6). Right: Dependence on μ_W for one-cold encoded labels, showing the 95% confidence interval.

If supervised learning breaks symmetry via developing a non-trivial one-point function (mean), but we see that symmetry at initialization helps training in this experiment, then what concept is missing?

It is that symmetry breaking at initialization could be in the wrong direction, i.e., the initialization mean is quite different from the desired trained mean, which (if well trained) approximate ground truth labels. In our experiment, the initialization mean is

$$G_i^{(1)}(x) = \mathbb{E}[f_i(x)] = 50\mu_{W^1}\, \mathbb{E}_{W^0}[\text{ReLU}(W_{ij}^0 x_j)] \neq 0, \qquad (18)$$

which will in general be non-zero along all output components. It is "in the wrong direction" since class labels are one-hot encoded and therefore have precisely one non-zero entry. Furthermore, even for means in the right direction, the magnitude could be significantly off.

In the second experiment, we test this idea by imposing a better match between the initialization mean and the class labels. To do so, we keep the network fixed and instead one-cold encode the class labels, i.e., instead of class i being encoded by the unit vector $e_i \in \mathbb{R}^D$, it is encoded by $\mathbb{1} - e_i$, where $\mathbb{1}$ is the vector of ones. At initialization, we find that $\mathbb{E}_{W^0}[\text{ReLU}(W_{ij}^0 x_j)] \sim 0.5\text{--}1.0$ for Fashion-MNIST, and therefore $G_i^{(1)}(x) \sim 25\mu_{W^1}\text{--}50\mu_{W^1}$ is of the right order of magnitude to match the ones in the one-cold vectors for $\mu_{W^1} \sim 0.02\text{--}0.04$. Relative to the first experiment, this experiment differs only in the one-cold encoded class labels and the fixed value

$k = 10$, which ensures complete symmetry breaking in the prior for $\mu_{W^1} \neq 0$.

We see from Figure 1 (*right*) that performance improves until $\mu_{W^1} \sim 0.02\text{--}0.04$ but then monotonically decreases for larger μ_{W^1}. By construction, the symmetry breaking is much closer to the correct direction than in the first experiment, but the magnitude of the initialization means affects performance: the closer they are to the $D - 1$ ones in the one-cold encoding, the better the performance. The latter occurs for $\mu_{W^1} \sim 0.02\text{--}0.04$ according to our calculation, which matches the experimental result.

5.   Conclusion

We introduce symmetry-via-duality, a mechanism that allows for the determination of symmetries of neural network functional densities P_f, even when the density is unknown. The mechanism relies crucially on two facts: (i) that symmetries of a statistical system may also be determined via their correlation functions and (ii) that the correlators may be computed in parameter space. The utility of parameter space in determining symmetries of the network density is a hallmark of duality in physical systems, in this case, Parameter-Space/Function-Space duality.

We demonstrated that invariance of correlation functions ensures the invariance of DfP_f, which yields the invariance of the density P_f itself in the absence of a Green–Schwarz mechanism. Symmetries were categorized into input and output symmetries, the analogs of spatial and internal symmetries in physics, and a number of examples of symmetries were presented, including $SO(D)$ and $SU(D)$ symmetries at both input and output. In all calculations, the symmetry transformation induces a transformation on the input or output that may be absorbed into a transformation of network parameters θ_T, and invariance of the correlation functions follows from invariance of $D\theta_T P_{\theta_T}$. The invariance of $D\theta P_\theta$ also follows, since θ_T are by definition the only parameters that transform.

The mechanism may also be applied at any point during training, since it relies on the invariance of P_θ. If duality is used to ensure the symmetry of the network density at initialization, then the persistence of this symmetry during training requires that P_θ

remains symmetric at all times. Under continuous time gradient descent, the flow equation for P_θ yields conditions preserving the symmetry of P_θ. We also demonstrated that symmetry could be partially broken in the initialization density, that symmetry-via-duality may also apply in the case of non-independent parameters, and that the Neural Tangent Kernel may be invariant under symmetry transformations.

Our analysis allows for different amounts of symmetry in the network density at initialization, leading to increasing constraints on the density with increasing symmetry. Accordingly, it is natural to ask whether this affects training. To this end, we performed Fashion-MNIST experiments with different amounts of network density symmetry at initialization. The experiments demonstrate that symmetry breaking helps training when the associated mean is in the direction of the class labels, and entries are of the same order of magnitude. However, if symmetry is broken in the wrong direction or with too large a magnitude, performance is worse than for networks with symmetric initialization density.

Acknowledgments

We thank Sergei Gukov, Joonho Kim, Neil Lawrence, Magnus Rattray and Matt Schwartz for discussions. We are especially indebted to Sébastian Racanière, Danilo Rezende and Fabian Ruehle for comments on the manuscript. J.H. is supported by NSF CAREER grant PHY-1848089. This work is supported by the National Science Foundation under Cooperative Agreement PHY-2019786 (the NSF AI Institute for Artificial Intelligence and Fundamental Interactions).

Appendix

A. Proofs and Derivations

A.1.   *Symmetry from correlation functions*

We begin by demonstrating the invariance of network correlation functions under transformations that leave the functional measure and density invariant. Consider a transformation

$$f'(x) = \Phi(f(x')) \tag{A.1}$$

that leaves the functional density invariant, i.e.,

$$D[\Phi f]\, e^{-S[\Phi f]} = Df\, e^{-S[f]}. \tag{A.2}$$

Then, we have

$$\mathbb{E}[f(x_1)\ldots f(x_n)] = \frac{1}{Z_f} \int Df\, e^{-S[f]}\, f(x_1)\ldots f(x_n) \tag{A.3}$$

$$= \frac{1}{Z_f} \int Df e^{-S[f']}\, f'(x_1)\ldots f'(x_n) \tag{A.4}$$

$$= \frac{1}{Z_f} \int D[\Phi f]\, e^{-S[\Phi f]}\, \Phi(f(x_1'))\ldots$$
$$\times\, \Phi(f(x_n')) \tag{A.5}$$

$$= \frac{1}{Z_f} \int Df\, e^{-S[f]}\, \Phi(f(x_1'))\ldots$$
$$\times\, \Phi(f(x_n')), \tag{A.6}$$

$$= \mathbb{E}[\Phi(f(x_1'))\ldots\Phi(f(x_n'))], \tag{A.7}$$

where the second to last equality holds due to the invariance of the functional density. This completes the proof of (3); see, e.g., Ref. [50] for a QFT analogy.

For completeness, we wish to derive the same result for infinitesimal output transformations, where the parameters of the transformation depend on the neural network input; in physics language, these are called infinitesimal gauge transformations.

The NN output, transformed by an infinitesimal parameter $\omega_a(x)$, is $f'(x) = \Phi(f(x')) = f(x') + \delta_\omega f(x')$, where $\delta_\omega f(x') = -\iota\omega_a(x')T_a f(x')$; T_a is the generator of the transformation group. Corresponding output space log-likelihood transforms as $S \mapsto S - \int dx' \, \partial_\mu j_a^\mu(x') \, \omega_a(x')$, for a current $j_a^\mu(x')$ that may be computed. The transformed n-pt function at $O(\omega)$ is given by

$$\mathbb{E}[f'(x_1) \cdots f'(x_n)] = \frac{1}{Z} \int Df \Phi(f(x_1') \cdots f(x_n')) e^{-S}$$

$$= \frac{1}{Z} \int Df \Big([f(x_1') \cdots f(x_n')] + \delta_\omega[f(x_1') \cdots$$

$$\times f(x_n')]\Big) e^{-S - \int dx' \partial_\mu j_a^\mu(x')\omega_a(x')}$$

$$= \mathbb{E}[f(x_1') \cdots f(x_n')] + \mathbb{E}[\delta_\omega[f(x_1') \cdots f(x_n')]]$$

$$- \int dx' \, \partial_\mu \mathbb{E}[j_a^\mu(x') \, f(x_1') \cdots f(x_n')] \, \omega_a(x'),$$

where we obtain second and last equalities under the assumption that functional density is invariant, following (A.2), and invariance of function-space measure, $Df = Df$, respectively.

Following the ω-independence of LHS of (A.8), $O(\omega)$ terms on RHS must cancel each other, i.e.,

$$\int dx' \Big[\partial_\mu \, \mathbb{E}[j_a^\mu \, f(x_1') \cdots f(x_n')]$$

$$+ \mathbb{E}\Big[\sum_{i=1}^n f(x_1') \cdots T_a f(x_i') \cdots f(x_n')\Big]$$

$$\times \delta(x' - x_i')\Big] \omega(x') = 0, \tag{A.8}$$

for any infinitesimal function $\omega(x')$. Thus, the coefficient of $\omega(x')$ in the above integrand vanishes at all x', and we have the following by divergence theorem:

$$-\iota \int dx' \, \mathbb{E}\Big[\sum_{i=1}^n f(x_1') \cdots T_a f(x_i') \cdots f(x_n')\Big] \delta(x' - x_i')$$

$$= \int_\Sigma ds_\mu \mathbb{E}[j_a^\mu \, f(x_1') \cdots f(x_n')]. \tag{A.9}$$

Taking hypersurface Σ to infinity does not affect the integral in (A.9), therefore in $\lim_{R_\Sigma \to \infty}$, if $\mathbb{E}[j_a^\mu f(x_1') \cdots f(x_n')]$ dies sufficiently fast, we obtain

$$\iota \sum_{i=1}^n \mathbb{E}[f(x_1') \cdots T_a f(x_i') \cdots f(x_n')] = 0 = \delta_\omega \mathbb{E}[f(x_1') \cdots f(x_n')],$$

(A.10)

a statement of invariance of correlation functions under infinitesimal input-dependent transformations.

Thus, we obtain the following invariance under finite/tesimal, input-dependent/independent transformations, whenever $Df = Df'$:

$$\mathbb{E}[f'(x_1) \cdots f'(x_n)] = \mathbb{E}[f(x_1') \cdots f(x_n')].$$

(A.11)

(A.11) is same as (3), completing the proof.

A.2. *SU(D) output symmetry*

We show the detailed construction of $SU(D)$ invariant network densities, for networks with a complex linear output layer, when weight and bias distributions are $SU(D)$ invariant.

The network is defined by $f(x) = L(g(x, \theta_g))$, for a final affine transformation L on last post-activation $g(x, \theta)$; x and θ_g are the inputs and parameters until the final linear layer, respectively. As $SU(D)$ is the rotation group over complex numbers, $SU(D)$ invariant NN densities require complex-valued outputs, and this requires complex weights and biases in layer L. Denoting the real and imaginary parts of complex weight $\mathbf{W}$ and bias $\mathbf{b}$ in layer L as W^1, W^2, b^1, b^2, respectively, we obtain $\mathbf{W}, \mathbf{b}$ distributions as $P_{\mathbf{W},\mathbf{W}^\dagger} = P_{W^1} P_{W^2}$ and $P_{\mathbf{b},\mathbf{b}^\dagger} = P_{b^1} P_{b^2}$. The simplest $SU(D)$ invariant structure is

$$\text{Tr}[\mathbf{W}^\dagger \mathbf{W}] = \mathbf{W}_{\alpha\beta}^* \mathbf{W}_{\alpha\beta} = W_{\alpha\beta}^1 W_{\alpha\beta}^1 + W_{\alpha\beta}^2 W_{\alpha\beta}^2$$

$$= \text{Tr}(W^{1^T} W^1) + \text{Tr}(W^{2^T} W^2),$$

(A.12)

and similarly for bias. To obtain an SU-invariant structure in $P_{\mathbf{W},\mathbf{W}^\dagger}$ as a sum of SO-invariant structures from products of P_{W^1}, P_{W^2}, all three PDFs need to be exponential functions, with equal coefficients in P_{W^1}, P_{W^2}. Therefore, starting with $SO(D)$-invariant real and imaginary parts $W^1, W^2 \sim \mathcal{N}(0, \sigma_W^2)$ and $b^1, b^2 \sim \mathcal{N}(0, \sigma_b^2)$, one can obtain the simplest $SU(D)$ invariant complex weight and bias distributions, given by $P_{\mathbf{W}, \mathbf{W}^\dagger} = \exp(-\mathrm{Tr}[\mathbf{W}^\dagger \mathbf{W}]/2\sigma_W^2)$, $P_{\mathbf{b}, \mathbf{b}^\dagger} = \exp(-\mathrm{Tr}[\mathbf{b}^\dagger \mathbf{b}]/2\sigma_b^2)$, respectively.

We want to express the network density and its correlation functions entirely in terms of complex-valued outputs, weights and biases, therefore, we need to transform the measures of W^1, W^2, b^1, b^2 into measures over $\mathbf{W}, \mathbf{b}$. As $DW^1 DW^2 = |J| D\mathbf{W} D\mathbf{W}^\dagger$, for Jacobian of $\begin{bmatrix} W^1 \\ W^2 \end{bmatrix} = \begin{bmatrix} \frac{1}{2} & \frac{1}{2} \\ \frac{i}{2} & -\frac{i}{2} \end{bmatrix} \begin{bmatrix} \mathbf{W} \\ \mathbf{W}^\dagger \end{bmatrix}$, we obtain $DW^1 DW^2 Db^1 Db^2 = |J|^2 D\mathbf{W} D\mathbf{W}^\dagger D\mathbf{b} D\mathbf{b}^\dagger$, and $|J|^2 = 1/4$. With this, the n-pt function for any number of fs and $f^\dagger$s becomes the following:

$$G^{(n)}_{i_1, \ldots, i_n}(x_1, \ldots, x_n) = \mathbb{E}[f_{i_1}(x_1) \cdots f_{i_r}(x_r) f^\dagger_{i_{r+1}}(x_{r+1}) \cdots f^\dagger_{i_n}(x_n)]$$

$$= \frac{1}{4Z_\theta} \int D\mathbf{W} D\mathbf{W}^\dagger D\mathbf{b} D\mathbf{b}^\dagger D\theta_g \left[\mathbf{W}_{i_1 j_1} g_{j_1}(x_1, \theta_g) + \mathbf{b}_{i_1} \right] \cdots$$

$$\times \left[\mathbf{W}_{i_r j_r} g_{j_r}(x_r, \theta_g) + \mathbf{b}_{i_r} \right]$$

$$\times \left[g^\dagger_{j_{r+1}}(x_{r+1}, \theta_g) \mathbf{W}^\dagger_{j_{r+1} i_{r+1}} + \mathbf{b}^\dagger_{i_{r+1}} \right] \cdots$$

$$\times \left[g^\dagger_{j_n}(x_n, \theta_g) \mathbf{W}^\dagger_{j_n i_n} + \mathbf{b}^\dagger_{i_n} \right] e^{-\frac{\mathrm{Tr}(\mathbf{w}^\dagger \mathbf{w})}{2\sigma_W^2} - \frac{\mathrm{Tr}(\mathbf{b}^\dagger \mathbf{b})}{2\sigma_b^2}} P_{\theta_g}, \qquad (A.13)$$

where Z_θ is the normalization factor. We emphasize that the transformation of f_i and $f_j^\dagger$ only transforms two indices inside the trace in $\mathrm{Tr}(\mathbf{W}^\dagger \mathbf{W})$; it is invariant in this case and also when all four indices transform.

From the structure of $P_{\mathbf{W}, \mathbf{W}^\dagger}$ and $P_{\mathbf{b}, \mathbf{b}^\dagger}$, only those terms in the integrand of (A.13), that are functions of $W^\dagger_{i_s} W_{i_s}$ and $b^\dagger_{i_t} b_{i_t}$ alone and not in product with any number of $W_{i_u}, W^\dagger_{i_u}, b_{i_u}, b^\dagger_{i_u}$ individually, result in a non-zero integral. Thus, we have the only non-vanishing correlation functions from an equal number of fs and $f^\dagger$s. We hereby redefine the correlation functions of this complex-valued network as

$$G^{(2n)}_{i_1, \ldots, i_{2n}}(x_1, \ldots, x_{2n}) := \mathbb{E}[f_{i_1}(x_{p_1}) \cdots f_{i_n}(x_{p_n})$$

$$\times f^\dagger_{i_{n+1}}(x_{p_{n+1}}) \cdots f^\dagger_{i_{2n}}(x_{p_{2n}})], \qquad (A.14)$$

where $\{p_1, \ldots, p_{2n}\}$ can be any permutation of set $\{1, \ldots, 2n\}$.

A.3. *SU(d) input symmetry*

We now show an example of neural network densities invariant under $SU(d)$ input transformations, provided that input layer parameters are drawn from an $SU(d)$ invariant distribution.

We will take a linear input layer and turn off bias for simplicity, as it may be trivially included as in $SU(D)$ output symmetry. $SU(d)$ group acts on complex numbers, therefore network inputs and input layer parameters need to be complex; such a network function is $f_i = g_{ij}(\mathbf{W}_{jk}x_k)$. The distribution of $\mathbf{W}$ is obtained from products of distributions of its real and imaginary parts W^1, W^2. Following $SU(D)$ output symmetry demonstration, the simplest $SU(d)$ invariant $P_{\mathbf{W},\mathbf{W}^\dagger}$ is obtained when $W^1, W^2 \sim \mathcal{N}(0, \sigma_W^2)$ are both $SO(d)$ invariant; we get $P_{\mathbf{W},\mathbf{W}^\dagger} = \exp(-\mathrm{Tr}[\mathbf{W}^\dagger\mathbf{W}]/2\sigma_W^2)$. The measure of $\mathbf{W}$ is obtained from the measures over W^1, W^2 as $DW^1 DW^2 = |J| D\mathbf{W} D\mathbf{W}^\dagger$, with $|J| = 1/2$. Following a similar analysis as (A.2), the only non-trivial correlation functions are

$$
\begin{aligned}
G^{(2n)}_{i_1,\ldots,i_{2n}}(x_1,\ldots,x_{2n}) &:= \mathbb{E}[f_{i_1}(x_{p_1}) \cdots f_{i_n}(x_{p_n}) f^\dagger_{i_{n+1}}(x^\dagger_{p_{n+1}}) \cdots \\
&\quad \times f^\dagger_{i_{2n}}(x^\dagger_{p_{2n}})] \\
&= \frac{1}{2Z_\theta} \int D\mathbf{W} D\mathbf{W}^\dagger D\theta_g \, g_{i_1 j_1}(\mathbf{W}_{j_1 k_1} x^{p_1}_{k_1}) \cdots g_{i_n j_n}(\mathbf{W}_{j_n k_n} x^{p_n}_{k_n}) \\
&\quad \times (x^{\dagger p_{n+1}}_{k_{n+1}} \mathbf{W}^\dagger_{k_{n+1} j_{n+1}}) g^\dagger_{j_{n+1} i_{n+1}} \cdots (x^{\dagger p_{2n}}_{k_{2n}} \mathbf{W}^\dagger_{k_{2n} j_{2n}}) \\
&\quad \times g^\dagger_{j_{2n} i_{2n}} e^{-\frac{\mathrm{Tr}(\mathbf{W}^\dagger \mathbf{W})}{2\sigma_W^2}} P_{\theta_g},
\end{aligned}
$$

where $\{p_1, \ldots, p_{2n}\}$ is any permutation over $\{1, \ldots, 2n\}$, and we have changed the x subscript label to a superscript to make room for the indices.

Under input rotations $x_i \mapsto S_{ij}x_j$, $x^\dagger_k \mapsto x^\dagger_l S^\dagger_{lk}$ by $S \in SU(d)$, the correlation functions transform into

$$
\begin{aligned}
G'^{(2n)}_{i_1,\ldots,i_{2n}}(x'_1,\ldots,x'_{2n}) &= \mathbb{E}[f_{i_1}(S_{k_1 l_1} x^{p_1}_{l_1}) \cdots f_{i_n}(S_{k_n l_n} x^{p_n}_{l_n}) f^\dagger_{i_{n+1}} \\
&\quad \times (x^{\dagger p_{n+1}}_{l_{n+1}} S^\dagger_{l_{n+1} k_{n+1}}) \cdots f^\dagger_{i_{2n}}(x^{\dagger p_{2n}}_{l_{2n}} S^\dagger_{l_{2n} k_{2n}})] \\
&= \frac{1}{2Z_\theta} \int D\mathbf{W} D\mathbf{W}^\dagger D\theta_g \, g_{i_1 j_1}(\mathbf{W}_{j_1 k_1} S_{k_1 l_1} x^{p_1}_{l_1}) \cdots g_{i_n j_n}
\end{aligned}
$$

$$\times (\mathbf{W}_{j_n k_n} S_{k_n l_n} x_{l_n}^{p_n})(x_{l_{n+1}}^{\dagger p_{n+1}} S_{l_{n+1} k_{n+1}}^{\dagger} \mathbf{W}_{k_{n+1} j_{n+1}}^{\dagger}) g_{j_{n+1} i_{n+1}}^{\dagger} \cdots$$

$$\times (x_{l_{2n}}^{\dagger p_{2n}} S_{l_{2n} k_{2n}}^{\dagger} \mathbf{W}_{k_{2n} j_{2n}}^{\dagger}) g_{j_{2n} i_{2n}}^{\dagger} P_{\mathbf{W}, \mathbf{W}^{\dagger}} P_{\theta_g}$$

$$= \frac{1}{2Z_\theta} \int |S^{\dagger -1}||S^{-1}| D\tilde{\mathbf{W}} D\tilde{\mathbf{W}}^{\dagger} D\theta_g \, g_{i_1 j_1}(\tilde{\mathbf{W}}_{j_1 l_1} x_{l_1}^{p_1}) \cdots g_{i_n j_n}$$

$$\times (\tilde{\mathbf{W}}_{j_n l_n} x_{l_n}^{p_n})(x_{l_{n+1}}^{\dagger p_{n+1}} \tilde{\mathbf{W}}_{l_{n+1} j_{n+1}}^{\dagger})$$

$$\times g_{j_{n+1} i_{n+1}}^{\dagger} \cdots (x_{l_{2n}}^{\dagger p_{2n}} \tilde{\mathbf{W}}_{l_{2n} j_{2n}}^{\dagger}) g_{j_{2n} i_{2n}}^{\dagger} P_{S^{-1}\tilde{\mathbf{W}}, \tilde{\mathbf{W}}^{\dagger} S^{\dagger -1}} P_{\theta_g}$$

$$= \mathbb{E}[f_{i_1}(x_{p_1}) \cdots f_{i_n}(x_{p_n}) f_{i_{n+1}}^{\dagger}(x_{p_{n+1}}^{\dagger}) \cdots f_{i_{2n}}^{\dagger}(x_{p_{2n}}^{\dagger})]$$

$$= G_{i_1, \ldots, i_{2n}}^{(2n)}(x_1, \ldots, x_{2n}). \tag{A.15}$$

The crucial second-to-last equality holds for $|(S^{\dagger})^{-1}||S^{-1}| = 1$, as is the case here; further, we need $P_{\mathbf{W}, \mathbf{W}^{\dagger}} = P_{\tilde{\mathbf{W}}, \tilde{\mathbf{W}}^{\dagger}}$; this stipulation holds true when $\text{Re}(\mathbf{W}), \text{Im}(\mathbf{W}) \sim \mathcal{N}(0, \sigma_W^2)$, due to the SU-invariance of $\text{Tr}(\mathbf{W}^{\dagger} \mathbf{W})$.

A.4. *Translation input symmetry*

We demonstrate an example of network densities that remain invariant under continuous translations on input space, when the input layer weight is deterministic and input layer bias is sampled from a uniform distribution on the circle, $b \sim \mathcal{U}(S^1)$. We will map the weight term to the circle by taking its mod 1 (i.e., %1).

The network output $f_i(x) = g_{ij}((W_{jk} x_k)\%1 + b_j)$ transforms into $f'(x') = g_{ij}((W_{jk} x_k)\%1 + b_j')$ under translations of inputs $x_k \mapsto x_k + c_k$, where $b_j' = (W_{jk} c_k)\%1 + b_j$. With a deterministic W, the network parameters are given by $\theta = \{\phi, b\}$, and $Db' = Db$. The transformed n-pt function is

$$G_{i_1, \ldots, i_n}^{'(n)}(x_1, \ldots, x_n) = \mathbb{E}[f_{i_1}'(x_1') \cdots f_{i_n}'(x_n')]$$

$$= \frac{1}{Z_\theta} \int Db D\phi \, g_{i_1 j_1}((W_{j_1 k_1} x_{k_1} + W_{j_1 k_1} c_{k_1})\%1 + b_{j_1}) \cdots$$

$$\cdots g_{i_n j_n}((W_{j_n k_n} x_{k_n} + W_{j_n k_n} c_{k_n})\%1 + b_{j_n}) P_b P_\phi$$

$$= \frac{1}{Z_\theta} \int Db' D\phi \, g_{i_1 j_1}((W_{j_1 k_1 x_{k_1}})\%1 + b_{j_1}') \cdots$$

$$\times \ g_{i_n j_n}((W_{j_n k_n} x_{k_n}) \% 1 + b'_{j_n}) P'_b P_\phi$$

$$= \mathbb{E}[f_{i_1}(x_n) \cdots f_{i_n}(x_n)] = G^{(n)}_{i_1,\ldots,i_n}(x_1,\ldots,x_n), \qquad \text{(A.16)}$$

where the crucial third-to-last equality holds when $P_b = P_{b'}$. This stipulation is true as $\mathbb{E}[b^k] = \mathbb{E}[b'^k]$ for any k when $b \sim \mathcal{U}(S^1)$ and W is deterministic; since the layer is valued on the circle with circumference 1, we know that any bias value is equally probable. Thus, b and b have identical moment generating functions and $P_b = P_b$.

A.5. *Sp(D) output symmetry*

We also demonstrate an example of network densities that remain invariant under the compact symplectic group $Sp(D)$ transformations on output space.

The compact symplectic $Sp(D)$ is the rotation group of quaternions, just as SU is the rotation group of complex numbers. Thus, a network with linear output layer would remain invariant under compact symplectic group, if last linear layer weights and biases are quaternionic numbers, drawn from $Sp(D)$ invariant distributions. We define the network output $f_i(x) = W_{ij} g_j(x, \theta_g) + b_i$ as before, with parameters $W_{ab} = W_{ab,0} + iW_{ab,1} + jW_{ab,2} + kW_{ab,3}$ and $b_a = b_{a,0} + ib_{a,1} + jb_{a,2} + kb_{a,3}$ such that Hermitian norms $\text{Tr}(W^\dagger W) = W^\dagger_{ab} W_{ab} = \sum_{i=0}^3 W^2_{ab,i}$ and $\text{Tr}(b^\dagger b) = b^\dagger_a b_a = \sum_{i=0}^3 b^2_{a,i}$ are compact symplectic $Sp(D)$ invariant by definition, where the conjugate of a quaternion $q = a + ib + jc + kd$ is $q^* = a - ib - jc - kd$. The distributions of W, b are obtained as products of distributions of the components W_0, W_1, W_2, W_3 and b_0, b_1, b_2, b_3, respectively. Following the $SU(D)$ symmetry construction, we can obtain the simplest $Sp(D)$ invariant $P_{W,W^\dagger}$ and $P_{b,b^\dagger}$ when these are the functions of the Hermitian norm, and PDF of each component P_{W_i} is an exponential function of $SO(D)$ invariant term $\text{Tr}(W_i^T W_i)$ with equal coefficient, similarly with bias. Starting with $W_0, W_1, W_2, W_3 \sim \mathcal{N}(0, \sigma_W^2)$ and $b_0, b_1, b_2, b_3 \sim \mathcal{N}(0, \sigma_b^2)$, we get $Sp(D)$ invariant quaternionic parameter distributions $P_{W,W^\dagger} = \exp(-\text{Tr}(W^\dagger W)/2\sigma_W^2)$ and $P_{b,b^\dagger} = \exp(-\text{Tr}(b^\dagger b)/2\sigma_b^2)$. We also obtain the measures over W, b from measures over W_i and b_i, e.g., $DW DW^\dagger = |J| DW_0 DW_1 DW_2 DW_3$. Following an analysis similar to (A.2), it can be shown that the only non-trivial correlation functions of this quaternionic-valued network are

$$
G^{(n)}_{i_1,\cdots,i_{2n}}(x_1,\ldots,x_{2n}) = \frac{|J|^2}{Z_\theta} \int DW\,DW^\dagger\,Db\,Db^\dagger\, f_{i_1}(x_{p_1})\cdots
$$

$$
\times\, f_{i_n}(x_{p_n})\,f^\dagger_{i_{n+1}}(x_{p_{n+1}})\cdots f^\dagger_{i_{2n}}(x_{p_{2n}})e^{-\frac{\mathrm{Tr}(W^\dagger W)}{2\sigma_W^2}-\frac{\mathrm{Tr}(b^\dagger b)}{2\sigma_b^2}}P_{\theta_g},
$$

$$
\text{(A.17)}
$$

for $\{p_1,\ldots,p_{2n}\}$ any permutation over $\{1,\ldots,2n\}$. Under $Sp(D)$ transformation of outputs $f_i \mapsto S_{ij}f_j$, $f^\dagger_k \mapsto f^\dagger_l S^\dagger_{lk}$, by $S \in Sp(D)$ in quaternionic basis, the correlation functions transform as

$$
G'^{(2n)}_{i_1\ldots i_{2n}}(x'_1,\ldots,x'_{2n}) = \mathbb{E}\left[S_{i_1 j_1} f_{j_1}(x_{p_1})\cdots S_{i_n j_n} f_{j_n}(x_{p_n})\right.
$$

$$
\left.\times\, f^\dagger_{j_{n+1}}(x_{p_{n+1}})S^\dagger_{j_{n+1}i_{n+1}}\cdots f^\dagger_{j_{2n}}(x_{p_{2n}})S^\dagger_{j_{2n}i_{2n}}\right]
$$

$$
= \frac{|J|^2}{Z_\theta}\int DW\,DW^\dagger\,Db\,Db^\dagger\,D\theta_g\, S_{i_1 j_1}(W_{j_1 k_1}g_{k_1}(x_{p_1},\theta_g)+b_{j_1})\cdots
$$

$$
\times\, S_{i_n j_n}(W_{j_n k_n}g_{k_n}(x_{p_n},\theta_g)+b_{j_n})(g^\dagger_{k_{n+1}}(x_{p_{n+1}},\theta_g)
$$

$$
\times\, W^\dagger_{k_{n+1}j_{n+1}}+b^\dagger_{j_{n+1}})S^\dagger_{j_{n+1}i_{n+1}}\cdots(g^\dagger_{k_{2n}}(x_{p_{2n}},\theta_g)
$$

$$
\times\, W^\dagger_{k_{2n}j_{2n}}+b^\dagger_{j_{2n}})
$$

$$
S^\dagger_{j_{2n}i_{2n}}P_{W,W^\dagger}P_{b,b^\dagger}P_{\theta_g} = \frac{|J|^2}{Z_\theta}\int |S^{-1}||S^{\dagger-1}|D\tilde{W}\,D\tilde{W}^\dagger\,D\tilde{b}\,D\tilde{b}^\dagger\,D\theta_g
$$

$$
\times\, (\tilde{W}_{i_1 k_1}g_{k_1}(x_{p_1},\theta_g)+\tilde{b}_{i_1})\cdots(\tilde{W}_{i_n k_n}g_{k_n}(x_{p_n},\theta_g)+\tilde{b}_{i_n})
$$

$$
\times\, (g^\dagger_{k_{n+1}}(x_{p_{n+1}},\theta_g)\tilde{W}^\dagger_{k_{n+1}i_{n+1}}+\tilde{b}^\dagger_{i_{n+1}})\cdots(g^\dagger_{k_{2n}}(x_{p_{2n}},\theta_g)
$$

$$
\times\, \tilde{W}^\dagger_{k_{2n}i_{2n}}+\tilde{b}^\dagger_{i_{2n}})P_{S^{-1}\tilde{W},\tilde{W}^\dagger S^{\dagger-1}}P_{S^{-1}\tilde{b},\tilde{b}^\dagger S^{\dagger-1}}P_{\theta_g}
$$

$$
= \mathbb{E}\left[f_{i_1}(x_{p_1})\cdots f_{i_n}(x_{p_n})f^\dagger_{i_{n+1}}(x_{p_{n+1}})\cdots f^\dagger_{i_{2n}}(x_{p_{2n}})\right]
$$

$$
= G^{(2n)}_{i_1\cdots i_{2n}}(x_1,\ldots,x_{2n}). \tag{A.18}
$$

The crucial second-to-last equality holds when $|S^{-1}| = 1$, $P_{W,W^\dagger} = P_{\tilde{W},\tilde{W}^\dagger}$, and $P_{b,b^\dagger} = P_{\tilde{b},\tilde{b}^\dagger}$. These stipulations hold true, for example, when $S \in Sp(D)$, $W_0, W_1, W_2, W_3 \sim \mathcal{N}(0, \sigma_W^2)$, and $b_0, b_1, b_2, b_3 \sim \mathcal{N}(0, \sigma_b^2)$, due to the invariance of $\text{Tr}(W^\dagger W)$ in $P_{W,W^\dagger} = \exp(-\text{Tr}(W^\dagger W)/2\sigma_W^2)$, and similarly for $P_{b,b^\dagger}$.

A.6.   *Preserving symmetry during training: Examples*

We study further the example of an $SO(D)$ output symmetry from Section 2. Turning off the bias for simplicity, the network function is

$$f_i(x) = W_{ij} g_j(x), \tag{A.19}$$

with parameters $\theta = \{W, \theta_g\}$; transformations of f_i may be absorbed into W, i.e., $W = \theta_T$.

The network density remains symmetric during training when the updates to P_θ preserve symmetry; for this example, we showed in Section 3 that it occurs when $\mathcal{L}$ is invariant and

$$\frac{\partial P_\theta}{\partial \theta_i} = I_P \, \theta_i \qquad \frac{\partial \mathcal{L}}{\partial \theta_i} = I_{\mathcal{L}} \, \theta_i. \tag{A.20}$$

Let the initial density be $P_\theta(0) = \exp[-\sum_{j=1}^k a_j (\text{Tr}(\theta^T \theta))^j]$ for $a_j \in \mathbb{R}$. This clearly satisfies the first condition in (A.20). An example of SO-invariant loss function is

$$\mathcal{L} = \sum_{x,y} (f_i(x) f_i(x) - y_j y_j)$$

$$= \sum_{x,y} (W_{il} g_l(x) W_{ik} g_k(x) - y_j y_j), \tag{A.21}$$

where $\partial \mathcal{L}/\partial \theta_g$ is invariant because $\mathcal{L}$ is and θ_g does not transform. Furthermore,

$$\frac{\partial \mathcal{L}}{\partial W_{mn}} = 2 \, W_{mk} \left(\sum_{x,y} g_k(x) g_n(x) \right), \tag{A.22}$$

which satisfies the second condition in (A.20), since the first index is the one that transforms when W absorbs the transformation of f_i.

B. More General SO Invariant Network Distributions

We will now give an example of an $SO(D)$ invariant non-Gaussian network distribution at infinite width, as parameters of the initialized $SO(D)$ invariant GP become correlated through training. Such a network distribution can be obtained up to perturbative corrections to the initialized network distribution, if the extent of parameter correlation is small.

Training may correlate last layer weights θ_{ij} of a linear network output $f_i = \theta_{ij} g_j(x, \theta_g)$ initialized with $\theta_{ij} \sim \mathcal{N}(0, \sigma_\theta^2)$, such that at a particular training step, we get $\mathcal{P}_\theta = e^{-\frac{1}{2\sigma_\theta^2}\theta_{\alpha\beta}^2 - \lambda_\theta\,\theta_{ab}\theta_{ab}\theta_{cd}\theta_{cd}}$ independent from P_{θ_g}, with small λ_θ. Correlation functions of this network distribution can be obtained by perturbative corrections to correlation functions of the network distribution at initialization. For example, the 2-pt function of the correlated network distribution is given by

$$G_{i_1 i_2}^{(2),\mathrm{NGP}}(x_1, x_2)$$

$$= \frac{\int D\theta D\theta_g\, \theta_{i_1 j_1}\theta_{i_2 j_2}[1 - \lambda_\theta\,\theta_{ab}^2\theta_{cd}^2] g_{j_1}(x_1, \theta_g) g_{j_2}(x_2, \theta_g)\, e^{-\frac{1}{2\sigma_\theta^2}\theta_{\alpha\beta}^2}\mathcal{P}(\theta_g)}{\int D\theta D\theta_g\,[1 - \lambda_\theta\,\theta_{ab}^2\theta_{cd}^2] e^{-\frac{1}{2\sigma_\theta^2}\theta_{\alpha\beta}^2}\mathcal{P}(\theta_g)}$$

$$= \Bigg[\sum_{i_1 j_1}\mathbb{E}[\theta_{i_1 j_1}^2] - \lambda_\theta\Bigg(\sum_{i_1 j_1 \neq ab \neq cd}\mathbb{E}[\theta_{i_1 j_1}^2]\mathbb{E}[\theta_{ab}^2]\mathbb{E}[\theta_{cd}^2]$$

$$+ \sum_{i_1 j_1 \neq ab}(\mathbb{E}[\theta_{i_1 j_1}^2]\mathbb{E}[\theta_{ab}^4] + 2\,\mathbb{E}[\theta_{i_1 j_1}^4]$$

$$\times\, \mathbb{E}[\theta_{ab}^2]) + \mathbb{E}[\theta_{i_1 j_1}^6])\Bigg]\Bigg[1 - \lambda_\theta\Bigg(\sum_{ab}\mathbb{E}[\theta_{ab}^4] + \sum_{ab \neq cd}\mathbb{E}[\theta_{ab}^2]\mathbb{E}[\theta_{cd}^2]\Bigg)\Bigg]^{-1}$$

$$\times\, \mathbb{E}[g_{j_1}(x_1, \theta_g)\, g_{j_1}(x_2, \theta_g)] + O(\lambda_\theta^2)$$

$$= G_{i_1 i_2}^{(2),\mathrm{GP}}(x_1, x_2) - \lambda_\theta \sum_{i_1 j_1 \neq ab}\Big(\mathbb{E}[\theta_{i_1 j_1}^6] - \mathbb{E}[\theta_{i_1 j_1}^2]\mathbb{E}[\theta_{i_1 j_1}^4]$$

$$-2\,(\mathbb{E}[\theta_{i_1 j_1}^2])^2\mathbb{E}[\theta_{ab}^2] + 2\,\mathbb{E}[\theta_{i_1 j_1}^4]\mathbb{E}[\theta_{ab}^2]\Big)$$

$$\times\, \mathbb{E}[g_{j_1}(x_1, \theta_g)g_{j_1}(x_2, \theta_g)] + O(\lambda_\theta^2). \tag{B.1}$$

$\mathbb{E}[\theta_{ij}^n]$ is evaluated using Gaussian $P_{\theta,\mathrm{GP}} = e^{-\frac{\theta_{\alpha\beta}^2}{2\sigma_\theta^2}}$ of initialized network distribution. $O(\lambda_\theta)$ terms in (B.1) scale as both $1/N$ and $1/N^2$, as can be seen after properly normalization of θ by $\sigma_\theta^2 \mapsto \frac{\sigma_\theta^2}{N}$; this 'mixed' $1/N$ scaling results from parameter correlations. (We set bias to 0 everywhere for simplicity; analysis for non-trivial bias follows a similar method.)

C. $SO(D)$ Invariance in Experiments

The correlator constraint (3) gives testable necessary conditions for a symmetric density. Consider a single-layer fully connected network, called Gauss-net due to having a Gaussian GP kernel defined by $f(x) = W_1(\sigma(W_0 x + b_0)) + b_1$, where $W_0 \sim \mathcal{N}(0, \sigma_W^2/\sqrt{d})$, $W_1 \sim \mathcal{N}(0, \sigma_W^2/\sqrt{N})$ and $b_0, b_1 \sim \mathcal{N}(0, \sigma_b^2)$, with activation $\sigma(x) = \exp(W_0 x + b_0)/\sqrt{\exp(2(\sigma_b^2 + \sigma_W^2/d))}$.

To test for $SO(D)$ invariance via (3), we measure the average elementwise change in n-pt functions before and after an $SO(D)$ transformation. To do this, we generate 2-pt and 4-pt correlators at various D for a number of experiments and act on them with 1000 random group elements of a given $SO(D)$ group. Each group element is generated by exponentiating a random linear combination of generators of the corresponding algebra, namely,

$$R_b = \exp\left(\sum_{i=1}^p \alpha_i \cdot T^i\right), \qquad (\text{C.1})$$

for $b = 1, \ldots, 1000$, $p = \dim(SO(D)) = D(D-1)/2$, $\alpha_i \sim \mathcal{U}(0, 1)$ and T^i are generators of $\mathfrak{so}(D)$ Lie algebra; i.e., $D \times D$ skew-symmetric matrices written in a simple basis.[2] For example, for $D = 3$, we take

---

[2] The generators are obtained by choosing each of the $\frac{D(D-1)}{2}$ independent planes of rotations to have a canonical ordering with index i, determined by a (p, q)-plane. Each ith plane of rotation has a generator matrix $[T^i]_{D \times D}$ with $T_{pq}^i = -1$, $T_{qp}^i = 1$, for $p < q$, rest 0. For instance, at $D = 3$, there are 3 independent planes of rotation formed by direction pairs $\{2, 3\}$, $\{1, 3\}$ and $\{1, 2\}$. For each ith plane defined by directions $\{p, q\}$, general $SO(3)$ elements $[R^i]_{3 \times 3}$ have

the standard basis for $\mathfrak{so}(3)$,

$$T^1 = \begin{bmatrix} 0 & 0 & 0 \\ 0 & 0 & -1 \\ 0 & 1 & 0 \end{bmatrix}, \qquad T^2 = \begin{bmatrix} 0 & 0 & -1 \\ 0 & 0 & 0 \\ 1 & 0 & 0 \end{bmatrix}, \qquad T^3 = \begin{bmatrix} 0 & -1 & 0 \\ 1 & 0 & 0 \\ 0 & 0 & 0 \end{bmatrix} \qquad (C.2)$$

to generate group elements of $SO(3)$.

We define the elementwise deviation $\mathcal{M}_n = \mathrm{abs}(G'^{(n)} - G^{(n)})$ to capture the change in correlators due to $SO(D)$ transformations. Here, $G'^{(n)}{}_{i_1,\cdots,i_n}(x_1,\ldots,x_n) := R_{i_1 p_1} \cdots R_{i_n p_n} G^{(n)}_{p_1,\cdots,p_n}(x_1,\ldots,x_n)$ is the SO-transformed n-pt function; both $\mathcal{M}_n$ and $G^{(n)}$ have the same rank.

Error bounds for deviation $\mathcal{M}_n$ are determined as $\delta\mathcal{M}_n = \sqrt{(\delta G'^{(n)})^2 + (\delta G^{(n)})^2}$ using the standard error propagation formulae, $\delta G^{(n)}$ equals the average (elementwise) standard deviation of n-pt functions across 10 experiments and $\delta G'^{(n)}$ is calculated as follows:

$$\delta G'^{(n)} = \frac{1}{D^n} \frac{1}{1000} \sum_{b=1}^{1000} \left[\sum_{t=(i_1,p_1)}^{(i_n,p_n)} (R^b_{i_1 p_1} \cdots \delta R^b_t \cdots R^b_{i_n p_n} G^{(n)}_{p_1,\ldots,p_n})^2 \right.$$

$$\left. + (R^b_{i_1 p_1} \cdots R^b_{i_n p_n} \delta G^{(n)})^2 \right]^{1/2}. \qquad (C.3)$$

We have changed the R subscript label b to superscript to make room for the indices. δR_{ij} denotes the average error in generated group elements R; it is captured by computing $R^T R$ for our experimentally generated matrices R and measuring the magnitude of the off-diagonal elements, which are expected to be zero. We measure an average magnitude of $\mathcal{O}(10^{-18}) =: \delta R$ in these off-diagonal elements.

We take the deviation tensors $\mathcal{M}_n$ over 10 experiments for $SO(3)$ and $SO(5)$ transformations of 2-pt and 4-pt functions at $D = 3, 5$, respectively; both correlators of each experiment are calculated using $4 \cdot 10^6$ and 10^6 network outputs, respectively. An elementwise average and standard deviation across 10 deviation tensors $\mathcal{M}_n$ are taken and then averaged over to produce the mean of the SO-transformation

---

$R^i_{pq} = -\sin\theta$, $R^i_{qp} = \sin\theta$, $R^i_{qq} = \cos\theta$, $R^i_{qq} = \cos\theta$, $R^i_{rr} = 1$ for $p < q$, $r \neq p, q$ and variable θ. Expanding each R^i in Taylor series, the coefficients of $\mathcal{O}(\theta)$ terms are taken to define the generators of $\mathfrak{so}(3)$ as in (C.2).

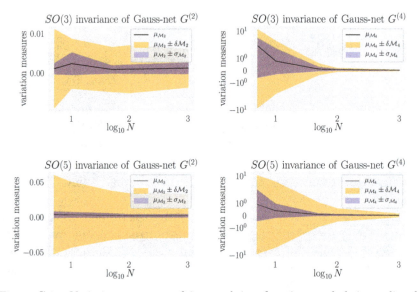

Figure C.1.   Variation measures of 2-pt and 4-pt functions and their predicted error bounds, for $SO(3)$ and $SO(5)$ transformations of $D = 3$ and $D = 5$ networks, respectively.

deviation $\mu_{\mathcal{M}_n}$ and its error $\sigma_{\mathcal{M}_n}$, respectively. We plot $\mu_{\mathcal{M}_n} \pm \sigma_{\mathcal{M}_n}$ (purple shaded area) in Figure C.1; this signal lies well within predicted error bounds of $\pm\delta_{\mathcal{M}_n}$ (in orange), although $\mu_{\mathcal{M}_n}$ deviates significantly from 0 at low widths, in contradiction to width independence of (3). This is due to the smaller sample size of parameters in low-width networks, and therefore small fluctuations in the weight and bias draws lead to more significant deviations from the "true" distribution of these parameters. A non-zero mean of the parameters caused by fluctuations leads to a non-zero mean of the function distribution $\langle f \rangle \neq 0$, thus breaking $SO(D)$ symmetry. We believe this is a computational artifact and does not contradict SO-invariance in (3).

D. Experiment Details

The experiments in Section 4 were done using Fashion-MNIST under the MIT License,[3] using 60000 data points for each epoch split with

---

[3]The MIT License (MIT) Copyright © 2017 Zalando SE, https://tech.zalando. com.

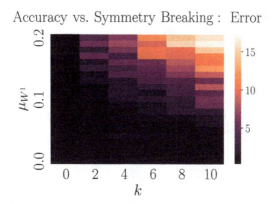

Figure C.2.   Error in the data from Figure 1. Color represents the % of variation across 20 experiments of the same configuration, computed as the standard deviation normalized by the mean.

a batch size of 64 and test batch size of 1000. Each experiment was run on a 240GB computing node through the Discovery Cluster at Northeastern University and took between 1 and 1.5 hrs to train 20 epochs. The experiments were repeated 20 times for each configuration and were run with 21×6 configurations for the left plot in Figure 1 and 11 for the right plot. The error in the left plot of Figure 1 is shown in Figure C.2.

The experiments in Appendix (A.6) were done on the same cluster, with the same memory nodes. These took around 24 hours on 10 compute nodes to generate models for each of the D values. The n-pt functions then took another 6 hours on a single node each.

E. Comments on Functional Densities

Functional integrals are often treated loosely by physicists: they use them to great effect and experimental agreement in practice, but they are not rigorously defined in general; see, e.g., Ref. [51].

We follow in this tradition in this work but would like to make some further comments regarding cases that are well defined, casting the discussion first into the language of Euclidean QFT and then bringing it back to machine learning.

First, the standard Feynman functional path integral for a scalar field $\phi(x)$ is

$$Z = \int D\phi \, e^{-S[\phi]}, \tag{E.1}$$

but in many cases, the action $S[\phi]$ is split into free and interacting pieces

$$S[\phi] = S_F[\phi] + S_{\text{int}}[\phi], \tag{E.2}$$

where the free action $S_F[\phi]$ is Gaussian and the interacting action $S_{\text{int}}[\phi]$ is non-Gaussian. The free theory, which has $S_{\text{int}}[\phi] = 0$, is a Gaussian process and is therefore well defined. When interactions are turned on, i.e., the non-Gaussianities in $S_{\text{int}}[\phi]$ are small relative to some scale, physicists compute correlation functions (moments of the functional density) in perturbation theory, truncating the expansion at some order and writing approximate moments of the interacting theory density in terms of a sum of well-defined Gaussian moments, including higher moments.

Second, it is also common to put the theory on a lattice. In such a case, the function $\phi : \mathbb{R}^d \to \mathbb{R}$ is restricted to a concrete collection of points $\{x_i\}$, $i = 1, \ldots, m$, with each $x_i \in \mathbb{R}^d$. Instead of considering the random function $\phi(x)$ drawn from the difficult-to-define functional density, one instead considers the random variable $\phi(x_i) =: \phi_i$, and the joint distribution on the set of ϕ_i defines the lattice theory. One sees this regularly in the Gaussian process literature: evaluated on any discrete set of inputs, the Gaussian process reduces to a standard multivariate Gaussian.

In this work, we study functional densities associated with neural networks and have both the perturbative and especially the lattice understanding in mind when we consider them. In particular, for readers uncomfortable with the lack of precision in defining a functional density, we emphasize that our results can also be understood on a lattice, though input symmetries may be discrete subgroups of those existing in the continuum limit. Furthermore, any concrete ML application involves a finite set of inputs, and for any fixed application in physics or ML, one can simply choose the spacing between lattice points to be smaller than the experimental resolution.

References

[1] A. Jacot, F. Gabriel and C. Hongler, Neural tangent kernel: Convergence and generalization in neural networks. In *NeurIPS* (2018).

[2] R. M. Neal, *Bayesian Learning for Neural Networks*. PhD Thesis, University of Toronto (1995).

[3] J. Lee, L. Xiao, S. S. Schoenholz, Y. Bahri, R. Novak, J. Sohl-Dickstein and J. Pennington, Wide neural networks of any depth evolve as linear models under gradient descent, *ArXiv*, abs/1902.06720 (2019).

[4] T. S. Cohen, M. Geiger and M. Weiler, Intertwiners between induced representations (with applications to the theory of equivariant neural networks) (2018).

[5] M. Mohamed, G. Cesa, T. S. Cohen and M. Welling, A data and compute efficient design for limited-resources deep learning (2020).

[6] L. Falorsi, P. de Haan, T. R. Davidson, N. De Cao, M. Weiler, P. Forré and T. S. Cohen, Explorations in homeomorphic variational auto-encoding (2018).

[7] T. S. Cohen and M. Welling, Group equivariant convolutional networks (2016).

[8] M. Weiler, M. Geiger, M. Welling, W. Boomsma and T. Cohen, 3D steerable CNNS: Learning rotationally equivariant features in volumetric data (2018).

[9] F. B. Fuchs, D. E. Worrall, V. Fischer and M. Welling, Se(3)-transformers: 3D roto-translation equivariant attention networks (2020).

[10] H. Maron, H. Ben-Hamu, N. Shamir and Y. Lipman, Invariant and equivariant graph networks (2019).

[11] H. Maron, O. Litany, G. Chechik and E. Fetaya, On learning sets of symmetric elements (2020).

[12] H. Maron, E. Fetaya, N. Segol and Y. Lipman, On the universality of invariant networks (2019).

[13] N. Thomas, T. Smidt, S. Kearnes, L. Yang, L. Li, K. Kohlhoff and P. Riley, Tensor field networks: Rotation- and translation-equivariant neural networks for 3D point clouds (2018).

[14] S. Ravanbakhsh, J. Schneider and B. Poczos, Equivariance through parameter-sharing (2017).

[15] R. Kondor, Z. Lin and S. Trivedi, Clebsch-gordan nets: A fully fourier space spherical convolutional neural network (2018).

[16] I. Higgins, D. Amos, D. Pfau, S. Racaniere, L. Matthey, D. Rezende and A. Lerchner, Towards a definition of disentangled representations (2018).

[17] R. Kondor and S. Trivedi, On the generalization of equivariance and convolution in neural networks to the action of compact groups (2018).

[18] B. Anderson, T.-S. Hy and R. Kondor, Cormorant: Covariant molecular neural networks (2019).

[19] A. Bogatskiy, B. Anderson, J. T. Offermann, M. Roussi, D. W. Miller and R. Kondor, Lorentz group equivariant neural network for particle physics (2020).

[20] D. E. Worrall, S. J. Garbin, D. Turmukhambetov and G. J. Brostow, Harmonic networks: Deep translation and rotation equivariance (2017).

[21] T. S. Cohen, M. Weiler, B. Kicanaoglu and M. Welling, Gauge equivariant convolutional networks and the icosahedral CNN. *CoRR*, abs/1902.04615 (2019).

[22] E. J. Bekkers, B-spline CNNS on lie groups, *CoRR*, abs/1909.12057 (2019).

[23] C. M. Bender, J. J. Garcia, K. O'Connor and J. Oliva, Permutation invariant likelihoods and equivariant transformations, *CoRR*, abs/1902.01967 (2019).

[24] K. Rasul, I. Schuster, R. Vollgraf and U. Bergmann, Set flow: A permutation invariant normalizing flow, *CoRR*, abs/1909.02775 (2019).

[25] D. J. Rezende, S. Racanière, I. Higgins and P. Toth, Equivariant hamiltonian flows (2019).

[26] J. Köhler, L. Klein and F. Noé, Equivariant flows: Exact likelihood generative learning for symmetric densities, *arXiv e-prints*, arXiv:2006.02425 (June 2020).

[27] G. Kanwar, M. S. Albergo, D. Boyda, K. Cranmer, D. C. Hackett, S. Racanière, D. J. Rezende and P. E. Shanahan, Equivariant flow-based sampling for lattice gauge theory, *Phys. Rev. Lett.* **125**(12) (September 2020), 121601.

[28] D. Boyda, G. Kanwar, S. Racanière, D. J. Rezende, M. S. Albergo, K. Cranmer, D. C. Hackett and P. E. Shanahan, Sampling using $SU(N)$ gauge equivariant flows, *Phys. Rev. D* **103**(7) (2021), 074504.

[29] P. Betzler and S. Krippendorf, Connecting dualities and Machine Learning, *Fortsch. Phys.* **68**(5) (2020), 2000022.

[30] S. Krippendorf and M. Syvaeri, Detecting symmetries with neural networks, (2020), 3.

[31] J. Halverson, A. Maiti and K. Stoner, Neural networks and quantum field theory, *Mach. Learn.* (March 2021).

[32] O. Cohen, O. Malka and Z. Ringel, Learning curves for overparametrized deep neural networks: A field theory perspective, *Phys. Rev. Res.* **3**(2) (April 2021), 023034.

[33] J. A. Zavatone-Veth and C. Pehlevan, Exact priors of finite neural networks (2021).

[34] C. KI Williams, Computing with infinite networks, in *Advances in Neural Information Processing Systems*, pp. 295–301 (1997).

[35] J. Lee, Y. Bahri, R. Novak, S. S. Schoenholz, J. Pennington and J. Sohl-Dickstein, Deep neural networks as gaussian processes (2017).

[36] O. Cohen, O. Malka and Z. Ringel, Learning curves for deep neural networks: A gaussian field theory perspective (2020).

[37] A. G. de Matthews, M. Rowland, J. Hron, R. E. Turner and Z. Ghahramani, Gaussian process behaviour in wide deep neural networks, *ArXiv*, abs/1804.11271 (2018).

[38] G. Yang, Tensor programs I: Wide feedforward or recurrent neural networks of any architecture are Gaussian processes, *arXiv e-prints*, pp. arXiv:1910.12478 (October 2019).

[39] G. Yang, Scaling limits of wide neural networks with weight sharing: Gaussian process behavior, gradient independence, and neural tangent kernel derivation, *ArXiv*, abs/1902.04760 (2019).

[40] R. Novak, L. Xiao, J. Lee, Y. Bahri, D. A. Abolafia, J. Pennington and J. Sohl-Dickstein, Bayesian convolutional neural networks with many channels are Gaussian processes, *ArXiv*, abs/1810.05148 (2018).

[41] A. Garriga-Alonso, L. Aitchison and C. E. Rasmussen, Deep convolutional networks as shallow Gaussian processes, *ArXiv*, abs/1808.05587 (2019).

[42] E. Dyer and G. Gur-Ari, Asymptotics of wide networks from Feynman diagrams, *ArXiv*, abs/1909.11304 (2020).

[43] S. Yaida, Non-Gaussian processes and neural networks at finite widths, *ArXiv*, abs/1910.00019 (2019).

[44] J. Polchinski, Dualities of fields and strings, *Stud. Hist. Phil. Sci. B* **59** (2017), 6–20.

[45] N. Seiberg and E. Witten, Electric — magnetic duality, monopole condensation, and confinement in $N = 2$ supersymmetric Yang-Mills theory, *Nucl. Phys. B* **426** (1994), 19–52. [Erratum: *Nucl. Phys. B* 430 (1994), 485–486].

[46] J. M. Maldacena, The Large N limit of superconformal field theories and supergravity, *Adv. Theor. Math. Phys.* **2** (1998), 231–252.

[47] M. B. Green and J. H. Schwarz, Anomaly cancellation in supersymmetric D=10 gauge theory and superstring theory, *Phys. Lett. B* **149** (1984), 117–122.

[48] D. Kunin, J. Sagastuy-Breña, S. Ganguli, D. L. K. Yamins and H. Tanaka, Neural mechanics: Symmetry and broken conservation laws in deep learning dynamics, *CoRR*, abs/2012.04728 (2020).

[49] H. Xiao, K. Rasul and R. Vollgraf, Fashion-mnist: A novel image dataset for benchmarking Machine Learning algorithms, *CoRR*, abs/1708.07747 (2017).

[50] P. Di Francesco, P. Mathieu and D. Senechal, *Conformal Field Theory*. Graduate Texts in Contemporary Physics. New York: Springer-Verlag (1997).

[51] Kevin 1977 Costello. *Renormalization and Effective Field Theory*. Mathematical surveys and monographs; v. 170. Providence, R.I.: American Mathematical Society (2011).

Chapter 9

Supervised Learning of Arithmetic Invariants

Thomas Oliver

Teesside University, Middlesbrough, Tees Valley, TS1 3BX, UK

t.oliver@tees.ac.uk

Abstract

We survey some recent implementations of supervised learning techniques on large sets of arithmetic data. As part of our methodological review, we perform some rudimentary statistical learning algorithms by hand on simplified problems. We incorporate a self-contained number-theoretic background which places a significant emphasis on conjectures and examples relevant to the machine learning context.

1. Introduction

We begin by explaining the terms used in the title. For our purposes, machine learning is a collection of algorithms by which a computer may solve problems without specific programming to do so. Supervised learning is a basic paradigm of machine learning, in which the problem solving strategy developed is based upon an existing set of solutions. For example, the solution offered by a naive Bayes classifier is that with the highest probability calculated using naive assumptions about the training data and Bayes theorem. The term arithmetic refers to the study of integers. By an arithmetic invariant, we mean a label for an object within some family developed as part of this study. For example, the class number is an invariant in the family of number fields or the rank is an invariant in the family of elliptic curves.

The arithmetic structures of interest in this paper are number fields and low genus algebraic curves defined over $\mathbb{Q}$. Supervised learning strategies were applied to data of this nature in the series [7–9]. The algorithms were implemented with [15], using data from [11]. While the invariants are of mathematical nature — and may be computed through an array of methods suggested by the underlying theory — the machine learning approach treats them as nothing more than labels. There is of course some practical computational value to an accurate and instantaneous machine learning approach and moreover potential theoretical value based on insights into what underlies a successful strategy. For example, one might hope that understanding the inner-workings of an interpretable machine learning model could yield new insights into open conjectures, such as the Gauss class number problem for real quadratic fields, the finiteness of the Tate–Shafarevich group for elliptic curves or the Sato–Tate conjecture for higher genus curves.

We conclude this Introduction with an overview of the subsequent sections. In Section 2, we offer a self-contained review of the arithmetic invariants appearing in the sequel. In Section 3, we discuss several open conjectures, which served as the primary motivation for the experimentation in [7–9]. Experts in number theory might choose to skip Sections 2 and 3. In Section 4, we overview the supervised learning strategies featured in [7–9], and we implement simplified versions of them by hand on toy problems. An expert in machine learning might choose to skip Section 4. In Section 5, we touch upon some deeper arithmetic theory connected to the machine learning experiments. In Section 6, we conclude this chapter and refer the curious reader to recent developments.

2. Arithmetic Invariants

The primary objective of this section is to define some basic arithmetic invariants. As a supplementary objective, we offer examples pertinent to the design of the machine learning experiments in [7–9].

This is a self-contained crash course intended only to contextualize later sections. For a more thorough treatment, the reader is directed to [14] for number fields, [12,13] for elliptic curves and [1] for genus 2 curves.

2.1. *Number fields*

Let $\mathbb{Q}$ denote the field of rational numbers. A field extension $F/\mathbb{Q}$ is a $\mathbb{Q}$-vector space whose dimension is referred to as the degree and denoted by $[F : \mathbb{Q}]$. A number field is a finite degree field extension of $\mathbb{Q}$.

Example 2.1. If F is a number field with $[F : \mathbb{Q}] = 2$, then, for some square-free $d \in \mathbb{Z}$, we may write

$$F = F_d = \mathbb{Q}\left(\sqrt{d}\right) = \left\{a + b\sqrt{d} : a, b \in \mathbb{Q}\right\}.$$

A number field is necessarily an algebraic extension of $\mathbb{Q}$. Given a number field F, a defining polynomial $P_F(x) \in \mathbb{Q}[x]$ is an irreducible polynomial such that $F = \mathbb{Q}[x]/(P_F(x))$.

Example 2.2. Let d be a square-free integer. Perhaps the most obvious defining polynomial for $F_d = \mathbb{Q}\left(\sqrt{d}\right)$ is $x^2 - d$. Furthermore, if $p_0, p_1, p_2 \in \mathbb{Q}$ satisfy $p_1^2 - 4p_0p_2 = d$, then $p_0 + p_1x + p_2x^2$ is also a defining polynomial for F_d.

For each F, there is an infinitude of defining polynomials. As per [11], a normalized defining polynomial is a monic defining polynomial with integer coefficients such that $\sum_{i=1}^n |\alpha_i|^2$ is minimized, where α_i are the complex roots.

Example 2.3. The polynomials $x^2 - x - 1$ and $x^2 - 5$ both define the quadratic number field $F_5 = \mathbb{Q}\left(\sqrt{5}\right)$. The squares of the roots of $x^2 - x - 1$ (resp. $x^2 - 5$) sum to $11/4$ (resp. 10). In fact, $x^2 - x - 1$ is a normalized defining polynomial for F_5.

More generally, the following table records normalized defining polynomials $P_d(x)$ for the range specified.

$P_d(x)$	d square-free, $-20 < d < 20$
$x^2 - d$	$-17, -14, -13, -10, -6, -5, -2, -1, 2, 3, 6,$ $7, 10, 11, 14, 15, 19.$
$x^2 - x - (d-1)/4$	$-19, -15, -11, -7, -3, 5, 13, 17.$

The integers in the second row are precisely the square-free $d \neq 1$ congruent to 1 mod 4.

Given a number field F of degree $[F : \mathbb{Q}] = m$, we will use the following notation for a normalized defining polynomial:

$$P_f(x) = \sum_{n=0}^{m} p_m x^m. \tag{1}$$

A real (resp. imaginary) embedding of F is a field homomorphism $F \to \mathbb{R}$ (resp. $F \to \mathbb{C}$ whose image is not contained in $\mathbb{R}$). We denote by r_1 (resp. r_2) the number of real (resp. conjugate pairs of complex) embeddings of F. We have $r_1 + 2r_2 = [F : \mathbb{Q}]$. We refer to the pair (r_1, r_2) as the signature of F.

Example 2.4. Consider $F_d = \mathbb{Q}\left(\sqrt{d}\right)$ for d square-free. If $d > 0$ (resp. $d < 0$), then F_d has signature $(2, 0)$ (resp. $(0, 1)$) and we refer to F_d as real quadratic (resp. imaginary quadratic).

The ring $\mathcal{O}_F$ of integers in a number field F is the integral closure of $\mathbb{Z}$ in F. As a $\mathbb{Z}$-module, $\mathcal{O}_F$ has rank $[F : \mathbb{Q}]$. An integral basis for F is a $\mathbb{Z}$-basis for $\mathcal{O}_F$.

Example 2.5. If $F = F_d$ for d square-free, then we will write $\mathcal{O}_d = \mathcal{O}_F$. If d is congruent to either 2 or 3 mod 4, then $\mathcal{O}_d = \mathbb{Z}\left[\sqrt{d}\right]$. If d is congruent to 1 mod 4, then $\mathcal{O}_d = \mathbb{Z}\left[(1 + \sqrt{d})/2\right]$.

An order in F is a subring of F which is also a lattice in F. The ring $\mathcal{O}_F$ is the maximal order in F.

Example 2.6. Let $F = F_5$. Recall from Example 2.5 that $\mathcal{O}_F = \mathbb{Z}[(1 + \sqrt{5})/2]$. The proper subring $\mathbb{Z}\left[\sqrt{5}\right]$ is an order in F.

Orders will briefly appear again in Section 2.2.

If $[F : \mathbb{Q}] = m$, then let $\{b_1, \ldots, b_m\}$ be an integral basis for F, and let $\{e_1, \ldots, e_m\}$ be the set of real and complex embeddings of F. Consider the matrix

$$\begin{pmatrix} e_1(b_1) & \cdots & e_1(b_m) \\ \vdots & \ddots & \vdots \\ e_m(b_1) & \cdots & e_m(b_n) \end{pmatrix}. \tag{2}$$

The discriminant Δ_F of F is the square of the determinant of the matrix in Equation (2).

Example 2.7. For square-free d, we denote by Δ_d the discriminant of F_d. If d is congruent to 1 (resp. 2 or 3) mod 4, then Δ_d is equal to d (resp. $4d$). This agrees with the discriminant of the normalized defining polynomials in Example 2.3. If we order square-free d by the absolute value of the corresponding discriminant Δ_d, then the list begins as follows: $d = -3, -1, 5, -7, \pm 2, -11, 3, 13, -15, 17, -19, -5, \ldots$

If $f \in \mathbb{Z}$ is the discriminant of a quadratic field, then we refer to f as a fundamental discriminant.

Example 2.8. Ordered by their absolute value, the first few fundamental discriminants are as follows: $-3, -4, 5, -7, \pm 8, -11, 12, 13, -15, 17, -19, -20, 21, -23, \pm 24, 28, 29, \ldots$

We will not use fundamental discriminants until Example 2.23.

A number field F is necessarily a separable extension of $\mathbb{Q}$, that is, the defining polynomial has distinct roots in the algebraic closure. We refer to the field F as Galois if it is also a normal extension of $\mathbb{Q}$, that is, if every irreducible polynomial over $\mathbb{Q}$ with a root in F splits into linear factors over F.

Example 2.9. The first examples of non-Galois number fields have extension degree 3. For example, the following cubic polynomial $x^3 - x^2 + 1$ defines a non-Galois number field. The properties of this number field are recorded at [11, Number field 3.1.23.1].

The Galois closure F^{Gal} of a number field F is the smallest number field (with respect to inclusion) containing F which is Galois over $\mathbb{Q}$.

Example 2.10. The number field in Example 2.9 has Galois closure with normalized defining polynomial $x^6 - 3x^5 + 5x^4 - 5x^3 + 5x^2 - 3x + 1$.

The Galois group of a number field F with Galois closure F^{Gal} is the group of automorphisms $\sigma : F^{\text{Gal}} \to F^{\text{Gal}}$ such that, for all $\alpha \in \mathbb{Q}$, $\sigma(\alpha) = \alpha$.

Example 2.11. The following table lists the number field F with minimal $|\Delta_F|$ having the specified Galois group.

Order	Group	Normalized Defining Polynomial
2	C_2	$x^2 - x + 1$
3	C_3	$x^3 - x^2 - 2x + 1$
4	C_4	$x^4 - x^3 - x^2 - x + 1$
4	$C_2 \times C_2$	$x^4 - x^2 + 1$
5	C_5	$x^5 - x^4 - 4x^3 + 3x^2 + 3x - 1$
6	C_6	$x^6 - x^5 + x^4 - x^3 + x^2 - x + 1$
6	S_3	$x^3 - x^2 + 1$

The unit group $\mathcal{O}_F^\times$ of $\mathcal{O}_F$ is a finitely generated abelian group with cyclic torsion subgroup of order w_F and rank $r_F = r_1 + r_2 - 1$. To ease terminology, we will refer to $\mathcal{O}_F^\times$ as the units of F, the rank of $\mathcal{O}_F^\times$ as the rank of F and a set of generators for the rank-part of $\mathcal{O}_F^\times$ as the fundamental units of F. We denote by w_F the size of the torsion subgroup in $\mathcal{O}_F^\times$.

Example 2.12. If $F = F_d$ for d square-free, then we will write $w_d = w_F$. If $d \notin \{-1, -3\}$, then the units in F are ± 1 and so $w_d = 2$.

Example 2.13. If $d < 0$, then F has rank 0 and w_d is equal to 4 (resp. 6 and resp. 2) if $d = -1$ (resp. $d = -3$ and resp. $d \notin \{-1, -3\}$), with generator as per the following table:

Square-Free $d < 0$	-1	-3	Other
Generator for $\mathcal{O}_d^\times$	$\sqrt{-1}$	$(1 + \sqrt{-3})/2$	-1

Example 2.14. If $d > 0$, then F has rank 1 and any unit may be written as $\pm \epsilon_d^m$ for a fundamental unit ϵ_d and $m \in \mathbb{Z}$. The first few fundamental units for square-free $d > 0$ are as follows:

Square-free $d > 0$	2	3	5	6	7	10
ϵ_d	$1 + \sqrt{2}$	$2 + \sqrt{3}$	$(1 + \sqrt{5})/2$	$5 + 2\sqrt{6}$	$8 + 3\sqrt{7}$	$3 + \sqrt{10}$

If $\alpha \in \mathcal{O}_F$, then we denote the ideal it generates by (α). An ideal $I \leq \mathcal{O}_F$ is principal if it is generated by a single element.

Example 2.15. The ideal $\left(3, 1 + \sqrt{-5}\right) \leq \mathcal{O}_{-5}$ is non-principal.

The norm $N(I)$ of an ideal $I \leq \mathcal{O}_F$ is the size of the quotient ring $\mathcal{O}_F/I$. If $I = (\alpha)$ is a principal ideal, then $N(I) = \prod_{i=1}^{n} e_i(\alpha)$ with e_i as in Equation (2).

Example 2.16. The non-principal ideal from Example 2.15 has norm 3.

Example 2.17. If $F = \mathbb{Q}(\sqrt{d})$ and $I = (a + b\sqrt{d})$ is a principal ideal for some $a, b \in \mathbb{Z}$, then $N(I) = a^2 - db^2$.

A fractional ideal J is an $\mathcal{O}_F$-submodule of F such that there is a non-zero $\beta \in \mathcal{O}_F$ satisfying $\beta J \subset \mathcal{O}_F$. A principal fractional ideal is a factional ideal generated by a single element of F. The fractional ideals (resp. principal fractional ideals) of $\mathcal{O}_F$ form a group $\mathcal{J}_F$ (resp. $\mathcal{P}_F$) under multiplication. We refer to the quotient group $\mathcal{J}_F/\mathcal{P}_F$ as the ideal class group of F. We will denote the cardinality of the ideal class group by h_F, which is known as the (ideal) class number.

Example 2.18. If $F = F_d$ for square-free d, then we will write $h_d = h_F$. If $d < 0$, then it is known that $h_d = 1$ precisely when $d \in \{-1, -2, -3, -7, -11, -19, -43, -67, -163\}$. This fact will be relevant again in Section 2.2. The following table documents the class number h_d of $\mathbb{Q}\left(\sqrt{d}\right)$ for all square-free $-50 < d < 0$.

h_d	Square-free $-50 < d < 0$
1	$-1, -2, -3, -7, -11, -19, -43.$
2	$-5, -6, -10, -13, -15, -22, -35, -37.$
3	$-23, -31.$
4	$-14, -17, -21, -30, -33, -34, -39, -42, -46.$
5	$-47.$
6	$-26, -29, -38.$
7	
8	$-41.$

Example 2.19. The analogous table for $0 < d < 50$ looks rather different.

h_d	Square-free $0 < d < 50$
1	$2, 3, 5, 6, 7, 11, 13, 14, 17, 19, 21, 22, 23, 29, 31, 33, 37, 38, 41,$ $43, 46, 47.$
2	$10, 15, 26, 30, 34, 35, 39, 42.$

Remark 2.20. *Typically, the class number is introduced as quantifying the failure of unique factorization in $\mathcal{O}_F$. We have chosen to eschew this narrative.*

A proper ideal $\mathfrak{p} \leq \mathcal{O}_F$ is a prime ideal if, whenever the product $\alpha\beta$ of two elements $\alpha, \beta \in \mathcal{O}_F$ is in $\mathfrak{p}$, we have either $\alpha \in \mathfrak{p}$ or $\beta \in \mathfrak{p}$.

Example 2.21. Let p be a prime number and let d be a square-free integer. The principal ideal $(p) \leq \mathcal{O}_d$ is prime if and only if Δ_d is not a square mod p. If (p) is prime, then we refer to p as inert. If p does not divide Δ_d and Δ_d is a square mod p, then (p) is a product of two distinct prime ideals and p is said to be split. If p divides Δ_d, then (p) is the square of a prime ideal and p is said to be ramified.

To a number field F, one associates its Dedekind zeta function $\zeta_F(s)$. For complex numbers $\text{Re}(s) > 1$, it is both a sum and a product:

$$\zeta_F(s) = \sum_{0 \neq I \leq \mathcal{O}_F} N(I)^{-s} = \prod_{\mathfrak{p} \leq \mathcal{O}_F} \left(1 - N(\mathfrak{p})^{-s}\right)^{-1}, \tag{3}$$

in which the sum (resp. product) is over the non-zero (resp. prime) ideals of $\mathcal{O}_F$.

Example 2.22. If $F = \mathbb{Q}$, then, for $\mathrm{Re}(s) > 1$, we recover $\zeta_F(s) = \sum_{n=1}^{\infty} n^{-s}$, that is, the Riemann zeta function $\zeta(s)$.

Example 2.23. For square-free d, we will write $\zeta_d(s) = \zeta_{F_d}(s)$. We have

$$\zeta_d(s) = \prod_{p \text{ split}} \left(1 - p^{-s}\right)^{-2} \prod_{p \text{ inert}} \left(1 - p^{-2s}\right)^{-1} \prod_{p \text{ ramified}} \left(1 - p^{-s}\right)^{-1}.$$

If d is a fundamental discriminant, then we have $\zeta_{F_d}(s) = \zeta(s)L(\chi_d, s)$, where χ_d is a Dirichlet character and

$$L(\chi_d, s) = \sum_{n=1}^{\infty} \chi_d(n) n^{-s}. \tag{4}$$

A given Dedekind zeta function $\zeta_F(s)$ does not uniquely determine a number field F.

Example 2.24. Let N_1 (resp. N_2) be the number field which has normalized defining polynomial $x^8 - 24x^4 - 3$ (resp. $x^8 - 3$). These degree 8 number fields are recorded at [11, number field 8.2.36691771392.1] (resp. [11, number field 8.2.36691771392.2]). Although these fields are not isomorphic, it is known that $\zeta_{N_1}(s) = \zeta_{N_2}(s)$. Non-isomorphic number fields with matching Dedekind zeta functions are said to be arithmetically equivalent. Arithmetically equivalent number fields have identical signatures and discriminants, and their Galois closures have isomorphic Galois groups. One the other hand, it is not necessarily the case that arithmetically equivalent number fields have equal class number.

For $n \in \mathbb{Z}_{>0}$, letting a_n denote the number of ideals in $\mathcal{O}_F$ with norm n, we may write

$$\zeta_F(s) = \sum_{n=1}^{\infty} a_n n^{-s}. \tag{5}$$

We refer to the set $\{a_n\}_{n=1}^{\infty}$ as the Dirichlet coefficients of F.

Example 2.25. If $F = F_d$ for a fundamental discriminant d, then $a_n = \sum_{m|n} \chi_d(m)$. In particular, for prime p, we have $a_p = 1 + \chi(p)$. The ramified primes in F_d are precisely those such that $a_p = 1$.

Even if two number fields are not arithmetically equivalent, then they might still have several Dirichlet coefficients in common.

Example 2.26. The number fields $F_{-105} = \mathbb{Q}\left(\sqrt{-105}\right)$ and $F_{-210} = \mathbb{Q}\left(\sqrt{-210}\right)$ are non-isomorphic and not arithmetically equivalent. Their Dedekind zeta functions agree to 10 coefficients with the Riemann zeta function:

$$1 + 2^{-s} + 3^{-s} + 4^{-s} + 5^{-s} + 6^{-s} + 8^{-s} + 9^{-s} + 10^{-s} + \cdots$$

The next non-trivial term for F_{-105} (resp. F_{-210}) is 2×11^{-s} (resp. 12^{-s}).

The Dedekind zeta function exhibits meromorphic continuation to $\mathbb{C}$, which is holomorphic away from a simple pole at $s = 1$. The analytic class number formula is an expression for the residue at the unique simple pole:

$$\lim_{s \to 1}(s - 1)\zeta_F(s) = \frac{2^{r_1} \cdot (2\pi)^{r_2} \cdot \operatorname{Reg}_F \cdot h_F}{w_F \cdot \sqrt{|\Delta_F|}}, \tag{6}$$

in which the only notation yet to be explained is the regulator Reg_F. We will not give a complete definition of Reg_F, but we will be content with the following example.

Example 2.27. If $d > 0$ is a fundamental discriminant, then $\operatorname{Reg}_{F_d} = \log \epsilon_d$, where ϵ_d is as in Example 2.14. For square-free d, Equation (6) simplifies to

$$h_d = \begin{cases} \dfrac{w_d \sqrt{|d|}}{2\pi} L(1, \chi_d), & d < 0, \\[3mm] \dfrac{\sqrt{d}}{\log \epsilon_d} L(1, \chi), & d > 0. \end{cases} \tag{7}$$

Remark 2.28. *There exist arithmetically equivalent fields with different class numbers. Equation (6) implies only that the product* $\operatorname{Reg}_F \cdot h_F$ *is determined by* $\zeta_F(s)$.

If $\Gamma_{\mathbb{R}}(s) = \pi^{-s/2}\Gamma(s/2)$, $\Gamma_{\mathbb{C}}(s) = 2(2\pi)^{-s}\Gamma(s)$ and $\xi_F(s) = |\Delta_F|^{s/2}\Gamma_{\mathbb{R}}(s)^{r_1}\Gamma_{\mathbb{C}}(s)^{r_2}\zeta_F(s)$, then we have the functional equation $\xi_F(s) = \xi_F(1-s)$. It follows that $\zeta_F(s)$ vanishes to order r_F at $s = 0$ with leading Taylor coefficient

$$\lim_{s \to 0} s^{-r_F} \zeta_F(s) = -\frac{h_F \cdot \mathrm{Reg}_F}{w_F}. \tag{8}$$

2.2. *Elliptic curves*

An elliptic curve over $\mathbb{Q}$ is a pair (E, Q), where E is a non-singular curve of genus 1 defined over $\mathbb{Q}$ and $\underline{Q} \in E(\mathbb{Q})$. Each elliptic curve over $\mathbb{Q}$ may be described by a Weierstraß equation

$$y^2 + w_1 xy + w_3 y = x^3 + w_2 x^2 + w_4 x + w_6, \tag{9}$$

where $w_1, w_2, w_3, w_4, w_6 \in \mathbb{Q}$.

Remark 2.29. *Though the indexing in Equation* (9) *may seem strange, it is conventional. For example, see* [12, Section III.1].

Example 2.30. The following two Weierstraß equations define isomorphic elliptic curves over $\mathbb{Q}$ with distinguished point $(1, 0)$:

$$y^2 + y = x^3 - x^2, \quad y^2 + 2xy + 3y = x^3 + x^2 - 2x. \tag{10}$$

The discriminant Δ_W of a Weierstraß equation as in Equation (9) is the quantity

$$\begin{aligned}
\Delta_W = {} & - \left(w_1^2 + 4w_2 \right)^2 \left(w_1^2 w_6 + 4w_2 w_6 - w_1 w_3 w_4 + w_2 w_3^2 - w_4^2 \right) \\
& - 8 \left(2w_4 + w_1 w_3 \right)^3 - 27 \left(w_3^2 + 4w_6 \right) \\
& + 9 \left(w_1^2 + 4w_2 \right) \left(2w_4 + w_1 w_3 \right) \left(w_3^2 + 4w_6 \right).
\end{aligned} \tag{11}$$

There is an infinitude of discriminants for the same curve, depending on the chosen Weierstraß equation. A minimal Weierstraß equation for an elliptic curve E is a Weierstraß equation as per Equation (9), with $w_1, w_2, w_3, w_4, w_6 \in \mathbb{Z}$, so that $|\Delta_W|$ is minimized. We refer to the discriminant of a minimal Weierstraß equation as the discriminant of E and denote it by Δ_E.

Example 2.31. The Weierstraß equation $y^2 + y = x^3 - x^2$ is minimal for the curve in Example 2.30, which has discriminant -11. The properties of this curve are recorded at [11, Elliptic curve 11a3].

Let p be a prime integer and let E be an elliptic curve. Reducing a minimal Weierstraß equation for E modulo p yields an algebraic curve over the finite field $\mathbb{F}_p$. If the reduction is singular (resp. non-singular), then E is said to have bad (resp. good) reduction at p.

Example 2.32. The curve in Example 2.30 has bad reduction only at the prime $p = 11$.

If E has bad reduction at a prime p, then there are various subsequent possibilities for the reduction type. The basic distinction is between additive (when the reduction has a cuspidal singularity) and multiplicative (when the reduction has a nodal singularity). In the additive case, the cusp has only one tangent, whereas in the multiplicative case, the node has two distinct tangents. If a curve has multiplicative reduction at p, then it is said to be split (resp. non-split) if the tangents are (resp. are not) defined over $\mathbb{F}_p$.

Example 2.33. The curve in Example 2.30 has split multiplicative reduction at $p = 11$.

The conductor $N_E \in \mathbb{Z}_{>0}$ of an elliptic curve has the form

$$N_E = \prod_{p \text{ bad}} p^{e_p}, \tag{12}$$

in which p ranges over the primes of bad reduction for E and the exponent $e_p \in \mathbb{Z}_{>0}$ depends on p and the reduction of E mod p. We defer to [13, Section IV.10] for the definition of e_p and content ourselves here with only the following example.

Example 2.34. Let p be a prime of bad reduction for an elliptic curve E. If E has multiplicative reduction at p, then $e_p = 1$. If $p \geq 5$ and E has additive reduction at p, then $e_p = 2$. If $p = 2$ (resp. $p = 3$) and E has additive reduction at p, then $e_p \in \{2, \ldots, 8\}$ (resp. $\{2, \ldots, 5\}$).

Example 2.35. The curve in Example 2.30 has conductor $N_E = 11$.

It is well known that the rational points $E(\mathbb{Q})$ form a finitely generated abelian group. We refer to the rank (resp. torsion subgroup) of this group as the rank r_E (resp. torsion subgroup $E(\mathbb{Q})_{\text{tors}}$) of E. An elliptic curve E has finitely many rational points if and only if $r_E = 0$.

Example 2.36. The curve in Example 2.30 has rank $r_E = 0$ and torsion subgroup $E(\mathbb{Q})_{\text{tors}} \cong \mathbb{Z}/5\mathbb{Z}$.

An isogeny from one elliptic curve E_1 to another E_2 is a nonconstant morphism $\phi : E_1 \to E_2$ such that $\phi(O) = O$.

Example 2.37. If E_1 is isogenous to E_2, then $r_{E_1} = r_{E_2}$. One the other hand, torsion subgroups are not isogeny invariants. For example, the curve in Example 2.30 is isogenous to the curve with minimal Weierstraß equation $y^2 + y = x^3 - x^2 - 7820x - 263580$ which has trivial torsion subgroup. The properties of the latter curve are recorded at [11, Elliptic curve 11a2].

An endomorphism of E is an isogeny $E \to E$. We denote the set of endomorphisms of E by $\text{End}(E)$.

Example 2.38. For an integer m, we may define the isogeny

$$[m] : E \to E$$
$$[m](P) = P + P + \cdots + P.$$

This yields an embedding $\mathbb{Z} \hookrightarrow \text{End}(E)$. The set $\text{End}(E)$ is the ring of characteristic zero with no zero divisors.

We say that E is generic if $\text{End}(E) = \mathbb{Z}$. If E is not generic, that is, its endomorphism ring is strictly larger than $\mathbb{Z}$, then we will refer to E as exceptional.

Example 2.39. To justify the terminology, we note that only around 0.2% of curves with conductor bounded by 1,000,000 in [11] are generic. The curve in Example 2.30 is generic.

Example 2.40. The Weierstraß equation $y^2 + y = x^3 - 270x - 1708$ defines an exceptional elliptic curve with conductor 27 (the smallest possible). The properties of this curve are recorded at [11, Elliptic curve 27a1].

For any exceptional elliptic curve E defined over $\mathbb{C}$, it can be shown that $\text{End}(E)$ is an order in an imaginary quadratic field F_d for some $d < 0$. By way of contrast to the generic endomorphisms defined in Example 2.38 — which are given by integer multiplication — exceptional curves are usually said to exhibit complex multiplication.

For E to be defined over $\mathbb{Q}$, the imaginary quadratic field F_d must have $h_d = 1$.

Example 2.41. The exceptional curve in Example 2.40 has CM by the ring $\mathbb{Z}\left[\frac{1+\sqrt{-27}}{2}\right]$. We caution the reader that 27 is not square-free.

If E has good reduction at p, then we define the local zeta function of E at p to be

$$Z\left(E/\mathbb{F}_p, T\right) = \exp\left(\#E(\mathbb{F}_p)T^k/k\right). \tag{13}$$

It is known that $Z\left(E/\mathbb{F}_p, T\right)$ may be rewritten as a rational function of the form

$$Z\left(E/\mathbb{F}_p, T\right) = \frac{L_p(T)}{(1-T)(1-pT)}, \tag{14}$$

where

$$L_p(T) = 1 - (p+1-\#E(\mathbb{F}_p))\,T + pT^2 \in \mathbb{Z}[T]. \tag{15}$$

For a good prime p, we introduce the notation

$$a_p = p + 1 - \#E(\mathbb{F}_p) \tag{16}$$

so that we have $L_p(T) = 1 - a_p T + pT^2$.

For $X \in \mathbb{R}$, we denote by $\pi_E(X)$ the set of primes $p \leq X$ such that E has good reduction at p. We are interested in the limiting distribution of $p^{-1/2}a_p$ as p varies in $\pi_E(X)$. This distribution is encapsulated in the moment sequence $(M_n)_{n=1}^{\infty}$, where

$$M_n = \lim_{X\to\infty} \left(\frac{1}{\#\pi_E(X)} \sum_{p\in\pi_E(X)} \left(p^{-1/2}a_p\right)^n\right). \tag{17}$$

It is known that there are only two possibilities for the moment sequences:

$$M_n = \begin{cases} 1,0,1,0,2,0,5,0,14,0,42,0,132,\ldots, & E \text{ generic,} \\ 1,0,1,0,3,0,10,0,35,0,126,0,462,\ldots, & E \text{ exceptional.} \end{cases}$$

The L-function of an elliptic curve E is defined by taking an Euler product of the form

$$L(E/\mathbb{Q}, s) = \prod_{p \mid N_E} \left(1 - a_p p^{-s}\right)^{-1} \prod_{p \nmid N_E} \left(1 - a_p p^{-s} + p^{-2s}\right)^{-1}, \quad (18)$$

which converges for $\text{Re}(s) > 2$. Expanding the product in Equation (18) yields a Dirichlet series for $L(E, s)$.

Example 2.42. An elliptic L-function determines an elliptic curve only up to isogeny. The non-isogenous elliptic curves [11, Elliptic curve 2310.a] (resp. [11, Elliptic curve 2310.b]) share their first 10 Dirichlet coefficients:

$$1^{-s} - 2^{-s} - 3^{-s} + 4^{-s} - 5^{-s} + 6^{-s} - 7^{-s} - 8^{-s} + 9^{-1} + 10^{-s}.$$

The 11th term is 11^{-s} (resp. -11^{-s}).

2.3. *Genus 2 curves*

A smooth, projectively integral genus 2 curve over $\mathbb{Q}$ is defined by a Weierstraß equation of the form

$$y^2 + h(x)y = f(x),$$

for $f(x), h(x) \in \mathbb{Z}[x]$ with $\deg(f) \leq 6$ and $\deg(h) \leq 3$.

As with elliptic curves, there is a notion of discriminant which varies with the choice of Weierstraß equation. A minimal Weierstraß equation is one for which the absolute value of the discriminant is minimized. The discriminant of a genus 2 curve is the discriminant of a minimal Weierstraß equation.

Example 2.43. The Weierstraß equation $y^2 + (x^3 + x + 1)y = x^5 + x^4$ is minimal with discriminant -169. The properties of this curve are recorded at [11, Genus 2 curve 169.1.169.1].

While an elliptic curve may have infinitely many rational points (iff its rank is positive), a genus 2 curve may only have finitely many. The Jacobian of a genus 2 curve is a 2-dimensional abelian variety, the rational points on which we define a finitely generated abelian group. We refer to the rank (resp. torsion subgroup) of this group as the rank (resp. torsion subgroup) of the curve.

Example 2.44. The genus 2 curve in Example 2.43 has rank 0 and torsion subgroup $\mathbb{Z}/19\mathbb{Z}$.

We say that a genus 2 curve over $\mathbb{Q}$ has good reduction at a prime p if its Jacobian has an integral model whose reduction mod p defines a smooth 2-dimensional variety over $\mathbb{F}_p$. Otherwise, we say that the curve has bad reduction at p.

Example 2.45. The genus 2 curve in Example 2.43 has bad reduction only at $p = 13$.

The conductor of a genus 2 curve is a positive integer divisible only by the primes of bad reduction. The exponent of a prime appearing in the conductor depends on the reduction type.

Example 2.46. The genus 2 curve in Example 2.43 has conductor 169.

3. Arithmetic Conjectures

In this section, we discuss conjectural properties of the arithmetic objects previously introduced. These conjectures formed the motivation for our machine learning endeavors in [7–9].

3.1. *Class numbers of real quadratic fields*

Recall that there is a known finite list of square-free $d < 0$ such that F_d has class number 1. As for $d > 0$, it is unknown whether or not the analogous list is finite. Verifying the infinitude of this list is known as the Gauss class number problem for real quadratic fields.

The following table lists the class number of F_d for all square-free d in the range specified.

h_d	$0 < d < 60$
1	$2, 3, 5, 6, 7, 11, 13, 14, 17, 19, 21, 22, 23, 29, 31, 33, 37, 38, 41, 43, 46,$ $47, 53, 57, 59.$
2	$10, 15, 26, 30, 34, 25, 29, 42, 51, 55, 28.$

As d grows, class number 1 seems to persist while larger class numbers begin to appear. The following table lists the class number of F_d for all square-free d in the range specified.

h_d	$100 < d < 160$
1	$101, 103, 107, 109, 113, 118, 127, 129, 131, 133, 134, 137, 139,$ $141, 149, 151, 152, 157 158.$
2	$102, 104, 105, 106, 110, 111, 114, 115, 122, 123, 138, 143, 146, 154,$ $155, 159.$
3	$142.$
4	$130, 145.$

Real quadratic fields F_d of class number 1 occur for square-free $d > 0$ larger orders of magnitude; see, for example, the following table.

h_d	$1000 < d < 1060$
1	$1006, 1013, 1019, 1021, 1031, 1033, 1039, 1041, 1046, 1049,$ $1051, 1057.$
2	$1001, 1005, 1037.$
3	
4	$1003, 1010, 1011, 1015, 1042, 1045.$
5	
6	
7	$1009.$
8	$1023.$

In all three tables, not only does class number 1 appear, it moreover seems to dominate. This can be quantified by the so-called Cohen–Lenstra heuristics, which states that around 76% of real quadratic fields with prime discriminant has class number 1 [2].

Example 3.1. For square-free d, recall that $\Delta_d \in \{d, 4d\}$. If Δ_d is prime, then d must be a prime congruent to 1 mod 4. For every prime $p \equiv 1 \mod 4$ such that $p < 229$, we have $h_p = 1$. We note that $h_{229} = 3$.

Remark 3.2. *Cohen–Lenstra also developed heuristics applicable to imaginary quadratic fields* [2]. *For example, around 43% of imaginary quadratic fields are expected to have class number divisible by* 3. *In particular, there is a bias in the distribution of* $\{h_d \bmod 3 : d < 0\}$.

3.2. *Ranks of elliptic curves over* $\mathbb{Q}$

Another question regarding the possible infinitude of a set concerns $\{r_E : E$ elliptic curve over $\mathbb{Q}\}$. Opinions on whether or not this set is infinite have varied over time, as reviewed in [4, Introduction]. On one hand, broadly accepted statistical models based on random matrix theory indicate that the set is finite. On the other hand, if $\mathbb{Q}$ is replaced by a function field, then the analogous set is known to be infinite.

Example 3.3. An explicit elliptic curve with rank ≥ 28 was found by Elkies in 2006. In [4], an elliptic curve with rank exactly 20 is given.

While the Euler product of an elliptic L-function converges only for $\mathrm{Re}(s) > 2$, if E is defined over $\mathbb{Q}$, then $L(E, s)$ is known to admit analytic continuation to $\mathbb{C}$ and functional equation relating the value at s to $2 - s$:

$$\Lambda(E, s) = \left(\frac{\sqrt{N}}{2\pi}\right)^{-s} \Gamma(s) L(E, s) = \pm \Lambda(E, 2 - s). \qquad (19)$$

So far, the story is similar to that of Dedekind zeta functions reviewed earlier. Pursuing this comparison further, one might wish for an expression for the leading Laurent coefficients comparable to Equation (6) or (8). The conjecture of Birch–Swinnerton-Dyer asserts that $L(E, s)$ vanishes to order r_E at $s = 1$, with leading Taylor coefficient

$$\frac{L^{(r)}(E, 1)}{r!} = \frac{\#\mathrm{TS}(E) \cdot \Omega_E \cdot \mathrm{Reg}_E \cdot T_E}{(\#E(\mathbb{Q})_{\mathrm{tors}})^2}, \qquad (20)$$

in which we have not defined the Tate–Shafarevich group $\mathrm{TS}(E)$, the real period Ω_E, the elliptic regulator Reg_E and the Tamagawa product T_E. To do so clearly would take us too far off course, but we will content ourself with the following example.

Example 3.4. Let E denote the elliptic curve with Weierstraß equation $y^2 + y = x^3 - x$ from Example 2.31. We have $r_E = 0$, $\#\mathrm{TS}(E) = 1$, $\Omega_E \approx 6.3460$, $\mathrm{Reg}_E = 1$, $T_E = 1$, $\#E(\mathbb{Q})_{\mathrm{tors}} = 5$ and

$$L(E, 1) \approx \frac{6.3460}{25} = 0.25384.$$

We will dwell on the Tate–Shafarevich group only long enough to note that implicit in Equation (20) is the assertion that $\mathrm{TS}(E)$ is finite. While finiteness of $\mathrm{TS}(E)$ is conjectural, it is known that, if $\mathrm{TS}(E)$ is finite, then its order is a square integer.

3.3. *Moment sequences for genus 2 curves over* $\mathbb{Q}$

The local zeta function of a genus 2 curve C is defined as in Equation (13) with E replaced by C. Equation (14) remains valid, with $L_p(T)$ taking the form

$$1 + a_{1,p}T + a_{2,p}T^2 + a_{1,p}p^3 T^3 + p^2 T^4,$$

for some $a_{1,p}, a_{2,p} \in \mathbb{Z}$.

For $X \in \mathbb{R}$, we denote by $\pi_C(X)$ the set of primes $p \leq X$ such that C has good reduction at p. For $i \in \{1, 2\}$, we are interested in the limiting distribution of $p^{-1/2}a_{i,p}$ as p varies in $\pi_C(X)$. This distribution is encapsulated in the moment sequence $(M_{i,n})_{n=1}^\infty$, where

$$M_{i,n} = \lim_{X \to \infty} \left(\frac{1}{\#\pi_C(X)} \sum_{p \in \pi_E(X)} \left(p^{-1/2}a_{i,p} \right)^n \right). \tag{21}$$

It is conjectured that there are 34 possibilities for the moment sequences $(M_{i,n})_{n=1}^\infty$ attached to genus 2 curves over $\mathbb{Q}$ (see [6,10]).

The 34 distributions may be specified using the canonical Haar measure on a compact Lie group known as the Sato–Tate group. The Sato–Tate group $\mathrm{ST}(C)$ of a genus 2 curve is a subgroup $\mathrm{USp}(4)$ satisfying certain axioms. If $\mathrm{ST}(C) = \mathrm{USp}(4)$, then C is said to be generic. Otherwise, C is said to be exceptional.

Example 3.5. The curve with Weierstraß equation $y^2 + (x^3 + 1)y = x^2 + x$ (resp. $y^2 + (x^3 + 1)y = x^4 + x^2$) has Sato–Tate group $\mathrm{USp}(4)$ (resp. $\mathrm{SU}(2) \times \mathrm{SU}(2)$). The properties of these curves are recorded at [11, Genus 2 curve 249.*a*.249.1] (resp. [11, Genus 2 curve 294.*a*.294.1]).

Remark 3.6. *An elliptic curve may also be assigned a Sato–Tate group. A generic elliptic curve over $\mathbb{Q}$ has Sato–Tate group $\mathrm{SU}(2)$, and an exceptional elliptic curve over $\mathbb{Q}$ has Sato–Tate group the normalizer $N(U(1))$ of $U(1)$ in $\mathrm{SU}(2)$. As with elliptic curves, the Sato–Tate group of a genus 2 curve corresponds to the structure of the endomorphism ring of its Jacobian.*

4. Supervised Learning Strategies

In this section, we describe three basic supervised learning classifiers, namely, naive Bayes, random forest and logistic regression. For each classifier under discussion, we offer simplified (but detailed) worked examples using small amounts of arithmetic data and recall the outcomes of previous experiments using much larger datasets.

We will also touch upon the k-nearest neighbors and linear regression classifiers. As with the previous sections, more thorough treatments are available, for example [5].

4.1. *Abstract setup*

Throughout this section, we will be given a set of training vectors $A = \{\underline{a}_j = (a_{j1}, \ldots, a_{jd}) : j = 1, \ldots, J\}$, a set of output classes $C = \{C_k : k = 1, \ldots, K\}$ and a training map $T : A \to C$ which assigns a class to each vector. The integers d, J and K will all vary with the context. Given an input vector $\underline{a} = (a_1, \ldots, a_d) \notin A$, the intention is to assign a meaning to $T(\underline{a})$. We interpret this process as predicting an output class for $\underline{a}$. In what follows, we will review three specific strategies for doing so.

4.2. *Naive Bayes classifier*

On the face of it, the naive Bayes classifier is entirely reasonable: given an input vector, naive Bayes chooses the output class with maximal probability. What is arguably less reasonable is the manner in which this probability is estimated, as we will see in the following.

The "Bayes" in "naive Bayes" refers to the fact that the probability of a class given its features is calculated via Bayes theorem.

That is, given an vector $\underline{a}$, the probability of class C_k is given by

$$P(C_k|\underline{a}) = \frac{P(C_k)P(\underline{a})}{P(\underline{a})} = \frac{P(C_k, a_1, \ldots, a_d)}{P(\underline{a})},$$

where $P(C_k, a_1, \ldots, a_d)$ is the joint probability. The "naive" in "naive Bayes" refers to the subsequent (and possibly unreasonable) assumption that the components a_i of $\underline{a}$ are independent variables. Under this assumption, we have

$$P(C_k|\underline{a}) = \rho \prod_{i=1}^{d} P(a_i|C_k),$$

for some $\rho \in \mathbb{R}_{>0}$.

In the article [7], a naive Bayes classifier was shown to distinguish between various Sato–Tate groups of genus 2 curves to high accuracy. One technical obstacle was the small amount of training data for certain Sato–Tate groups. To circumvent this, the classifiers were trained on random matrix datasets (in line with the Sato–Tate conjecture stated in [6,10]).

The following examples demonstrate simple implementations of a naive Bayes classifier on data from the theory of arithmetic curves.

Example 4.1. Let $\mathbf{E}_1$ (resp. $\mathbf{G}_1$) denote the family of exceptional (resp. generic) isogeny classes for elliptic curves over $\mathbb{Q}$. The following table lists the first *five* isogeny classes in $\mathbf{E}_1$, labeled as on [11], alongside the corresponding first 10 values of a_p (p prime). In the final row, we count the number of times $a_p = 0$ for each p.

Isogeny Class	a_5	a_7	a_{11}	a_{13}	a_{17}	a_{19}	a_{23}	a_{29}	a_{31}	a_{37}
27a	0	−1	0	5	0	−7	0	0	−4	11
32a	−1	0	0	6	2	0	0	−10	0	2
36a	0	−4	0	2	0	8	0	0	−4	−10
49a	0	0	4	0	0	0	8	2	0	−6
64a	2	0	0	−6	2	0	0	10	0	2
#$\{a_p = 0\}$	3	3	4	1	2	3	4	2	3	0

The following table lists *five* randomly chosen isogeny classes in $\mathbf{G}_1$ with conductor $25 < N < 65$, labeled as on [11], alongside the corresponding first 10 values of a_p (p prime). In the final row, we again count the number of times $a_p = 0$ for each p.

Isogeny Class	a_5	a_7	a_{11}	a_{13}	a_{17}	a_{19}	a_{23}	a_{29}	a_{31}	a_{37}
$26a$	-3	-1	6	1	-3	2	0	6	-4	-7
$30a$	-1	-4	0	2	6	-4	0	-6	8	2
$35a$	-1	1	-3	5	3	2	-6	3	-4	2
$46a$	4	-4	2	-2	-2	-2	1	2	0	-4
$62a$	-2	0	0	2	-6	4	8	2	-1	10
$\#\{a_p = 0\}$	0	1	2	0	0	0	2	0	1	0

Consider the elliptic curve $33a$, which has

$$(a_5, a_7, a_{11}, a_{13}, a_{17}, a_{19}, a_{23}, a_{29}, a_{31}, a_{39})$$
$$= (-2, 4, 1, -2, -2, 0, 8, -6, -8, 6). \tag{22}$$

We immediately encounter the issue that some of these components have probability zero in our training data (for example, a_7 is never equal to 4). Based on arithmetic intuition that the classification of exceptional curves is related to $\#\{p : a_p = 0\}$, let us simplify the vectors by replacing the numerical value with the label z (resp. n) if it is zero (resp. non-zero) so that

$$(a_5, a_7, a_{11}, a_{13}, a_{17}, a_{19}, a_{23}, a_{29}, a_{31}, a_{39})$$
$$\mapsto (n, n, n, n, n, z, n, n, n, n). \tag{23}$$

The following table records the probability that the a_p would be labeled as per Equation (23), conditional on the assumption that $33a$ is exceptional.

p	5	7	11	13	17	19	23	29	31	39
$P(a_p \mid 33a \in \mathbf{E}_1)$	$\frac{2}{5}$	$\frac{2}{5}$	$\frac{1}{5}$	$\frac{4}{5}$	$\frac{3}{5}$	$\frac{3}{5}$	$\frac{1}{5}$	$\frac{3}{5}$	$\frac{2}{5}$	1

Assuming that the labels are independent variables, we deduce that $P(33a \in \mathbf{E}_1|(a_5, \ldots, a_{37}))$ is proportional to

$$\frac{4320}{9765625} \approx 0.0004. \tag{24}$$

The following table records the probability that the a_p would be labeled as per Equation (23), conditional on the assumption that $33a$ is generic.

p	5	7	11	13	17	19	23	29	31	39
$P(a_p|33a \in \mathbf{G}_1)$	1	$\frac{4}{5}$	$\frac{3}{5}$	1	1	1	$\frac{3}{5}$	1	$\frac{4}{5}$	1

Assuming again that the labels are independent variables, we deduce that $P(33a \in \mathbf{G}_1|(a_5, \ldots, a_{37}))$ is proportional to

$$\frac{144}{625} = 0.2304. \tag{25}$$

Comparing the values in Equations (24) and (25), we see that Naive Bayes predicts that $33a$ is generic. This prediction agrees with rigorous computation.

Example 4.2. Let us emulate Example 4.1 with genus 2 curves. Let $\mathbf{E}_2$ (resp. $\mathbf{G}_2$) denote the family of exceptional (resp. generic) isogeny classes for genus 2 curves over $\mathbb{Q}$. The following table lists the first five isogeny classes in $\mathbf{E}_2$, labeled as on [11], alongside the corresponding first 10 values of $(a_{1,p}, a_{2,p})$ (p prime). Inspired by the previous example, in the final row, we count the number of times $a_{1,p} = 0$ for each p.

Isogeny Class	$(a_{1,5}, a_{2,5})$	$(a_{1,7}, a_{2,7})$	$(a_{1,11}, a_{2,11})$	$(a_{1,13}, a_{2,13})$	$(a_{1,17}, a_{2,17})$
169a	$(0, -7)$	$(0, 7)$	$(0, 11)$	$(5, 5)$	$(-3, -8)$
196a	$(0, 10)$	$(-2, 1)$	$(0, 22)$	$(8, 42)$	$(-12, 70)$
256a	$(2, 2)$	$(0, -10)$	$(-2, 2)$	$(2, 2)$	$(4, 38)$
294a	$(2, 10)$	$(0, -1)$	$(-4, 22)$	$(6, 34)$	$(0, -2)$
324a	$(0, -5)$	$(2, -3)$	$(-3, -2)$	$(2, -9)$	$(6, 43)$
$\#\{a_{1,p} = 0\}$	3	3	2	0	1

The following table lists the first *five* isogeny classes in $\mathbf{G}_2$, labeled as on [11], alongside the corresponding first 10 values of (a_{p_1}, a_{p_2}) (p prime). In the final row, we again count the number of times $a_{1,p} = 0$ for each p.

Isogeny Class	$(a_{1,5}, a_{2,5})$	$(a_{1,7}, a_{2,7})$	$(a_{1,11}, a_{2,11})$	$(a_{1,13}, a_{2,13})$	$(a_{1,17}, a_{2,17})$
$249a$	$(0, 2)$	$(1, -2)$	$(-1, 2)$	$(0, -2)$	$(1, 28)$
$277a$	$(1, -2)$	$(-1, 3)$	$(2, 4)$	$(-3, 7)$	$(4, 28)$
$295a$	$(2, 6)$	$(-1, 0)$	$(-2, 14)$	$(2, -2)$	$(0, -10)$
$349a$	$(1, 7)$	$(2, 12)$	$(-1, -6)$	$(-2, 14)$	$(-3, 11)$
$353a$	$(-1, 2)$	$(0, -6)$	$(-2, 1)$	$(1, -8)$	$(-6, 27)$
$\#\{a_{1,p} = 0\}$	1	1	0	1	1

Consider isogeny class $360a$, which has

$$(a_{1,5}, a_{1,7}, a_{1,11}, a_{1,13}, a_{1,17}) = (1, 0, 0, 4, -4) \mapsto (n, z, z, n, n), \quad (26)$$

where the labeling is as in Example 4.1. The following table records the probability that a_p would be labeled as per Equation (26), conditional on the assumption that $360a$ is exceptional.

p		5	7	11	13	17
$P(a_{1,p}|360a \in \mathbf{E}_2)$		$\frac{2}{5}$	$\frac{3}{5}$	$\frac{2}{5}$	1	$\frac{4}{5}$

The following table records the probability that a_p would be labeled as per Equation (23), conditional on the assumption that $360a$ is generic.

p		5	7	11	13	17
$P(a_{1,p}|360a \in \mathbf{G}_2)$		$\frac{4}{5}$	$\frac{1}{5}$	0	$\frac{4}{5}$	$\frac{4}{5}$

Assuming that $a_{1,p}$ are independent, we deduce that $P(360a \in \mathbf{E}_2|(a_{5,1}, \ldots, a_{17,1}))$ is proportional to $\frac{48}{625}$, whereas $P(360a \in \mathbf{G}_2|(a_{5,1}, \ldots, a_{17,1})) = 0$. Naive Bayes therefore predicts that $360a$ is exceptional, which agrees with rigorous computation.

Though it is beyond the scope of the present text, we also highlight that an unsupervised principal component analysis was observed to distinguish between generic and non-generic genus 2 curves [7].

4.3. *Random forests and nearest neighbors*

For our purposes, a tree is a tool for partitioning $\mathbb{R}^d$ into hypercubes and associating an output class with each. For binary classifications ($K = 2$), one begins by choosing a split variable a_j and a split point s_j. This choice leads to a partition $\{a_j \leq s_1\} \cup \{a_j > s_j\}$. Subsequently, the regions $\{a_j \leq s_j\}$ and $\{a_j > s_j\}$ may each be split further using the variables a_i $(i \neq j)$ and so on. The choice of split variables and split points, and the assignment of output classes to each region, is reviewed in [5, 9.2.3].

The "forest" part of "random forest" is because the algorithm creates several trees. The "random" part of "random forest" is because, for each tree, a random choice of variables eligible to be split is made. Given an input vector, each tree in the forest makes a prediction based on the class of the vector in the corresponding partition of $\mathbb{R}^d$. The random forest classifier subsequently predicts the class predicted by a majority of trees.

As discussed in [5, Section 15.4.3], the random forest classifier has much in common with the k-nearest neighbors classifier. Given an input vector $\underline{a}$, the latter classifier makes its predictions by determining the k training vectors nearest to $\underline{a}$ and predicting the class to which the majority belong.

In [8], it is shown that a random forest classifier is able to distinguish real quadratic fields of class number 1 from those of class number 2. In the following examples, we implement the k-nearest neighbors algorithm on a small dataset of real quadratic fields. In Example 4.4, we will incorporate some class number 3 fields.

Example 4.3. Let $T = \{\text{squarefree } d > 0 : 200 < \Delta_d < 229\}$. The following table records the class number h_t and the Dirichlet coefficient vectors (a_2, a_3, a_4, a_5) associated with $\mathbb{Q}(\sqrt{t})$.

$t \in T$	h_t	a_2	a_3	a_4	a_5
201	1	2	1	3	2
51	2	1	1	1	2
205	2	0	2	1	1
209	1	2	0	3	2
213	1	0	1	1	0
217	1	2	2	3	0
55	2	1	2	1	1
221	2	0	0	1	2

For square-free $d_1, d_2 > 0$, let $D(d_1, d_2)$ denote the Euclidean distance between the corresponding 4-dimensional vectors (a_2, a_3, a_4, a_5). Consider $v = 58 \notin T$, which corresponds to the vector $\underline{a} = (1, 2, 1, 0)$. For each $t \in T$, the following table records the distance squared $D(v, t)^2$, the ranking of t from nearest to furthest, and the class number h_t as the "vote" for t.

t	$D(v,t)^2$	Vote	Ranking
201	10	1	7
51	5	2	=4
205	2	2	=2
209	13	1	8
213	2	1	=2
217	5	1	=4
55	1	2	1
221	9	2	6

Since $D(58, 205) = D(58, 213) = 2$ and $D(58, 51) = D(58, 217) = 5$, we have given equal ranking to $\{205, 213\}$ and $\{51, 217\}$. With $k \in \{1, 3, 5\}$, the k-nearest neighbor algorithm predicts $h_{58} = 2$, which agrees with rigorous computation.

Example 4.4. Let $D = \{\text{squarefree } d > 0 : 460 < \Delta_d < 490\}$ and decompose $D = T \cup V$, where

$$T = \{461, 465, 469, 118, 473, 119, 122, 489\}, \quad V = \{481, 485\}.$$

The following table records the class number h_t and the Dirichlet coefficient vectors (a_2, a_3, a_4, a_5) associated with $\mathbb{Q}\left(\sqrt{t}\right)$.

$t \in T$	h_t	a_2	a_3	a_4	a_5
461	1	0	0	1	2
465	2	2	1	3	1
469	3	0	2	1	2
118	1	1	2	1	0
473	3	2	0	3	0
119	2	1	0	1	2
122	2	1	0	1	0
489	1	2	1	3	2

Note that 481 (resp. 485) corresponds to the vector $(2, 2, 3, 2)$ (resp. $(0, 0, 1, 1)$). For all $t \in T$ and each $v \in V$, the following table records the distance squared $D(v, t)^2$, the ranking of t from nearest to furthest and the class number h_t as the "vote" for t.

$t \in T$	$D(481, t)^2$	$D(485, t)^2$	Vote	Ranking for 481	Ranking for 485
461	12	1	1	7	1
465	2	9	2	2	= 6
469	8	5	3	= 3	4
118	9	6	1	= 5	5
473	8	9	3	= 3	= 6
119	9	2	2	= 5	= 2
122	13	2	2	8	= 2
489	1	10	1	1	8

It can be shown rigorously that $h_{481} = h_{485} = 2$. No value $k < 5$ predicts the correct value of h_{481} via k-nearest neighbors. On the other hand, the 3-nearest neighbors prediction for h_{485} is correct.

Example 4.5. Let's try to make a tree-based classification algorithm using the first table in Example 4.3. Viewing the a_5 column, we observe that the split point 0 yields the region $\{a_5 \leq 0\}$ containing 2 data points both with class number 1, and the region $\{a_5 > 0\}$ containing 6 data points of which 2 (resp. 4) have class number 1 (resp. 2). Subsequently, the a_4 column yields the partition

$$\{a_5 \leq 0\} \cup (\{a_5 > 0\} \cap \{a_4 \leq 2\}) \cup (\{a_5 > 0\} \cap \{a_4 > 2\}).$$

In each region, all data points have the same class number, that is, 1, 2 and 1, respectively. Applying this tree to $v = 58$ again yields class number $h_{58} = 2$.

4.4. *Logistic and linear regressions*

The "logistic" in "logistic regression" is due to the involvement of the (standard) logistic sigmoid function:

$$\sigma(x) = \frac{1}{1 + e^{-x}}.$$

The "regression" in "logistic regression" is based on the fact that it aims to fit a coefficient vector $\underline{\beta}$ such that the value of $\sigma(\underline{\beta} \cdot \underline{v})$ is indicative of the class of $\underline{v}$. In our description of the regression process, we will focus on the case of two classes C_1 and C_2. If, for $j = 1, \ldots, J$, the vector $\underline{a}_j$ belongs to class C_j, then the vector $\underline{\beta}$ is chosen to satisfy

$$\sum_{i=1}^{N} \left(y_i - P(C_i|\underline{a}_i, \underline{\beta})\right) = 0, \tag{27}$$

where $y_i = 1$ (resp. $y_i = 0$) corresponds to class C_1 (resp. C_2). It is assumed that the probabilities are of the form

$$P(C_1|\underline{a}_i, \underline{\beta}) = \exp(\underline{\beta} \cdot \underline{a}_i)\sigma(-\underline{\beta} \cdot \underline{a}_i), \quad P(C_2|\underline{a}, \underline{\beta}) = \sigma(-\underline{\beta} \cdot \underline{a}_i)$$

so that Equation (27) is nonlinear in β.

By first fitting a logistic regression model and then rounding the fitted sigmoid function to the nearest integer, it was shown in [9] that one may accurately predict the ranks of low genus curves over $\mathbb{Q}$. More precisely, a logistic regression classifier was able to distinguish between elliptic (resp. genus 2 curves) over $\mathbb{Q}$ with ranks in the set $\{0,1\}$ (resp. $\{0,1,2\}$). A different example of a logistic sigmoid model (for the ranks of degree 6 number fields) is reviewed in [8].

As explained in [5, Section 4.4.5], the logistic regression model shares some commonalities with generalized linear regression models. In the following example, we investigate a linear regression model for elliptic curve rank. The predictions are not as accurate as those using the techniques in [9], owing to the simplicity of the model.

Example 4.6. Let us consider isogeny classes of elliptic curves with conductor $53 \leq N_E \leq 58$. The isogeny classes in the sample $54a, 55a, 56a$ (resp. $53a, 57a, 58a$) have rank 0 (resp. rank 1). We construct an input matrix A rows $(1, a_5, a_7)$ and an output matrix R with rows $(1,0)$ (resp. $(0,1)$) if rank is 0 (resp. 1). In both A and R, the rows are ordered by N_E.

$$
A = \begin{pmatrix} 1 & 0 & -4 \\ 1 & 3 & -1 \\ 1 & 1 & 0 \\ 1 & 2 & -1 \\ 1 & -3 & -5 \\ 1 & -3 & -2 \end{pmatrix}, \quad R = \begin{pmatrix} 0 & 1 \\ 1 & 0 \\ 1 & 0 \\ 1 & 0 \\ 0 & 1 \\ 0 & 1 \end{pmatrix}.
$$

The linear regression model predicts the rank of an unseen elliptic curve by first computing $(1, a_5, a_7)P$, where

$$
P = (A^T \cdot A)^{-1} \cdot A^T \cdot R = \frac{1}{2080} \begin{pmatrix} 1664 & 416 \\ 246 & -246 \\ 1440 & -1440 \end{pmatrix},
$$

where A^T is the transpose of the matrix A. For an unseen curve with associated coefficients (a_5, a_7), we compute the 2-dimensional vector $(1, a_5, a_7) \cdot P$ and predict its rank to be 0 (resp. 1) if its first (resp. second) co-ordinate is the larger of the two. The following table records the predicted and actual rank of the remaining isogeny classes in our conductor range.

Isogeny Class	a_5	a_7	Prediction	Actual	Correct?
54b	-3	-1	1	0	no
56b	-4	1	0	0	yes
57b	2	1	0	0	yes
57c	-2	0	0	0	yes
58b	1	-2	1	0	no

5. Number-Theoretic Considerations

We have reviewed the success in machine-learning certain arithmetic invariants first presented in [7–9] and furthermore carried out simplified algorithms by hand in small cases. In this final section, we consider deeper arithmetic ideas connected to the machine learning experiments that are not necessarily reflected in the data or detected by the classifiers.

5.1. *Parity*

Let E denote an elliptic curve over $\mathbb{Q}$, and let $w(E) \in \{\pm 1\}$ denote the sign in Equation (19). As reviewed in [3], the parity conjecture asserts that

$$(-1)^{r_E} = w(E).$$

In [9], it was demonstrated that a logistic regression classifier trained on finitely many Dirichlet coefficients $\{a_p : p \leq X\}$, for some choice of X, could distinguish between elliptic curves over $\mathbb{Q}$ of rank 0 and those of rank 1. Conditional on the parity conjecture, the same can clearly be achieved by computing the sign of the functional equation. Of course, the methodologies are rather different, and the parity conjecture alone does not explain the accuracy of the machine learning approach.

In [8], it is shown that a random forest classifier may distinguish between real quadratic fields of class numbers 1 and those of class number 2. As we now explore, the fact that 1 and 2 are of different parity leads to a pure mathematical approach to making a similar distinction.

The narrow class group of a number field F is the quotient $\mathcal{J}_F/\mathcal{P}_F^+$, where $\mathcal{P}_F^+$ is the group of principal fractional ideals $a\mathcal{O}_F$ such that $\sigma(a)$ is positive for every embedding $\sigma : F \to \mathbb{R}$. The narrow class number h_F^+ is the cardinality of the narrow class group.

Example 5.1. If $F = F_d$ is a quadratic number field, then we write $h_d^+ = h_F^+$. The first few $d > 0$ such that $h_d^+ = 1$ are $5, 8, 13, 17, 29, 37, 41, 53, 61$.

It was shown by Gauss that the 2-rank of the narrow class group of F_d is equal to $\omega(\Delta_d) - 1$, where $\omega(\Delta_d)$ is the number of distinct primes dividing the discriminant Δ_d. Since these primes are precisely those that ramify, the corresponding Dirichlet coefficients a_p in the Dedekind zeta function are equal to 1. One may therefore devise strategies for distinguishing between narrow class numbers 1 and 2 by enumerating occurrences of $\{a_p = 1\}$ among the coefficient vectors $(a_2, \ldots, a_J)$. As above, this alone does not explain the accuracy of the machine learning approach for the analogous problem for class numbers.

5.2. *Counting zeros*

We have seen that the question of determining the parity of the narrow class number of a number field can be related to counting instances of $a_p = 1$. As was already hinted in Example 4.1, one can determine the endomorphism type of an elliptic curve over $\mathbb{Q}$ by counting instances of $a_p = 0$. Indeed, as reviewed in [13, Chapter 2], if E has CM by the ring of integers $\mathcal{O}_F$ in a quadratic imaginary field F, then

$$L(E/\mathbb{Q}, s) = L(\psi_{E/F}, s), \tag{28}$$

where $\psi_{E/F}$ is a Hecke character on the idele group $\mathbb{A}_F^\times$. In this case, it follows from the Chebotarev density theorem that, asymptotically, 50% of the a_p vanish. One can therefore distinguish between exceptional and generic elliptic curves by counting occurrences of $\{a_p = 0\}$.

The L-functions of exceptional genus 2 curves may also be expressed in terms of simpler L-functions, and a more refined analysis of $\{a_p = 0\}$ could be employed to classify the Sato–Tate groups.

6.   Conclusion

In this chapter, we have overviewed the utility of standard supervised learning algorithms when applied to arithmetic data. We have reviewed the background theory and implemented several toy examples by hand. There are several natural questions stemming from the results documented, and we will conclude by noting two broad themes. First, one might seek to interpret the mechanism underlying such accurate classifiers. One attempt to do that can be found in the recent article [16], though many aspects remain unexplored. Second, one could consider the application of unsupervised learning strategies to arithmetic datasets. One recent implementation of the most basic of unsupervised learning algorithms yielded the new "murmurations" phenomenon for elliptic curves [17].

References

[1] J. W. S. Cassels and E. V. Flynn, *Prolegomena to a Middlebrow Arithmetic of Curves of Genus* 2, London Mathematical Society Lecture Note Series 230 (1996).

[2] H. Cohen and H. W. Lenstra, *Heuristics on Class Groups of Number Fields*, Lecture notes in Math., Vol. 1068, pp. 33–62 (1985).

[3] T. Dokchitser, *Notes on the Parity Conjecture*, Advanced Courses in Mathematics - CRM Barcelona, Vol. 201–249 (2013).

[4] N. D. Elkies and Z. Klagsbrun, *New Rank Records for Elliptic Curves Having Rational Torsion*, The Open Book Series, Vol. 4, pp. 233–250 (2020).

[5] T. Hastie, R. Tibshirani and J. Friedman, *The Elements of Statistical Learning*, Springer Series in Statistics, 2nd edn. (2008).

[6] F. Fité, K. S. Kedlaya, V. Rotger and A. V. Sutherland, Sato–Tate distributions and Galois endomorphism modules in genus 2, *Compos. Math.* **148**(5) (2012), 1390–1442.

[7] Y. H. He, K. H. Lee and T. Oliver, Machine-learning the Sato–Tate conjecture, *Journal of Symbolic Computation*, to appear.

[8] Y. H. He, K. H. Lee and T. Oliver, Machine-learning number fields, arXiv:2011.08958.

[9] Y. H. He, K. H. Lee and T. Oliver, Machine-learning arithmetic curves, arXiv:2012.04084.

[10] K. S. Kedlaya and A. V. Sutherland, Hyperelliptic curves, *L*-polynomials, and random matrices, *Contemp. Math.* **487** (2019), 119–162.

[11] LMFDB collaboration, The *L*-functions and modular forms database (December 2021).

[12] J. Silverman, *The Arithmetic of Elliptic Curves*, Springer Graduate Texts in Mathematics 106, 2nd edn. (2008).

[13] J. Silverman, *Advanced Topics in the Arithmetic of Elliptic Curves*, Springer Graduate Texts in Mathematics 151 (1994).

[14] I. Stewart and D. Tall, *Algebraic Number Theory and Fermat's Last Theorem*. CRC Press, 3rd edn. (2001). https://doi.org/10.1201/9781439864081.

[15] Wolfram Research, Inc., *Mathematica 12.1*. Champaign, Illinois (2020).

[16] M. Amir, Y. H. He, K. H. Lee, T. Oliver, and E. Sultanow, Machine Learning Class Numbers of Real Quadratic Fields, arXiv:2209.09283.

[17] Y. H. He, K. H. Lee, T. Oliver, and A. Pozdnyakov, Murmurations of elliptic curves, arXiv:2204.10140.

Chapter 10

Calabi–Yau Volumes, Reflexive Polytopes and Machine Learning

Rak-Kyeong Seong

Department of Mathematical Sciences, and Department of Physics,
Ulsan National Institute of Science and Technology,
50 UNIST-gil, Ulsan 44919, South Korea

seong@unist.ac.kr

Abstract

We review recent work on calculating systematically the minimum volumes of large classes of Sasaki–Einstein manifolds in $2n + 1$ dimensions corresponding to toric Calabi–Yau $(n + 1)$-folds. These non-compact Calabi–Yau $(n + 1)$-folds are characterized by n-dimensional convex lattice polytopes known as toric diagrams. The review summarizes the discovery of a universal lower bound on the minimum volume for toric Calabi–Yau $(n + 1)$-folds and a more restricted upper bound when the corresponding toric diagrams are reflexive polytopes. The review also covers the pioneering application of machine learning techniques in 2017, including a convolutional neural network that takes as its input the toric diagram, in order to identify new exact formulas for the minimum volume. We give a brief overview of how these discoveries on the minimum volume have implications for recent developments in identifying supersymmetric gauge theories in diverse dimensions that are realized by brane configurations based on the corresponding toric Calabi–Yau

365

$(n + 1)$-folds. We put a particular emphasis on brane configurations known as brane tilings and brane brick models.

1. Introduction

Calabi–Yau manifolds have played a special role in the study of supersymmetric gauge theories in various dimensions. In particular, when these supersymmetric gauge theories are taken to be world-volume theories of D-branes probing Calabi–Yau singularities, the interplay between Calabi–Yau geometry and gauge theories has been particularly fruitful.

For example, the worldvolume theories of D3-brane probing toric Calabi–Yau 3-fold singularities [1–4] are $4d$ $\mathcal{N} = 1$ supersymmetric gauge theories that are realized in terms of IIB brane configurations known as brane tilings [5–7]. In this context, the AdS/CFT correspondence [1,8,9] on $AdS_5 \times Y$ provides us with a direct relationship between the minimum volume of the Sasaki–Einstein 5-manifolds Y and the central charges of the corresponding superconformal field theories [10–12]. More recently, interest has grown in studying world-volume theories of D1-branes probing toric Calabi–Yau 4-fold singularities as a way to better understand $2d$ $\mathcal{N} = (0, 2)$ gauge theories. These $2d$ theories are now known to be realized by a IIA brane configuration called the brane brick model [13–22].

With these developments in mind, the following review concentrates on two research papers [23,24] that systematically computed and studied the minimum volumes of various Sasaki–Einstein base manifolds in $2n + 1$ dimensions corresponding to toric Calabi–Yau $(n + 1)$-folds. These works were motivated by the role played by the minimum volume under the AdS/CFT correspondence in relation to $4d$ theories and toric Calabi–Yau 3-folds. In particular, the goal in Ref. [23] was to gain new insights into what role the minimum volume for higher-dimensional toric Calabi–Yau 4- and 5-folds plays in relation to lower-dimensional gauge theories realized by brane configurations such as brane brick models.

In parallel, Ref. [24] introduced for the first time machine learning techniques, including the use of convolutional neural networks (CNNs), in order to identify a new formula for the direct computation of minimum volumes for toric Calabi–Yau 3-folds. This idea to train a neural network in order to find new ways to calculate geometric invariants that have a field theoretic interpretation in the context of string theory was pioneering in the research field in 2017. In fact, Ref. [24] illustrated that even simple machine learning model setups are surprisingly capable of predicting well geometric invariants such as the minimum volume for toric Calabi–Yau 3-folds. In the spirit of interpretable and explainable AI, Ref. [24] even shed light on the trained models by giving explicit new formulas for the minimum volume for a large set of toric Calabi–Yau 3-folds as well as depictions of the parameters of the trained neural network. This was a milestone in the study of toric Calabi–Yau manifolds in string theory and, as predicted in Ref. [24], led to various other applications of similar machine learning techniques in string theory, some of the first being Refs. [25–27]. Today, these steps led to the creation of an entirely new research field where machine learning techniques play an integral role in the toolbox of researchers in string theory.

In this review, we will give in Section 2 a brief summary on non-compact toric Calabi–Yau $(n + 1)$-folds and their connection to supersymmetric gauge theories in various dimensions. We will then proceed with a summary on calculating volume functions for Sasaki–Einstein manifolds from Hilbert series [28] characterizing corresponding toric Calabi–Yau $(n + 1)$-folds. These volume functions parameterized by Reeb vector components are then used to identify the minimum volume. In Section 3, we review the results in Ref. [23], including results on new lower and upper bounds on the minimum volume corresponding to toric Calabi–Yau $(n + 1)$-folds in various dimensions. In Section 4, we conclude the review with a summary of the results in Ref. [24], including the pioneering application of machine learning techniques in order to identify new methods for the computation of the minimum volume for toric Calabi–Yau 3-folds.

2. Background

In the following review, we exclusively concentrate on non-compact toric Calabi–Yau $(n + 1)$-folds whose base is a Sasaki–Einstein $(2n + 1)$-manifold. We give a brief summary on the construction of non-compact toric Calabi–Yau $(n + 1)$-folds in terms of toric diagrams and the algebro-geometric characterization of these manifolds in terms of Hilbert series. The following review summarizes how the Hilbert series calculation leads to the volume function and the minimum volume of the Sasaki–Einstein $(2n + 1)$-base manifolds.

2.1. *Non-compact toric Calabi–Yau $(n + 1)$-folds*

For a given convex lattice polytope Δ_n in dimension n [29–31], one can define a toric variety $X(\Delta_n)$ [32,33]. The convex lattice polytope Δ_n, which is also known as the toric diagram of $X(\Delta_n)$, with its extremal lattice points forms a convex polyhedral cone σ. Toric geometry tells us that the affine toric variety $X(\Delta_n)$ is the spectrum of the semigroup algebra of the dual cone of σ.

The complex cone over the toric variety $X(\Delta_n)$ is the non-compact toric Calabi–Yau $(n + 1)$-fold whose base manifold is a $(2n + 1)$ real dimensional Sasaki–Einstein manifold Y_{2n+1}. Generally, we can write down the metric of the toric Calabi–Yau $(n + 1)$-fold in terms of the metric of the Sasaki–Einstein manifold as follows:

$$\mathrm{d}s^2(X(\Delta_n)) = \mathrm{d}r^2 + r^2 \mathrm{d}s^2(Y_{2n+1}). \tag{1}$$

For example, for toric Calabi–Yau 3-folds, the metric for the Sasaki–Einstein 5-manifolds $Y^{p,q}$ [34,35] is known explicitly in terms of positive integers p and q. The metric is particularly useful for the calculation of the Sasaki–Einstein base manifold's volume function [12,36]. In the following review, we will concentrate on an alternative more algebro-geometric method of calculating the volume function as a limit of a certain equivariant index of the Calabi–Yau $(n + 1)$-fold, also known as the Hilbert series [36]. For this section, let us first concentrate on a particular class of toric Calabi–Yau $(n + 1)$-folds whose toric diagrams are reflexive polytopes.

2.1.1. *Reflexive polytopes and Fano varieties*

The work in Ref. [23] concentrates on a particular class of toric Calabi–Yau $(n + 1)$-folds whose toric diagrams are reflexive polytopes. Two convex lattice polytopes in n dimensions are taken to be equivalent if there is a $GL(n; \mathbb{Z})$ matrix that relates the vertices of the polytopes to each other. We note that equivalent convex lattice polytopes correspond to the same toric Calabi–Yau n-fold.

While there are infinitely many convex lattice polytopes in a given dimension n, there are only finitely many if the convex lattice polytopes are reflexive. A convex lattice polytope Δ_n is considered to be reflexive if the dual polytope Δ_n° is also a convex lattice polytope in $\mathbb{Z}^n$. Given a convex lattice polytope Δ_n, its dual is defined as follows:

$$\Delta_n^\circ = \{\vec{v} \in \mathbb{Z}^n | \vec{m} \cdot \vec{v} \leq -1 \ \forall \ \vec{m} \in \Delta_n\}. \tag{2}$$

A special feature of reflexive polytopes is that reflexive polytopes and their duals have a unique interior lattice point at the origin $(0, \ldots, 0) \in \mathbb{Z}^n$. Reflexive polytopes were first studied by Batyrev and Borisov [40,41] in relation to mirror symmetry [37–39,42,43].

If a convex lattice polytope is reflexive, the corresponding toric variety is known to be a Gorenstein toric Fano variety $X(\Delta_n)$ or in short a Fano n-fold. Kreuzer and Skarke [37–39] have fully classified the finite set of reflexive polytopes up to dimension $n = 4$. The number of distinct reflexive polytopes up to dimension $n = 4$ is shown in Table 1. For example, in $n = 3$, there are 4318 reflexive polytopes that each correspond to a toric Calabi–Yau 3-fold.

A subset of these reflexive polytopes is known to be regular. A polytope Δ_n is called regular if every cone σ in the fan $\Sigma(\Delta_n)$, generated by the positive hull of the n-cones over all faces of Δ_n, has generators that form part of a $\mathbb{Z}$-basis. For example, this means in $n = 2$ that every boundary edge of a regular Δ_2 does not contain any internal points, and in $n = 3$, the boundary triangles of regular Δ_3 do not contain any internal points. While reflexive polytopes Δ_n correspond to toric Fano n-folds, regular reflexive polytopes correspond to smooth toric Fano n-folds [40,44–46] (see Figure 1). Table 1 shows how many of the reflexive polytopes are also regular in a given dimension n.

Table 1. The classification of reflexive polytopes and distinct regular reflexive polytopes in dimension $n \leq 4$ [37–39].

d	Number of Polytopes	Number of Regular Polytopes
1	1	1
2	16	5
3	4,319	18
4	473,800,776	124

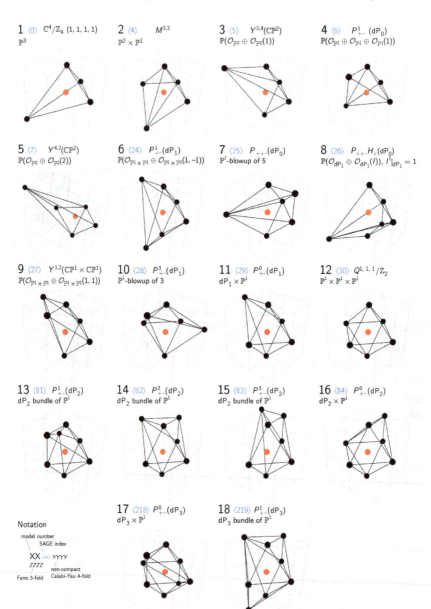

1 ⟨0⟩ $\mathbb{C}^4/\mathbb{Z}_4$ (1, 1, 1, 1)
$\mathbb{P}^3$

2 ⟨4⟩ $M^{3,2}$
$\mathbb{P}^2 \times \mathbb{P}^1$

3 ⟨5⟩ $Y^{2,4}(\mathbb{CP}^2)$
$\mathbb{P}(\mathcal{O}_{\mathbb{P}^2} \oplus \mathcal{O}_{\mathbb{P}^2}(1))$

4 ⟨6⟩ P^1_{+-} (dP$_0$)
$\mathbb{P}(\mathcal{O}_{\mathbb{P}^1} \oplus \mathcal{O}_{\mathbb{P}^1} \oplus \mathcal{O}_{\mathbb{P}^1}(1))$

5 ⟨7⟩ $Y^{4,2}(\mathbb{CP}^2)$
$\mathbb{P}(\mathcal{O}_{\mathbb{P}^2} \oplus \mathcal{O}_{\mathbb{P}^2}(2))$

6 ⟨24⟩ P^1_{+-}(dP$_1$)
$\mathbb{P}(\mathcal{O}_{\mathbb{P}^1 \times \mathbb{P}^1} \oplus \mathcal{O}_{\mathbb{P}^1 \times \mathbb{P}^1}(1, -1))$

7 ⟨25⟩ P_{++-}(dP$_0$)
$\mathbb{P}^1$-blowup of 5

8 ⟨26⟩ P_{++} H_+(dP$_0$)
$\mathbb{P}(\mathcal{O}_{dP_1} \oplus \mathcal{O}_{dP_1}(l))$, $l^2|_{dP_1} = 1$

9 ⟨27⟩ $Y^{1,2}(\mathbb{CP}^1 \times \mathbb{CP}^1)$
$\mathbb{P}(\mathcal{O}_{\mathbb{P}^1 \times \mathbb{P}^1} \oplus \mathcal{O}_{\mathbb{P}^1 \times \mathbb{P}^1}(1, 1))$

10 ⟨28⟩ P^3_{+-}(dP$_1$)
$\mathbb{P}^1$-blowup of 3

11 ⟨29⟩ P^0_{+-}(dP$_1$)
dP$_1 \times \mathbb{P}^1$

12 ⟨30⟩ $Q^{1,1,1}/\mathbb{Z}_2$
$\mathbb{P}^1 \times \mathbb{P}^1 \times \mathbb{P}^1$

13 ⟨81⟩ P^1_{+-}(dP$_2$)
dP$_2$ bundle of $\mathbb{P}^1$

14 ⟨82⟩ P^2_{+-}(dP$_2$)
dP$_2$ bundle of $\mathbb{P}^1$

15 ⟨83⟩ P^3_{+-}(dP$_2$)
dP$_2$ bundle of $\mathbb{P}^1$

16 ⟨84⟩ P^0_{+-}(dP$_2$)
dP$_2 \times \mathbb{P}^1$

17 ⟨218⟩ P^0_{+-}(dP$_3$)
dP$_3 \times \mathbb{P}^1$

18 ⟨219⟩ P^1_{+-}(dP$_3$)
dP$_3$ bundle of $\mathbb{P}^1$

Notation

model number
⟍ SAGE index
XX ⟨m⟩ YYYY
ZZZZ ╱
╱ non-compact
Fano 3-fold Calabi–Yau 4-fold

Figure 1.   The 18 regular reflexive polytopes in $n = 3$ dimensions corresponding to toric non-compact Calabi–Yau 4-folds and related smooth Fano 3-folds [22].

2.1.2.   *Gauge theories and the volume*

The work in Ref. [47] studies $4d$ $\mathcal{N} = 1$ supersymmetric gauge theories corresponding to toric Calabi–Yau 3-folds whose toric diagrams are reflexive have been identified. These $4d$ $\mathcal{N} = 1$ supersymmetric gauge theories are worldvolume theories of D3-branes that probe the associated singular toric Calabi–Yau 3-folds. Because of their association to toric Calabi–Yau 3-folds, these $4d$ $\mathcal{N} = 1$ supersymmetric gauge theories can be realized also as a Type IIB brane configuration of D5-branes and NS5-branes as shown in Table 2. These brane configurations are known as brane tilings [6,7] and in the mathematics literature as dimer models [48,49]. It was noted in Ref. [47] that there are exactly 30 brane tilings associated with the 16 reflexive polygons in dimension $n = 2$. Some of the toric Calabi–Yau 3-folds with reflexive toric diagrams are associated with multiple brane tilings due to the existence of Seiberg duality [7,50,51] between brane tilings and the corresponding $4d$ $\mathcal{N} = 1$ supersymmetric gauge theories.

More recently, $2d$ $(0,2)$ supersymmetric gauge theories corresponding to toric Calabi–Yau 4-folds have been constructed systematically. These $2d$ supersymmetric gauge theories can be considered as worldvolume theories of D1-branes probing the singular toric Calabi–Yau 4-folds. They are realized in terms of Type IIA brane configurations, which are known as brane brick models as summarized in Table 3 [15–22]. These brane brick models are the analog of brane tilings and feature interesting gauge theory phenomena in 2 dimensions such as Gadde–Gukov–Putrov triality [52]. In Ref. [22], it was shown that all of the 18 smooth Fano 3-folds have a corresponding $2d$ $(0,2)$ supersymmetric gauge theory realized by a brane brick model. The work in Ref. [22] showed that the lattice of generators of the moduli space of the brane brick models forms a

Table 2.   Type IIB configurations where D5-branes are suspended from an NS5-brane that wraps a holomorphic surface Σ are known as brane tilings. This configuration is T-dual to a D3-brane probing a toric Calabi–Yau 3-fold corresponding to Σ.

	0	1	2	3	4	5	6	7	8	9
D5	×	×	×	×	×	·	×	·	·	·
NS5	×	×	×	×	——	Σ	——		·	·

Table 3.   Type IIA configurations where D4-branes are suspended
from an NS5-brane that wraps a holomorphic surface Σ are known
as brane brick models. This configuration is T-dual to a D1-brane
probing a toric Calabi–Yau 4-fold corresponding to Σ.

	0	1	2	3	4	5	6	7	8	9
D4	×	×	×	·	×	·	×	·	·	·
NS5	×	×	——————— Σ ———————						·	·

convex lattice polytope in $\mathbb{Z}^3$ which is the exact dual polytope of the
regular reflexive toric diagrams associated with the 18 smooth Fano
3-folds.

Parallel to the development of identifying supersymmetric gauge
theories corresponding to toric Calabi–Yau $(n + 1)$-folds, the focus
was also on calculating the volume of the Sasaki–Einstein $(2n + 1)$-
manifolds corresponding to the toric Calabi–Yau $(n + 1)$-folds. In
particular, in dimension $n = 2$, the volume of the Sasaki–Einstein
5-manifolds was shown to be related to the central charge a-function
of the corresponding $4d$ $\mathcal{N} = 1$ theory via the AdS/CFT correspondence [10–12,53]. In particular, Ref. [12] showed that the minimization of the volume of the Sasaki–Einstein 5-manifolds determines the
manifold's Reeb vector. Following this, volume minimization can be
interpreted as the geometric dual of a-maximization [12,54,55] in the
context of $4d$ theories corresponding to toric Calabi–Yau 3-folds.

The work in Ref. [36] identified a method of computing the volume
function of Sasaki–Einstein manifolds using an equivariant index of
the associated Calabi–Yau cone that counts holomorphic functions.
This index is also known as the Hilbert series of the Calabi–Yau
$(n + 1)$-fold. In the case of $n = 2$ and $n = 3$, where the toric Calabi–
Yau 3-folds and 4-folds are associated with brane tilings and brane
brick models, respectively, the Hilbert series can be considered as the
generating function of gauge invariant operators of the corresponding
supersymmetric gauge theories [28,56]. As a result, the Hilbert series
can be directly calculated as part of the moduli space computation of
brane tilings and brane brick models. In the following review section,
we summarize an alternative method of calculating the Hilbert series
directly from the toric diagram of the corresponding toric Calabi–Yau
$(n + 1)$-folds, as described in Ref. [23].

2.2. The Hilbert series and volume functions

Given a general projective variety X realized as an affine variety in $\mathbb{C}^k$, the Hilbert series is defined as the generating function for the dimension of the graded pieces of the coordinate ring of the form

$$\mathbb{C}[x_1, \ldots, x_k]/\langle f_i \rangle, \tag{3}$$

where f_i are the defining polynomials of the variety X. Accordingly, we can write the Hilbert series of X as a rational function with the following expansion:

$$g(t) = \sum_{m=0}^{\infty} \dim_{\mathbb{C}}(X_m)t^m, \tag{4}$$

where t is the fugacity counting the degree of the m-th graded piece X_m, which can be thought of as the number of algebraically independent degree m polynomials on the variety X.

In the case when the affine variety X is toric, the Hilbert series of the corresponding toric Calabi–Yau $(n + 1)$-fold can be directly computed from the associated toric diagram Δ_n [36]. Given Δ_n and a triangulation of Δ_n that consists of unit $(n - 1)$-simplices which involve all external and internal points of the convex lattice polytope Δ_n,[1] the Hilbert series takes the following form:

$$g(t_1, \ldots, t_{n+1}) = \sum_{i=1}^{r} \prod_{j=1}^{h} (1 - \vec{t}^{\,\vec{u}_{i,j}})^{-1}, \tag{5}$$

where the index $i = 1, \ldots, r$ runs over the n-dimensional simplices of the triangulation of Δ_n and the index $j = 1, \ldots, h$ runs over the faces of each such simplex. We note that each $\vec{u}_{i,j} \in \mathbb{Z}^{n+1}$ is the outer normal vector to the j-th face of the fan that is associated with the i-th simplex in the triangulation of Δ_n. The $n + 1$ fugacities correspond to the $n + 1$ components of the vector $\vec{u}_{i,j}$ and accordingly, we have $\vec{t}^{\,\vec{u}_{i,j}} = \prod_{a=1}^{n} t_a^{\vec{u}_{i,j}(a)}$, where $\vec{u}_{i,j}(a)$ is the a-th component of $\vec{u}_{i,j}$. In other words, the grading of the Hilbert series in Equation (5) is such that the a-th fugacity t_a corresponds a-th coordinate of $\vec{u}_{i,j}$.

---

[1] Such triangulations are also known as FRS triangulations [57–59].

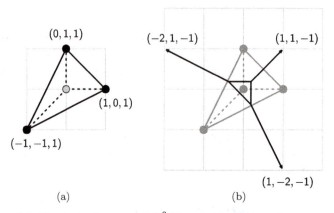

$(0,1,1)$ $(-2,1,-1)$ $(1,1,-1)$

$(1,0,1)$

$(-1,-1,1)$

$(1,-2,-1)$

(a)   (b)

Figure 2.   (a) The toric diagram of $\mathbb{C}^3/\mathbb{Z}_3$, also known as the cone over $\mathbf{dP}_0$. (b) The toric diagram has a unique triangulation which gives rise to internal and external normal vectors $\vec{u}_{i,j}$. The three external normal vectors are shown in this figure.

In the formula for the Hilbert series in Equation (5), it is also important to note that the toric diagram Δ_n is on a hyperplane which is a distance 1 away from the $(n+1)$-dimensional origin $(0,\ldots,0)$. As a result, this sets the $(n+1)$th coordinate of $\vec{u}_{i,j}$ to be 1. Taking all these notes into account, we emphasize that the Hilbert series defined in Equation (5) varies under $GL(n;\mathbb{Z})$ on the toric diagram Δ_n. Equally affected is the Hilbert series under changes in the triangulation of Δ_n which is used in Equation (5). Neither $GL(n;\mathbb{Z})$ transformation of Δ_n nor changes to the triangulation of Δ_n affect the minimum volume of the Sasaki–Einstein manifold which is associated with the toric Calabi–Yau $(n+1)$-fold corresponding to Δ_n.

Figure 2 shows the toric diagram for $\mathbb{C}^3/\mathbb{Z}_3$, also known as the cone over $\mathbf{dP}_0$, which has the following points on $\mathbb{Z}^2$ as its toric points,

$$v_1 = (1,0,1), \quad v_2 = (0,1,1), \quad v_3 = (-1,-1,1), \quad v_4 = (0,0,1). \quad (6)$$

There is a unique triangulation of the toric diagram for $\mathbb{C}^3/\mathbb{Z}_3$ that splits Δ_2 into three sub-simplices that involve all toric points in Equation (6). The unique triangulation is given by

$$\{\{v_1, v_2, v_4\}, \ \{v_1, v_3, v_4\}, \ \{v_2, v_3, v_4\}\}. \quad (7)$$

Using the Hilbert series formula in Equation (5), we can then write down the Hilbert series for $\mathbb{C}^3/\mathbb{Z}_3$ as follows:

$$g(t_i) = \frac{1}{(1 - t_2)(1 - t_1^{-1}t_2)(1 - t_1 t_2^{-2} t_3^{-1})}$$
$$+ \frac{1}{(1 - t_1)(1 - t_1 t_2^{-1})(1 - t_1^{-2} t_2 t_3)}$$
$$+ \frac{1}{(1 - t_1^{-1})(1 - t_2^{-1})(1 - t_1 t_2 t_3^{-1})}. \tag{8}$$

By setting the fugacities $t_1, \ldots, t_3$ all to 1, the Hilbert series can be unrefined resulting in

$$g(t) = \frac{1 + 7t + t^2}{(1 - t)^3}. \tag{9}$$

According to Stanley [60], the palindromic numerator in Equation (9) indicates that the corresponding variety is Calabi–Yau (Gorenstein).

Having in mind that the minimum volume is a geometric invariant of the toric Calabi–Yau $(n + 1)$-fold, in the following paragraph, we proceed with the review of the volume computation using the Hilbert series of $X(\Delta_n)$.

2.2.1. *Volume function and the minimum volume*

The volume of a real $(2n + 1)$-dimensional Sasaki–Einstein base manifold Y can be calculated from the Einstein–Hilbert action on Y [12,36]. The volume takes the form of a strictly convex function and has the following general form:

$$\text{vol}[Y] = \int_Y d\mu = 2n \int_{r \leq 1} \frac{\omega^n}{n!}, \tag{10}$$

where ω is the Kähler form and $d\mu$ is the Riemannian measure on the toric Calabi–Yau cone. The Killing vector field on the Sasaki–Einstein base manifold Y is called the Reeb vector and the volume of the base Y is a function of the Reeb vector components b_i [12].

The volume function takes the form

$$V(b; Y) := \frac{\text{vol}[Y]}{\text{vol}[S^{2n+1}]},$$ (11)

where $\text{vol}[S^{2n+1}] = \frac{2\pi}{(n+1)!}$ is the volume of S^{2n+1}. The ratio in Equation (11) is known to be always an algebraic number as we will see shortly when we make the connection to the Hilbert series of the corresponding toric Calabi–Yau $(n + 1)$-fold. In this review, when we talk about the volume of a toric Calabi–Yau $(n + 1)$-fold, we refer to the above volume of the corresponding Sasaki–Einstein base Y.

The volume function is obtained as the leading order in the μ-expansion of the Hilbert series when one re-writes the Hilbert series using $t_i = \exp[-\mu b_i]$. We can pick the leading order using the following limit:

$$V(b_i; Y) = \lim_{\mu \to 0} \mu^n g(t_i = \exp[-\mu b_i]),$$ (12)

which gives us the volume function for the Sasaki–Einstein base Y [12,36,61]. Because the Reeb vector is always in the interior of the toric diagram Δ_n and because Δ_n is placed on a hyperplane that is a distance 1 apart from the $(n + 1)$-dimensional origin $(0, \ldots, 0)$, one of the components of the Reeb vector can be chosen to be

$$b_n = n.$$ (13)

Using the Hilbert series expression in Equation (8) for $\mathbb{C}^3/\mathbb{Z}_3$, we can write the volume function of the corresponding Sasaki–Einstein base as follows:

$$V(b_i; \mathbb{C}^3/\mathbb{Z}_3) = \frac{-9}{(b_1 - 2b_2 - 3)(-2b_1 + b_2 - 3)(b_1 + b_2 - 3)},$$ (14)

where b_i are the Reeb vector components and $b_3 = 3$.

At critical values of the Reeb vector components b_i^*, the volume function has a global minimum value [12,55],

$$V_{\min} = \min_{b_i^*, \, b_n = n} V(b_i; Y).$$ (15)

For toric Calabi–Yau 3-folds and the corresponding Sasaki–Einstein 5-manifolds, the process of volume minimization is known to be dual to the process of a-maximization [12]. The AdS/CFT correspondence relates the central charge a-function of the corresponding $4d$ superconformal field theory with the volume minimum of the corresponding Sasaki–Einstein 5-manifold as follows [10–12]:

$$a(R;Y) = \frac{\pi^3 N^2}{4V(R;Y)}, \tag{16}$$

where the $U(1)$ R-charges R of the $4d$ superconformal field theory can be expressed in terms of Reeb vector components b_i. Computing the minimum volume under volume minimization is equivalent to computing the maximum of $a(R;Y)$ under a-maximization and therefore the minimum volume has a physical interpretation under the AdS/CFT correspondence.

In Ref. [23], we used volume minimization to compute the volume minimum of all toric Calabi–Yau $(n+1)$-folds whose toric diagrams are reflexive polytopes in dimensions $n = 2$ and $n = 3$. The computation was extended to a subset of the 473,800,776 toric Calabi–Yau 5-folds whose toric diagrams are reflexive polytopes in dimension $n = 4$. This is the largest systematic attempt to fully understand the distribution of minimum volumes of Sasaki–Einstein manifolds corresponding to toric Calabi–Yau $(n+1)$-folds. The study led to interesting findings that we summarize in the following section.

Additionally, following the systematic calculation of the minimum volumes for toric Calabi–Yau $(n+1)$-folds in Ref. [23], a natural question is whether the minimum volume can be computed following alternative methods given the fact that the search for the exact global minimum of the volume function in Equation (12) becomes increasingly more difficult with larger toric diagrams Δ_n and larger dimension n. Motivated by this problem, in 2017, we pioneered the application of machine learning methods in Ref. [24] with the explicit aim to identify a new method of calculating the volume minimum for any toric Calabi–Yau $(n+1)$-fold. The following sections review the results in Refs. [23,24] and connect them to current developments in this research direction.

3.   Bounds on the Minimum Volume

In Ref. [23], the minimum volume $V_{\min}$ corresponding to all toric Calabi–Yau 3-folds and 4-folds whose toric diagrams are reflexive polytopes has been computed. Following this computation, the minimum volume $V_{\min}$ was found to have an upper and a lower bound of the following form:

$$\frac{1}{\chi(X(\Delta_n))} \leq V_{\min} \leq m_{n+1} \int c_1(X(\Delta_n))^n, \qquad (17)$$

where $\chi(X(\Delta_n))$ is the Euler number of the completely resolved toric variety $X(\Delta_n)$ and $C = \int c_1(X(\Delta_n))^n$ is the Chern number of $X(\Delta_n)$. The Euler number $\chi(X(\Delta_n))$ and the Chern number $C = \int c_1(X(\Delta_n))^n$ are both integers and their calculation is outlined in Ref. [23].

The upper bound in Equation (17) depends on a gradient $m_{n+1} \in \mathbb{R}$ which for $n = 2$ is $m_3 \sim 3^{-3}$ and for $n = 3$ is $m_4 \sim 4^{-4}$, where we observe that $m_n > m_{n+1}$. A further finding with regard to Equation (17) is that the lower bound is valid for all toric Calabi–Yau $(n + 1)$-folds, whereas the upper bound depending on m_{n+1} is a feature of toric Calabi–Yau $(n + 1)$-folds with reflexive toric diagrams Δ_n. In particular, the lower bound is saturated when the toric Calabi–Yau $(n+1)$-fold is an abelian orbifold of $\mathbb{C}^n$. A proof on why the lower bound is saturated for abelian orbifolds of $\mathbb{C}^n$ is given in Ref. [23].

Figure 3 shows the minimum volumes $V_{\min} = V(b_i^*; Y)$ against the Chern number $C = \int c_1(X(\Delta_2))^2$ as well as the inverse minimum volume $1/V_{\min} = 1/V(b_i^*; Y)$ against the Euler number $\chi(X(\Delta_2))$ for the 16 toric Calabi–Yau 3-folds with reflexive toric diagrams Δ_2. We can see that the lower bound for $V_{\min}$ is saturated when the toric Calabi–Yau 3-folds are abelian orbifolds of $\mathbb{C}^3$. As shown in Figure 3, there are exactly five abelian orbifolds of $\mathbb{C}^3$ for which $\chi(X(\Delta_2)) = 1/V_{\min}$. These abelian orbifolds are of the following form [62–64]:

$$\mathbb{C}^3/\mathbb{Z}_3 \, (1,1,1), \ \ \mathbb{C}^3/\mathbb{Z}_4 \, (1,1,2), \ \ \mathbb{C}^3/\mathbb{Z}_6 \, (1,2,3),$$

$$\mathbb{C}^3/\mathbb{Z}_4 \times \mathbb{Z}_2 \, (1,0,3)(0,1,1), \ \ \mathbb{C}^3/\mathbb{Z}_3 \times \mathbb{Z}_3 \, (1,0,2)(0,1,2). \quad (18)$$

For toric Calabi–Yau 3-folds, the bounds in Equation (17) on the volume minimum have also an interpretation in terms of the maximum central charge $a_{\max} = a(R^*; Y)$ of the corresponding $4d\ \mathcal{N} = 1$ theories. Following the relationship between the volume and central

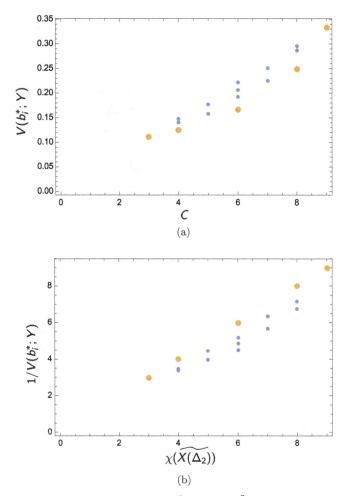

Figure 3. (a) The Chern number $C = \int c_1(X(\Delta_2))^2$ against the minimum volume $V_{\min} = V(b_i^*; Y)$ and (b) the Euler number $\chi(X(\Delta_2))$ against the inverse of the minimum volume $1/V_{\min} = 1/V(b_i^*; Y)$ for the 16 reflexive toric Calabi–Yau 3-folds. The toric Calabi–Yau 3-folds that saturate the bound $\chi(X(\Delta_2)) = 1/V_{\min}$ are highlighted in orange; the rest of the points are in blue.

charge in Equation (16), we can rewrite the bounds in Equation (17) for reflexive toric Calabi–Yau 3-folds as follows:

$$m_3 \int c_1(X(\Delta_2))^2 \le a_{\max} \le \frac{1}{\chi(X(\Delta_2))}. \tag{19}$$

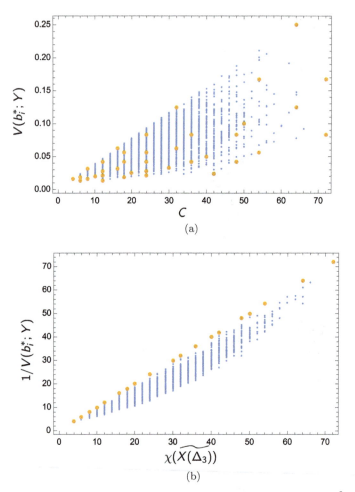

Figure 4.   A plot (in blue) of (a) the Chern number $C = \int c_1(X(\Delta_3))^3$ against the minimum volume $V_{\min} = V(b_i^*; Y)$ and (b) the Euler number $\chi(X(\Delta_3))$ against the inverse of the minimum volume $1/V_{\min} = 1/V(b_i^*; Y)$ for the 4319 reflexive toric Calabi–Yau 4-folds. The toric Calabi–Yau 4-folds that saturate the bound $\chi(X(\Delta_3)) = 1/V_{\min}$ are highlighted in orange.

Similarly, for the 4318 reflexive toric Calabi–Yau 4-folds, Figure 4 shows the minimum volumes $V_{\min}$ against the Chern number $C = \int c_1(X(\Delta_3))^3$ as well as the inverse minimum volume $1/V_{\min}$ against the Euler number $\chi(X(\Delta_3))$. Again, we can see that the lower bound is saturated as expected when the toric Calabi–Yau 4-fold is an abelian orbifold of $\mathbb{C}^4$. There are exactly 48 abelian orbifolds of

$\mathbb{C}^4$ whose toric diagrams are reflexive and their minimum volumes saturate the lower bound in Equation (17). They are indicated as orange points in Figure 4.

In Ref. [23], for a subset of the 473,800,776 reflexive toric Calabi–Yau 5-folds, the minimum volume bound in Equation (17) was confirmed to be satisfied. It would be interesting to complete the calculation of the minimum volumes for all reflexive toric Calabi–Yau 5-folds in future work. Furthermore, although minimum volumes corresponding to toric Calabi–Yau 3-folds have a natural interpretation in terms of the corresponding $4d$ theories through the central charge a, there is still work to be done in order to have a better understanding on what role the minimum volumes corresponding to higher-dimensional toric Calabi–Yau $(n+1)$-folds play in the context of, for example, brane brick models representing $2d$ supersymmetric gauge theories.

We investigate these questions in an upcoming work and proceed with the review of our work in Ref. [24], where we for the first time applied machine learning techniques in string theory in order to find an alternative method of calculating minimum volumes for toric Calabi–Yau $(n + 1)$-folds.

4. Machine Learning the Minimum Volume

In Ref. [24], we applied machine learning techniques in order to identify alternative methods for computing the minimum volume corresponding to toric Calabi–Yau $(n + 1)$-folds. In particular, we focused on toric Calabi–Yau 3-folds whose toric diagrams are 2-dimensional convex polygons Δ_2. We used two standard machine learning models, and a combination of both, in order to estimate a minimum volume function for toric Calabi–Yau 3-folds.

4.1. *Multiple linear regression*

The first model is based on multiple linear regression, where the inverse of the minimum volume formula is estimated to take the following form:

$$1/V_{\min}^{\text{MLR}}(\Delta_2) = \sum_{i=1}^{10} \omega_i f_i(\Delta_2) + \omega_0, \tag{20}$$

where $\omega_i \in \mathbb{R}$ are the weights of the linear regression model that need to be found and f_i are the components of the 9-dimensional feature vector that we use for this model. Note that we take as the target the inverse of the minimum volume given that the inverse provides us with a wider range for the target space of the model. The feature vector f has the following form:

$$f = (I, E, V, IE, IV, EV, I^2, E^2, V^2), \tag{21}$$

where I, E and V are the number of internal, boundary and corner lattice points of the toric diagram Δ_2, respectively.

By minimizing the mean least squares of the following form:

$$\text{argmin}_\omega \frac{1}{N} \sum_{\Delta_2} \left(1/V_{\min}(\Delta_2) - 1/V_{\min}^{\text{MLR}}(\Delta_2)\right)^2, \tag{22}$$

where N is the number of toric diagrams Δ_2 in the training dataset of the model, we obtain the following estimates for the weights in Equation (20):

$$\begin{aligned}
&\omega_1 = 1.9574, \quad \omega_2 = 0.8522, \quad \omega_3 = -0.7658, \quad \omega_4 = -0.0138, \\
&\omega_5 = -0.0020, \quad \omega_6 = -0.0104, \quad \omega_7 = -0.0120, \quad \omega_8 = -0.0523, \\
&\omega_9 = -0.0478, \quad \omega_0 = 1.3637.
\end{aligned}$$

$$\tag{23}$$

The optimization problem of minimizing the mean least squares in Equation (22) is iteratively solved using stochastic gradient descent. The dataset used to solve this optimization problem consists of $15,151$ $GL(2,\mathbb{Z})$-distinct toric diagrams that fit into a 5×5 lattice square. We split the dataset into a training set (75%) and a test set (25%).

We note that the characterization of each toric diagram Δ_2 in the training data in terms of the three integers numbers I, E and V is not unique. In fact, there are 645 unique feature combinations from the $15,151$ toric diagrams in our dataset. As a result, the proposed formula for the inverse of the minimum volume in Equation (20) models the statistical expectation $E(V_{\min}(\Delta_2))$ of the inverse of the minimum volume for a set of toric Calabi–Yau 3-folds with the same I, V and E numbers.

According to the training done in Ref. [24], the results in Equations (20) and (23) estimate the inverse of the minimum volume for a given toric Calabi–Yau 3-fold from its toric diagram Δ_2 with an expected predicted error of around 2.2%. This in 2017, when the work in Ref. [24] was done, was a good indication that the minimum volume for a toric Calabi–Yau 3-fold can be obtained with a surprisingly good accuracy in terms of numbers of special lattice points that characterize the corresponding toric diagram Δ_2.

4.2. *Convolutional neural network (CNN)*

In the second part of Ref. [24], we introduced a convolutional neural network [65,66] in order to directly take the whole image of the toric diagram Δ_2 as the input for the calculation of the minimum volume for toric Calabi–Yau 3-folds. This is in contrast to the manually constructed features in Equation (21) for the multiple linear regression model. A convolutional neural network is able to optimize kernels for features in the input image and therefore automates feature extraction in the input data.

In Ref. [24], the CNN is first coupled to the original multiple linear regression model as illustrated in Figure 5. The coupling is such that the output of the linear regression is added via a single ReLU unit, also known as a rectified linear unit, to the outputs of the convolutional neural network. We use a ReLU unit because the final output of the coupled model is the inverse of the minimum volume which has to be a positive number. Such a coupled model is also known in the literature as a wide and deep convolutional neural network (WDCNN).

Accordingly, the inverse of the minimum volume for a given toric Calabi–Yau 3-fold with toric diagram Δ_2 is modeled by the following function:

$$1/V_{\min}^{\text{WDCNN}}(\Delta_2) = \max\left(\omega_1^f/V_{\min}^{\text{MLR}}(\Delta_2) + \sum_{i=1}^{o} \omega_{2i}^f \, m_i(\Delta_2) + \omega_0^f, 0\right),$$
(24)

where m_i is the i-th output of the CNN and ω^f are the weights of the final layer in the coupled model. The input layer for the CNN

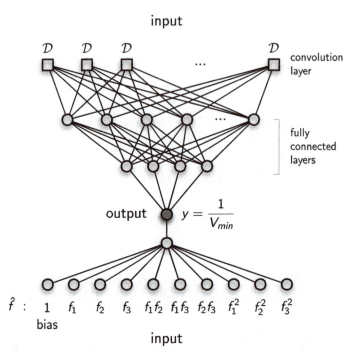

Figure 5.   The wide and deep model that couples a multiple linear regression model with a CNN.

is 2-dimensional and consists of 32 filters of size 3×3 with linear activation. It takes the toric diagram Δ_2 centered on a 9×9 lattice square as the input. The filters of the input layer are convolved against the input and produce a $2d$ activation map of the filter. As a result, the layer learns spatially localized features of the input toric diagrams. Figure 6 shows the 32 convolutional filters acting on the average input of the training dataset in the CNN. The convolutional layer is followed by two relatively smaller fully connected layers of sizes 12 and 4 with tanh activation. Overall, the CNN part of the model has four outputs m_i which are then, as described above, coupled to the output of the multiple linear regression model.

Similar to the multiple linear regression model, the wide and deep CNN model is trained on the training dataset by minimizing the mean squared error in Equation (22) using stochastic gradient descent. The resulting trained model in Equation (24) is found to approximate the minimum volume with an averaged predicted error

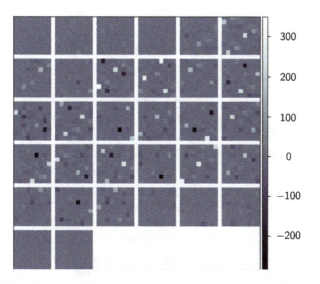

Figure 6.   Visualization of the 32 convolutional filters acting on the average input of the CNN. The color shading refers to the output of the convolutional layer.

of 0.9%. If only the CNN is used without the coupling to the multiple linear regression part of the wide and deep model, the predicted average error increases to exactly 1% as reported in Ref. [24].

5.   Conclusion

In [24], we introduced, parallel to the work in [25], machine learning and neural networks as new useful additions to the toolbox in string theory. Following the work in [23], the dataset of minimum volumes of Sasaki–Einstein base manifolds for toric Calabi–Yau 3-folds seemed particularly useful in our endeavor to test whether the usual minimum volume computation [12,36] can be replaced by discovering an approximate functional relationship between the minimum volume and known other topological data of toric Calabi–Yau 3-folds. In our work in [24], it was surprising to see that even simple machine learning models were effective enough to show that such an approximate functional relationship exists between the minimum volume and certain topological quantities of toric Calabi–Yau 3-folds. This was the first example of such a functional relationship identified by machine learning in string theory.

Following this result, in the conclusion section of our work in [24], we further predicted that other datasets that occur in string theory can be tested for similar functional relationships. We mentioned in [24] as examples the rich datasets involving complete intersection Calabi–Yaus (CICYs) [67] parameterized by configuration matrices and the rich database of hyperbolic 3-manifolds corresponding to knots [68]. Following our work in [24], both datasets have been explored with the use of machine learning techniques in [69] and [70], respectively, further confirming that machine learning techniques can lead to new interesting results in string theory.

As a final comment for this review article, it is important to note that our work in [24] not just tried to run a machine learning model on a dataset in string theory and measure its performance but also tried to explain the machine learning models used to approximate the minimum volume for toric Calabi–Yau 3-folds. This was done in part not only by explicitly writing down the learned weights for the multiple linear regression models giving an explicit and reusable formula for the minimum volume but also by trying to peak into the neural network by illustrating the convolution filters of the CNN model as shown in Figure 5. With the development of new machine learning techniques, we believe that this way of using machine learning will play a greater role in the future in fundamental sciences. In line with this principle, we hope to report on new results in the near future.

Acknowledgments

R.K.-S. would like to thank Y.-H. He, D. Krefl and S.-T. Yau for the collaboration on the two research papers that are reviewed in this chapter. R.K.-S. is supported by a Basic Research Grant from the National Research Foundation of Korea (NRF-2022R1F1A1073128). He is also supported by a Start-up Research Grant for new faculty at UNIST (1.210139.01), an UNIST AI Incubator Grant (1.230038.01) and an UNIST Fundamental Science Research Grant (1.220123.01), as well as an Industry Research Project funded by Samsung SDS in Korea. He is also partly supported by the BK21 Program ("Next Generation Education Program for Mathematical Sciences", 4299990414089) funded by the Ministry of Education in Korea and the National Research Foundation of Korea (NRF).

References

[1] J. M. Maldacena, The large N limit of superconformal field theories and supergravity, *Adv. Theor. Math. Phys.* **2** (1998), 231 [hep-th/9711200].

[2] E. Witten, Anti-de Sitter space and holography, *Adv. Theor. Math. Phys.* **2** (1998), 253 [hep-th/9802150].

[3] I. R. Klebanov and E. Witten, Superconformal field theory on three-branes at a Calabi–Yau singularity, *Nucl. Phys.* **B536** (1998), 199 [hep-th/9807080].

[4] A. Hanany and A. Zaffaroni, On the realization of chiral four-dimensional gauge theories using branes, *JHEP* **9805** (1998), 001 [hep--th/9801134].

[5] A. Hanany and A. M. Uranga, Brane boxes and branes on singularities, *JHEP* **9805** (1998), 013 [hep-th/9805139].

[6] A. Hanany and K. D. Kennaway, Dimer models and toric diagrams, hep-th/0503149.

[7] S. Franco, A. Hanany, K. D. Kennaway, D. Vegh and B. Wecht, Brane Dimers and Quiver Gauge theories, *JHEP* **1** (2006), 096 [hep--th/0504110].

[8] D. R. Morrison and M. R. Plesser, Nonspherical horizons. 1, *Adv. Theor. Math. Phys.* **3** (1999), 1 [hep-th/9810201].

[9] B. S. Acharya, J. M. Figueroa-O'Farrill, C. M. Hull and B. J. Spence, Branes at conical singularities and holography, *Adv. Theor. Math. Phys.* **2** (1999), 1249 [hep-th/9808014].

[10] S. S. Gubser, Einstein manifolds and conformal field theories, *Phys. Rev. D* **59** (1999), 025006 [hep-th/9807164].

[11] M. Henningson and K. Skenderis, The Holographic Weyl anomaly, *JHEP* **07** (1998), 023 [hep-th/9806087].

[12] D. Martelli, J. Sparks and S.-T. Yau, The geometric dual of a-maximisation for toric Sasaki–Einstein manifolds, *Commun. Math. Phys.* **268** (2006), 39 [hep-th/0503183].

[13] H. Garcia-Compean and A. M. Uranga, Brane box realization of chiral gauge theories in two-dimensions, *Nucl. Phys. B* **539** (1999), 329 [hep-th/9806177].

[14] K. Mohri, D-branes and quotient singularities of Calabi–Yau fourfolds, *Nucl. Phys.* **B521** (1998), 161 [hep-th/9707012].

[15] S. Franco, D. Ghim, S. Lee, R.-K. Seong and D. Yokoyama, 2d (0,2) Quiver Gauge theories and D-Branes, *JHEP* **9** (2015), 072 [1506.03818].

[16] S. Franco, S. Lee and R.-K. Seong, Brane brick models, toric Calabi–Yau 4-folds and 2d (0,2) Quivers, *JHEP* **2** (2016), 047 [1510.01744].

[17] S. Franco, S. Lee and R.-K. Seong, Brane brick models and 2d (0, 2) triality, *JHEP* **5** (2016), 020 [1602.01834].

[18] S. Franco, S. Lee, R.-K. Seong and C. Vafa, Brane brick models in the mirror, *JHEP* **2** (2017), 106 [1609.01723].

[19] S. Franco, S. Lee and R.-K. Seong, Orbifold reduction and 2d (0,2) Gauge theories, *JHEP* **3** (2017), 016 [1609.07144].

[20] S. Franco, S. Lee, R.-K. Seong and C. Vafa, Quadrality for supersymmetric matrix models, *JHEP* **7** (2017), 053 [1612.06859].

[21] S. Franco, D. Ghim, S. Lee and R.-K. Seong, Elliptic genera of 2d (0,2) Gauge theories from Brane brick models, *JHEP* **6** (2017), 068 [1702.02948].

[22] S. Franco and R.-K. Seong, Fano 3-folds, reflexive polytopes and Brane brick models, *JHEP* **8** (2022), 2203.15816.

[23] Y.-H. He, R.-K. Seong and S.-T. Yau, Calabi–Yau volumes and reflexive polytopes, Commun. Math. Phys. **361** (2018), 155 [1704.03462].

[24] D. Krefl and R.-K. Seong, Machine learning of Calabi–Yau volumes, *Phys. Rev. D* **96** (2017), 066014 [1706.03346].

[25] Y.-H. He, Deep-learning the landscape, *Phys. Lett. B* **774** (2017), 564–568. 1706.02714.

[26] F. Ruehle, Evolving neural networks with genetic algorithms to study the String Landscape, *JHEP* **8** (2017), 038 [1706.07024].

[27] J. Carifio, J. Halverson, D. Krioukov and B. D. Nelson, Machine learning in the String Landscape, *JHEP* **9** (2017), 157 [1707.00655].

[28] S. Benvenuti, B. Feng, A. Hanany and Y.-H. He, Counting BPS operators in gauge theories: Quivers, syzygies and plethystics, *JHEP* **11** (2007), 050 [hep-th/0608050].

[29] B. Nill, Gorenstein Toric Fano varieties, *Manuscripta Math.* **116** (2005), 183.

[30] C. F. Doran and U. A. Whitcher, From polygons to string theory, *Math. Mag.* **85** (2012), 343.

[31] H. Skarke, How to classify reflexive Gorenstein cones, in *Strings, Gauge Fields, and the Geometry Behind: The Legacy of Maximilian Kreuzer*, A. Rebhan, L. Katzarkov, J. Knapp, R. Rashkov and E. Scheidegger, eds., pp. 443–458 (2012). Doi: [1204.1181].

[32] W. Fulton, Introduction to toric varieties, *Annals of Mathematics Studies*, Princeton, NJ: Princeton University Press (1993).

[33] D. Cox, J. Little and H. Schenck, Toric varieties, graduate studies in mathematics, *Am. Math. Soc.* (2011).

[34] D. Martelli and J. Sparks, Toric geometry, Sasaki–Einstein manifolds and a new infinite class of AdS/CFT duals, *Commun. Math. Phys.* **262** (2006), 51 [hep-th/0411238].

[35] S. Benvenuti, S. Franco, A. Hanany, D. Martelli and J. Sparks, An infinite family of superconformal Quiver Gauge theories with Sasaki–Einstein duals, *JHEP* **6** (2005), 064 [hep-th/0411264].

[36] D. Martelli, J. Sparks and S.-T. Yau, Sasaki–Einstein manifolds and volume minimisation, *Commun. Math. Phys.* **280** (2008), 611 [hep--th/0603021].

[37] M. Kreuzer and H. Skarke, On the classification of reflexive polyhedra, *Commun. Math. Phys.* **185** (1997), 495 [hep-th/9512204].

[38] M. Kreuzer and H. Skarke, Classification of reflexive polyhedra in three dimensions, *Adv. Theor. Math. Phys.* **2** (1998), 847 [hep-th/9805190].

[39] M. Kreuzer and H. Skarke, Complete classification of reflexive polyhedra in four dimensions, *Adv. Theor. Math. Phys.* **4** (2002), 1209 [hep-th/0002240].

[40] V. V. Batyrev, Toroidal Fano 3-folds, *Math. USSR-Izvestiya* **19** (1982), 13.

[41] V. V. Batyrev and L. A. Borisov, On Calabi–Yau complete intersections in Toric varieties, arXiv e-prints (1994) alg [alg-geom/9412017].

[42] V. V. Batyrev, Dual polyhedra and mirror symmetry for Calabi–Yau hypersurfaces in toric varieties, *J. Alg. Geom.* **3** (1994), 493 [alg-geom/9310003].

[43] P. Candelas, X. de la Ossa and S. H. Katz, Mirror symmetry for Calabi–Yau hypersurfaces in weighted P**4 and extensions of Landau-Ginzburg theory, *Nucl. Phys. B* **450** (1995), 267 [hep-th/9412117].

[44] V. V. Batyrev, On the classification of Toric Fano 4-folds, arXiv Mathematics e-prints (1998) math/9801107 [math/9801107].

[45] G. Ewald, On the classification of Toric Fano varieties, *Discrete Comput. Geom.* **3** (1988), 49.

[46] K. Watanabe and M. Watanabe, The classification of Fano 3-folds with torus embeddings, *Tokyo J. Math.* **5** (1982), 37.

[47] A. Hanany and R.-K. Seong, Brane Tilings and reflexive polygons, *Fortsch. Phys.* **60** (2012), 695 [1201.2614].

[48] R. Kenyon, Local statistics of lattice dimers, in *Annales de l'Institut Henri Poincare (B) Probability and Statistics*, Vol. 33, pp. 591–618, Elsevier (1997).

[49] R. Kenyon, An introduction to the dimer model, ArXiv Mathematics e-prints (2003) [math/0310326].

[50] N. Seiberg, Electric - magnetic duality in supersymmetric nonAbelian gauge theories, *Nucl. Phys. B* **435** (1995), 129 [hep-th/9411149].

[51] B. Feng, A. Hanany and Y.-H. He, D-brane gauge theories from toric singularities and toric duality, *Nucl. Phys. B* **595** (2001), 165 [hep--th/0003085].

[52] A. Gadde, S. Gukov and P. Putrov, (0, 2) trialities, *JHEP* **3** (2014), 076 [1310.0818].

[53] A. Butti and A. Zaffaroni, From toric geometry to quiver gauge theory: The Equivalence of a-maximization and Z-minimization, *Fortsch. Phys.* **54** (2006), 309 [hep-th/0512240].

[54] K. A. Intriligator and B. Wecht, The exact superconformal R symmetry maximizes A, *Nucl. Phys. B* **667** (2003), 183 [hep-th/0304128].

[55] A. Butti and A. Zaffaroni, R-charges from toric diagrams and the equivalence of a-maximization and Z-minimization, *JHEP* **11** (2005), 019 [hep-th/0506232].

[56] B. Feng, A. Hanany and Y.-H. He, Counting Gauge invariants: The Plethystic program, *JHEP* **3** (2007), 090 [hep-th/0701063].

[57] A. P. Braun and N.-O. Walliser, A new offspring of PALP. 1106.4529.

[58] R. Altman, J. Gray, Y.-H. He, V. Jejjala and B. D. Nelson, A Calabi–Yau database: Threefolds constructed from the Kreuzer-Skarke list, *JHEP* **2** (2015), 158 [1411.1418].

[59] C. Long, L. McAllister and P. McGuirk, Heavy tails in Calabi–Yau moduli spaces, *JHEP* **10** (2014), 187 [1407.0709].

[60] R. Stanley, Hilbert functions of graded algebras, *Adv. Math.* **28** (1978), 57.

[61] Y. Tachikawa, Five-dimensional supergravity dual of a-maximization, *Nucl. Phys. B* **733** (2006), 188 [hep-th/0507057].

[62] A. Hanany, D. Orlando and S. Reffert, Sublattice counting and orbifolds, *JHEP* **6** (2010), 051 [1002.2981].

[63] J. Davey, A. Hanany and R.-K. Seong, Counting orbifolds, *JHEP* **6** (2010), 010 [1002.3609].

[64] A. Hanany and R.-K. Seong, Symmetries of Abelian orbifolds, *JHEP* **1** (2011), 027 [1009.3017].

[65] Y. LeCun, Y. Bengio and G. Hinton, Deep learning, *Nature* **521** (2015), 436.

[66] J. Schmidhuber, Deep learning in neural networks: An overview, *Neural Netw.* **61** (2015), 85.

[67] P. Candelas, A. M. Dale, C. A. Lutken and R. Schimmrigk, Complete intersection Calabi-Yau manifolds, *Nucl. Phys. B* **298** (1988), 493.

[68] V. F. R. Jones, A polynomial invariant for knots via von Neumann algebras, *Bull. Am. Math. Soc.* **12** (1985), 103.

[69] K. Bull, Y.-H. He, V. Jejjala and C. Mishra, Machine learning CICY threefolds, *Phys. Lett. B* **785** (2018), 65 [1806.03121].

[70] V. Jejjala, A. Kar and O. Parrikar, Deep learning the hyperbolic volume of a knot, *Phys. Lett. B* **799** (2019), 135033 [1902.05547].

Epilogue

The publication of this book has very serendipitously coincided with the latest excitement surrounding OpenAI's ChatGPT. Academics are certainly trying it out with great curiosity and guarded optimism. While still in its infancy and prone to many errors, ChatGPT and the likes thereof will indubitably be transformative. Already, the consensus in universities seems to be that it can perform as well as an undergraduate with a passable mark. This is not only true of essay writing in the humanities but, surprisingly, is the case for the mathematical sciences. Conversely, many of my colleagues in the mathematics and physics departments across the world are currently asking it to design, solve and typeset their exams: what used to take many hours can now be done in minutes, and it is good enough for first- and second-year undergraduate level courses.

All of this beckons the question as to what the nature and structure of mathematics are. Christian Szegedy at Google Deepmind speculated that by 2000, computers beat humans in chess, by 2015–2017, AlphaGo and AlphaZero beat humans in Go, by 2020, AlphaFold beat scientists in protein biology, and so by the 2030s, AlphaMath will beat humans in proving theorems. Of course, most mathematicians are more reserved in their optimism and foresee many more decades before AI can generate significant new theorems in mathematics with detailed proofs or new formulae in theoretical physics with supporting derivations. Nonetheless, it is astounding and perhaps frightening that such speculations are no longer outlandish.

It is the purpose of this book — one of the first of its kind — to extend this dialog between mathematicians, theoretical physicists and AI experts, to present and celebrate some of the initial results, and to anticipate countless future collaborations. We hope that machine learning will become a critical tool to the practicing mathematician as calculus or algebra in the years to come.

Index